I0592315

Wharton B. Marriott

Vestiarvm Christianvm

he origin and gradual development of the dress of holy ministry in the chvrch

Wharton B. Marriott

Vestiarvm Christianvm
he origin and gradual development of the dress of holy ministry in the chvrch

ISBN/EAN: 9783337285623

Printed in Europe, USA, Canada, Australia, Japan

Cover: Foto ©Lupo / pixelio.de

More available books at **www.hansebooks.com**

VESTIARIVM CHRISTIANVM

DIPTYCH OF S⸍ PAUL

g the Apostolic Throne and giving Benediction to a Bishop

VESTIARIVM CHRISTIANVM

The Origin and Gradual Development

OF

THE DRESS OF HOLY MINISTRY

IN THE CHVRCH

BY THE

REV. WHARTON B. MARRIOTT, M.A., F.S.A.

(Sometime Fellow of Exeter College, Oxford, and Affiftant Mafter at Eton)

Select Preacher in the Univerfity,

and Preacher, by licenfe from the Bifhop, in the Diocefe, of Oxford.

London

RIVINGTONS, WATERLOO PLACE

HIGH STREET | TRINITY STREET

Oxford | Cambridge

1868

PREFACE.

HISTORICAL or antiquarian inveſtigation is one thing, theological controverſy is another. There is time, and there is place,
for both; but not for both the ſame time and the ſame place,
without diſadvantage to the former of the two. Under this
conviction I have ſtudiouſly put aſide, in the Treatiſe which
follows, all reference to the paſſing controverſies of theſe days,
and have made it my one object to collect every fact of
importance bearing upon the ſubject immediately before me, to
ſet it before my readers in ſuch a way, as ſhall enable them to
form their own eſtimate of its value, and at the ſame time to
offer, for whatever may be its worth, the interpretation which
I myſelf believe to be the true one.

And even now that my work is complete, a work that originated in the controverſies of theſe days, and that touches, as I
believe, upon thoſe controverſies in many points of the greateſt
importance, I ſtill think it better, on many grounds, to adhere
to the ſame courſe. The objects I have in view will, I believe,
be beſt attained, if I leave the monuments, here reproduced, to
tell their own tale, and to produce conviction by their own
force, without any attempt on my part to apply their leſſons in
detail to queſtions of Ritual, or of Doctrine, now diſputed in
the Church.

But there is one duty which I muſt take this opportunity of
diſcharging, though it is beyond my power to do ſo adequately.
I have to expreſs my grateful thanks to all thoſe (they are very
many) from whom, in various ways, I have received aſſiſtance
in my work. Among theſe I may be allowed to refer more

particularly to the Truftees, and the Officers, of the Britifh Mufeum. To Mr. Newton as an old friend, to Mr. Bond, and Mr. A. Franks, with no other claim but that of a common intereft in antiquarian ftudy, I have often had recourfe, and never without receiving the readieft and the moft efficient help.

To Mr. Woodward, Her Majefty's Librarian at Windfor, I have to acknowledge many fpecial obligations. And I know that I fhall do fo in the manner that will be moft acceptable to him, if I take this opportunity of faying, that in making available for literary ftudy the refources of the Library under his charge, he is but carrying out the exprefs commands of H.R.H. the Prince Confort, under the fanction of the Queen. It was the Prince's defire, that as foon as the arrangement of the Library, commenced under his direction, fhould be fufficiently advanced, it fhould be made acceffible for purpofes of ftudy as far as might be confiftent with its fpecial character. As one of the firft to have profited, as I have moft largely, by the per-miffion thus given, I venture to exprefs my grateful acknow-ledgments, and to make known this additional illuftration of the generous confideration for others, and regard for the interefts of Literature, which were confpicuous in the lamented Prince.

I have received communications of much intereft and value in reference to particular queftions, from Mr. Droop, Mr. Wilfhere, the Rev. J. C. Wynter, Mr. W. Simpfon, and others. I have gladly availed myfelf of the information fo received.

For the Illuftrations of this Volume I have been dependent, mainly, upon two very fkilful Photographers, Mr. Prefton and Mr. Saunders; and on a Copyift, all but photographically exact, Mr. A. Reid, of the South Kenfington Mufeum. I am alfo greatly indebted to Signor Scifoni, of Rome, for Drawings made from MSS. in the Vatican Library and elfewhere.

I ought not to conclude without faying, how much I owe to more than one foreign writer whofe books I have laid under contribution. Treating though they do of fubjects keenly controverted for the laſt three hundred years, they write in a ſpirit of loyal devotion to the Truth, and the Truth alone, ſuch as others, differing widely from them in doctrinal prepoſſeſſions, might well defire to imitate. In ſaying this, I refer particularly to Dr. Hefele, and the Chevalier De Roffi, from both of whom I have learnt much, and hope to learn much more.

I have frequently made uſe of the admirable Compendium of Profeſſor Weiſs, and of the ſpecial Treatiſe on Liturgical Veſt- ments by Dr. Bock. This latter work contains minute in- formation, not to be found elſewhere, as to the material, ſhape, and ornamentation, of Mediæval Veſtments.

Nor muſt I paſs over without mention yet another writer, Dr. Rock, a fellow-countryman of my own. His learned work, "The Church of our Fathers," contains much intereſting informa- tion on the early Hiſtory of Veſtments in this country. He writes, as thoſe who know him will not need to be told, with a doctrinal object in view, with which the writer of the preſent Treatiſe cannot ſympathiſe. But I gladly bear teſtimony to the extenſive reſearch, of which his work gives proof; and I regret that my own book was all but completed before I had any opportunity of confulting his pages.

And now I have only to ſend forth my work to the light, with the expreſſion of my earneſt hope, that it may contribute, in ſome ſmall meaſure at leaſt, to a more accurate knowledge of the Paſt ; and, in ſo doing, help in its degree to the guidance of the Church, in our own days, through the difficulties of theſe preſent times, and of the uncertain but not unhopeful Future that awaits Her.

ETON,
January 29, 1868.

ERRATA.

Page xii., note o. quoted in App. A. *erase.*

— xxxii., line 13.   For St. Clement *read* St. James

— xxxviii., note τ.   For given in the Canons *read* conceded by long custom

— lviii., line 10.   For fought *read* ought

— lxv., note θ.   For No. 27 *read* No. 26

— lxxviii., line 14.   For Vienna *read* Vienne

— lxxxviii., note ψ.   For 1430 *read* 1438

— 15, line 13.   For and thefe of *read* and of thefe

— 22, line 22.   *Remove comma after* pectore

— 42, line 2 of the text.   For κατηγοράσας *read* κατηγορήσας

— 88, note 157 *in fin.*   For Cap. fupra *read* Cf. fupra

— 106, line 6.   *Infert comma (in place of full ftop) after* confecrantur

— ,, note 206.   For or its place *read* for its place

— 148, line 3.   For orma *read* forma

— 149, line 3.   For cum integra fit *read* cum unica fit

— 151, line 3.   For fubjects *read* fubject—for then *read* them

— ,, line 12.   For meniti *read* muniti

— 168, note 144.   For to homage *read* of homage

— 181, note 374.   For facco *read* fucco

— 196, line 22.   For appear *read* wear

— 207, note 427.   For utuntur *read* utantur

— 209, note 429.   *After* Archbifhop of Milan *infert* (in the fourth century)

— 222, note 454, line 1.   *Omit* which

— 226, note 464.   For baulekin *read* baudekin

— 246, plate lxiii.   This is fo numbered in order to correfpond with the number on the plate itfelf.   The number ought to have been lxii. both on the plate and in the defcription.

— 247, line 19.   For p. xliii. The Prophet Malachi *read* p. xxxiv. The Prophet Malachi
[To the Lift of Woodcuts there given fhould have been added the following:—

— xliii.   A Reprefentation of Our Lord, from the fame MS. as that laft defcribed.]

— 248.   *Erafe the words,* the coin juft below the roll, the marriage dowry

CONTENTS.

---

* Of the extracts fo marked Tranflations only are given, particular paffages of the Original being added in the Notes.

† Of the extracts fo marked the original only is given in full, tranflations of particular paffages, and illuftrative notes, being fubjoined.

AUTHORS AND EDITIONS

QUOTED OR REFERRED TO IN THIS TREATISE.

Acta Sanctorum (AA.SS.) The Bollandist Collection. Fol. Antwerp.
Acta Sanctorum Ordinis Benedicti. 4 voll. Fol. Paris. 1733.
Alcuinus (Albinus Flaccus). Liber de Divinis Officiis. Apud Hittorpium, q. v.
Alemannus (Nicolaus). De Lateranensibus Parietinis. 4to. Romæ. 1625.
Amalarius Metensis. De Ecclesiasticis Officiis. Apud Hittorpium, q. v.
Ambrosii D. Opera. Basle. Fol. 1567.
Ammianus Marcellinus. Rom. Imperatorum Historiæ. 8vo. Paris. 1544.
Anastasius Bibliothecarius. Apud Muratorium (tom. III.), q. v.
Antiquités de l'Empire de Russie. 6 voll. Fol. St. Petersburgh.
Aringhi Roma Subterranea. 2 voll. Fol. Romæ. 1651.
Artemidori Daldiani Oneirocritica. 8vo. Lutetiæ. 1603.
Assemani (Steph. Evod.) Bibliotheca Medicea. Florentiæ. Fol. 1742.
Augustini S. (Hipponens. Epi.) Opera. Migne's Edition. 12 voll. 4to. Paris. 1841.

Baronii * Annales Ecclesiastici. 12 voll. Fol. Antwerp. 1618.
Bartolinus (Bartolus). De Pænula. Apud Grævium, q. v.
Basilii S. (Seleuciæ Epi.) Opera. 3 voll. 8vo. Paris. 1839.
Bayfius (Lazarus) De Re Vestiaria. Apud Grævium, q. v.
Bedæ Venerabilis Opera. 12 voll. 8vo. London 1843.
Belethi Rationale Divinorum Officiorum. Apud Durandum, q. v.
Bellarmini (Cardinalis) Opera Omnia. 6 voll. Fol. Coloniæ. 1620.
Bellorius (G. P.). Veteres Arcus Augustorum. Fol. Romæ. 1690.
Bellorius (G. P.). Colonna Traiana. Fol. 1673.
Bertramni (al Ratramni) Liber de Corpore et Sanguine Domini. London. 12mo. 1688.
Bock (Dr. Fr.). Geschichte der liturgischen Gewänder des Mittelälters. 2 voll. 8vo. Bonn. 1866.
Boissardus (J. J.). Urbis Romanæ Antiquitates. Fol. Frankfurt. 1597.
Braunius. De Habitu Sacerdotali Hebræorum. 4to. Amst. 1680.
Byzantine Architecture. See "Texier."

Cælestinus Papa. Apud Labbe Concil. Tom. ii., p. 1618.
Cæsarii Arelatensis Vita. Apud Baronium (Tom. vi.), q. v.
Capitolinus (Julius). Apud Historiæ Augustæ Scriptores, q. v.
Chrysostomi S. Opera. 12 voll. 4to. Paris. 1735.
Ciampini (Joannis) Vetera Monimenta. Romæ. 1699.
† Ciceronis (M. T.) Opera. 2 voll. Fol. Paris. 1539.
Clementis Alexandrini Opera. Potter. 2 voll. Fol. Oxon. 1715.
Codex Theodosianus. Ritter. Lipsiæ. Fol. 1741.
Cotelerius, J. B. Ecclesiæ Græcæ Monumenta. 4 voll. 4to. Paris. 1677.
Councils. See Labbe, Harduin, Raynaldus, Spelman.

---

* Sometimes quoted from later editions.

† Of the ordinary Classical Authors, to which every Scholar has ready access, I have included in this List those only which present any difficulty in the verification of References.

D'Agincourt (Seroux). Histoire de l'Art par les Monuments. 6 voll. Fol. Paris. 1823.

Damianus (Petrus). Apud Migne, q. v. P. C. C. tom. 144.

De la Bigne (Margarinus). Maxima Bibliotheca Veterum Patrum. 28 voll. Fol. Lugduni. Genuæ. 1677, 1707.

De Rossi. Roma Sotterranea. Fol. Roma. 1864.

———— Imagines Selectæ Deiparæ Virginis. Fol. Romæ. 1863.

Didron, A. N. Annales Archéologiques. 4to. Paris. 1844, etc.

Donatus. Apud Wetstenium (Nov. Test. Græc. 2 voll. Amsterdam. 1752.)

Ducange. See Dufresne.

*Dufresne, C. (Du Cange) Glossarium Med. et Inf. Latinitatis. 3 voll. Fol. Paris. 1628.

———————— Glossarium Med. et Inf. Græcitatis. Lugdun. 1688.

Durandi (R. D. G.) Rationale Divinorum Officiorum. 4to. Lugduni. 1672.

Du Saussay. Panoplia Sacerdotalis. Apud Martigny, q. v.

Duval (Amaury). Monuments des Arts du Dessin. 4 voll. Fol. Paris. 1829.

Ennodii (Magni Felicis) Carmina. Apud Sirmondum (tom. i.), q. v.

Epiphanii (Constantiæ Episc.) Opera. 2 voll. Fol. Paris. 1622.

Eusebii Pamphili Hist. Eccles. Libri x. 4 voll. 8vo. Oxon. 1847.

Ferrandus Diaconus. Apud Thomassinum, q. v.

Ferrarius (Octavius) De Re Vestiaria. Apud Grævium, q. v.

Ferrarius, F. B. De Veterum Acclamationibus. Apud Grævium, q. v.

Ffoulkes. Manual of Ecclesiastical History. Oxford. 1851.

———— Christendom's Divisions. Part II. 8vo. London. 1867.

Florovantis (Benedicti) Antiquiores Pontificum Romanorum Denarii. 4to. Romæ. 1734.

Fortunati (Venantii) Carminum, etc. Libri XI. 4to. Mogunt. 1617.

Garrucci (Raffaelle) Vetri Ornati in Oro. Roma. 1864.

Gay (Victor). Apud Didron, q. v.

Gell (Sir W.). Pompeiana. 2 voll. 4to. 1832.

Genebrardi (Gilbert) Chronographia. Fol. Lugduni. 1609. [There are several other Editions of the Chronographia, in which the *Church History* of Genebrard is omitted, and replaced by the shorter compendium of Arnaldus Pontacus. Of four copies in the British Museum, only the one above described contains the passage referred to in p. lxxxiii., note θ, of this Treatise.]

Germanus Patriarcha Constantinop. Rerum Ecclesiasticarum Theoria. Apud De La Bigne (tom. xiii.), q. v.

Gieseler. Ecclesiastical History. Davidson's Translation. Edinburgh. 1848.

Goar. Euchologion Græcorum. Fol. Paris. 1647.

Gurius, A. F. Thesaurus Veterum Diptychorum. 3 voll. Fol. Florentiæ. 1759.

Grævii Thesaurus Romanarum Antiquitatum. 12 voll. Fol. Venet. 1732.

Gregorii D. cogn. Magni Opera. 4 voll. Fol. Paris. 1705. [Sometimes quoted from the Edition of 1586. Fol. Paris.]

Gregorii Papæ I. Sacramentorum Liber. Ed. Hugo Menardus. 4to. Paris. 1642.

Gregorii Nazianzeni Opera. Fol. Paris. 1630.

Gregorii Turonensis Opera. Fol. Paris. 1699.

Harduini Conciliorum Collectio. 12 voll. Fol. Paris. 1715.

Hefele, Dr. C. J. Beiträge zur Kirchengeschichte, u. s. w. 2 voll. 8vo. Tubingen. 1864.

Hefner-Altenek. Trachten des Christlichen Mittelalters. 3 voll. 4to. Frankfurt. 1840—1854.

Hegesippus apud Hieronymum, q. v.

Hemans, C. J. Ancient Christianity and Sacred Art. 12mo. London and Florence. 1866.

Herodiani Historiarum Libri Sex. Aldus. 1523.

Hieronymi, S. Eusebii, Opera. 4 voll. Fol. Paris. 1693.

Histoire Littéraire de la France. 22 voll. 4to. Paris. 1733—52.

Historiæ Augustæ Scriptores. Fol. Hanoviæ. 1611.
Hittorpius de Divinis Catholicæ Ecclefiæ Officiis. Fol. Coloniæ. 1568.
Honorii Auguftodunenfis Opera. Biblioth. Mag. vet. Patrum. Tom xx.
Hook (Dr. W. F.). Lives of the Archbishops of Canterbury. 8vo. London. 1860
Hugo de S. Victore. Apud Migne P. C. C. tom. 175—177.

Innocentii III. Pont. Max. Opera. Fol. Coloniæ. 1552.
Joannis Damafceni Liber De Hærefibus, apud Cotelerium, q. v.
Joannes Diaconus. [D. Gregorii Vita, etc.] Apud Gregorii Magni Opp., q. v.
Joannes Ravennas apud Gregorii Magni Opera, q. v.
Jofephi (Flavii) Opera. 2 voll. Fol. Oxon. 1720.
Ivo, St. De Rebus Ecclefiafticis Sermones. Apud Hittorpium, q. v.

King, Dr. J. G. Rites and Ceremonies of the Greek Church in Ruffia. 4to. London. 1772
Kirchen Ordnung zu Brandenburg, u. s. w. See Note 458.
Knight (Gally). Ecclefiaftical Architecture of Italy. Fol. London. 1842.
Knox (Alex.), Remains of. 4 voll. 8vo. London. 1837.
Kreutz (Johann). La Bafilica di San Marco. Fol. Venice. 1843.

Labbe. Concilia Sacrofancta. 16 voll. Fol. Paris. 1671.
Lampridius (Ælius) apud Hiftoriæ Auguftæ Scriptores, q. v.
Louandre et Maugé. Les Arts Sompteux. 4to. Paris. 1852—58.
Lucilii Satirarum quæ fuperfunt. Ed. F. J. Doufa. Lugduni. 1597.
Luitprandi Epi. Hiftoria. Muratori. R. S. S. Tom. ii.
——————— Legatio. Apud Pertz Mon. Germ. Hift.

Mabillon. Mufeum Italicum. 2 voll. 4to. Paris. 1689.
Manfi. Sacrofancta Concilia. 29 voll. Fol. Venet. et Lucæ. 1728—1752.
Marriott, W. B. Eirenica. 8vo. London. 1865.
Martene (Edmund). De Antiquis Ecclefiæ Ritibus. 4 voll. Fol. Venet. 1788.
————- Thefaurus Novus Anecdotorum. 5 voll. Fol. Paris. 1717.
Martigny. Dictionnaire des Antiquités Chrétiennes. 8vo. Paris. 1865.
Martini (Epi. Bracarens.) Capitula. Apud Labbe (q. v.) Tom. v. p. 912.
Menardus (Hugo). D. Gregorii Papæ Sacramentorum Liber. 4to. Paris. 1642.
Menologium Græcorum. Urbini. 1727. 3 voll. Fol. 1727.
Migne. Patrologiæ Curfus Completus. Series Latina. 221 voll. 4to. Paris. 1844—64
Millin. Voyage en Italie. Apud Martigny, q. v.
Mümmfen (Theodor). The Hiftory of Rome. London. 1864.
Monete dei Romani Pontefici, ecc. Domenico Promis. Torino. 1858.
Montfaucon. L'Antiquité Expliquée. 15 voll. Fol. Paris. 1719—1724.
Muratorius, L. A. Rerum Italicarum Scriptores. 28 voll. Fol. Mediolani. 1723—51.

Nicephori Callixti Hiftoria Ecclefiaftica. 2 voll. Fol. Paris. 1630.
Nicolai, PP. 1. Refponfa ad Bulgaros. Apud Labbe. Tom. viii.

Ordines Romani. Apud Mabillon (Mufeum Italicum), q. v.

Paley (F. A.). Fafti of Ovid. 8vo. London. 1854.
Palmer (Rev. W.). Differtation on Primitive Liturgies, prefixed to Antiquities of the Englifh Ritual.
    2 voll. 8vo. Oxford. 1832.
Perret. Catacombes de Rome. 6 voll. Fol. Paris. 1851, etc.
Pertz (G. H.). Monumenta Germaniæ Hiftorica. 18 voll. Fol. Hanoviæ. 1826—1863.
Philonis Judæi Opera. Fol. Paris. 1640.
Photii Bibliotheca. Fol. Rothomag. 1653.
Piftolefe (Erafmo). Il Vaticano Illuftrato. 6 voll. Fol. Roma. 1829.
Plutarchi Chæronenfis Opufcula. H. Stephanus. 1572.

Pollux (Julius). Onomasticon. 2 voll. Fol. Amsterd. 1706.
Polycrates, Bp. of Ephesus. Apud Eusebium, q. v.
Procopii Historiarum Libri viii. 2 voll. Fol. Paris. 1662.
Promis Domenico (Memoria di). See " Monete."
Prudenti Clementis Opera. Paris. MDCLXXXVII.
Pugin. Glossary of Ecclesiastical Ornament. Fol. London. 1846

Rabanus Maurus. De Instit. Clericorum. Apud Hittorpium, q. v.
Radberti (Paschasii) Opera. Fol. Paris. 1618.
Ramboux (J. A.). Beiträge zur Kunstgeschichte des Mittelalters. Fol. Köln. 1860.
Raynaldi Annales Ecclesiastici (Continuatio Baronii). 8 voll. Fol. Colon. Agrip. 1693.
Raynaudus (Theophilus). De Pileo. Apud Grævium, q. v.
Regino (Abbas Prumiensis). De Disciplina Ecclesiastica. Migne P. C. C. Tom. 132.
Renaudot. Liturgiarum Orientalium Collectio. 2 voll. 4to. Paris. 1716.
Riculfus Eps. Apud Migne P. C. C. Tom. 132.
Rock, Dr. Church of our Fathers. 3 vols. 8vo. London. 1849.
Rubenius (Albertus). De Re Vestiaria. Apud Grævium, q. v.

Salviani et Vincentii Lirinensis Opera. Ed. Baluzius. Paris. 8vo. 1669.
Salzenberg. Altchristliche Baudenkmale von Constantinopel. Fol. Berlin. 1854.
Senecæ (L. Annæi) Opera. Coloniæ. 1614.
Sirmondi (Jacobi) Opera Varii. Tom. v. Fol. Paris. 1696.
Spartianus. Apud Historiæ Augustæ Scriptores, q. v.
Spelman. Concilia, Decreta, etc. Fol. London. 1639.
Stephani Tornacensis Epistolæ. Apud Migne P. C. L. Tom. 212.
Strutt. Manners and Customs, etc. 2 vols. 4to. London. 1775.
Suetonii. De XII Cæsaribus Libri VIII. J. Casaubon. Fol. Paris. 1610.
Symeon (Archbishop of Thessalonica). Fol. Jassii. 1683.

Tertulliani (Q. S. F.) Opera. Semler. 5 voll. 8vo. Magdeburg. 1773.
Texier and Pullan. Byzantine Architecture. Fol. London. 1864.
Theodoreti Epi. Cyri Opera. 5 voll. 8vo. Halæ. 1771.
Theodulfi Epi. Apud Sirmondum (Tom. ii.), q. v.
Thomassini Vetus et Nova Ecclesiæ Disciplina. Mogont. 4to. 1787.
Trebellius Pollio. Apud Historiæ Augustæ Scriptores, q. v.

Valentini (Agostino). Basilica Vaticana Illustrata. 6 voll. Fol. Roma. 1845.
Vopiscus (Flavius). Apud Historiæ Augustæ Scriptores, q. v.

Walafrid Strabo De Rebus Ecclesiasticis. Apud Hittorpium, q. v.
Weiss, H. Kostümkunde. Tracht und Geräth in Mittelalter. Stuttgart. 1864.
————————— Tracht u. s. w. des Alterthums. II. Abtheil. Stuttgart. 1860.
Westwood, J. O. Miniatures and Ornaments of Anglo-Saxon and Irish Manuscripts. Fol.
    London (Quaritch). 1868.
Wyatt, M. D. Notices of Sculptures in Ivory. London. 1856.

THE ORIGIN AND GRADUAL DEVELOPMENT OF ECCLESIASTICAL DRESS.

INTRODUCTION.

CHAPTER I.

THE queſtion, what veſtments are to be regarded as proper to offices of holy miniſtry in Chriſt's Church, is one that of late has been keenly debated, and is ſtill for various reaſons exciting confiderable intereſt.

There are thoſe who believe that the dreſs of Chriſtian miniſtry was from the firſt, under Divine guidance, and, by Apoſtolic authority, modelled, in detail, upon the dreſs of the Aaronic prieſthood. But, after all that has been written in difproof of this opinion of late years, efpecially by learned Roman Catholic writers, whofe bias would naturally incline them to its fupport, this belief muſt be regarded as an opinion due to doctrinal prepoſſeſſions on the part of the few who ſtill maintain it, rather than as one which admits of ferious fupport upon hiſtorical grounds.

On the other hand, it may be faid with truth, that there were features of analogy between the two types of dreſs, although the points of difference were in primitive times far more ſtrongly marked than the points of refemblance.

Among thoſe [a] who have examined the queſtion upon

---

[a] See, for example, the concife ſtate- | Nearly the fame conclufions are main-
ment of Jacobus Sirmondus quoted in | tained by Dr. Hefele in his eſſay on
the fecond part of this volume (p. 47). | the " Liturgical Veſtments " [Beitrāge

purely antiquarian or hiftorical evidence, the more general opinion is fuch as this : —That in the Apoftolic age there was no effential difference between the drefs worn by Chriftians in ordinary life, and that worn by bifhops, priefts, or other clerics, when engaged in offices of holy miniftration. But that after the lapfe of three or four centuries the drefs of ordinary life became changed, while that worn in ecclefiaftical offices remained in form unchanged, though ever more and more richly decorated. That from thefe caufes a marked diftinction was gradually brought about between the drefs of the clergy and that of the laity (to fay nothing of the monaftic orders who were diftinguifhed from them both); that, as time went on, the ordinary drefs of the clergy themfelves came to be diftinguifhed, in form, in colour, and in name, from that in which they miniftered; while at length yet a further diftinction was introduced as between the drefs of the more ordinary miniftrations, and the more fplendid Veftments referved for the higheft Offices of all, and for occafions of fpecial folemnity.

There is much in this fecond ftatement which is undoubtedly true. But the evidence to be alleged in the following treatife will fhow, that important modifications of that ftatement, and additions to it, muft be made, if we wifh to convey an exact idea of what was the Primitive and Apoftolic type of miniftering drefs, and what the fucceffive ftages of its gradual development. The moft important of thefe modifications and additions of which I fpeak, it may be well, before proceeding further, briefly here to indicate.

---

zur Kirchengefchichte &c., von Dr. C. J. Hefele, Tubingen, 1864.] Even Dr. Bock, who with great erudition and much ingenuity, traces out refemblances between the Roman veftments *now in ufe* and thofe of the Levitical priefthood, is conftrained by the force of facts to admit that this refemblance was brought about by changes firft made after the clofe of the eighth century. [Gefchichte der liturgifchen Gewänder des Mittelalters, Band i. cap. vi. p. 413.] Compare Thomaffinus, *Vetus et nova Ecclefiæ Difciplina.* Part i. Lib. ii. cap. xliii. 299.

Dividing the hiftory of the Church, for the purpofes of this inquiry, into three periods, we may regard the firft, or Primitive Period, as extending to the clofe of the four firft centuries. The fecond, or Tranfition Period, as of four hundred years more, to the clofe of the eighth century. The third period may be confidered as extending to the prefent time, but as fubdivided, in refpect of the churches of the Weft, by the age of the Reformation.

The First, or Primitive Period.

In the Primitive Period, of about 400 years, the drefs of Chriftian miniftry was in form, in fhape, in diftinctive name, identical with the drefs worn by perfons of condition, on occafions of joyous feftival, or folemn ceremonial. And this was a drefs which in fuch wife differed from the Habit of every-day life, and of ordinary wear, that it was marked out plainly in the eyes of all as a garb proper to occafions of religious worfhip, and of folemn affembly in the Prefence of God.

In the centuries that have elapfed fince the clofe of that firft Period, modifications of the Primitive type, and additions to it, have been made from time to time. Thefe modifications and additions have varied in degree, and in kind, in various branches of the Church. And when traced (as they admit of being traced) to their caufes, they are found to reflect faithfully important changes through which fuch churches have paffed, either inwardly, by reafon of innovations upon Primitive Doctrine, or outwardly through viciffitudes of political pofition. For a ftriking example of what is here afferted, we may do well to confine our attention for the prefent to the Churches of the Weft, as being thofe in which we ourfelves have chief concern, and as affording ampler materials for investigation than do the Eastern Churches.

The Second, or Primitive Period.

Passing on then to the Second Period (from *circ.* 400 to 800 A.D.) the facts which come before us are these. When in the fifth century overwhelming tides of invasion from the North swept in succession over the face of Southern Europe, the purity of the old Latin speech, and the dignity of the old Roman garb, became, for the first time, distinctive marks to which the inheritors of the older civilisation of Rome clung with affection, as separating them, even in outward semblance, from the revolutionary barbarism about them. And, accordingly, after this older costume had disappeared from common use, it was still preserved in the state dresses of Roman official dignitaries, and in the vestments which alone were considered seemly for such as ministered in the various offices of the Church. During this period of transition, the slight but significant distinctions, both of dress and Insignia, which from very early times had been employed in the Church, were not unfrequently the subjects of special regulation, and were modified and added to by degrees.

The Third Period.

Passing now to the Third Period, we shall find that in the sudden but very brief revival of learning and of art which marks the age of Charlemagne, the peculiarities of ecclesiastical dress began to attract the special attention of the more learned ecclesiastics of the time. Certain points of analogy between the older vestments of the Levitical priesthood and the ministering

dreſs of the Church, had been made the ſubjeƈt of occaſional
alluſion even in earlier writers.   But now for the firſt time
was the attempt made to trace out in detail a correſpondence
between the 'eight veſtments' of the Jewiſh high-prieſt, and
thoſe of Chriſtian miniſtry.   The idea once embraced took
ſtrong hold upon the mind of churchmen.   And as, in the
ninth century, the points of difference between the two types
of dreſs were, to ſay the leaſt, quite as evident, as the marks of
reſemblance, changes and additions were rapidly made with a
view to aſſimilating, as far as might be, the Chriſtian to
the older Levitical type.   So that, if we take the eleventh or
twelfth century as the period for compariſon, inſtead of the
age of the Apoſtles, the theory of an analogy in detail between
the Levitical and the Chriſtian veſtments admits of being
maintained with great plauſibility.

The type of dreſs which was thus at length eſtabliſhed
has been maintained in the Roman Church, with very ſlight
modifications only, to the preſent time.   But when, after the
revival of ancient learning, the Church of England reformed
her faith and her diſcipline, upon the authority of Holy
Scripture and the model of the Primitive Church, conſiderable
changes were made among ourſelves in that Mediæval and
Roman type of dreſs.   And the reſult has been that the cuſtomary miniſtering dreſs of the Engliſh clergy during the laſt
three hundred years, has been in colour and general appearance,
though not in name, all but exaƈtly identical with that which
we find aſſigned to the Apoſtles in the earlieſt monuments of
Chriſtendom, and which, upon ſimilar evidence, we ſhall find
reaſon to conclude was, in point of faƈt, the dreſs of Chriſtian
miniſtry in the primitive ages of the Church.

Such is, in general terms, the reſult to which the monuments of ſucceſſive centuries, and the teſtimony of ſucceſſive
writers, ſeem to point.   And now, as a firſt ſtep towards eſta-
bliſhing by direƈt evidence the various ſtatements above made,

it will be well to remind ourſelves what was the prevailing
type of dreſs, and what the nature of official Inſignia, in that
firſt age of Chriſtianity with which our inquiry begins.

But this opens up a ſomewhat wide ſubject, to which it
will be well to devote a ſeparate chapter.

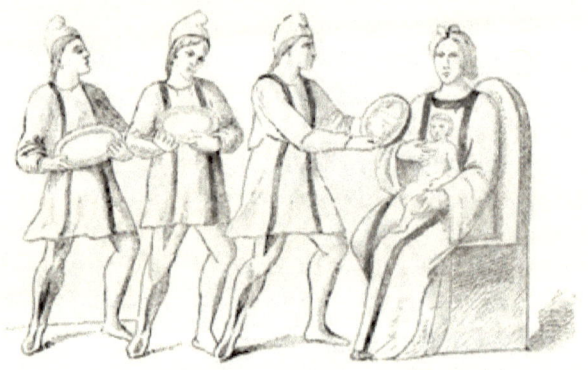

CHAPTER II.

CIVIL DRESS IN THE FIRST CENTURY.

WITH a view to the queſtion now before us, it is important to obſerve that the dreſs of ordinary life, in the firſt[β] century of our era, was in all eſſential reſpects the ſame[γ] in Syria, in Aſia Minor, in Greece, and in Rome.

Nor have we far to ſeek in order to determine what this was. In the various monuments of ancient art in which repreſentations of civil dreſs have been preſerved to us, we find

---

[β] I ſpeak here of the *firſt* century, becauſe it is then that *in ſome way or other* the queſtion of a dreſs proper to offices of Chriſtian miniſtry muſt firſt have been practically determined. But what is ſtated above of the firſt century will apply to the firſt four hundred years of the Chriſtian era. Throughout that time there were changes of faſhion at Rome as between Toga and Pallium, and Pænula and Caracalla, and the like, but the general characteriſtics of the dreſs above deſcribed remained but little changed.

[γ] The following paſſage will ſerve to ſuggeſt the true cauſe of the general reſemblance here noticed. "Greece and Rome may be regarded as the medium through which, in the deſigns of Providence, a flood of *Eaſtern civiliſation* was deſtined to overſpread the other-

wiſe barbarous Weſt . . . The influence of Rome . . . has never yet ceaſed, though the *eſſentially Eaſtern characteriſtics* of Pelaſgic Rome have long ſince paſſed away. In truth, it is not eaſy to contemplate, even in imagination, a people walking about in ſandals and white blankets, living in houſes which retained, amidſt all their incomparable ſplendour and luxury, the primitive Eaſtern arrangement of a central fireplace and a hole in the roof above it; reclining, like Turks or Arabs, on cuſhions at their meals; burning their dead like Hindus, and with all the idol acceſſories both in their homes and their temples (to ſay nothing of the impure rites), which ſtill mark the pantheiſm of the unchanging Eaſt." — *Preface to Paley's Faſti*, p. xiv.

on examination two prevailing types, the characteristics of
which can be recognised at a glance. They may be described
respectively as the dress of active exertion, and the dress of
dignified leisure, of festivity, or of solemn state. And of these
two leading types two articles of dress are respectively characteristic. The χίτων, or *tunica*, the *chetoneth* of Holy Scripture, is the dress of activity. That same χίτων, or tunic, *with
the addition of some full and flowing supervesture*, is the dress of
dignity or of solemn state.

Of these two main constituents of ancient dress, common to
both men and women, the Tunic was fitted somewhat closely to
the body, and, when need required, was girt up so as to leave
the lower limbs more or less free. It admitted, accordingly,
of but little variety in shape, though it did admit, of course,
of variety in material and in texture. And because of this
simplicity the names by which it was known vary comparatively
little. But there was a longer form of the tunic suited for
occasions of state, known as the χίτων ποδήρης, *tunica talaris*,
that is, "reaching to the feet," or "to the ankles," as well as
the shorter tunic commonly worn.

The supervesture, on the other hand, the prevailing form
of which was that of a large blanket, or of a Highland plaid,
admitted, as does such a plaid now, of the greatest variety in
arrangement,—admitted too of every degree of splendour in
respect of material, texture, and ornamentation. And to this
portion of ancient dress we find, accordingly, a great variety
of names assigned, indicative, many of them, of special modifications of the general type. Now a supervesture of this
kind, full and flowing, was in the nature of things unsuited to
energetic action, and even incompatible[3] with it. It was,

---

3 Hence the frequent allusions in
ancient authors to the throwing off of
the outer garment (ἱμάτιον) when active
exertion was required. Hom. Il. B.
183, is the earliest instance. Compare
note 128, p. 73. (Part ii.)

therefore, affociated in men's minds either with the peaceful [
occupations of rulers, ftatefmen, and councillors, or with thofe
more folemn occafions of feftivity or of worfhip, when, in the
prefence of the father of their houfe or of the chief of their
tribe, or of God, at once their Father and their King, men
gathered together in folemn affembly, and with a natural in-
ftinét of propriety put on their more beautiful apparel.
Better illuftrations of thefe two types of drefs cannot be found
than in two reprefentations of our Lord which are of frequent
occurrence in the early Catacombs. When He is reprefented
(fee Plate XIII.) as "The Good Shepherd," the figure (of
claffical origin, and nearly refembling the Ἑρμῆς κριόφορος of
Calamis) is that of an aétual fhepherd, clad in the χίτων only,
and that girt up, and reaching barely to the knee. But when
He is reprefented, not allegorically but direétly, as fitting in
the midft of His difciples or of the Jewifh doétors, [as giving
food, which He Himfelf had bleffed, to the feeding of great
multitudes,* as bleffing young children,* or raifing dead La-
zarus to life ; * in all thefe cafes alike both our Lord Himfelf
and the Twelve (when they, too, are reprefented) are clad in
what men then deemed a drefs appropriate to all fuch occafions,

---

[This accounts for the idiomatic
ufe of the word *toga ;* as in the *cedant
arma togæ* of Cicero, or in the words
preferved by S. Ifidore of Seville
(*Etym.* lib. xix.) as addreffed to
Roman citizens by the Senate, "*De-
pofitis togis, Quirites, ite ad faga.*"
[The *fagum* being a fhort *military*
cloak.] Herein, too, note the preg-
nant implication of the clofing epithet
in the well-known line,—

"Romanos rerum dominos gentemque togatam ;"

" Lords of the world, a nation clad in
garb of peaceful rule."

{ See Plates XIV. and XV. The

firft of the two has by fome antiquaries
been interpreted as reprefenting our
Lord among the Jewifh doétors. Compare Plate XII.

* This fubjeét, fuggeftive of the
deeper truths which underlie the mi-
racle of the loaves, and which are dwelt
upon by our Lord Himfelf in His fubfequent difcourfe (John, chap. vi.), is
one of very frequent occurrence in the
earlier frefcoes of the Roman Catacombs. See Aringhi, R. S. tom. ii. pp.
59, 91, 95, 101, 249, 269, 333, &c.
* See Plate XI.
* Aringhi, R. S. tom. ii. pp. 87,
123, 183, 205, 269, &c.

b

viz. in a full and flowing fuper-veftment worn over the χίτων, or tunic already fpoken of.

Long Garments when Worn.

This diftinction between the long, full, and ftately robes of which I have laft fpoken, and the fhorter, clofer, and more convenient drefs of active life, is one which meets us again and again both in the literature of antiquity, and in early monuments of art. It is one, too, which it is fpe-cially neceffary to bear in mind in reference to the queftions on which we are now engaged. And with a view to thefe the following points fhould fpecially be noticed.

The wearing of long garments by *men*, except for fpecial reafons and on exceptional occafions, was, as is well known, regarded as a proof of effeminacy.ˣ

But, on the other hand, on occafions of ftately ceremony, — efpecially of religious ceremony,— this wearing of long garments (τὸ ποδηροφορεῖν in Greek phrafe) was regardedλ as a natural and appropriate mode of marking the ceffation from laborious exertion proper to occafions of folemnity. Hence

---

ˣ In the *Eaft*, the tunic was as a rule worn longer than by the Romans. But even there the fame feeling may be traced. Thus Clement of Alexandria, referring to Homer's well-known epithet for the Ionian people, fays, οὓς Ὅμηρος ἰκθηλύνων ἑλκεσιπέπλους καλῦ (*Pædag.* ii. p. 233). Compare p. 238 : τὸ σύρειν τὰς ἐσθῆτας ἐπ' ἄκρους καθιεὶς τοὺς πόδας κομιδῇ ἀλαζονικὸν, ἐμποδὼν τῇ ἐνεργείᾳ τοῦ περιπατῶν γινόμενον. For the Weft, St. Auguftine's authority may fuffice (*De Doct. Chrift.* lib. iii.). He fays, *Talares ac manicatas tunicas habere olim apud Romanos opprobrium.* Compare Cicero's reproach againft the companions of Catiline as being con-fpicuous *manicatis ac talaribus tunicis, velis amictos non togis.*

λ As to the length of the *tunic*, the following is the *locus claffcus* commonly referred to. Quintilian, *De Or.* lib. xi., *Cui lati clavi jus non erit, ita cin-gatur, ut tunicæ prioribus oris infra genua paulum, pofterioribus ad medios poplites ufque proveniant. Nam infra mulierum eft, fupra centurionum.* In other words, women wear a tunic reaching to the feet (*talaris*); foldiers, a fhort tunic, girt up above the knee; the orator, in his forenfic habit, is to obferve a medium between the two.

their ufe in reprefentations alike of the laft farewell fpoken by a father over his daughter's grave (Pl. I.), by an emperor prefiding at a facrifice (Plate III.), by a bridegroom (Plate V. *bis*), pledging troth to his bride.

And in all the monuments of art bearing upon this matter it will be found that a long tunic is almoft invariably worn whenever any fuperveftment of ftate,^μ or official dignity,^ν is worn above it.

CHANGE IN THE USE OF THE TOGA.

A further point of importance to the underftanding of our prefent fubject is this, that the older ufage of the *toga* had ceafed, and a new etiquette with regard to it had become

---

μ Hence explain Artemidorus, *On-eirocritica*, ii. 3 (p. 886), ἐν μὲν ταῖς ἑορταῖς καὶ πανηγύρεσιν οὔτε ποικίλα οὔτε γυναικεῖα βλάπτει τινὰ ἐσθής. Artemidorus, who will be often quoted upon the fubject now before us, was a native of Afia Minor, a Greek by birth and education, a Roman by domicile, and a witnefs therefore who combines the traditions both of Greece and Rome. He practifed as a phyfician at Rome early in the fecond century. The *Oneirocritica* is a treatife (as the title implies) on the interpretation of dreams, and abounds with curious details as to the drefs and coftume of that age.

ν The only exception is in military drefs, and that for obvious reafons. And becaufe in military drefs, therefore alfo in the drefs of *emperors ;* the original idea of the *imperator* being that of the firft citizen of the republic in his character of commander of the

Roman armies. When appearing in that character he wears a fhort military cloak fo arranged, generally, as to leave the *right, or fword arm*, wholly free from wrift to fhoulder. But when he appears as *Pontifex Maximus* (as often on coins), and engaged in facrifice, or as *Princeps Senatus*, he wears the full and flowing veftments, *Toga* and *Tunica talaris*, which were regarded as proper to religious ceremonial and to the ftately dignity of a citizen prince — *rerum dominus, gentifque togatæ*, to paraphrafe Auguftus' own quotation. Hence explain Lampridius in *Alex. Severo : Accepit prætextam* (h. e. togam prætextam) *etiam tum cum facra faceret, fed loco Pontificis Maximi, non Imperatoris.* For the two types of imperial drefs compare the two principal figures in Plates III. and IV., and fee the fame diftinctions illuftrated in the various figures on the diptych of St. Paul forming the frontifpiece to this volume.

eſtabliſhed, before the introduction of Chriſtianity into Rome. Under the republican *régime*, the free citizen, who as ſuch had a right to ſhare, and commonly did ſhare, in the moſt exalted functions of government in a municipality which gave law to the "world," would never appear in Forum, in Senate (if ſuch his rank), or in aſſembly of the people, without the characteriſtic dreſs (note ξ, p. ix), which marked him out as one of the "maſters of the world." But when, after the eſtabliſhment of the empire, the whole powers of government at home and abroad came to be concentrated in the hands of one man, and of his nominees, the general uſe of the *toga* was at once abandoned; and the far more convenientξ ſuper-veſtments, the *lacerna*,ο or the *pallium*,π ſubſtituted for it. Auguſtus attempted, but in vain, to reſiſt an innovation

---

ξ Tertullian (*De Pallio*, p. 214) alludes to the many inconveniences involved in the uſe of the Toga. "Quid te prius in toga ſentias, indutum anne onuſtum? Habere veſtem, an bajulare? Si negabis, domum conſequar; videbo quid ſtatim a limine properes. Nullius profecto alterius indumenti depoſitio quam [*i.e.* magis quam] togæ gratulatur."

ο The *Lacerna* (χλάμυς, μανδύας, or ἐφεστρίς) was originally regarded as a garment proper to ſoldiers, and was conſidered therefore wholly unſeemly in republican times within the walls of Rome. But under the empire it came into general uſe even in the city. Martial alludes to it as worn by ſpectators at the games. Epig. iv. 2, quoted in Appendix A.

π The word *Pallium* has a great variety of meanings (note 125) both in claſſical and in eccleſiaſtical Latin (notes 127, 129, 157, 195, 227) At Rome in the firſt century the word when ſpecifically uſed ſerved to deſig-

nate the characteriſtic *Greek* dreſs (the ἱμάτιον) in contradiſtinction from the *toga*, the national dreſs of Latium. The *pallium* varied in ſize (as did the *toga*) according to the wealth and dignity of the wearer, and the occaſion of greater or leſs ceremony on which it was worn. But there was one marked diſtinction between it and the *toga*, that the former was (when opened out) either ſquare or oblong; the latter either circular or oval. [This muſt be ſaid with ſome reſerve, *ut in re adhuc ſub judice*.] The following paſſages will illuſtrate what has been ſaid. Suetonius *in Auguſto*, cap. 98: "Ceteros continuos dies, inter varia munuſcula, togas inſuper ac pallia diſtribuit, lege propoſita (*i.e.* making it a condition), ut Romani Græco, Græci Romano habitu uterentur." Valerius Maximus, lib. ii. cap. 2, ſpeaking of the Romans when in Greece perſiſting in uſing Latin in the law courts: "Nulla non in re pallium togæ ſubjici debere arbitrabantur." See Plate V. *bis*.

which was due not to any mere caprice of fafhion, but to the complete change in the ftatus of Roman citizens brought about by Auguftus himfelf. But what was in his own power he did, aided as he was by thofe traditionary affociations which connected the *toga* in Roman minds with the whole courfe of their hiftory even from earlieft times. It was ftill thought of as the diftinctively Roman drefs,*e* in contraft with the Greek *pallium* (ἱμάτιον); it was ftill regarded as the proper drefs for ceremonial ufe on all occafions of ftate, of focial or religious celebration. Thus it was contrary to etiquette to dine with the emperor, except in a *toga*. Advocates *r* were ftill required to wear it; and Clients,*v* at leaft on important occafions, in attendance upon their Patrons.

---

e Suetonius, fpeaking of Auguftus: *Vifa quondam pullatorum* (the ordinary *lacerna* was of a dark colour) *turba, dedit negotium Ædilibus ne quem paterentur in Foro aut in Curia nifi pofitis lacernis togatum confiftere.* It was on the like occafion that he is reprefented as quoting, with indignation, the well-known line of Virgil, commented on in note *ι*, p. ix.

ϭ Spartianus *in Severo.* "Habuit etiam aliud omen imperii, cum rogatus ad cœnam Imperatoriam palliatus veniffet, *qui togatus venire debuiffet*, togam præfidiariam ipfius Imperatoris accepit."

r To this probably refers Juvenal, Sat. viii.

"Veniet de plebe togata
Qui juris nodos et legum ænigmata folvat."

And fo Ovid, *Remed. Amor.* 150.

"Da vacuæ menti, quo teneatur, opus.
Sunt fora, funt leges, funt, quos tuearis,
amici.

Vade per urbanæ fplendida [al. candida] caftra togæ."

On this paffage I may note in paffing that *fplendida*, which is probably the true reading, would convey to a Roman ear nearly the fame meaning as *candida*, which, as a various reading, is probably a glofs upon the former word. Compare Seneca, Epift. v. "Non *fplendeat* toga; ne fordeat quidem." And for *candidus*, equivalent to λαμπρὸς, fee note 19.

v Hence the phrafe, *opera togata*, ufed of "full-drefs" ceremonial in general, and more particularly of the ceremonious attendance upon perfons high in office or in ftation. Hence explain Martial, Lib. iii. Ep. 46.

"Exigis a nobis operam fine fine togatam;
Non eo, libertum fed tibi mitto meum."

And, again, Lib. ix. Ep. 101:

"Denariis tribus invitas, et mane togatum
Obfervare jubes atria, Baffe, tua;
Deinde hærere tuo lateri, præcedere fellam,
Ad vetulas tecum plus minus ire decem."

THE TOGA AS A GARMENT OF RELIGION.

But for our preſent purpoſe it is of ſpecial importance to note the uſe of the *toga* on occaſions which were more particularly of a religious character. It was worn (but then black, or at leaſt of dark colour) at funerals by mourners; while in a *white* toga were the dead themſelves carried out to burial. It was worn by thoſe who took part in public ſacrifices, [φ] as in the earlier times it had ever been. To this uſe of the *toga* Martial alludes when in writing to a friend (iv. Ep. lxv.) he congratulates him on the eaſy life he leads; and on this among other things, that living away from Rome, as he does, in a country town, he has not to take his *toga* out more than once or twice a month on " temple days," ſo to ſay.

> " Egiſti vitam ſemper, Line, municipalem,
> Qua nihil in vita dulcius eſſe poteſt.
> Idibus, et raris togula eſt excuſſa Kalendis."

And a ſimilar uſage of the *toga* is alluded to by Tertullian (*De Cor. Mil.* p. 358). He is ſpeaking of a particular kind of *Corona* (or chaplet, note 54, p. 32) known as *Corona Hetruſca*. *Hoc vocabulum*, he writes, *eſt coronarum, quas gemmis, et foliis ex auro quercinis, ob Jovem inſignes, ad deducendas thenſas cum palmatis togis ſumunt.*

SUMMARY.

Paſſages to a ſimilar effect might be multiplied if need were. But enough has been ſaid to determine the two points which it is of chief importance to my preſent purpoſe to make clear. Firſt, that the uſe of long, full, and flowing gar-

---

[φ] See, for example, the figure of the Emperor preſiding at a ſacrifice in Plate III. And ſee note ı above.

ments, was regarded in the Roman world generally, in the firſt century, as ſpecially appropriate to all ceremonial occaſions, whether civil or religious. And, ſecondly, that at Rome the *toga* had ceaſed to be worn as a garb of ordinary life, but was retained as the habit of ceremony, both civil and religious.

I need only add that where Greek dreſs prevailed, the *pallium* (ἱμάτιον), in its fuller and more dignified form, occupied the ſame place relatively, as a dreſs of ceremonial, as did the *toga* in Rome itſelf, and in thoſe parts of the Roman world which adhered to Roman uſage.

CHAPTER III.

§ 1. Associations of Colour in the First Four Centuries.

Enough has been said in the laft chapter on the fubject of Drefs in general to allow of our proceeding now to a further queftion, that of the Colour, which, in the primitive age, was thought appropriate to the Drefs of Chriftian Miniftry.

The earlieft monuments bearing upon this queftion, whether in literature, or in early Chriftian art, point to the conclufion that that Drefs was white.

And before we proceed to any more detailed examination of thofe monuments, it will be well to take note of the ideas which prevailed in the ancient world upon this fubject of Colour, and of the caufes to which that feeling may be traced.

In this place I fhall do little more than ftate the general refults to which the language of antiquity points; referring to an Appendix χ the more detailed ftatement of the evidence bearing upon this queftion.

§ 2. Associations of Colour in Classical Writers.

And, firft, a few words as to the feeling of the ancient world generally upon this matter of Colour, apart from, and antecedent to, any exclufively Chriftian influences.

χ See Appendix A.

Black and fombre ✤ colours, bright and gaudy colours, and laftly, white, thefe are the three main divifions with which we have to deal. And each of thefe had, in the minds of men generally, a certain accepted fignificance in the times of which we now are fpeaking, and that both in the Eaft and in the Weft.

Black or dark garments, by a natural affociation, have ever been regarded as the expreffion of mourning.ω They were alfo worn for obvious reafons of economy and of convenience by the poor, and by labouring men in general.

White, on the other hand, was the colour thought appropriate to joyous feftivity of all kinds. Donatus (commenting on Terence) fpeaks for the general feeling upon this fubject when he fays, that "Bright white garments are for them that rejoice, and fombre clothing to them that grieve." *Læto veftitus candidus : ærumnofo obfoletus.*

A further point fhould here be noticed, that not among the Jews ɑ only, but in the ancient world generally, white was regarded as the colour efpecially appropriate to things divine, and to religious worfhip. Thus Plato, β when fpeaking of the kind of offerings which may with moft fitnefs be made to the gods, fays, that "*White colours will be moft feemly for gods, as in other things, fo alfo in this of woven garments offered*

✤ μίλαινα or φαία ἐσθὶς, in Greek writers: *atræ, nigræ, fufcæ, pullæ, veftes*, in the Weft; or to exprefs a meaning nearly, though not exactly the fame, *fordidæ* and *obfoletæ*.

ω It may be well, however, to note that in fome exceptional cafes white was for women a colour of mourning; as to a certain extent it ftill is among ourfelves. This, however, was only the cafe where, as an ordinary rule, bright and gay colours were worn. In all ages, and in all countries, the

conventional figns of mourning are to be explained by remembering that they confift in a reverfing (more or lefs complete) of the habit of ordinary life. Thus where the hair is ordinarily worn fhort it is a fign of mourning to let it grow long; where the hair is generally long, as with women, it is a fign of mourning to cut it off.

ɑ See Appendix A, Part II.

β Περὶ νόμων, xii. p. 956. Appendix A, No. 1.

c

to them.   Dyed garments," he adds, *" fhould not be offered, fave only as ornaments of war."*[γ]

Brilliant[δ] and gaudy colours, laftly, had fome more fpecial affociations of which a few words may be faid before proceeding further.

And firft, thefe more brilliant colours which could only be added to wool by art, and were very coftly, were naturally affociated in men's minds with ideas either of the fplendour and luxury of the more wealthy, or of the ornate coftume appropriated to defignation of royal or official dignity.   More efpecially was this the cafe with regard to purple,[ε] which from its exceeding coftlinefs was referved, commonly, for defignation of imperial rank, or to be worn by thofe, who from delegated office, or fpecial privilege of favour, were allowed to wear imperial colours.   Thus the Emperor Commodus, near the clofe of the fecond century, writes to Albinus,[ζ] then high in

---

γ He refers of courfe to red, or colours approaching to red (*blood-red*), which have ever had a fpecial affociation with the idea of war. The red fhirt of Garibaldi's troops, of which we heard fo much not long fince, was the fignal for battle with the Legions of the Republic two thoufand years ago.

δ Ποικίλαι, ἀνθηραί, ἐσθῆτες with the Greeks, anfwering to the *pictæ veftes* of Roman writers. With thefe are con-trafted in ancient writers ἰδιόχροα εἵμ-ατα, or *nativi colores*, the natural colours belonging to various kinds of wool. Some curious information as to the varieties of *natural colour* in wools, will be found in the Treatife of La-zarus Bayfius, *De Re Veft.* p. 563. Apulia was famous for its white wools; Spain for black; Liguria (the city Pollentia is fpecially named) for red; and Tarentum for the various

fhades of tawny yellow defignated by the epithet *fulvus.*

ε The *purpura* itfelf varied in price according to the varieties of quality and of manufacture [See Ferrarius *De Re Veft.* lib. ii. cap. 7.]. The Ty-rian δίβαφον was the moft coftly; next to it the Tarentine dye; and, laftly, a much cheaper dye of home manufacture, fuch as was ufed at Rome in the earlier and fimpler days of the Republic, and was retained (owing to the confecration imparted by long cuf-tom) in the dreffes of fome of the Roman magiftracies to a much later time.

ζ Capitolinus *in Albino, Hift. Aug. Sane ut tibi aliquod Imperialis majeftatis accedat, habebis utendi coccinei pallii fa-cultatem, habiturus et purpuram, fed fine auro.*

his favour, and in command of the Roman forces in Britain, and tells him that in order to confer upon him fomething of imperial greatnefs, he gives him licenfe to wear a fcarlet mantle (*pallium coccineum*) *even in the prefence of the emperor*, and to wear the purple, but without decorations of gold.

The higher magiftrates, too, under the empire, as previoufly under the republic, wore, on ftate occafions, a *toga* bordered (*prætexta*) with purple. This was always the cafe when they prefided at the public games;" occafionally alfo, when taking part, officially, in public facrifice.'

It is worth noting that at Rome the *toga prætexta* (or *toga piEta*), which, with the embroidered tunic (*tunica palmata*) worn beneath it, was referved for thefe ftate occafions, was not the private property of the various magiftrates on whom it devolved to wear it, but belonged to the State, and was laid up in the Temple of Jupiter Capitolinus, or in the Palatium. The Emperor Gordian' was the firft to make a change in this refpeft, and to provide himfelf, while yet a private citizen, with a *tunica palmata* and *toga piEta* of his own.

Not to dwell further upon particulars of this kind, let us now further take note that as bright and brilliant colours"

" See the Confular Diptychs photographed among the Illuftrations of this volume. Plates XXII., XXIII.

é Thus, for inftance, Appian ('Ἐμφύλια, iii. *apud Ferrarium*) fpeaks of Afellius wearing, as prætor, ἱερὰν καὶ ἐπίχρυσον ἐσθῆτα, ὡς θυσίᾳ περικείμενος, a facred veftment, adorned with gold, as being occupied in facrifice. Compare the mention of that ἱερὰ στολὴ which was fent by Conftantine to Bifhop Macarius of Jerufalem, *infra*, p. 42.

ᵢ Capitolinus *in Gordiano*, *Hift. Aug.* p. 370. *Palmatam tunicam et togam piEtam primus Romanorum privatus fuam propriam habuit : cum ante Im-*

peratores etiam de Capitolio acciperent, vel de Palatio. The dreffes kept in the Palatium would be thofe of the Pontifex Maximus, whofe official refidence was part of the "Palace of Auguftus."

× I may notice here one exceptional affociation of idea with purple, that of having "*a certain affinity with death*," as Artemidorus (quoted in Appendix A) has noted. We may trace the fame feeling in the ufe of purple (violet) as a colour of mourning in the Greek Church (See p. 174), and in court etiquette.

are fuch as naturally attract the eye and draw attention to thofe who wear them, garments of brilliant colour, *if not worn in official coftume*, were regarded, not by Chriftians only, but in the ancient[λ] world generally, as immodeft and meretricious.

DRESS OF HEATHEN PRIESTHOOD.

Before we pafs on further, it may be well to ftate, that while white garments were, as we have feen, regarded as fpecially appropriate to religious folemnity of all kinds, they were not in heathen notion regarded as the infignia *of the higher official priefthoods.*[μ] Two reafons there were why this fhould not be. One, that where white drefs was worn, or at leaft might be worn, *by all*, fome diftinctive drefs was required, when the object was to mark out one or another as the poffeffor of any fpecial hierarchical dignity. The other reafon was this, that there were fpecial confecrations of colour, fo to fpeak, to particular divinities, either from natural or conventional affociations, which made of thefe colours a kind of livery appropriate to fuch gods. When we find purple fpoken of as fpecially characteriftic of Priefts of Dionyfus[ν] (or Bacchus), or of Mars, we can hardly doubt that in this there was thought had of the purple vine, or of the juice of the grape, in the one cafe, of the blood of the battle-field in the other. And fo, too, in thofe many other inftances in which purple is found affociated with the drefs of thofe honorary priefthoods, whether in Afia Minor, in Greece, or in Italy,

---

[λ] One paffage may fuffice in confirmation. Pliny, alluding to the dyes produced in Gaul [then as now proverbial for love of gay drefs: cf. Martial, Epig. xiv. 129], fpeaks of them as furnifhing *per quod facilius matrona adultero placeat, corruptor infidictur*

nuptæ (*Hift. Nat.* xxii. cap. 11).

[μ] Evidence for the ftatements here following, concerning the coftume of heathen priefthood, will be found in Appendix A. See No. 12, to 18.

[ν] See Appendix A, No. 15.

of which we find fuch frequent mention in antiquity.‡ In almoft all of them the tunic of official coftume had its ftripes of purple ; in almoft all, the fuper-veftment, whatever its fhape might be, was either bordered (*prætexta*) with rich ornament, or wholly made of purple, of fcarlet, or of both combined. And here again the reafon may probably be traced to the idea of fetting forth authority,ᵉ as of a royal priefthood, by the royal purple of official drefs. The actual facrificers, on the other hand, wore not thofe flowing veftments. Amid thofe fouler forms of heathenifm which prevailed in many parts of the Eaft, the nakednefs of the priefts was a natural accompaniment to rites of revolting groffnefs. But even in Italy and Greece the drefs of the actual facrificers was for obvious reafons a very fcanty one. They were *nudi* (or γυμνοί) in the conventional ᵀ fenfe of the word ; at times, too, if we may judge by monuments, not in a conventional fenfe only. [See the figures of the facrificing priefts in Pl. III., and the central figure in Pl. VI. ; and contraft with thefe the figure of the Greek ἀρχιερεὺς in Pl. VII.]

§ 3. Associatons of Colour to the Mind of Christians
OF THE PRIMITIVE TIME.

The various ideas above fpoken of as affociated generally

---

‡ See Appendix A, No. 12 to 18.

ᵉ The Priefts of whom I here fpeak were regarded in the later Republican Conftitutions, both of Greece and Rome, as inheritors of that "royal Priefthood" which had formerly been vefted in their kings. Hence the retention of the royal title, "Ἀρχων Βασιλεὺς, *Rex Sacrificulus*, for religious ceremony, in cities where in any other connection the title of king would not have been endured.

ᵀ A man clad in a tunic only, without fuper-veftment of any kind, was a fight common enough in the country ; but in capital cities, and in important towns, for a man of pofition fo to appear would have been thought as ftrange as it would be for one in like pofition now to walk down Regent Street in his fhirt-fleeves. Hence the various meanings of the words *nudus* and γυμνός. It may mean (often does mean) " clad in tunic only ; " it *may* mean (fometimes does mean) actually naked.

in men's minds with particular colours, or claſſes of colours, had come to be ſo aſſociated, not from any ſingularity of faſhion peculiar to any one age or country, but as the reſult of natural cauſes, and of the ordinary conditions of civiliſed ſociety.

The uſe of thoſe gay and brilliant colours, for example, of which we laſt ſpoke, is to be explained preciſely in the ſame way, whether they were worn as decorations of official coſtume, for the greater dignity of a court, or to miniſter to vanity, or worſe than vanity, by thoſe who aſſumed them only for the ſake of perſonal decoration. In all caſes the effect at leaſt was the ſame, that of attracting the eyes of men to him or to her who wore them, and of marking them out from others among whom they moved. And this effect was the more eaſily ſecured becauſe the great coſtlineſs of thoſe more brilliant colours was ſuch, as to prevent their being adopted by any but a very few.

In going on now to conſider the language of early Chriſtian writers upon this ſubject of colour, we muſt bear in mind that they were influenced not only by thoſe traditionary feelings which were common to the ancient world, but alſo by the language of Holy Scripture, by the uſages of the Church of which they formed a part, and laſtly by a natural repugnance to all that favoured of heathen forms of worſhip.

The witneſſes of chief importance for this firſt period of four hundred years, are St. Clement of Alexandria,ᵉ Tertullian, and St. Jerome.

The firſt of theſe, a native,ᶠ there is a reaſon to think, of Athens, but reſident during the greater part of his life at Alexandria, had "viſited the cities, and learnt to know the mind of many men." He had travelled in Magna Græcia,

---

ᵉ Quoted in Appendix A, No. 36 to 43; Tertullian, *ibid.* No. 44 to 46; St. Jerome, *infra*, p. 34.

ᶠ The date of his birth is uncertain, but he died A.D. 220.

in Paleſtine, in Syria, in Egypt ; and everywhere he had ſought
to the moſt learned of every land, that he might add to the
ſtores of varied knowledge which he had acquired. And as
a witneſs, therefore, for the feeling of primitive Chriſtendom
in a matter ſuch as this, it would be difficult, nay, not
poſſible, to find one better qualified than is he.

The book from which I quote is the Παιδαγωγὸς, " The
Divine Guide in the path of Chriſtian Life." In the ſecond
and third books of that treatiſe he has frequently occaſion
to ſpeak on the ſubjeƈt of dreſs, of perſonal ornament, and
the like. And we find him giving expreſſion again and again,
and in the ſtrongeſt manner, to preciſely the ſame feelings
in reſpeƈt both of bright and brilliant colours, and of white,
which we have already traced elſewhere, and adding thereto
much that reminds at once of the new atmoſphere of religious
thought, which now at length we breathe.

For to St. Clement too, as to others to whom we have
been liſtening, theſe dyed garments, coloured like unto
flowers, form a fitting ͳ garb only for women that are without modeſty, and men that are without manhood. In his eyes
they favour of falſehood, and of treachery ; they are proofs
of a corrupted taſte, they are ſigns of an evil diſpoſition.
But, on the other hand, white to him is the appropriate
garb "for men of peaceful heart and inwardly illuminate."
White he deems the colour befitting all ſolemnity and reverence ; and he quotes with delight the *" excellent Plato,"*
" herein as in other things a follower of Moſes," as one in
opinion with himſelf upon this matter.

But it may be objeƈted to the relevancy of all this, and
of much elſe to the ſame effeƈt which might be quoted, that
he is ſpeaking of theſe brilliant colours as worn in ordinary
life, not of any ſuch when conſecrated to the ſervice of the
Chriſtian ſanƈtuary.

ͳ For the expreſſions which follow, ſee Appendix A, Nos. 36 to 43.

Most true. It would not become me to say in reply that the reason of this silence is that he had never heard or dreamt of any such consecration. For this would be assuming the very point in dispute. But I will appeal to all my readers, let their prepossessions on this question be what they may, and I will ask whether on any other supposition it is possible to account for his using language such as this which follows. Had he known of vestments "coloured like unto flowers" being used in highest offices of Christian ministration, could he possibly have said, as now we may hear him say, that together with the dealers in costly ointments and the preparers of incense, *the dyers of various wools should be banished one and all from the Commonwealth of Truth?* Could he in that case have said, as in fact he does, that *" these colours bright like flowers are fit only for the worshippers of Bacchus, for the mummeries of heathen mysticism, for the vanities of the stage?"* One only answer can be given to such a question, by any save those (to use St. Clement's own words) to whose imagination, as unto men mad, white and black are both alike.

I will not now detain my reader by further quotations, in proof of the feeling of the primitive age in respect of those varieties of colour of which alone we have spoken hitherto. Those who would pursue the subject further will find the means of doing so in the passages collected in the Appendix. At present I have only to point out, that in the moral scale of colours, as recognised at the time of which we speak, there was a middle point between the solemnity of a pure or brilliant white, and the luxurious extragavance of the more costly dyes. Sober colours there were, or, as commonly they were called, natural or native colours,ᵛ which were recognised as fitted for the every-day garb of the sober-minded Christian

---

ᵛ *Nativi colores,* ἰδιόχροα ἱμάτια, are terms of frequent occurrence. Compare note δ, p. xviii.

man or woman.φ Such ſober colours we may ſee depicted in the
ſeries of plates (XVIII. to XXI.) from the Church of St. George
at Theſſalonica, among the illuſtrations of this volume. And
with this hint to guide us, in addition to what has already
been ſaid in earlier pages of this Introduction, we ſhall have
no difficulty, I think, in apprehending the general nature, at
leaſt, of the dreſs, which in the paſſage now following is
deſcribed.

§ 4. THE DRESS OF CHRISTIAN MEN AND WOMEN WOR- SHIPPING IN THE ASSEMBLIES OF THE CHURCH.

It is St. Clement that ſpeaks : —

" The wife and the huſband ſhould take their way unto the
church, in ſeemly apparel, with unaffected gait, and ſpeech
reſtrained ; having love unfeigned ; pure in body and pure
in heart ; fitly decked for prayer to God. And this further
let the woman have : let her wholly cover her head, (unleſs
perchance ſhe be at home), for ſo dreſſed ſhe will have reſpect,
and be withdrawn from gazing eyes. And if thus with
modeſty, and with a veil, ſhe covereth her own eyes, ſhe ſhall
neither be miſled herſelf, nor ſhall ſhe draw others, by the
expoſure of her face, into the dangerous path of ſin. For
this willeth the Word ; ſeeing that it is meet for the woman
that ſhe pray with covered head. . . . But then ſo as
they, who are joined to Chriſt, adorn themſelves, in a more
ſolemn faſhion, for aſſemblies of the church, even ſuch ſhould
they ever be, even ſo be faſhioned, all the days of their life.
' To be, not ſeem to be,' let that be their watchword ; gentle,
reverend, full of holy love, at one time not leſs than at
another.

φ " As there is a dreſs," ſays St.
Clement, " proper to ſoldiers, to ſai-
lors, to magiſtrates, ſo is there a garb
befitting the ſobriety of the Chriſtian."

" But it is not ſo indeed.   Somehow doth it come about,
that, with change of place, they change both their habit and
their manners ; even as the polypus is ſaid to change each one
his colour, to the ſemblance of the rock whereby he dwells."
[*Pædag.* lib. iii. p. 300.]

From a Syriac MS. of the year 586 A.D.

CHAPTER IV.

Direct Evidence as to the Dress of Christian Ministry
during the Four First Centuries.

In the two laſt Chapters ſufficient has been ſaid to enable the
reader to appreciate, at their true value, the facts which will
preſent themſelves, now that we enter upon the conſideration
of the direct evidence applicable to the queſtion before us.

That evidence naturally divides itſelf under two heads;
and of theſe we may firſt conſider that afforded by the earlieſt
monuments of Chriſtian art.

I will aſk the reader to refer to the ſeries of Plates numbered XIV., XV., and XVII., among the illuſtrations of this
volume, and to bring to bear upon their interpretation thoſe
general diſtinctions, as to form and colour, with which we have
been hitherto occupied. He will ſee, I think, at once, that
the dreſs there portrayed is one, which, in thoſe earlieſt ages
now in queſtion, would be ſuggeſtive to the mind by its
form of occaſions of eſpecial ſolemnity, and by its colour
of a garb ſuited, as none elſe could be, to ſuch as ſhould
miniſter before God in the courts of His houſe.

Of thoſe Plates, the two firſt are repreſentative (the firſt,
probably, and without doubt the ſecond) of our Lord ſeated
on a central Throne, with His Apoſtles on either hand, ſeated,
or ſtanding, about Him. In another very ſimilar freſco [x] to
theſe, the twelve Apoſtles, ſeated on ſecondary θρόνοι, or apoſtolic

[x] Given by Perret in his great work on the *Catacombs*, vol. iii. Pl. xxxv.

thrones, on either fide of our Lord (nearly as in Pl. XIV.),
realife exactly one of the pictures of the heavenly kingdom
fet forth to us by our Lord Himfelf; a kingdom which is
upon earth, though not " of " ↓ the earth, wherein He, our
Lord, fitteth upon His " throne of glory," while to the
twelve, by delegation from their Lord, it is given to fit upon
twelve thrones, judging (*i.e.* ruling) ⸗ the twelve tribes of the
fpiritual Ifrael.

And this type of Apoftolic drefs, I may obferve in paffing,
is preferved by the traditions of the Church, and efpecially
appropriated to the Twelve, throughout almoft all the later
centuries of Chriftian art.⸗

For our prefent purpofe, however, it is yet more important
to note, that in the earlieft Chriftian reprefentation of any of
the more folemn acts of religion by bifhops, priefts, or deacons
(I refer to Pl. XVII.), the drefs attributed to them is, as
might have been expected on *à priori* grounds, almoft an
exact counterpart of that which we have already feen attributed
to the Apoftles.

In few words, one who examined thofe early monuments
of the primitive age, with a competent knowledge of the
habits, and the affociations of colour, characteriftic of that
time, would come to the conclufion that the drefs he there
faw was exactly fuch as we have pointed to in the three preceding Chapters. He would fee there a garb which thus far
differed from the drefs ordinarily worn, that by its form and
colour it would at once fuggeft the folemn office of them who
wore it, whether as drawing near on behalf of God's people
unto God, or as His fervants and meffengers delivering to
His people the meffages of the Divine word, and the facra-
ments of His Divine grace.

↓ *ix* expreffing origin. See *Eire-* | in *Eirenica*, pp. 186, 187.
nica, p. 75, note 14. | ⸗ See Plates XIX., XLV.
⸗ Matt. xix. 28, commented on

And now we have only to turn, in the ſecond place, to the ſecond ſource of available evidence which is open to us, and we ſhall find the ſtrongeſt confirmation of the concluſions juſt ſtated. The contemporary references to any dreſs of actual miniſtry in the Church, are, in the firſt four centuries, very few. But what there are, point all (or almoſt all*) to the ſame concluſion. In the ſecond part of this treatiſe will be found all the chief paſſages from early writers that can be brought to bear upon this queſtion. And among theſe there are ſome to which, as containing a direct reference to the ſubject now before us, I will now aſk more particular attention.

The firſt occurs in the Commentary β of St. Jerome on Ezekiel, cap. xliv. His ſubject there had led him to ſpeak of the dreſs worn by "Egyptian prieſts, not only within their temples, but without alſo." He then adds (ſee note 53, p. 31), *Porro religio divina alterum habitum habet in miniſterio, alterum in uſu vitaque communi.* "Moreover that worſhip which is of God has one habit in (holy) miniſtry, another for the uſage of common life." In a note on that paſſage (note 53) I have pointed out, that the primary reference at leaſt of theſe words is (as context ſhows) to Jewiſh rather than to Chriſtian obſervances. But a compariſon with other paſſages of the ſame author will juſtify the belief expreſſed in the note to which I allude, viz. that St. Jerome has purpoſely here choſen a very incluſive term, "*religio divina,*" as having in his mind the uſages of the Church in his own time, as well as thoſe of the Jewiſh prieſthood in times paſt. I ſhould not myſelf reſt any weight upon a paſſage of ſuch doubtful reference. But as writers on ritual habitually quote this paſſage (and generally without any reference to its context), it may be well to point out that *the utmoſt* the paſſage will prove is this, that there was a difference of ſome kind between the habit worn in ordinary life, and that which was recogniſed as proper

---

* See Appendix B.   β See Part II., p. 28, *ſqq.*

to ſervices of holy miniſtry. And this I for one ſhould regard as ſo ſelf-evident (I might almoſt ſay) as to require
no proof from iſolated paſſages ſuch as this.

A difference there was beyond all doubt, but in what did
that difference conſiſt ?

Another paſſage in the ſame commentary will advance us
yet one further ſtep, and a ſomewhat more ſecure one, in
replying to this queſtion. At p. 30 (ſee alſo note 51) will
be found a ſomewhat clearer intimation of what St. Jerome
thought to be the " *habitus religionis.*" Having to ſpeak
of the holy veſtments worn by the Levitical prieſts, and which
they were required to put off before leaving the ſanctuary,
he adds, " *By all which we learn, that we too ought not to enter
into the moſt holy place in our everyday garments, juſt ſuch as we
will, when they have been defiled from the uſage of ordinary life ;
but with a clean conſcience, and in clean garments* (mundis veſtibus) *hold in our hands the ſacraments of the Lord.*"

The word *mundus,*[γ] which he here employs as the characteriſtic epithet for the dreſs of Chriſtian miniſtry, is one
which to no dreſs could more fitly be applied, than to one
white, bright, and of ſtately ſolemnity, ſuch as that which is
preſented to us in the Plates to which I have referred. And
if any doubt ſtill remain as to what was the colour, which in
St. Jerome's time (the cloſe of the fourth century) was thought
proper to the higheſt offices of Chriſtian miniſtry, that doubt
will be removed by yet a third paſſage (ſee p. 57, Part II.),
in which, when defending the uſages of the Church againſt
the ſtrictures of Pelagius, he aſks, what offence there would
be againſt God if " *in the adminiſtration of the holy things* (ſacri-
ficiorum) *biſhop, preſbyter, and deacons, and other officers of the
Church* (reliquus eccleſiaſticus ordo) *ſhould come forward dreſſed
in white garments.*"

γ On the meaning of *mundus* ſee note 57, p. 34.

Before we quit this fubject of colour it may be proper
to notice an argument by which fome among ourfelves have
fought to found a claim to antiquity for the " fplendid " veftments now worn in the Roman Church. Unable to refift the
force of evidence which they found abfolutely incorfiftent
with the idea of the primitive drefs of Chriftian miniftry
having been modelled upon that of the Levitical priefthood,
they yet contend for " fplendid " dreffes, brilliant in colour,
having been worn as Euchariftic veftments even in primitive
times. The two paffages to which they refer are a " rubric,"
(fo to call it) in the Liturgy appended to the " Apoftolical
Conftitutions," and one which fpeaks of Conftantine the Great
having fent a " facred veftment" (ἱερὰν στολὴν) made of gold
tiffue, to Macarius, Bifhop of Jerufalem. As for this laft
piece of evidence the reader has only to refer to the original
paffage (p. 42) in which this ftory is firft told, to fee that it
proves nothing about Euchariftic veftments at all, for Conftantine fent it to be worn in the adminiftering of holy baptifm. He will find too that the fucceffor of Macarius, Cyril
Bifhop of Jerufalem, fold³ this veftment not very long after,
and that it paffed into the hands of a ftage-dancer. The
truth is, that this cuftom of emperors diftributing fplendid
garments, as marks of honour, had now become common in
the Weft, as it long continued to be ; and Conftantine, with
his half-heathen, half Chriftian notions about religion, may
not improbably have fent to Macarius one of the ἱεραὶ στολαί
which had been laid up (as was the cuftom of the times) in
fome Roman temple, for the ufe on feftal days, of Flamen,
of Pontiff, or of Augur. If fo, I may add, it was probably
taken from his own *Veftiarium Pontificium*, from the ftore

---

³ Nicephorus, the Byzantine hif-
torian, alluding to this ftory many
centuries later, fays that fome fuppofed
that Bifhop Cyril fold it in time of
famine in order to feed the poor.

But he adds, that it is difficult to fuppofe this could have been, elfe why
was not this defence offered at the
time in excufe to the emperor?

of ſplendid veſtments reſerved for the emperor's uſe in his character of *Pontifex Maximus.*

The other paſſage referred to deſerves particular notice, were it only as affording a notable proof of the little weight to be attached to iſolated phraſes of ancient authors, quoted, as they often are, in Engliſh, without reference to the original language, or to the context in which they occur; or, as in this caſe, of paſſages from Liturgies, the framework of which may be very ancient, but which have been largely interpolated from time to time, as, on the moſt concluſive evidence it is evident that they have been.

In the inſtance before us, a rubrical direction is quoted from the Liturgy of St. Clement, preſcribing that the prieſt ſhould commence his office λαμπρὰν ἐσθῆτα μετενδύς. This expreſſion proves, as it is argued, that *ſplendid* garments were in uſe for Chriſtian miniſtry from an early period of the third century, to which this Liturgy may not improbably be aſſigned.

The ſimple anſwer is this. Firſt as regards the authority quoted, it is for the moſt part impoſſible to determine whether any particular paſſage in any of the Liturgies, *as they now come into our hands,* is a portion of the original Liturgy or not. We know, both by direct teſtimony,⸱ and by internal evidence, that even thoſe Liturgies whoſe framework is really ancient, have been largely added to from time to time; and that the rubrical directions more particularly are in almoſt all caſes

---

⸱ There is a remarkable paſſage in Walafrid Strabo bearing upon this point and worthy of eſpecial attention (*De Rebus Eccl.*). After deſcribing the great ſimplicity with which in primitive times maſs was celebrated, he goes on to ſay that as time went on, *multi apud Græcos et Latinos miſſæ ordinem, ut ſibi viſum eſt, ſtatuerunt.*

The Romans, he ſays, having received their "Uſe" from St. Peter, *ſuis quique temporibus, quæ congrua judicata ſunt addiderunt.* On the endleſs variation in the various MSS. of the Greek Liturgies, and the uncertainties of the Rubrics, ſee the Introduction to Goar's *Euchologium Græcorum.*

of comparatively recent date. Therefore, even if the meaning of the Rubric here quoted really were what thofe who quote it fuppofe, nothing would really be proved as to the ufage of the Church at the time (poffibly the third century) in which, *in its earlieft form*, the Liturgy was originally compofed.

But, fecondly, in point of fact, the meaning of the paffage (whether genuine or not) is *exactly the reverfe* of what an uncritical reader might fuppofe. For the word λαμπρός, which means literally " fhining " (λάμπειν), is the word habitually ufed" in the later Greek writers in fpeaking of a " fhining " or gliftening white ; correfponding to the Latin *candidus.* And this difpofes of the only plaufible objection which, as far as I know, has been made to the conclufion already ftated.

On a review, then, of the whole evidence from early literature bearing upon this queftion, we fhould conclude, without doubt, that the drefs appropriate to the moft folemn offices of holy miniftry, during the primitive age, was white.

And if we turn next to the monumental evidence, whether in the frefcoes of the Roman Catacombs,* or in the mofaics of early churches at Rome,* Ravenna,* Conftantinople,* we fhall find that it confirms in the ftrongeft manner the conclufion, which by a feparate path we fhall have already reached.

And laftly, I may add, that the traditions of the Church, both in literature and in art, for nearly a thoufand years after the. primitive period with which we are now occupied, bear witnefs incidentally to the fame conclufion. Again and again,* even in mediæval writers, do we find recognition of

---

* See note 19, p. 9. And to the paffages there referred to, add No. 3, p. 176 in Appendix A, and note τ, p. xiii.

* See Plates XI., XII., XIV., XV., XVII.

* See Plate XXIX.

* See Plate XXVIII.

λ See Weifs, fig. 65 ('Tracht und Geräth u. s. w.), p. 125. And with this compare the figure of St. James given in Pl. LXIII.

μ See, for example, Hugo à S. Victore, quoted p. 131 ; and Symeon of Theffalonica, quoted p. 171, l. 8.

white veftments as being the *proper* garb of Chriftian miniftry.   And in the later' art monuments exhibited in this
volume, it will be feen, that the drefs attributed to the Apoftles
in the frefcoes of the Roman Catacombs, and in early monuments of the Eaft, is reproduced century after century as
their fpecial charaéteriftic, long after the general type of
miniftering drefs had been altogether changed.

On every ground, then, we may accept without hefitation
a conclufion, in which all the beft authorities on the fubjeét are
agreed; and hold that white was the colour appropriated in
primitive times to the drefs of Chriftian miniftry.

' See, for example, Pl. XXXVIII., XLV.

From a Syriac MS. of the year 586 A.D.

CHAPTER V.

ORNAMENT OF THE PRIMITIVE DRESS OF CHRISTIAN MINISTRY.

OF OFFICIAL INSIGNIA GENERALLY.

THE points of chief importance concerning the primitive drefs of holy miniftration have been examined in the preceding chapters. But there are ftill fome minor particulars which it feems defirable here to notice, with a view to the fuller underftanding of the art monuments of antiquity, and of allufions which frequently are made in the pages of old writers.

§ 1. ORNAMENT OF PRIMITIVE VESTMENTS.

And, firft, a few words muft be faid concerning the peculiar ornament which may be feen in almoft all the more ancient reprefentations of drefs figured in this volume.

A fpecial intereft attaches to this ornament, owing to the fact that in appearance and in colour (though not in name), it prefents an almoft exact refemblance to the fcarf or ftole now cuftomarily worn in the Englifh Church.

On the walls‡ of Roman Catacombs, and in the mofaics of early churches at Rome,⁴ Ravenna, and elfewhere, the long ϖ

---

‡ See Plates XI., XII., XIV., XV., XVI., XVII.

⁴ See Plates XXVIII., and for Ravenna, fee Plate XXIX.

ϖ Occafionally alfo the fhort tunic, when for fpecial reafons this is affigned, exceptionally, to dignified perfons.

See, for example, the figures of the Magi in the woodcut at p. vi. Regarded as juft arriving from *a journey*, they have a fhort tunic (*itineri habilis*, fee note 203, p. 105) affigned to them. But this ornament is added as an indication of dignity.

tunic of more ſolemn dreſs is almoſt invariably repreſented with the addition of an ornamental ſtripe, extending from between the neck and ſhoulders, on either ſide, to the lower edge of the tunic. In ſome caſes ſimilar ſtripes are repreſented running round the lower extremity of the ſleeve. [Pl. V. and XXVIII.]

Similar ornaments are to be ſeen in other repreſentations of Roman dreſs, as, for example, in ſome of the illuſtrations of the Vatican Virgil, dating from the fourth century.

But this ornament is by no means peculiar to the coſtume of Rome. We find on the walls of the Catacombs, not only our Lord and His Apoſtles, but Abraham, Moſes, the "Three Children," and other Eaſterns, wearing a tunic ſo ornamented. But from this, if this were all, we could not infer more with certainty, than that the Chriſtian painters of the ſecond, third, or fourth centuries, to whom thoſe freſcoes are to be traced, believed this ornament to be common in the Eaſt as it was among themſelves. But, in point of faĉt, we have abundant evidence, both in literature and in art, which proves that they were right in ſo thinking. The ornamental tunics of heathen prieſthood, for example, in the Tyrian colonies, and in Tyre itſelf, were diſtinguiſhed, as we have ſeen, by ſtripes of purple. And the ſeventy tranſlators in their rendering of Iſaiah, iii. 21, ſpeak of garments which are ſtriped (μεσοπόρφυρα) and bordered (περιπόρφυρα) with purple. And the ſtripes of purple there ſpoken of differed only in colour and material, but not in form, from the ſimple ornament commonly worn on the full-dreſs tunic of ordinaryᵉ people.

So common, indeed, is this particular kind of ornament

ᵉ Compare the comment of St. Baſil, tom. i. p. 661, D. Τὸν ἐν τῇ ἐσθῆτι κόσμον τῶν καλλωπιζομένων γυναι- | κῶν ὡς περίεργον διαβάλλει, πορφύραν πότε μὲν κατὰ τὰ ἄκρα παρυφαινόντων, πότε δὲ κατὰ τὸ μέσον αὐτὴν ἐντιθέντων.

in early monuments, both in the East[e] and in the West, that I cannot but suppofe it to have originated in fome fimple caufe, incident to the prevailing form of the garment now in queftion. It may be conjectured that in joining together the various "breadths," of linen or woollen ftuff, out of which the tunic was to be made, a feam was made from between the neck and fhoulders on either fide down to the lower edge; and that thefe ornamental ftripes were fo fewn on as to hide (compare p. 3, l. 27) what would otherwife have been unfightly, and yet admit of being eafily removed when the tunic itfelf needed wafhing.

What has been faid hitherto points onward to a further point of intereft concerning the ecclefiaftical drefs of the primitive age. We know that various grades of rank were diftinguifhed at Rome, from very early times, by the colour and by the relative width of the ornamental ftripes worn upon the tunic by fenators, and by knights. Whether two fuch were worn, ftole-wife, or one only, is uncertain. But, however, this may be, the broad *clavus* was the diftinctive mark of a fenator; the narrow *clavus* of a knight. And it is wholly in accordance with this, that in one of the monuments figured in this volume (fee Plate XIV), the black *lora* (or "*clavi*") on the *tunica talaris*, worn by our Lord, are confiderably larger than thofe worn by the fix perfons (probably Apoftles) in the midft of whom He is feated.

Facts fuch as thefe would lead us antecedently to expect, that diftinctions between the higher and the lower offices of

---

[e] A remarkable example may be feen in a very ancient frefco in a rock-church at Urgub, in Mefopotamia. See Texier, B.A., Pl. V. One of the principal figures (reprefenting, probably, one of the Old Teftament prophets) feen approaching with reverence to the Holy Child before him, is dreffed in a white tunic under an outer garment of reddifh brown. And this white tunic (στιχάριον, it would probably be called by thofe who originally drew it) has narrow black ftripes by way of ornament, which exactly correfpond with the *lora*, or ornamental ftripes, of the Roman Dalmatic.

the Chriftian miniftry might probably be indicated, in early times, by means of thefe ornamental ftripes.[r] The hiftory of the " dalmatic," which was juft fuch an ornamented tunic as that now defcribed, ftrongly confirms the probability that this was really the cafe ; and of this we fhall fhortly have occafion to fpeak more at length.

For the prefent it is only neceffary to add, that thefe ornamental ftripes vary in colour, according to the colour of the drefs upon which they are worn. But in all the examples of *white* drefs, worn by Apoftles or by ecclefiaftics, belonging to the firft 600 years of Chriftian hiftory, thefe ftripes, as far as I have obferved, are invariably black.

But it was not only by thefe ornaments on the tunic that difference of official rank could be indicated. We have abundant evidence to fhow, that, at Rome, almoft every modification of the ordinary drefs had a certain well-underftood fignificance in the eyes of men. The unufual fulnefs, or the fcant dimenfions, of *toga* or of *pallium*, were as fignificant then, as is the long graceful train that fweeps the ground now worn by ladies of fafhion, when contrafted with the fhorter, fimpler drefs of thofe who, from motives of economy, or for any other reafon, ftudy convenience and comfort rather than ftately beauty and grace. And as with the outer garment (whether *toga* or *pallium*), fo with the tunic alfo. Nay, fo minute and rigorous was the etiquette of drefs at Rome under the Empire, that people of any pofition varied the kind of fhoes which they wore, according to the nature of the upper garment in which they might be clad. And we fhall find, when we come to examine the later monuments bearing upon the fubject here under difcuffion, that diftinctions fuch as thefe, familiar to Romans and to Greeks under the imperial

---

[r] As among ourfelves, for example, the right of wearing a " fcarf" is given, in the Canons, to fuch as are members of Cathedral bodies, and to the chaplains of noblemen.

fyftem, were reproduced from time to time in the regulations made for the miniftering drefs of the Church.

§ 2. OFFICIAL INSIGNIA.

But diftinctions of drefs, minute and varied though they may be, are, for the moft part, not fufficient of themfelves to ferve as expreffions for all thofe diverfities of rank and office, which are characteriftic of highly civilifed ftates. Therefore is it that in fuch ftates the cuftom has at all times obtained, of marking out, by conventional fymbols, both grades of relative dignity, and varieties of official occupation. Of thefe conventional fymbols, two claffes may be particularly noticed : thofe which are worn upon the head, fymbols moftly of *authority;* and thofe borne in the hand, fymbols, for the moft part, of fpecial departments of activity.

Ornaments, firft, of the head. To the head, the crown and apex of the human form, itfelf the nobleft and moft god-like of all created things,—to the head, which with a nod, or with a glance, or with an uttered word, can give expreffion to the Sovereign Will which therein fits enthroned,—to this, by a natural inftinct, men have ever affigned the fymbols of power to rule, whether with a fupreme and all-embracing rule, as did great kings, or in fpecial departments of delegated authority, as did others in their name.

But the hand, alfo, the organ and inftrument of that fovereign will, furnifhes fignificant expreffion, by appropriate fymbols, of the various fields of fpecial activity in which the powers of man find exercife. The fceptre *v* of the king, the lituus of the augur, the written fcroll of philofopher or man

---

v It is not an eafy matter to determine what was the *original* affociation of idea in confequence of which the word σκῆπτρον, for example, fuperadded to its primitive meaning of a " ftaff," or ftout ftick, that of " fceptre " or fymbol of royalty, actual or delegated. In what we read in the Iliad of fuch a

of law, the inftruments of facrifice of the heathen prieft, the
paftoral ftaff of Chriftian bifhop, or the book of the Gofpels
held in his hand, thefe, and other fuch, are fignificant, each
of fome fpecial department of official miniftration, to which
prominence is given by the mere fact of fuch fymbolic reprefentation.

We may apply thefe general principles to the fubject immediately before us. In Egyptian monuments we find the
fymbols of priefthood to be either fuch as could be worn upon
the head, a high cap or mitre, indicative of authority ; or
fuch as could be carried in the hand. And thefe laft, again,
are of two kinds : inftruments of facrifice, marking them out
as facrificers ; or *a roll of papyrus infcribed with hieroglyphics,*
indicative of their office as keepers and expounders of divine
knowledge. And at an interval of fome two thoufand years,
we find the fame fymbolic language employed in Chriftian
art. On the walls of the Catacombs the Divine power of our
Lord is fymbolifed by "the rod of power" which He holds,
when working miracles; His office as "The Word," the
revealer of Divine truth to man, by the infcribed fcroll which
He holds, or by the two open *capfæ* on His right hand and
on His left, filled each with written fcrolls, and reprefentative,
we cannot doubt, of the Old and New Teftament [Pl. XII.].
And, laftly, His own revelation of Himfelf as the true Manna,
as the Bread of Life, as one whofe Body offered on the Crofs,
and whofe Blood thereon outpoured, are the food of them
that hunger, and the refrefhment of them that thirft : this, too,
is fet forth again and again in the feven bafkets filled with

---

σκᾶπτρον being laid, and that with a
heavy hand, upon the fhoulders of
Therfites, we have, if I miftake not,
an indication of the original ufe from
which this "ftaff" was derived. In
the rude affemblies wherein a warrior
chief gathered about him his armed

followers for council of battle or, in
time of peace for judgment of wrong
done, the "right of the ftaff" would be
frequently exercifed, both for the main-
tenance of order, and for the punifhment of offenders.

bread which He hath bleffed and broken ; in loaves, marked with a crofs, which He bears in His own bofom.

But that which now more fpecially concerns us is the queftion of the Jnfignia, with which, in early Chriftian monuments, either the Apoftles themfelves, or their fucceffors in offices of Chriftian miniftry, were invefted. One ϕ fuch monument there is, and one only I believe, in which the Apoftles are reprefented as wearing a peaked cap, fuch as in ancient times was known as a τιάρα (fee note 84, p. 52). This reprefentation would ferve to indicate the "*royal* priefthood" with which the Lord had invefted them. And thus the monument, of which J now fpeak, offers an exact parallel to one or two exceptional paffages in ancient authors, in which this fame idea is either alluded χ to, or (as by Epiphanius)ψ expreffly ftated.

A fimilar fuggeftion of power *to rule*, committed to the Twelve, under Chrift, and by delegation from Him, is fet forth by the apoftolic thrones on which they are fometimes reprefented as feated. [See Frontifpiece, and compare note χ, p. xxviii.]

With thefe exceptions (the firft of which appears to have been unobferved hitherto by writers on ritual), the infignia of Apoftles, in the early monuments of Chriftian art, are fuch, as mark them out as the deliverers of a Divine meffage, of the " Word of God," to man. This their office is indicated by the "fcroll" † held in their hand, a "*volumen*" (note 79, p. 50) in the original fenfe of the word. At times, however, we find in place of this fcroll a " martyr's crown," or chaplet, held in the hand. Thus, in a remarkable monument, of which

---

ϕ Ciampini, *Vet. Mon.* tom. i. Pl. LXX.

χ See the letter of Bifhop Polycrates, quoted at p. 38, and compare note 62. And fee further, on this fide of the queftion, the paffage referred to in Appendix B.

ψ See the paffage quoted at p. 40, and refer to note 65.

† See Pl. XII., XIII., XXIX., and the figure of St. Peter, Pl. XLV.

f

there is a drawing in the collection at Windfor, our Lord is reprefented between St. Paul (at His right hand) and St. Peter (on the left) ; and while St. Paul holds the fcroll of an apoftle, St. Peter holds in his hands the chaplet (*corona*) which defignates his martyrdom.

The fpecial defignations by which particular Apoftles were indicated (as ftill they are) in the later and more developed fymbolifm of Chriftian art, are not met with in the primitive period with which we are now concerned.

Paffing on now from the Apoftles themfelves to the various orders of the Chriftian miniftry, we find that a chair † of ftate (*fedes* or καθέδρα), or "epifcopal throne," ferves to mark the authority to rule committed to a bifhop; while his office as a teacher of Divine truth is indicated by the Book of the Gofpels, which he holds in his left hand. From a paffage of great intereft in a fermon attributed to St. Chryfoftom (fee note 89, p. 53), we learn that at the confecration of bifhops,*ω* the book of the Gofpels was laid upon their heads, as being "the true evangelical tiara," and as a fign to the bifhop himfelf, that "*though he be head of all, yet doth he act in fub-jection to God's laws; though he be ruler of all, yet is he too under rule to the law; though in all things a fetter forth of the Word, yet is he himfelf, to that Word, in fubjection.*"

The paftoral ftaff is firft mentioned as one of the dif-tinctive infignia* of a bifhop, in the acts of the Fourth

---

† See Pl. XVII., and for full de-tails fee Martigny D. A. C. *in voc.* Chaire.

ω τῶν ἱερῶν is the expreffion ufed. But context fhows that by *ἱερὸς* here, as after in early writers, is meant a bifhop. Compare note 90, p. 54, and fee Index *in voc.*

α The various infignia above men-tioned (the "ftaff" only excepted) may be feen in the Frontifpiece to this volume (a diptych of St. Paul), and in Pl. XI. (the "virga" or rod of power), XV., XVII. (the "throne" there re-prefented, as in Aringhi, is, I fhould think, incorrectly drawn), XXIX. (the earlieft example, as far as I know, of a "crozier," is there feen), XXX., XXXI. Later examples of fuch in-fignia may be feen in almoft all later Plates publifhed in this volume.

Council of Toledo (fee *infra*, p. 75). But it does not appear to have been found in monuments of Chriftian art till the tenth century. Its fymbolifm is well fet forth in a paffage of Honorius, quoted later in this volume (p. 140). And whatever be the date of its firft ufe as one of the diftinctive infignia of a bifhop, it ferves, more fully and expreffively perhaps than any other fuch fymbol, to fet forth that paftoral afpect of the minifterial office, which at all times, and in all places, has conftituted its fureft paffport to the hearts and affections of God's people.

From a Syriac MS. of the year 586 A.D.

CHAPTER VI.

The Transition Period from 400 to 800 a.d.

We enter now upon the fecond of the three periods, into which, for the purpofes of this inquiry, the hiftory of the Chriftian Church has been divided. This, and the fucceeding period, may be treated much more briefly than the firft, in which I have been obliged to occupy what is in fome meafure new ground,—new, at leaft, in connexion with the queftion, with which, in thefe pages, we are occupied.

At the very outfet of this fecond period two facts arreft our attention, as having had a momentous influence on the hiftory of the Church generally. And this influence may be traced, as in other particulars of far more intrinfic importance, fo alfo in this of ecclefiaftical drefs with which here we are more efpecially concerned.

The two facts of which I fpeak are, the dualization of the Roman empire, fomewhat earlier in date, but to be traced in its effects throughout this period; and the firft outburft, in the year 408, of that great flood of barbarian invafion, whofe fucceffive waves fpread, with overwhelming force, over the face of Southern Europe. Goths, Vandals, Lombards, a " triple wave of woe," poured down in fucceffion, from the North, upon the rich land which lay open, and almoft undefended, to their attacks; and the older Roman civilifation was all but deftroyed,—would have been deftroyed altogether, had not the ſpiritual force, that was in the Church, proved a more effectual ſafeguard, than the degenerate valour of the imperial armies.

The firſt of the two events above mentioned requires ſpecial notice in this place, becauſe the eſtabliſhment of the imperial ſyſtem in the "new Rome" of the Boſphorus, ſerves to account for the development of both civil and eccleſiaſtical dreſs, in nearly parallel lines, at Conſtantinople and at Rome, during the period of 400 years with which we now are occupied. Let the reader examine the two monuments of conſular coſtume, one of the Eaſt, the other of the Weſt, among the illuſtrations of this volume (Plates XXII. and XXIII.), and he will ſee at a glance, that not the official titles only, but the coſtume and inſignia of the older Rome of the Seven Hills, had been transferred, before the date of thoſe monuments, to the New Rome of the Boſphorus. And at Conſtantinople, not leſs than at Rome, modifications were brought about, during this tranſition period, in the dreſs of Chriſtian miniſtry, owing to the application to eccleſiaſtical uſe of peculiarities of coſtume and of inſignia, which were of the Empire, before they were of the Church.

And now, for reaſons already indicated, we will confine our attention, for the preſent at leaſt, to the churches of the Weſt. And we ſhall have no difficulty in ſeeing how the political circumſtances of thoſe times were outwardly reflected, on the one hand, in the revolution effected in the general coſtume of civil life, and, on the other, in the ſpirit of conſervatiſm, which maintained, in official coſtume at Rome, and in the miniſtering habits of the Church generally, that type of dreſs, characteriſtic of the older Roman civiliſation, of which we have already treated at length in the earlier chapters of this Introduction.

A complete change was brought about, this firſt we have to note, in the ordinary coſtume of civil life. The type of dreſs by which the invaders from the north were diſtinguiſhed, differed widely from that older Roman habit (Eaſtern in its character), of which we ſpoke in the earlier chapters of this Introduction.   The new dreſs was a dreſs for ſoldiers (a *ſagum*, or ſhort mantle, its prevailing form, worn over a ſhort tunic like a Highland kilt); the old dreſs, as we have ſeen (note ε, p. ix.) a dreſs of citizens.   The contraſt between the new and the old type of dreſs may be ſeen at a glance, on comparing the dreſs of the Emperor Charlemagne in Pl. XXXIII. with that of the Emperor Juſtinian (which is of the older type with Byzantine additions) in Pl. XXVIII.   And in a leſs exalted rank, we may compare the figure of the layman, in Pl. XXXVII., and that of Beno de Rapiza (ſomewhat later in date), in Pl. XLIII., with thoſe of the courtiers in attendance on Juſtinian in the S. Vitale moſaic already referred to; with that of Gordianus (a ſenator), in Pl. XXV., or with thoſe of the ſeveral laymen repreſented in the moſaics of the Church of St. George in Theſſalonica (Pl. XVIII. to XXI.).

The contraſt between theſe two types of dreſs was matter of obſervation at the time; and adhering to the "old ways" was regarded as a mark of orthodoxy.   That this was the caſe as late as the cloſe of the ſixth century, we have the evidence of the biographer (a very well-informed one) of St. Gregory the Great.   Speaking of the houſehold of the good biſhop, whoſe life he writes, he ſays, "That not one among them, from the leaſt to the greateſt, had any taint of 'barbariſm' (uſing the word in its Latin ſenſe) either in ſpeech or in dreſs; but the *toga* or the *trabea*, of old Latin uſage, maintained diſtinctly the old Latin ſpirit, in that palace to which Latium had given a name." [β]

<hr>

β Joan. Diac. Vita S. Gregorii, lib. ii. cap. 13. " Nullus Pontifici famulantium a minimo uſque ad maximum barbarum quodlibet in ſermone vel habitu præferebat ; ſed togata Quiritium more vel trabeata Latinitas ſuum Latinum (Latium ?) in ipſo Latiali palatio ſingulariter obtinebat."

A paffage fuch as this, even if it ftood alone, would prepare us, after the facts that have already been confidered, to find that even as late as St. Gregory's time the old types of drefs were ftill maintained, with little change, at Rome itfelf, however much they might be modified where the new influences were predominant. And in diftinctly ecclefiaftical drefs, we find, accordingly, that, in fome of the Roman monuments of that period, fcarcely any difference is to be detected between the reprefentations dating from that time, and thofe which we meet with in the "Ciclo Biblico" of the earlier Roman Catacombs. In the mofaic of the Church of St. Lorenzo (Pl. XXIX.), dating from juft before the pontificate of St. Gregory, not only the Apoftles, but the then Bifhop of Rome, Pelagius, have the fame white veftments, with black *lora*, which we have already feen in earlier monuments (Pl. XIV. and XV.). And if Anaftafius is to be underftood literally when he fays, that Pelagius II. "made" (*fecit*) the Cemetery of St. Hermes, it muft follow that the remarkable frefco reprefented in Pl. XVII. cannot be of earlier date than about the clofe of the fixth century.

I fpeak advifedly of "diftinctly ecclefiaftical drefs," becaufe we have to remember that the Bifhops of Rome, from the clofe of the fourth century, occupied a great civil pofition alfo in the ftate. Their civil power was indeed wholly anomalous and undefined, and in theory fubordinate to that of the *Præfectus Urbis*, Reprefentative of the Emperor ; but it was often very real, at a time when the titular magiftracies were for the moft part names and nothing more. And this will account for a phenomenon, fo ftrange at firft thought, as that of Chriftian bifhops affuming, as infignia of their office, decorations derived from the civil magiftracies of the old Roman republic. Thefe magiftracies were preferved firft, under the Imperial fyftem, as honorary diftinctions, conferred by the emperor ; and their infignia, at a later period ftill, were imitated in ecclefiaftical ufe at Rome and Conftantinople, and thence γ fpread to other churches.

A moft remarkable evidence of the clofe connection, to Roman ideas, between the drefs of high civil magiftracy and that of their own chief bifhop, is to be found in the monument reprefented in Pl. XXIV., in which St. Gregory the Great is reprefented with nearly the fame drefs and infignia as would have been his had he been "Conful" under the empire, inftead of "Præful,"³ in the Church. And the clofe refemblance between the dignified drefs of a fenator, and that of a bifhop of the Church, is well indicated in the plate ι immediately following (Pl. XXV.), in which, but for the Papal *pallium*, and the Book of the Gofpels, carried (as one of the *infignia* of a bifhop) in the left hand, it would be impoffible (as Cardinal Baronius remarked long ago) to diftinguifh which were the fenator, and which the bifhop.

LITERARY MONUMENTS.

Turning now from thefe art-monuments to the contemporary ι notices of ecclefiaftical drefs, to be met with in ancient literature, it may be well here to point out one or two

---

γ To this, as regards Rome, Thomaffinus bears teftimony. *De Ben.* tom. ii. p. 327. "Conftat ab ecclefia maxime Romana cæteras identidem varia extorfiffe privilegia, ut cum ipfis magnificentiora quædam divini cultus indumenta communicarentur. Antiquiffimas enim et pretiofiffimas has veftes et frequentius ufurpaverat, et retinuerat conftantius, urbs Imperii totius regina. Imperatoriæ etiam in vefte et ornatu magnificentiæ copia major facta fuerat Ecclefiæ Romanæ.

Ab ea ergo effundebantur hi veluti pompæ gloriæque facerdotalis rivuli in reliquum Chriftianum orbem."

³ This is a title frequently given to the Bifhops of Rome in the earlier Roman documents.

ι The paffages of chief importance are given in the later part of this work, pp. 42 to 87. Others will be found quoted in the chapter next following, in which the veftments in ufe at this period are feparately noticed.

features which are common to all, and which it is important to note for the better underſtanding of the preſent queſtion.

It will be found that paſſages quoted from writers of this period have reference, either to the veſtments of Levitical ⟨ prieſthood, or to the dreſs and inſignia which were regarded as proper to biſhops, prieſts, deacons, or others holding offices of miniſtry in the Church. And as regards the firſt of theſe two claſſes, thoſe in which the Levitical veſtments are deſcribed or referred to, a marked diſtinction will be obſerved between the writers of this period and thoſe of the ſucceeding centuries. If St. Jerome, St. Auguſtine, St. Chryſoſtom (or the writer ⁿ who bears his name), if St. Gregory, or Venerable Bede, deſcribe in detail the Levitical veſtments, they do ſo without giving the ſlighteſt intimation that the veſtments of Chriſtian miniſtry correſponded in number, in form, and colour, or in name, with thoſe of the older prieſthood. Oftentimes, on the contrary, the language they employ ſhows, that they recogniſed the marked contraſt between the two [Notes 94, 96, 101, 139]. But in the later writers, from the beginning of the ninth century [Notes 169, 170], we find, on the contrary, that the Levitical veſtments are ever mentioned as the prototypes, to which thoſe of Chriſtian prieſthood may be referred, and the names proper to the one are transferred, often upon the moſt imaginary grounds, to thoſe which were then in uſe for offices of Chriſtian miniſtry [Note 253].

But the claſs of paſſages, of which I have now been ſpeaking, affords only negative and indirect evidence upon the

---

⟨ See Nos. XII., XVI., XVII., XVIII., XIX., XX., XXVI., XXVII., XXIX. With theſe ſhould be included the paſſages from St. Jerome (pp. 10 to 35). For theſe, though they precede by a few years the cloſe of the fourth century, are the ſources to which, directly or indirectly, all the writers in the Weſtern Church are mainly indebted for their knowledge on the ſubject of the Levitical veſtments. For apparent exceptions to the general ſtatements of the text, ſee Appendix B.

ⁿ See note 80, p. 51.

hiſtory of the veſtments of the Church. Of more direct
intereſt are the paſſages, in which theſe laſt are enumerated
and deſcribed. And among theſe, in regard of the Weſt, I
may here mention, as of chief intereſt and importance, the
extracts (No. XXV., p. 68, *ſqq.*) from St. Iſidore of Seville,
and from the Acts (No. XXVIII., p. 75) of the Fourth
Council of Toledo held under his preſidency. For Eaſtern
uſage, ſome ſeventy years later, we have as a guide the
deſcription, given by St. Germanus of Conſtantinople (No.
XXX., p. 82, *ſqq.*), of the veſtments recogniſed in the Eaſt
at the time he wrote. Of theſe we ſhall have to ſpeak in
detail, in the following chapter.

But before proceeding further, I may mention two
paſſages as having a ſpecial intereſt for Engliſh readers. I
refer to the extracts from the *De Tabernaculo* of Venerable
Bede (p. 78, *ſqq.*), and to the nearly contemporary letter of
St. Boniface (Winifrid of Crediton) to Cuthbert, Archbiſhop
of Canterbury, quoted in note 209, p. 106.

Both of theſe paſſages date from an early period of the
eighth century. And both ſhow, though in different ways,
what was the feeling of thoſe times in reſpect of the queſtions
now under diſcuſſion. We ſee, on the one hand, a man
wiſe and learned, and of the greateſt piety, ſuch as Bede,
ſtill regarding the Levitical veſtments in the ſame light preciſely as had all the earlier Fathers. "The outward ſplendour," ſo he writes,[a] "which, in the former times, ſhone
brightly in ornamented veſtments, is now to be ſpiritually
underſtood ; inwardly conſpicuous in the hearts of Chriſtian
prieſts, and outwardly ſo alſo in their activity in all good
works." And it is matter of intereſt to obſerve from what
ſource he derived his thought, viz. *from the ſervice then in uſe
for the conſecration of biſhops.* In a very ancient MS. of the
Liber Sacramentorum of St. Gregory the Great, edited by the

---

[a] See note 135, p. 78, and Appendix B.

learned Benedictine Hugo Menardus, the ſame thought is
expreſſed nearly in the ſame words.' And with this again
agrees the deſcription given of St. Germanus of Paris by
Fortunatus (writing in the ſixth century) : —

> Senſim incedit velut alter Aaron,
> Non de veſte nitens, ſed pietate placens.
> Non lapides, coccus, clarum aurum, purpura, byſſus,
> Exornant humeros, ſed micat alma Fides.

The other paſſage, that from St. Boniface, " the apoſtle
of Germany," preſents great difficulties, the ſolution of which,
I own, I cannot as yet ſee. For the expreſſions that he uſes
indicate, on the one hand, that the " veſtimenta " which he
ſo ſtrongly condemns were in ſome way connected with *ſuperſtitious*ᵡ uſe (ſo at leaſt he deemed it) ; that they were of
recent introduction (ſo the general tone of his letter ſeems to
imply) ; and apparently alſo that they were brought into
England through ſome foreign ᵡ influence. On the other
hand, he ſpeaks of theſe as tending to luxury and unclean
living, and to evil companionſhips, among the younger members of the monaſtic houſes ; to the neglect of reading and of
prayer, and to the ruin of ſouls. Whatever may have been
the exact ſtate of circumſtances which called out this his
ſtrong denunciation, this much at leaſt is clear, that in the
Engliſh monaſtic houſes, early in the eighth century, there

ᵢ Illius namque Sacerdotii anterioris
habitus, noſtræ mentis ornatus eſt ; et
Pontificalem gloriam non jam honor
commendat veſtium, ſed ſplendor animarum. . . . Et idcirco huic
famulo tuo quem ad ſummi ſacerdotii
miniſterium elegiſti, hanc, quæſumus,
Domine, gratiam largiaris, ut *quicquid
illa velamina in fulgore auri, in nitore
gemmarum, in multimodi operis varietate ſignabant, hæc in ejus moribus actibuſque clareſcat.* D. Greg. Papæ

Sacram. Liber, p. 239. [The MS. is
not earlier than the eighth century,
and probably not much later. See
Menardus' Preface.] Other paſſages
to the ſame effect are quoted in Appendix B.

ᵡ *Veſtimentorum ſuperſtitionem, Deo
odibilem.* Cf. *infra*, note 299, p.
106.

ᵡ He ſpeaks of them as *tranſmiſſa*,
" ſent acroſs," by Antichriſt, and as
precurſors of his advent.

had been a great development of external ſplendour in dreſs, either ſecular ▪ or miniſterial, or both ; and that this had been defended upon ſome grounds of religion, which were regarded as ſuperſtitious and anti-Chriſtian by St. Boniface.

▪ Of the ſplendid ſecular dreſs affected by eccleſiaſtics in the eighth century, we have many notices in early writers. Compare note 336, p. 165.

From a Drawing in Her Majeſty's Collection.   [See Deſcription of Pl. XXXIII.]

*

CHAPTER VII.

Special Vestments and Insignia of Christian Ministry between 400 and 800 a.d.

We have already mentioned the two principal authorities for the Chriftian veftments of this period,—St. Ifidore,[1] and the Fourth Council of Toledo, for the Weft; St. Germanus[1] of Conftantinople, for the Eaft. We may take the enumerations, there given, as a bafis, in proceeding now to confider thefe veftments more in detail.

Ministering Vestments in the West.

The veftments and infignia mentioned in the Acts of the Council of Toledo, A.D. 633, are the Alb, the Planeta, the Orarium; and, in addition to thefe, the Epifcopal Ring, and Paftoral Staff, as the diftinctive infignia of a bifhop. Thefe Acts, however, determine, with certainty, only the veftments recognifed at that period in Spain. From other fources we learn the names of additional veftments, fuch as the Dalmatic, and the Pallium, connected more particularly with Rome; and of thefe alfo we will take the prefent opportunity of fpeaking.

---

[1] See *infra* pp. 68 and 75; and for S. Germanus, p. 82.

1. THE ALB.

The " tunica alba," or, as it is more briefly called,[ξ] the *alba*, is the term used of the long white tunic worn, as we have seen, from Apostolic times, by those who ministered in the Church. Even as early as the Fourth Council of Carthage,[o] we find a canon regulating its use as a garb to be worn, by deacons,[π] only at specified times. And by this name, probably for more than four centuries, rather than by *dalmatica*, was the tunic of holy ministration known in all the Latin churches, Rome only excepted.

Later notices of the " alb" occur in the Council of Narbonne[ρ] (A.D. 589), indicative of the growth of great irreverence in the celebration of the " mass," an irreverence which required to be checked by special enactment. And if we find in the Acts of the Council of Toledo, already alluded to, that the " alb" is there spoken of as the characteristic vestment of a *deacon*, it is not that bishops and presbyters did not wear a white tunic under the " planeta," but that the

---

[ξ] *Alba* is first used virtually as a substantive, in a passage from Vopiscus (*in Claudio*, 14 and 17), in which we read of an *alba subserica*, i.e. made of linen interwoven with silk, sent as a present by Trebellius Pollio to Claudius (*circ.* A.D. 265).

[o] Concil. Carthag. iv. Can. 41 (Labbe, vol. ii. p. 1203). *Ut diaconus tempore oblationis tantum vel lectionis alba utatur.* It is very doubtful whether there was ever such a Fourth Council of Carthage actually held. The Canons, however, which are attributed to this Council, are of about the date assigned, viz. towards the close of the fourth century.

[π] It is to this white vestment of Deacons that John the Deacon alludes (Vita S. Gregorii, lib. i. 25), saying, that on being ordained deacon, St. Gregory appeared *non solum nitore habitus, verum etiam claritate morum probabilium, divinis angelis adæquari.*

[ρ] See Labbe, tom. v. p. 1020. *Nec diaconus, aut subdiaconus certe, vel Lector, antequam missa consummetur, alba se præsumat exuere.*

deacon, having no fuper-veftment,[e] was fpecially defignated by the white alb in which he miniftered.

Before proceeding further it may be well to notice a fpecial form of the miniftering tunic, connected more efpecially with Roman ufe.

THE DALMATIC.

The Dalmatic[r] (fee Pl. VI. and XXVIII.) was a tunic with long and full fleeves, differing therein from the *colobium*, which had a very fhort and clofe fleeve, reaching a few inches only below the fhoulder.[v]

Like other garments appropriated at a comparative early time, to ecclefiaftical ufe at Rome, the Dalmatic had been in ufe by perfons high in fecular pofition, before it was adopted by the Church. In the Weft,[φ] the earlieft fecular traditions connected with it are peculiarly unfortunate. For the firft perfons recorded to have worn it are the Emperors Commodus († A.D. 190) and Heliogabalus († 223). Their biographer Lampridius[x] records, as an outrage upon all pro-

---

[e] Compare Pl. XXVIII. where Archbifhop Maximian wears a planeta over a dalmatic, whereas the two clerics in attendance on him are in dalmatics only. See alfo Pl. XVII.

[r] The full expreffion was *tunica dalmatica*, but this very rarely occurs, the word *dalmatica* being ufed as a fubftantive, as was "alba." The name was derived from the province of Dalmatia. See note 131.

[v] See, for example, the woodcut in p. xxxiv.

[φ] Of a different kind are the firft traditions in the Eaft, if the word διλμᾶτικιον, ufed by John Damafcene, be not an anachronifm. Speaking of

the pretences to fpecial fanctity made by the Pharifees, he mentions, *inter alia*, σχήματα ἰδιλοςκσκιυτικὰ τῆς ἰνδυσιας, διά τι τῆς ἀμπιχόνης, καὶ τῶν διλμᾶτικίων, ἤτουν κολοβίων, καὶ τοῦ πλατυσμοῦ τῶν Φυλακτηρίων, τούτιστι σαμάτων τᾶς πορφύρας, καὶ κρασπίδων, καὶ ρσίσκων ἰπὶ τα πτιρύγια τᾶς ἀμπιχόνης. [Cotelerii *Eccl. Græc. Monumenta Inedita*, vol. i. p. 284.]

[x] Lampridius *in Heliogabalo*, cap. 26. *Dalmaticatus in publico poft cenam fæpe vifus eft ; Gurgitem Fabium et Scipionem fe appellans, quod cum ea vefte effet cum qua Fabius et Cornelius a parentibus, ad corrigendos mores, adolefcentes in publicum effent producti.*

priety,↓ the fact of their being feen in public wearing this particular kind of tunic. Of the latter he writes, that he would often appear in public, after dinner, clad in a Dalmatic ; and calling himfelf a fecond Fabius or Scipio, " becaufe he wore a garment fuch as that in which Fabius and Cornelius, before they attained to manhood, were made by their own parents to appear in public, as a punifhment for fome offence committed." It may feem ftrange, at firft thought, to hear of precifely the fame garment being worn, " in public," only fome thirty years later, by a Chriftian bifhop. St. Cyprian of Carthage († 258), when led out to death, was wearing (if the " Acts " of his martyrdom may herein be trufted), firft a byrrhus,⍵ then, under that, a Dalmatic ; and again, under the Dalmatic, a " *linea*," or fhirt. That drefs was, of courfe, not that which he would ufe in offices of holy miniftry, but the feemly attire which he would wear on other occafions. And it is probable, for reafons already fully fet out in earlier chapters⍺ of this Introduction,

---

↓ The impropriety may have confifted either in coming out into the ftreets, *ficut erat*, in the dalmatic, in which he had reclined at table, without toga or pallium ; or poffibly in his wearing a *tunica manicata*. This laft would have been thought effeminate in the days of thofe older Fabii and Scipios. And hence the *punifhment* involved in making two high-fpirited boys appear in a tunic fit only for women. But I can hardly think, with Dr. Hefele, that a dalmatic worn by an emperor *under a fuper-veftment* (*toga, pallium*, or *lacerna*), would have been thought an outrage upon propriety in the third century of our era.

⍵ We hear elfewhere of a " byrrhus " as the fecular drefs of bifhops, and others of the clergy. St. Auguftine (*Serm. de Diverfis*, ccclvi., tom.

v. p. 1579, *fqq.*), for example, fays, that he could not wear a *byrrhus pretiofus*, even if it were given him. A byrrhus of coftly material *might perchance be fitting for a bifhop*, but not fitting for Auguftine, " *hominem pauperem de pauperibus natum.*" If good folk wifhed to give him what he fhould actually wear, it muft be fuch as he could wear " without blufhing." If it were more than this, he fhould fell it, and put the money into the common ftock. For other references, fee Raynaudus, *De Pilis*, &c., p. 1285. The *word* byrrhus, in older Latin *burrus*, is probably the Greek πυῤῥός. So St. Ifidore, Orig. lib. xix. cap. 24. *Birrus a Græco vocabulum trahit : illi enim birrum bibrum* [*leg.* πυῤῥόν] *dicunt.*

⍺ See Chapter II., p. vii., *fqq.*

that a bifhop, in fo important a place as Carthage, would habitually wear a long and ftately tunic, like the Dalmatic, which even ordinary perfons would at times affume, on occafions of unufual folemnity. And when worn, as by St. Cyprian, with a fuper-veftment over it, it would at once become appropriate to a folemn occafion, and to a perfon of dignified rank.

That the ufe of the Dalmatic, as a tunic of ceremony for ftate officials, and other fuch, continued at Rome itfelf fide by fide with its ecclefiaftical ufe, we have proof afforded in the defcription [β] given by John the deacon, of the drefs worn by Gordianus, a fenator, father of St. Gregory the Great [fee Pl. XXV]. That double ufage, fecular and ecclefiaftical, has continued ever fince. A Dalmatic is ftill worn as one of the imperial and royal coronation robes, both on the Continent and in England. Of its ufe as an ecclefiaftical veftment, in ancient and in modern times, we proceed now to fpeak.

The earlieft traditions [γ] on the fubject go back to the time of Conftantine. Sylvefter, then Bifhop of Rome, is faid to have ordered that the deacons fhould wear Dalmatics in place of the *colobia*, which had previoufly been in ufe in offices of holy miniftry. The fulleft account of the fubject is that of Rabanus Maurus (*infra*, p. 106, *fqq.*), written about the middle of the ninth century. He fays, that "In the earlieft times mafs was performed in the drefs of ordinary life, as fome Eafterns are faid to do even to this day. But

---

β Joan. Diac. Vita S. Gregor. lib. iv. cap. 84. *Gordiano . . . caftanei coloris Planeta, fub Planeta Dalmatica, in pedibus caligæ.*

γ See Rabanus Maurus (*infra*, p. 88), *De Inft. Cler.* lib i., 7 and 20; Amalarius *De Eccl. Off.* lib. ii. cap. 21 (*infra*, p. 99), and note 203, p. 105); Alcuinus *De Div. Off.* (*infra*,

p. 116); Honorius of Autun (*infra*, p. 137.) With thefe agrees Anaftafius, drawing as he did from the fame fources as the early writers above quoted. *De Vit. Pontif.* p. 105. In S. Sylveftro. "*Hic conftituit ut diaconi Dalmatica uterentur in ecclefia, et pallio linoftimo læva eorum tegeretur.*"

Stephanus,[δ] twenty-fourth Pope, directed that priests and
Levites should not employ their sacred vestments in the
ordinary usage of daily life, but reserve[213] them exclusively
for the Church.   And Sylvester ordained, that deacons should
wear Dalmatics in Church, and cover their left hands with a
pallium[214] of mixed linen and wool.   And at first (*primo*),
before Chasubles came into use, those of the priestly order
wore Dalmatics.   But afterwards, when they had begun to
wear Chasubles, they conceded the use of Dalmatics to deacons.
And yet, that pontiffs themselves sought to wear Dalmatics, is
clear from this, that Gregory[ι] and other Roman primates[ζ]
allowed the use of them to some bishops, forbade it in the
case of others.   And from this we may gather that in those
days that was not matter of general privilege, which now
almost all bishops, and some presbyters, regard as their
right, to wit, the wearing of a Dalmatic under the Chasuble."

This account, compared with the original passage quoted
by Anastasius from the *Gesta Pontificum* (note γ, p. lvii), leaves
some questions still open to doubt.   Both writers agree in
stating that St. Sylvester's ordinance had special reference to
deacons.   And it is *possible*, therefore, that the Dalmatic, or
full-sleeved tunic, may have been worn by bishops and priests
in the Roman Church, at an earlier period.   And so some
writers[n] have maintained.   But it appears more probable
that the fuller tunic was assigned to the deacons,[ι] because they

---

[δ] *Sed.* 253–257.

[ι] See, for example, the letter quoted
infra, p. 67.

[ζ] So Pope Zachary (*sed.* 741–752),
writing to Austrobert, Bishop of
Vienne: *Dalmaticam usibus vestris
misimus, ut, quia ecclesia vestra ab hac
sede doctrinam Fidei percepit, et morem
habitus sacerdotalis, ab illa etiam acci-
piat decorem honoris.*   For Pope Symmachus, at a much earlier date, see
below note *θ*.

[n] Visconti *De Apparatu Missæ*, lib.
iii. cap. 25.   Du Saussay, *Panoplia
Episc.* lib. vi. cap. 3 and 4.   *Apud*
Martigny, D. A. C. *in voc.* Dal-
matique.

[θ] With this would agree again the
concession of the Dalmatic to the
deacons of the Church of Arles, by
Pope Symmachus (*sed.* 498–514).
[*Vita Cæsarii Arelat. apud* Baron. Annal. tom. vi. p. 601, *ad ann.* 508].
" Ipse Pontifex præclara ejus (*sc.* S.

wore no fuper-veftment, fo that the fcantinefs of the older *colobium* was in their cafe fpecially confpicuous.

However this may be, it is clear that, as late as the eighth century, the Dalmatic, as a veftment of Chriftian miniftry, was regarded as fpecially belonging to the Roman Church ; and that it was only by fpecial privilege from Rome (or by invafion of that privilege) that it was worn in any of the diocefes fubject to the Roman See.

With this accords the fact, noticed by foreign ritualifts,' that, with fpecial exceptions only, the Dalmatic was not worn in the Gallican Church till, in the time of Hadrian I., her own Liturgy was difplaced (under preffure from the Crown) by that which was in ufe at Rome.

One word muft be faid, in conclufion, as to the ornaments of the Dalmatic at this period. From a paffage of St. Ifidore (quoted below at p. 74), it has been inferred by fome, that that all Dalmatics had *clavi* or ornamental ftripes, of *purple*.* But this is evidently a miftake. Of the very few ecclefiaftical Dalmatics, earlier than the year 600, whofe date λ and whofe colour I have been able to determine, none have any other than black ftripes. And even if exceptions fhould be found, no more would be proved than that the *clavi* of fuch dalmatics *might* be purple. The fhort notices of words like "*dalmatica*," which have been preferved to us by S. Ifidore, are often copied ftraight down from Scholiafts on Plautus,

---

Cæfarii) meritorum dignitate permo-
tus, non folum eum veriffime Metro-
politani honore præditum voluit, fed
etiam fpeciali quodam privilegio pallii ufum ei permifit, et *diaconos ejus
perinde ac Romanæ Ecclefiæ diaconos
Dalmaticis uti voluit.*"

ı Martigny D. A. C. *in voc.* Dal-
matique.

ᴈ Dr. Hefele, who is generally very
exact, has been led into error as to the

colour of the *clavi* on the Dalmatics in
the Ravenna mofaic (Pl. XXVIII).
They are black, not purple, as he fuppofes. See p. 206 of his treatife.

λ A mofaic, of which there is a
coloured drawing in the Windfor collection, reprefents the Apoftles with
red *clavi* upon their tunics. This
mofaic dates from the year 640, and is
the earlieft which I have found fo
ornamented.

Terence, and other old writers, and are not in all cafes to be regarded as the refults of careful refearch of his own. This being fo, I think it not impoffible, *μ* that his account (p. 74, note 131) of the Dalmatic (a veftment which does not appear to have been ufed in Spain) may be derived from fome fuch older fource ; and that the word *facerdotalis* may have referred (when originally penned by its actual author) to a tunic of heathen priefthood, fuch as we have feen to have been in not unfrequent ufe.

2. THE PÆNULA, CASULA, AND PLANETA.

Moft writers on ritual affume that the three words, with which this fection is headed, are but different names for one and the fame garment. There are many queftions of intereft involved in the inquiry whether this affumption is well grounded, or no. And I propofe therefore to ftate here the general refults of a careful inveftigation of the hiftory of thefe three words; and to fet out in full, in an Appendix, the evidence upon which thofe refults have been reached.

THE PÆNULA.

I give precedence to the Pænula, as being, in all probability, far the oldeft word of the three. We have *direct* evidence that garments, called by this name, were in ufe in Italy from the third ⁵ century before Chrift, to the fifth ° century of our era. In the Eaft the φαινόλης (the fame word

---

μ A contrary opinion to this is expreffed in note 131, p. 74. But that
note was written a year ago, when the
writer knew lefs of St. Ifidore's mode
of working than he does now. See

Appendix A, Nos. 12, 13, 14.
ꞵ See Appendix C.
⁵ Appendix C, No. 1.
° Appendix C, No. 22. Compare
what is faid under No. 23 and 25.

under another form) has had a ſtill wider range. We hear
of it firſt in a writer ⁊ of the fourth century B.C., but then
in a context which implies a belief, that ſuch a garment was
in uſe "*ante Agamemnona.*" And the ſame word, in its
Byzantine form (note 153) having been adopted in the Eaſt,
at an early period, ⁊ as the deſignation for the ſuper-veſtment
worn in offices of Chriſtian miniſtry, ſurvives even to this
day, both in the Greek Church itſelf, and, with ſlight modifications, in other Churches of the Eaſt. ⁊

Deferring, for the preſent, any further reference to its uſe
in the Eaſt, we ſhall do well to note here thoſe points only in
the hiſtory of the Pænula, which will illuſtrate its relation to
the Planeta or Caſula, the " Chaſuble " of Weſtern uſage.

And, firſt, for its form. Whether, in the later times of the
Roman empire, the primitive form of this garment was always
exactly adhered to, may reaſonably be doubted. But this at
leaſt is certain, that the prevailing idea, connected with this
word, was that of a garment which ſo completely enveloped ⁊
the whole perſon, as to interfere entirely with active exertion
of the arms. It was probably much ſuch a cloak as the
" poncho," which was in faſhion in England not many years
ago ; with this addition, however, that it was furniſhed with
a hood (as ſuch outdoor garments for common uſe generally
were) for protection of the head, if need were, from cold
or wet. This primitive ſhape of the garment is probably
that which was long retained in the Eaſt (as it ſtill is, I believe, in many parts of it), and which may be ſeen repreſented

---

⁊ Rhinthon, quoted by Julius Pollux. See Appendix C, No. 16.

⁊ The earlieſt *direct* evidence of
ſuch adoption, as far as I know, is the
paſſage of Patriarch Germanus, referred
to in Appendix C, No. 24.

⁊ In the Syriac Liturgies φαινόλιον
appears as Faino, Filono, or Phaino.
[Iſa-Bar-Hali, quoted by Renaudot,

Lit. Orient. Coll. ii, p. 55.] In the
Arabic verſion of the Coptic Liturgies
it is generally *Albornos,* "The Bur-
nous," with which we are more or
leſs familiar. But in Sclavonic the
Greek word reappears as *Pheloni.*

⁊ See Appendix C, No. 3 ; and
compare No. 16, and note 396.

in Pl. LVIII., No. 1 (St. Sampfon). But in the Weſt it is very poſſible that the older form may have been ſo far modified, that a garment ſuch as that ſhown in Pl. V. *bis* (No. 5), may really be intended for a Pænula, as moſt antiquaries believe. ᵛ

We have abundant evidence in Roman literature of the uſes to which the Pænula ſerved, and of its gradual exaltation in dignity from a garb of ſlaves or of peaſants ᵠ to one which even emperors ˣ might wear in travelling, and which was expreſſly preſcribed, in the fifth century of our era, as the dreſs of ſenators.↓

A Pænula, of ſome kind, was from very early times re-cogniſed as the proper dreſs for travellers.ᵘ But to wear a Pænula *as an ordinary dreſs*, in the city, would, in republican times, have been regarded as a grave breach of etiquette on the part of any one who pretended to the character of a gentleman. But the uſe of the Pænula in rainy or very cold weather, as an outer cloak to be worn over the ordinary dreſs, had in the firſt century of our era become well eſta-bliſhed even in Rome.ᵃ Yet even in the ſecond century of our era the older plebeian aſſociations ſtill clung about it, ſo that an emperor ᵝ could not appear in ſuch a dreſs in the city, be the weather what it would. In the third century ᵞ a ſpecial permiſſion was given by the Emperor Alexander Severus, by which ſenators were allowed to wear the Pænula in cold weather, even *intra Urbem*. But the ſame decree forbade its uſe by ladies, except when on a journey. It is not till yet two hundred years later ᵟ (A.D. 438) that we find

---

ᵛ See Octavius Ferrarius, p. 831; Bartolus Bartolinus, *De Pænula*, cap. iv.; Weiss, Koſtümkunde im Mitte-lalter, p. 14, fig. 8.

ᵠ Of ſlaves, Appendix C, No. 1; of peaſants, Appendix C, No. 4 (com-pare No. 9).

ˣ See Ferrarius D. R. V. pars ii. lib. ii. cap. 5.

↓ Appendix C, No. 22.

ᵘ Appendix C, Nos. 3, 5, 15.

ᵃ Appendix C, Nos. 7, 12, 13.

ᵝ Appendix C. No. 13.

ᵞ Appendix C, No. 15.

ᵟ Appendix C, No. 22.

the Pænula formally installed, in the place of the older toga, as the distinctive garment of peaceful dignity, and as such to be worn by senators, to the exclusion of the warlike "terrors" associated with the *chlamys*.[142]

An important question now arises, Was this Pænula the super-vestment adopted by the Western Church as the distinctive garb of bishops and priests in the highest offices of Christian ministry? By the Western Church *in Apostolic times*, or in the centuries immediately succeeding, most undoubtedly it was not. The proof of this may be seen in the Appendix.[1] And to what is there stated I may add here, that I have neither seen alleged by others, nor have I myself found, one passage of any Latin writer from the first century to the fourteenth, in which mention is made of the Pænula as the proper name of a vestment of Christian ministry. But, on the other hand, the usage of the *phænolion* by the Greek Church, and early monuments of ecclesiastical dress in the West, such as those in Pl. XXVIII., XXX., and XXXI., lead to the conclusion, that the super-vestment worn in the sixth century, though called Planeta, was not unlike *in form* to the Pænula of which we have been speaking. And it is of course *possible* that, in some local churches, the name Pænula may really have been employed rather than Planeta, as a designation for this vestment. All that can be said is that no evidence has ever yet been alleged to prove that such was the case.

THE CASULA.

There is no certain evidence of the word *casula* ever being employed in speaking of a vestment of Christian ministry before the ninth century of our era. If, therefore, the arrangement adopted in this treatise were strictly adhered to, this word would first come under discussion at a later period

---

1 See Appendix C, under No. 17.

than the present. But it will be convenient to give the earlier history of the word in this place, in order to make it clear how the Casula stands related to the Planeta and the Pænula.

And, first, for the origin of the word. There is no doubt that the derivation given by St. Isidore is the true one. ζ He regards it (see p. 74, note 130) as a diminutive of "*casa*," "a little house," or "hut." And we find, in point of fact, that the word had in his time the meaning of a "hut," or "booth,"[130] side by side with that of a garment, which is its more common meaning.

As regards its primitive shape we have no certain evidence to guide us, in respect of the first eight centuries, because, as far as we can now judge, the super-vestments in the monuments of ecclesiastical dress, dating from the sixth and seventh centuries, would have been originally called *Planetæ*, and not Chasubles. But there is a strong probability that *in form* the Casula of earlier times differed but little,ᶰ if at all, from the Planeta and the Pænula. What difference there was consisted chiefly in material, and possibly in ornament; the Casula being in those older days a garb chiefly worn by the poor, and, because worn by the poor, therefore also by monks. [Appendix C, No. 26, 28, 32, 33.]

ζ A passage of Philo Judæus, *De Victimis* (quoted by Alb. Rubenius D. R. V. lib. i. cap. 6) contains a curious anticipation of this application of the term *casula*, to a cloak. αἰγῶν δὲ αἱ τρίχες αἱ (*leg.* καὶ) δοραὶ συυφαινόμεναι τι καὶ συῤῥαπτόμεναι, φορηταὶ γεγόνασιν ὁδοιπόροις οἰκίαι, καὶ μάλιστα τοῖς ἐν στρατείαις, οὒς ἔξω πόλεως ἐν ὑπαίθρῳ διατρίβειν ἀναγκάζουσιν αἱ χρεῖαι τὰ πολλά. He is evidently describing the φαινόλης, which in his time was in use in the East as well as in Greece and Italy. And by speaking

of it as "*a portable house*" for travellers, he makes it very probable that he was acquainted with the term *casula*, as employed in the *lingua volgaris* for the same garment, by the Latin-speaking peoples.

ᶰ Among other points of resemblance the older Casula was, like the Pænula, a *vestis cucullata*, provided with a cowl or hood for the protection of the head. See the quotation from St. Isidore, p. 74. *Casula est vestis cucullata, &c.* And see, further, Appendix C, No. 38.

In the Appendix will be found all the earlieſt notices that have been preſerved to us, having reference to the Cafula. And their general reſult, it will be ſeen, is this. The word was originally uſed of a garment worn, in outdoor uſe, by men of the lower claſs,[*] as a protection againſt cold and wet. The ſame word was occaſionally employed (in the African provinces at leaſt) in ſpeaking of the cloak worn for ſimilar purpoſes by perſons in ſomewhat higher ſtation. Thus St. Auguſtine employs the word, in one place, in ſpeaking of the outdoor garment worn by a journeyman tailor at Hippo (before his own time). At another time, ſpeaking to an ordinary congregation (Sermo CVII.), he expreſſes his wonder that when men are careful that every thing about them ſhould be good of its kind, they care not that their own fouls ſhould be ſo alſo. "Thou chooſeſt not a bad houſe, but a good one,—nor a bad wife, but a good one,—nor a bad Cafula, or a bad ſhoe,—and why then art thou content that thine own foul be bad?" (See Appendix C, Nos. 26 and 27).

The *Cafula* was alſo, from the ſixth to the eighth century, recogniſed as the characteriſtic dreſs of monks; and was worn, in outdoor dreſs, by many biſhops, and by the clergy generally. St. Boniface (Appendix C, No. 36) in Council preſcribed it as the proper out-door dreſs of the clergy (note 416), forbidding the uſe of the Sagum, or ſhort cloak worn by the laity. (Appendix C, Nos. 27, 28, 29, 31.)

Laſtly, at the beginning of the ninth century,[*] we find the word Cafula uſed for the firſt time, as a deſignation for the veſtment previouſly known as *Planeta;* and from that time, down to the preſent, the word Cafula has in common uſage almoſt ſuperſeded the older term.

---

[*] See Appendix C, Nos. 27 and 32. [*] See p. 203, note 420.

The Planeta.

This laſt-named veſtment is that with which we are more properly concerned in reference to the tranſition period, between the fourth and the ninth centuries.

We hear of the Planeta firſt in the fifth century, and again in the ſeventh (ſee Appendix C, Nos. 38 and 42), as a dreſs too coſtly to be worn by monks. And with this agree later notices, from which (Appendix C, Nos. 39 and 41) we find that it was worn by laymen of rank, both in Rome itſelf and in the African Provinces, in the courſe of the ſixth century of our era.[x]

The firſt mention of it as worn in offices of Chriſtian miniſtry is found in the Acts of the Council of Toledo, early in the ſeventh century (ſee p. 75). But we find it there ſpoken of not as any new thing, but as the recogniſed habit of biſhops and preſbyters, diſtinguiſhing them from the deacons, who wore an alb only.

St. Iſidore, who preſided at that Council, and whoſe pen may be clearly traced (note 133) in the record of its acts, has given elſewhere a derivation of the word Planeta. In an enumeration of a great variety of garments worn in ordinary life, he comes to the mention of "*Caſula*" already noticed. And he proceeds in the ſame ſentence (ſee p. 74) as follows. "The Caſula is a garment provided with a cowl, the name being a diminutive from '*caſa*,' a houſe, becauſe, like a little houſe, it covers the whole man. . . . . In like manner, people ſay that in Greek *Planetæ* are ſo called, becauſe the border of the Planeta 'wanders' in vague lines about the body. For which cauſe ſome ſtars are called 'Planetæ,' as implying that their movements are erratic and divergent." Rabanus Maurus, in the ninth century, while adopting verbatim (ſee p. 91) St. Iſidore's derivation of the

---

[x] See, further, Appendix C, Nos. 40, 42, 44, 45.

word *Cafula,* fays, expreffly, " *hanc* (*fc.* Cafulam) *Græci Plane-tam vocant,*" identifying, diftinctly, the *Cafula* and the *Planeta.* In fo identifying them he was fo far right, that *in his own time* the diftinction between the two was no longer recognifed. But in the fixth and feventh centuries it is evident that they were diftinguifhed, the *Cafula* as the *humbler* and *fimpler* drefs, proper to poor men and to monks (Appendix C, No. 26); the Planeta as the handfomer and more coftly habit, worn in ordinary life at Rome, alike by fenators and by popes (Appendix C, No. 41); and in Spain certainly, if not elfewhere, the diftinctive veftment of bifhops and prefbyters.

The form of the Planeta (as an epifcopal veftment), at that time, may be feen in Pl. XXVIII., compared with Pl. XXX. and XXXI., and to thefe we may add Pl. XXV., in which St. Gregory and his father Gordianus, a Roman fenator, are both reprefented as wearing a Planeta.

SUMMARY OF EVIDENCE RELATING TO PÆNULA, CASULA, AND PLANETA, IN THE TRANSITION PERIOD.

On a review of the whole evidence as to thefe three garments, we arrive at the following conclufions.

Firft, that in general form the three differed little, if at all, the one from the other. But there is no evidence to fhow that a veftment of Chriftian miniftry was ever called Pænula in the Latin Churches; nor *Cafula* before the ninth century. That till about the clofe of the eighth century, "Planeta" was the name given to the fuper-veftment of Chriftian miniftry, which in form and in ufe correfponded to what at a later time was known as the Chafuble (*Cafula*).

That all thefe garments were worn, in ordinary life, by laymen as well as by ecclefiaftics; the Planeta, however, as worn by laymen, being regarded, in all probability, as a mark of official dignity.

3. The Orarium (the later "Stole.")

1. In the Acts of the Council of Toledo, which we have taken as our starting-point for the present period, we find the Orarium recognised as a distinctly ministerial vestment, worn by bishops, presbyters, and deacons; the Orarium of the deacon, however, being worn upon one (the left) shoulder only.

Whence this word Orarium, and what the origin of the vestment so called? To these questions such reply as *can* be given will appear upon consideration of the following facts.

For the origin and derivation of the word itself, we must look not to the technical connotations of the word, whether secular or ecclesiastical, but to what is older than these technicalities, the common usage of the word as a term of ordinary speech. So guided, we shall probably be right in thinking, that the word is connected with *os*, the mouth (of which *or* is the real root-form), or, in its plural form, *ora*, the face; and regard the term as originally equivalent to our own "handkerchief." (See Appendix E, No. 1).

But of the passages, *now extant*, in which the word occurs, those of earliest date (Appendix E, No. 1 *b*) employ it in a somewhat technical sense. We first hear of it in the pages of Trebellius Pollio, a writer of the fourth century, and a contemporary of Constantine. According to him the Emperor Gallienus (Imp. 260-268) sent to Claudius (his successor in the empire) as an imperial present, four *oraria sarabdena*. Not very many years later we hear of Aurelian (Imp. 270-275) being "the first who distributed *oraria* as presents to the people, to be used by them ' *ad favorem*,'" *i.e.*, probably as colours to be worn and waved at the circus, on occasion of public games, much in the same way as ribands of various colours are worn now, ' *ad favorem*,' among ourselves, whether

as emblems of political party, or (in contexts of another kind)
of rival univerfities, or of rival fchools.

Once more. At a period not very long fubfequent to
that laft named, we find, upon the Arch of Conftantine (fee
Pl. IV.), a reprefentation of the Emperor and his attendant
courtiers; and of thefe latter many are diftinguifhed by a
broad riband, or fcarf, worn over their other drefs, prefenting
nearly the appearance of the "riband" of the Order of
Knighthood, ftill worn as an honorary diftinction in our own
times. And the fcarf, or broad riband, fo worn, *correfponds,
in general appearance, to the Orarium of the earlieft ecclefiaftical monuments* in which this veftment is reprefented
(fee Pl. XXVIII., XXX., XXXI.), though in point of
arrangement fome difference is obfervable.

In another Roman monument (not ecclefiaftical), of
which an engraving is given by Boiffardus, a fimilar "fcarf"
is feen worn over the reft of the drefs by two of the principal
perfonages reprefented. But here the arrangement differs
confiderably from that feen in the plates, reproduced in this
Work, to which reference has juft been made; and approaches very clofely to the form of the later archiepifcopal
pallium, as it may be feen in Pl. XXV., XLII., &c.

To thefe facts fhould be added that to which I here allude
by anticipation, viz. the ufe of *pallia linoftima,*[λ] or cloths partly
of linen and partly of wool, employed at Rome from the
time of S. Sylvefter, as diftinctive infignia of deacons; and the
carrying of an ἐγχείριον, a napkin, or towel, to fimilar purpofe, by deacons in the Eaft.

And with all thefe facts before us we fhall probably not

λ See note 214, p. 108. The
fame words are employed (being taken
from the fame fource) by Anaftafius,
De V. R. P. p. 105. But this writer
records a precifely fimilar order made
by Zofimus (*fed.* 417 A.D.): *Hic*

*multas conftituit ecclefias, et fecit con-
ftitutum ut diaconi lævas tectas habe-
rent* [*hora facrificii,* fo one MS.] *de
pallis* (fic) *linoftimis, et per parochias
conceffa licentia cereos benedici.*

do wrong in concluding, that the ufe of "*oraria*," of "*pallia linoſtima*" (mappulæ or *manipuli*), of the *pallium pontificium*, in the Weſt—of ὠϛάϛιον, ἐγχείϛιον, ὠμοϛόϛιον, in the Eaſt—are all inſtances of the adaptation, with certain modifications, to Chriſtian ufe, as diſtinctive infignia in the church, of what had been previouſly uſed in fecular life as marks of fpecial privilege, or of official dignity.

The fact that the date of thefe adaptations, both in Eaſt and Weſt, is. not earlier than that of the "peace of the church," fo called, in the time of Conſtantine, adds confiderably to the probability of this conjecture, becaufe of the more fully developed organifation which then firſt became poſſible.

We need only add that the veſtment now known in the Weſtern Church as a "Stole," was called "Orarium" (not Stole) till the clofe of the Tranſition Period. It is in accordance with this fact that the Greek word ϛτολὴ is never uſed in the Latin fenfe of a "Stole," but retains, in ecclefiaſtical and Byzantine Greek, its older claſſical meaning. [Note 141, p 83.]

4. The Mappula and Papal Pallium.

The three veſtments already defcribed, the Alb (or the Dalmatic, as the cafe might be), the Planeta, and the Orarium, thefe alone can be defcribed as veſtments of Chriſtian miniſtry, properly fo called, recognifed in the Weſt during the Tranſition Period. But a few words muſt here be faid of two veſtments, connected more efpecially with the Roman Church, viz. the *Mappula* and the Papal Pallium.

From two letters on the fubject of the Mappula, which are quoted in the Second Part of this work (pp. 65 and 66), we learn that, even before St. Gregory's time, a cuſtom had obtained, that the clergy of the Metropolitan City fhould carry *Mappulæ*. The Roman clergy confidered this a diſtinctive privilege, to which no other church could lay claim;

and refented extremely the pretenfion to a fimilar right put forward by the clergy of Ravenna. St. Gregory, by way of appeafing the ftrife, gave his confent at laft that the principal deacons of the Church of Ravenna fhould wear them, but only when in attendance, on ceremonial occafions, upon the archbifhop. Compare Appendix C, No. 40, and note 418.

The matter is only fo far of importance, that it illuftrates a tendency of which we find many inftances at a later time. At Rome, the centre of the wealth, the luxury, the power, of the older empire, fpecial developments of outward drefs and infignia were brought about from time to time; and for the very reafon that thefe were connected, at firft, with the feat of government, and of the "Apoftolic fee," the clergy of other churches became defirous of the like diftinctions, and fo the example fet at Rome was fooner or later followed in the Weft generally. This we fhall find to have been the cafe with the Mappula of which now we are fpeaking. The Maniple, which, to the eyes of Latin writers of the ninth century, was one of the "facred veftments" of Chriftian miniftry, was but a development of this earlier *Mappula.*

A far greater hiftorical importance attaches to the "Pallium," in that new, and exclufively ecclefiaftical fenfe, in which we find it employed from the fifth century downward. Of the ordinary meaning of the word we have already had occafion to fpeak. (Note π, p. xii).

But the "Pallium" now in queftion is that known as the Papal or archiepifcopal Pallium, the earlieft form of which may be feen in Pl. XXVIII, the lateft μ in Pl. LXI. (No.

μ The fucceffive variations in the form of the Papal Pallium may be traced in the following among the illuftrations of this volume. For the beginning of the ninth century, fee above, p. lii, compared with Pl. XXXIII. and XL.; for the tenth century, Pl. XLII. (probably, alfo, XXXIX.) and XLIII.; for the eleventh, Pl. XLIV.; for the twelfth, the figures of popes in Pl. XLV. and XLVI. From the reprefentation of the modern Pallium, given in Pl. LXI., and of the "Orfrey" of the

16). The monuments lately difcovered by De Roffi in the Roman Catacombs (fee Pl. XXX., XXXI.), and which date, probably, from the eighth century, will fhow what, during this tranfition period, was reputed to have been the primitive form of this veftment. As there fhown, it is fimply *a white orarium worn outfide the planeta*, and croffed over the left hand, fo as to keep it from actual contact with the Book of the Gofpels, then the traditional infignia of a bifhop. It is very poffible that in the frefcoes in queftion it is an Orarium (and not a Pallium) which the painter defigned to reprefent. If he were accurately acquainted with the epifcopal drefs of the third century which he had to reprefent, he would no doubt have faid (and faid with truth) that it would have been an anachronifm for him to reprefent, in a drefs of *that time*, a veftment fuch as the Papal Pallium, which was then unknown to the Church.

We have only to confider for a moment the contract between the pofition of the Church in the firft three centuries, and that to which fhe attained after the age of Conftantine, in order to fee why the Papal Pallium, as a diftinctive veftment, fhould not have been known in that earlier period. While the empire was in antagonifm to the Church, as it was till the time of Conftantine, it was not in the nature of things that a completely organifed hierarchical fyftem fhould be developed, by the formal aggregation of diocefes into metropolitan provinces, the fubordination of metropolitans to patriarchs, of patriarchs to an œcumenical patriarch, or to the " Apoftolic fee." We find, accordingly, that the veftments worn in that earlier period were veftments for bifhops, prefbyters, deacons, the three orders of the Chriftian miniftry which had exifted from the very firft. But

---

priest's Chafuble fhown in the fame plate, it will be feen that the latter far more nearly refembles in fize and general appearance the Pallium of the eleventh century, than does the Pallium itfelf as now worn by an archbifhop.

from the period of the "peace of the church" under Constantine, the Christian hierarchy was developed in two directions—downwards in respect of the minor orders, sub-
deacons, acolytes, readers, and the like,—upwards, in a
graduated ascent, which, by flow degrees, and with much, at
times, of even bitter contest, culminated at length in the
recognition of the Bishop of Constantinople in "New Rome,"
as ecumenical Patriarch in the East, and of the Bishop of
Rome as having first place in precedence among all the patriarchal sees throughout the world. And it is in accordance
with these facts that we find so many of the early councils,
in the latter part of the fourth century, occupying themselves
with the regulation of distinctive vestments, or insignia, such
as marked off, on the one hand, the position of the deacon,
as one to be distinguished even in outward semblance (by the
wearing of an orarium) from that of the minor orders; and,
on the other hand, served to distinguish Metropolitans and
Patriarchs from the suffragan bishops of their respective provinces.

MINISTERING VESTMENTS IN THE EAST.

What has been already said of the various vestments
recognised in the West during the Period of Transition (400
to 800 A.D.), will apply, with slight modifications only, to
those of the East.

The vestments recognised at this time were the Sticharion, corresponding to the Alb, or rather to the Dalmatic

---

, For the *word* see note 346, p.
169. I may add, however, that as
one meaning of στοῖχος is a "line," it
is not improbable that this vestment
may have been so called from the

λῶρια (note 146), or coloured stripes,
by which it was decorated. We hear
of the Sticharion as a vestment of holy
ministry as early as the time of S.
Athanasius.

k

of the Weft; the Phænolion,‡ anfwering to the Planeta (the later "Chafuble"); and the Orarium,˙ a term common to both Eaft and Weft in refpect of the deacon's Scarf (or "Stole"), Pl. LIX., but which was known as Peritrachelion, or Epitrachelion, when worn pendent round the neck by bifhops or priefts. See Pl. LVI., No. 1, and the defcription.

And as we hear of Mappula and Pallium (fee above, p. lxx) in the Weft, fo alfo of ἐγχείριον (Napkin or Towel), and Omophorion in the Eaft. This laft veftment, from the fifth century, if not from an earlier time, down to the prefent, has been worn by Patriarchs and Metropolitans, and by almoft all bifhops in the Eaft. And if the reader will compare the confular drefs, reprefented in Pl. XXIII., with that attributed to Patriarchs in Pl. XLI., LVIII., and to St. James in Pl. LXIII., he will fee how clofe is the refemblance between the diftinctive ornament of the two coftumes. On the drefs, too, of Emperors of the Eaft, a fimilar ornament is confpicuous. And there can be little doubt that the imperial (or confular) Omophorion was the type upon which the patriarchal Omophorion was formed.

The paffages from early writers, of chief importance, bearing upon the ecclefiaftical drefs of the Eaft at this period, will be found in the later pages ᵗ of this volume.

The art-monuments dating from before 800 A.D. are but few. Thofe from the Church of St. George at Theffalonica,

---

‡ Called φιλόνιον by St. Germanus. See p. 84, note 143. For various forms of the Eaftern φιλόνιον, at various times, fee Plates XVIII., XIX., XX., XXVII., XLI., and the figure of St. Sampfon in Pl. LVIII. Several Phænolia, attributed by tradition to bifhops or patriarchs of the twelfth and following centuries, are accurately depicted in the firft volume of the *Antiquités de l'Empire Ruffe.*

˙ See note 144.

ᵗ See St. Ifidore of Pelufium, p. 94; St. Chryfoftom, or the author who bears his name (fee note 94), p. 51; St. Germanus, p. 82; and with thefe compare St. Symeon of Theffalonica, p. 168.

ſome of which are figured in this volume (Pl. XVIII., XIX., XX., XXI.), do not reprefent a dreſs of holy miniſtry, but of dignity, common, with very ſlight modifications only, to prieſts and people alike. Theſe moſaics date, probably, from the fourth century. Two centuries later in date are the moſaics of the great Church (St. Sophia) at Conſtantinople. And among thoſe which, from their poſition, have eſcaped deſtruction at the hands of the Turks, are ſome *e* of biſhops of the fourth century, dreſſed in white *r* veſtments (Sticharion and Phænolion), and with an Omophorion, reſembling in form that attributed to St. James, in the freſco reproduced in Pl. LXIII.

Upon a review of the whole evidence, literary *r* and monumental, bearing upon the queſtion, we ſhould conclude that the ſacred veſtments, recogniſed in the Greek Church in the eighth century, were the Sticharion, Girdle, Orarium,*v*

---

e See Salzenberg's *Alt-Chriſtliche Baudenkmale.* Pl. XXVIII. and XXIX. The biſhops reprefented are Anthenios, Biſhop of Nicomedia, † 311 ; Baſileios (St. Baſil the Great), † 379 ; Dionyſius the Areopagite, † 96 ; Nicolaus, Biſhop of Myra (one of the 318 at Micæa), † 330 ; and Gregorius of Armenia, † 325.

The Church of St. Sophia was built 532–538 A.D., and the moſaics are of the ſame date.

r The dreſs cloſely reſembles that attributed to St. James in Pl. LXIII., with this difference only, that in every caſe the Sticharion, or long tunic, has double ſtripes on either ſide, and running round the ſleeve, this latter fitting cloſely round the wriſt, inſtead of being full and looſe as is the ſleeve of the Roman dalmatic. In five out of the ſix figures, the *lora*, or

ſtripes, are two lines of purple and red ; in one (that of Gregory of Armenia) of red only. The croſſes on the Omophorion correſpond in colour, in every caſe, to thoſe of the *lora*.

r The paſſage of St. Germanus, quoted at p. 82, *ſqq.* preſents ſome difficulty owing to his mixing up the mention of garments worn in holy miniſtry with thoſe of ordinary uſage, ſuch as the Mandyas,[153] and the Cowl.[151]

v The ἰδὼν mentioned by St. Germanus (p. 86, note 154) as a part of the deacon's dreſs, is probably only another name for the Orarion, having reference to the material (linen) of which it was formed. The word is evidently ſo uſed in the paſſage, attributed to St. Chryſoſtom, quoted at p. 49, note 78.

and (ἐγχείριον °) Napkin, for deacons; the Sticharion, Girdle, Phænolion, and Peritrachelion, for priests; while the bishop, over and above these, wore an Omophorion as his distinguishing badge.

ᵠ The ἐγχείριον, mentioned by St. Germanus, as carried by the deacon, suspended from his Girdle, may have been of local use only, as was, at one time, the Mappula at Rome. But the use of the ἐγχείριον died out (or at least the mention of it as thus carried by the deacon); but that of the Mappula spread by degrees throughout the Western Churches.

From the Roma Subterranea of Aringhi.

CHAPTER VIII.

THE THIRD PERIOD, FROM THE YEAR 800 A.D. TO THE PRESENT TIME.

WE attain now to well-trodden ground, and have for the firft time ample materials for our guidance, in contemporary monuments, both of literature and of art, fuch as thofe publifhed in the later pages of this volume.

Thefe have been fo arranged in chronological order as to tell, in great meafure, their own tale. A few words only are needed by way of preliminary remark.

One who takes a review of the literature of the eighth and the ninth centuries can fcarcely fail to remark, how rapid, in the later period of the two, was the fucceffion of writers upon fubjects mainly relating to ritual. It is not difficult, on reflection, to account for this being fo. The reftoration of peace to Europe, confequent upon the victories of Charlemagne, gave men leifure for a devotion to ftudy, which had been all but impoffible amid the wars and rumours of wars, by which for nearly four hundred years the minds of men had been diftracted. The example, too, and the liberal patronage of that monarch, favoured the interefts of letters; and new fchools of learning were founded both in France and Germany, under the aufpices of our countryman Alcuin, or of fuch worthy inheritors of his learning as Rabanus Maurus [155] and Walafrid Strabo [204].

The circumftances of the time account for the direction then given to literary activity. It was not unnatural that in the Carlovingian age the minds of earneft men, fhocked by the contemplation of the awful corruption, both in Church and State, which everywhere met their gaze, fhould turn back with fond and reverential affeƈtion to the earlier and purer ages of the Church; and in the writings of thofe whom they, like ourfelves, fpoke of as "the Fathers," feek for guidance in building up anew the ruined fabric of the Church.

To caufes fuch as thefe may probably be traced the fudden outburft, early in the ninth century, of a new fpirit of inquiry into all that concerned the difcipline and the ritual of the Church. And the queftion of veftments was one which naturally, at that time, affumed a fpecial prominence. Churchmen, who had travelled widely, as then fome did, in Eaft as well as Weft, could hardly fail to notice the remarkable faƈt, that at Conftantinople as at Rome, at Canterbury as at Arles, Vienna or Lyons, one general type of miniftering drefs was maintained, varying only in fome minor details; and that this drefs everywhere prefented a moft marked contraftˣ to what was *in their time* the prevailing drefs of the laity. And as all knowledge↓ of claffical antiquity had for three centuries or more been well·nigh extinƈt in the Church, it was not lefs

---

χ See this illuftrated in piƈtures dating from the ninth or tenth century, fuch as thofe in Pl. XXXVII. and XLIII.

↓ At the clofe of the fixth century St. Gregory writes to a bifhop in Gaul, faying that he cannot fend him the Pallium till he gives up ftudying Grammar and teaching it to others (Ep. xi. 54). He himfelf, as he tells us, *knew nothing of Greek;* and at Conftantinople in his time there was no one who knew enough of Latin to tranflate one of his letters intelligibly (Ep. vii. xxx). With a few rare exceptions this ignorance of Greek continued in the Weft, till the fall of Conftantinople, in the fifteenth century, fent learned Greeks for a refuge into Italy, and fo contributed powerfully to the reftoration of learning, and the reformation of Weftern Chriftendom. When a Roman Cardinal fpoke in Greek (or in what paffed for Greek) at the Council of Florence, A.D. 1430, it was held to be (fo Raynaldus gravely tells us) clear proof of miraculous agency. I ftate thefe faƈts not for the purpofe of cafting a reproach upon the Church of paft ages; but becaufe this faƈt of prevailing ignorance of the ancient languages ferves to explain many of the phenomena (among them fome that are very painful) of the hiftory of the Church in mediæval times.

natural that they ſhould have ſought a ſolution of the phenomenon thus preſented to them, in a theory of Levitical origin,
which, from that time forward, was generally accepted. It
was not till the revival of claſſical learning, many centuries
later, that men were led to form a truer eſtimate of this and
of other kindred queſtions. The ſucceſſive documents, dating
from the ninth and the two following centuries, contained in
the later part of this volume, ſhow very plainly the progreſſive
development of this theory. Thus Rabanus Maurus, perhaps
the earlieſt of theſe writers, when ſpeaking of the older Levitical veſtments, and of their ſpiritual meaning, does but follow,
as he ſays, in the ſteps of the older writers. But in what he
ſays of the *habitus ſacerdotalis* of his own day, he makes a
kind of apology for ſpeaking *ſecundum modulum ingenioli ſui*
(ſee note [160]), as one who felt that he had entered upon new
and ſomewhat doubtful ground. And we have only to compare
the dreſs of a biſhop of the ninth century (as in Pl. XXXVII.)
with that of the Jewiſh high-prieſt (Pl. IX.), in order to ſee
what difficulties had to be got over in identifying the one with
the other. Some accordingly (as Walafrid Strabo) contented
themſelves with ſaying (p. 108) that *in number* the Chriſtian
veſtments correſponded to thoſe of the law; and with ſuch
vague reſemblances as that of the " plate of gold " being worn
only by the High-prieſt, as the pallium was worn only
by chief paſtors. But others, while recogniſing points of
ſtrong contraſt[u] between the two types of dreſs, too obvious
to be overlooked, ſought, by the moſt far-fetched compariſons[α]
to find features of likeneſs between them. And where this was
not poſſible, additions[β] were made from time to time to the

---

[u] Such as the abſence of *tiara* or
lamina aurea (p. 112 and Appendix E,
No. 12).

[α] As of the Amice to the Ephod
(ſee p. 111,[224]); of the Jewiſh Rational
'a jewel of twelve precious ſtones

worn on the breaſt] to the Pallium of
an Archbiſhop (Note [217]).

[β] As of an actual jewel to repreſent
the Rational (Note [236], p. 124, and
more certainly at p. 138, Note [283]),
and of a mitre with its *circulus aureus,*

" *Sacræ Veſtes* " of the Church, in order to create a ſimilarity where none had exiſted hitherto.

We find, accordingly, both in the literature and in the monuments of art, dating from the period now under conſideration, diſtinct evidence of the rapid development of the miniſtering dreſs of the Weſtern Church, from the beginning of the ninth to the end of the twelfth century.

Rabanus Maurus (p. 88), and Amalarius (p. 94), early in the ninth century, and the reputed Alcuin, probably in the tenth (p. 110, note 218), all ſpeak of eight γ veſtments as worn by biſhops, beſide the Pallium proper to archbiſhops. St. Ivo (p. 128), writing at the cloſe of the eleventh century, adds but one to the older enumeration, he being the firſt to ſpeak of the " *caligæ byſſinæ,*" " leggings," or ſtockings, made of linen, as among the ſacred veſtments. But within a period of about fifty years, at the moſt, from the time of St. Ivo's writing, we find in Honorius of Autun (note 296ᵃ, p. 142), the number of the ſacred veſtments exactly doubled. He reckons ſeven veſtments as proper to prieſts; ſeven more (fourteen in all) as belonging to biſhops; while two others, the Pallium and the Crozier, are appropriated to archbiſhops. Innocent III., by the further mention (p. 153) of a veſtment (the " *orale* " 314), and an ornament (the pectoral croſs 315), which he regarded as belonging excluſively to the Roman Pontiff, added yet more to the whole enumeration. And by him, accordingly, ſix veſtments are aſſigned to preſbyters, fifteen in all to biſhops, one, the Pallium, ſpecially to archbiſhops; making, with the two which he regarded as proper to the Biſhop of Rome, no leſs than eighteen in all.

With this rapid development of the veſtments in the

---

to repreſent the Tiara of the High-prieſt, Appendix G.

γ Walafrid Strabo (p. 106) men-

tions but ſeven, omitting, as he does, all mention of the Amice.

Roman Church, may be contrafted the fixity which, in this as in other matters, is characteriftic of "the unchanging Eaft." [a] Patriarch Simeon, writing in the fifteenth century, knows of but five veftments proper to a prieft, and of two more, making feven in all, as belonging to a bifhop.[357] And though he mentions the Pectoral Crofs,[312] and the Staff,[315] as infignia of a bifhop, he claffes them with the Mandyas, or Mantle, as part of the non-liturgical coftume, as in point of fact they are ftill regarded.

But to return to our more immediate fubject,—the hiftory of the veftments in the Weft,— it will be found that the multiplication of the "facred veftments," above fpoken of, was effected, partly by actual additions to the lefs elaborate drefs of earlier centuries, partly by the promotion, fo to fpeak, to facred rank, of articles of drefs, or of ornament, which had long been in ufe, but without being confecrated to fymbolical fignificance, or to any fpecially facerdotal ufage.

As the moft convenient way of bringing before my readers the general refults of the documents printed in full in the later pages of this volume, I have drawn out in an Appendix (fee Appendix F), an enumeration of the facerdotal veftments, at the time of their fulleft development in the Roman Church; with fuch brief notices to each as will indicate their origin, and the fucceffive modifications which they underwent.

For the prefent it will be fufficient to point out fome of the more general conclufions which refult from the whole inquiry.

---

[a] Yet there are not wanting indications that in the Eaft alfo, in particular inftances at leaft, and in the later mediæval times, the idea of directly imitating Levitical veftments was entertained. See, for example, the curious monument reproduced in Pl. LVII, and the Defcription at p. 245.

And, firſt, it will be ſeen, that of all the various types of miniſtering dreſs, now retained in different branches of the Church, there is one, and one only, which approaches cloſely both in form and diſtinctive ornament to that of primitive Chriſtendom, that dreſs being the Surplice (Appendix G, 5), with Scarf or Stole (ſee note on Pl. LXIII), now worn in the Engliſh Church.[1] The reader has only to refer to Pl. XV. and XVII., in which monuments of that ancient dreſs have been preſerved, in order to ſee that this is the caſe.[ʒ]

It appears further, that the original elements out of which the preſent miniſtering dreſs was developed, are common to the Greek, the Roman, and the Anglican Churches. But in the miniſtering dreſs of the Roman Church that primitive dreſs *has been overlaid by ſucceſſive additions,* till the older type can ſcarcely be recogniſed under the changed forms in which it now appears. See Pl. LXI. We, ourſelves, at the Reformation, had no ſooner thrown aſide thoſe mediæval additions, merely Roman in their character, than we placed ourſelves at one again with the Primitive Church, in this, as in other matters of far higher importance, in which a ſimilar courſe was purſued.

Of the additions which at various times have been made to the really primitive dreſs, ſome few, as the Orarium and Planeta, date from the fourth century. And theſe are common to both Eaſt and Weſt. But by far the greater number date from the ninth, to the middle of the twelfth, century;

---

[1] See particularly the central figure of the right-hand group (*ſpectator's* right) in Pl. XV. The dreſs of an Engliſh clergyman of the preſent day is there exactly delineated.

[ʒ] The only difference is that the black ſtripes repreſented on thoſe primitive veſtments were *attached to the tunic* inſtead of being ſeparate, as was the later Orarium, and the modern " Stole."

a period of darknefs, both intellectual [n] and moral, (efpecially fo at Rome itfelf), fuch as the Chriftian world has never known either before or fince.

It is not within the fcope of the prefent work to enter upon matter of theological controverfy. And I therefore only ftate here, as matter of hiftory, that this development of the facerdotal drefs was exactly coincident in time with the development of innovations in euchariftic doctrine, which were diftinctly mentioned for the firft [o] time early in the ninth century, and which culminated in the decree of the Eleventh Lateran Council,[ι,π] concerning tranfubftantiation, *anno* 1215. It was but natural that this fhould be. The formation of

---

[n] Baronius (Cardinal) ad ann. 900. "Incipit annus Redemptoris nongente-fimus . . . . quo et novum in-choatur Sæculum, quod fui afperitate ac boni fterilitate, ferreum, malique exundantis deformitate plumbeum, at-que inopia fcriptorum appellari con-fuevit obfcurum." [*Ann. Ecc.* tom. x. p. 629].

[o] *Id.* ad ann. 912, No. 14, p. 663. "Quæ tunc facies fanctæ Ecclefiæ Ro-manæ, quam fœdiffima, cum Romæ dominarentur potentiffimæ æque ac fordidiffimæ meretrices, quarum arbi-trio mutarentur Sedes, darentur Epi-fcopi, et quod auditu horrendum et infandum eft intruderentur in Sedem Petri earum Amafii Pfeudopontifices, qui non fint nifi ad confignanda tan-tum tempora in catalogo Romanorum Pontificum fcripti. Quis enim a fcortis hujufmodi intrufos fine lege, legitimos dicere poffet Romanos fuiffe Pontifices?" For a *contemporary* pic-ture of what Rome then was—a picture which more than juftifies fuch language as the above—fee the fixth book of the *Hiftoria Luitprandi Epifcopi.*

Genebrardus, Archbifhop of Aix (Chronographia, lib. iv. p. 553), fpeaks of this period of awful corrup-tion in the Papal See itfelf as lafting for 150 years, and through a fucceffion of fifty pontiffs.

[ι] In the treatife of Pafchafius Ru-bertus, of whom Cardinal Bellarmine (Opp. tom. vii. p. 121) writes, "*Hic auctor primus fuit qui ferio ac copiofe differuit de veritate Corporis ac San-guinis Domini in Euchariftia.*" By this, of courfe, he means that he is the earlieft writer who diftinctly main-tains *the Roman doctrine* on this fubject. So underftood, his affertion is perfectly exact. The doctrine of Pafchafius was thought fo ftrange, that Charles the Bald *called upon Ratramnus* (*al.* Ber-tramnus) *of Corbey to anfwer it*, which he did in a treatife which is of fpecial intereft to ourfelves, as having formed the mind of Ridley and Cranmer upon this particular queftion. For further particulars of intereft concerning it, fee *Knox's Remains*, vol. ii. p. 157, and *Chriftian Remembrancer*, July, 1867.

what was deemed a diftinctly facerdotal drefs, modelled in detail upon the veftments of Levitical priefthood, both promoted, and in its turn was promoted by, fuch developments of doctrine as thofe to which I refer.

With this much of Preface, I may afk my readers to proceed to the ftudy of the many monuments, both of primitive and of mediæval times, which are fet out in the later pages of this volume.

Ancient Glafs from the Roman Catacombs. See defcription at p. 247.

PASSAGES FROM ANCIENT AUTHORS.

I.

NAMES OF THE SACERDOTAL VESTMENTS AS ENUMERATED IN HOLY SCRIPTURE.

THE various paſſages[1] in Holy Scripture in which the veſtments of the Levitical prieſthood are deſcribed or referred to, need not be quoted at length, as they are eaſily acceſſible to all. But it will be convenient for purpoſes of reference to ſpecify the various names by which thoſe veſtments were known in the Apoſtolic age, and in thoſe which followed, whether in Greek, through the LXX., or in Latin, through the early Italic Verſions, and that of S. Jerome.

	LXX.	S. JEROME.	ENGLISH A. V.
1. The Linen Drawers.	περισκελῆ λινᾶ.	Feminalia linea.	Linen Breeches.
2. The White Tunic (of linen).	χιτὼν ποδήρης, or χιτὼν βύσσινος.	Tunica talaris, or linea ſtriɛta.	Coat, long robe.
3. The Girdle.	ζώνη.	Balteus, cingulum, or zona.	Girdle.
4. The Prieſt's Cap.	κίδαρις, or μίτρα.	Cidaris, or mitra.	Bonnet.
5. The Tunic of Blue worn under the Ephod.	χιτὼν κοσυμβωτός, or ὑποδύτης ὑπὸ τὴν ἐπωμίδα.	Tunica ſuperhumeralis.	Broidered coat, or Robe of the Ephod.
6. The Ephod, with the bands thereof.	ἐπωμίς. (The Girdle of the Ephod is not mentioned by LXX.)	Superhumerale and Balteus (Exod. xxxix. 5).	Ephod, and 'curious Girdle' of the Ephod.
7. The Breaſtplate, or Jewel of the Ephod.	λόγιον, or περιστήθιον.	Rationale.	Breaſtplate.
8. The Tiara, or High-Prieſt's Mitre, with the Plate of Gold.	κίδαρις, or μίτρα, with πέταλον.	Cidaris, or Tiara, with Lamna.	Mitre, with the Plate of Gold, or Holy Crown.

[1] The paſſages of chief importance are Exod. xxviii. xxix. and xxxix.; Lev. viii. and xvi. (compare below, note 17); Num. x 26–28; Ezek. xliv. 17, ſqq. In the Apocryphal Books, Ecclus. xlv., and 1 Macc. x. 21, where by ἡ ἱερὰ στολή is meant not one ſingle robe only (as in A. V. "put on him the holy robe"), but the entire inveſtiture of the high-prieſt.

II.

JOSEPHUS.

ON THE SACERDOTAL VESTMENTS OF THE LEVITICAL PRIESTHOOD.

1. Antiq. Jud. iii. 7.

[He begins by saying that there are vestments proper both to the ordinary priests known as Xαναiαι,[2] and to the 'Αναραβάχης,[3]—*i.e.* chief of priests or high-priest. These he proceeds to describe in detail.]

Dress of the Priests (of the second order).—1. *The Linen Drawers.* The dress of the priests is such as I shall now describe. When any one of them is about to engage in offices of priesthood he performs the ablutions required by the law, and then puts on, first, the garment called Μαναχασης,[4] equivalent in meaning to the Greek συνακτηρ. These are drawers made of linen, fastened about the middle, into which the feet are passed, as would be the case with Persian trousers. They do not reach higher than the waist, where they are securely fastened.

2. *The long white Tunic, and* (3) *the Girdle thereof.* Over these drawers he wears an under-garment of linen, made of byssus.[5] It is called Χεθομίνη,—that is, "made of linen;" for χεθών with us means flax. This garment is a full-length tunic (χιτών ποδήρης), fitted exactly[6] to the body, and with its sleeves fastened closely about the

---

[2] Xαναiας is, probably, the Hellenic representative of כהן.

[3] The reading here (as often is the case with foreign words in old MSS.) is probably corrupt. Various emendations have been proposed, as Ραβαγαδην, or Ραβαχοανη,—*i.e.* chief of the priests. But these are in the highest degree uncertain.

Heb. רבים.

[5] The Greek βύσσος = Heb. בוץ; which means sometimes (α) fine flax, sometimes (β) the fine linen thence prepared. It would seem to be used occasionally (γ) with a primary reference to its *bright white* colour (*candor*). Compare Note 19.

[6] τὰς χειρίδας περὶ τοῖς βραχίοσιν κατισφιγμένος. This closeness of fit, and the absence, generally, of all loosely-flowing garments, in the dress of the Levitical priesthood, is a characteristic necessarily entailed (for cleanliness sake) by the nature of their ministrations in respect of animal sacrifice.

arms. This they gird in to the breaft, not far from the armpit, paffing the girdle round the body, very high up.† This girdle is four fingers broad, and woven in open pattern, like the fcales of a ferpent. Upon it flowers are worked in divers colours of purple, blue, and white; but the woof is made of byffus only. When worn, the prieft begins by placing one end upon his cheft, and then paffes it twice round him, and faftens it: after which, if he is not engaged in the active duties of his miniftry, he lets it flow down full as far as the ankles. The beauty of the girdle is thus fully difplayed. But whenever he is required to bufy himfelf about the facrifices, or in other acts of miniftry, he throws it over his left fhoulder, and so wears it that its movements may not interfere with the work in which he may be engaged. This girdle was named by Mofes Ἀβανίθ, but by us of thefe days it is called Ἐμίαν, a name which we learnt from the Babylonians, by whom it is ftill employed. The tunic above fpoken of has no loofe folds in any part of it; but the opening for the neck is left of full fize, and is faftened up, upon the cheft and back, juft above either collar-bone, by ftrings attached to the border. Μασναβαζάνες is the name by which it is known.

4. *The Prieft's Cap.* On the head he wears a cap without any peak,[7] extending, not over the whole head, but over a little more than half of it. It is called μασναιμφθῆς. Its conftruction is fuch as to prefent the appearance of a turban,[8] being a band of linen weft, and of confiderable thicknefs, folded upon itfelf feveral times, and fo ftitched together. At top of this band there is a covering of fine linen (σινδών) which overlaps it and reaches to the forehead, and is fo arranged as to hide the ftitching of the thick band below, which would have been unfeemly if left expofed, and to lie flat upon the fkull. It is made to fit with great exactnefs, fo as not to fall off while the prieft is engaged in facrifice. Thus much as to the drefs of the priefts generally, as diftinct from that of the high-prieft.

---

† ὀλίγον τῆς μασχάλης ὑπεράνω τὴς ζώνην περιάγοντες. The tranflation above given is fuggefted for want of a better. To render the words with former tranflations, *paulo fupra axillas*, gives a meaning which is unintelligible as applied *to a girdle*.

[7] πίλος ἄκωνος. He mentions thus particularly the *abfence* of any " cone " or peak,

becaufe among the prieftly infignia of many heathen rites fuch a peak was confpicuous. See Pl. V. Or the contraft intended *may* be that of the high-prieft's tiara.

[8] τῇ κατασκευῇ τοιούτός ἐστιν ὡς στιφάνη δοκεῖν. The exact meaning of στιφάνη is doubtful.

Vestments worn by the High Priest only.

5. *The Tunic of blue with its Girdle.* The high-prieſt wears the veſtments already deſcribed, without omitting any; but over them he wears further a tunic of blue,[9] reaching to the feet, like that firſt deſcribed, and known in our tongue as the *μιιρ.* This is faſtened about him with a girdle of the ſame colours as that already deſcribed, but with gold thread alſo introduced. Along the lower border is a fringe attached, coloured and faſhioned ſo as to reſemble pomegranates; and with them golden bells deviſed with great beauty of appearance, and ſo arranged that, between each two bells a pomegranate is ſet, and between each two pomegranates a bell. This tunic is not formed in two ſeparate parts, faſtened together by a ſeam upon the ſhoulders and at the ſide, but conſiſts of one long piece, woven throughout, and has an opening ſlit for the neck, not horizontally, but length-wiſe (vertically) towards the cheſt and the middle of the back. Upon the opening thus made, an edging, or border, is ſewn, ſo as to con-ceal anything unſeemly in the opening thus made. A ſimilar ſlit is made at the wriſts.

6 and 7. *The Ephod and the Breaſtplate.* Over and above theſe he puts on, thirdly,[10] the ephod, as it is called, reſembling the *ἐπωμίς* of the Greeks. The faſhion of it is as follows:—It is woven for the ſpace of a cubit in depth of various colours, with wrought work of gold, and leaves the middle of the breaſt uncovered. It is furniſhed with ſleeves, and in its whole faſhion is conſtructed as a tunic. In the ſpace left void by the ephod itſelf, a piece of cut (ſquared) cloth is faſtened, wrought in divers colours like thoſe of the ephod. It is called Ἐσσήνς, and means in the Greek tongue "Oracle." This exactly fills up that ſpace which in the weaving of the ephod was left as an opening on the breaſt. It is united by golden rings at each corner to the ephod, which is itſelf provided with correſponding rings for the purpoſe, and the one ſet of rings is attached to the other by a band of blue cloth. And that the parts intervening between theſe rings might not hang looſe and out of ſhape, a plan was deviſed for

---

[9] χιτῶνα ἐξ ὑακίνθου πεποιημένον.

[10] He ſpeaks of the ephod as *third* among the diſtinctive veſtments of the high-prieſt, reckon-ing the tunic of blue as the firſt, and the girdle, or bands, belonging to this outer tunic (by which it was attached to the ephod) as the ſecond.

keeping all in place by (νἠματα ὑακίνϑινα) a ftitched edging of blue. The ephod has a clafp of fardonyx on either fhoulder, each of the two projecting ends being wrought in gold, fo as to fit in with the clafps. Upon thefe ftones are inferibed the names of the twelve fons of Jacob in the letters proper to our native language, fix on either ftone. The elder fons' names are on the right fhoulder, thofe of the younger on the left. So likewife on the breaftplate (or " Oracle ") there are fet twelve ftones of unufual fize and beauty, forming an ornament fuch as men generally could not poffibly obtain becaufe of its exceeding coftlinefs. Thefe ftones are arranged in lines, there being four rows, and each of thefe containing three ftones. They are worked into the ftuff on which they are fixed with a fetting of gold, whofe ornamental work is fo inferted into the ftuff as to hold together without giving way. Of the four rows the firft contains a fardonyx, a topaz, and an emerald; the fecond a carbuncle, a jafper, and a fapphire. In the third are, firft, a lyncurius, then an amethyft, and an agate ; making up nine in all, thus far. In the loweft row a chryfolite ftands firft ; afterwards an onyx, and, laftly, a beryl. On all thefe ftones letters were engraved, which ferved to defignate Jacob's fons, whom we regard as the heads of our twelve tribes. Each ftone bears a name of fome one patriarch, according to the order of birth. The rings already mentioned are too weak of themfelves to bear the weight of the ftones. Accordingly, the border of the breaftplate, where it reaches upwards towards the neck, is furnifhed with two larger rings, inferted into the principal texture. Thefe rings are to receive certain chains of wrought work, which, on the top of either fhoulder, met and were attached to cords of gold. The end of thefe cords was turned up, and reached [11] as far as a ring projecting from the hinder border of the ephod. Thus was the breaftplate fecured from all danger of giving way.

The ephod was alfo furnifhed with a girdle, wrought in divers colours and in gold, as already defcribed ; and this encircled the ephod, and was then brought back and faftened at the feam, and then hung down. The fringes of the ephod were bordered on either fide, and kept in place, by cylinders of gold.

8. *The High-prieft's Cap, or Mitre.* A cap,[12] fuch as that already

---

[11] ἀνέβαινε κρίκῳ τρείχοντι. I fufpect that the true reading is ἐνέβαινε, with the meaning | " was inferted into."

[12] πῖλος = Latin *pileus*, or *pileum*.

described as worn by the priests generally, was assigned to the high-priest also. But above this, and sewn on to it, he had another, made of blue, and richly ornamented. Round this cap ran a circlet of gold, wrought in three tiers,[13] and upon this circlet is a cup-shaped flower, exactly resembling what our own people call Saccharus, but is known to the Greek herbalists as Hyoscyamus. [Here follows in the original text a long description of the plant in question, which I have omitted as being very obscure, and not of importance to the questions now before us.] The golden circlet thus formed extends from the back of the head to either temple. But to the forehead itself the flower-shaped ornament, just described, does not extend. But there is here a plate[14] of gold, on which is engraved, in sacred letters,[15] the holy name of God. Thus have I described the adornment of the high-priest.

2. De Bello Judaico. (Lib. v. Cap. v. § 7.)

Those of the priests who, by reason of any bodily defect, did not engage in holy ministrations, were wont to appear, together with those who had no such defect, inside the enclosure, and received the portions due to them by right of birth, but wore the garments of ordinary life. For the sacred dress was worn only by one who ministered (at the altar). But those of the priests who were without

---

[13] στιφέχιται στίφανος χρύσιος ἐπὶ τριοτουχίαν κιχαλκιωμένος. No mention of this triple crown is made in H. S. But Josephus tells us (Antiq. Jud. xx. cap. 9), that Judas son of Hyrcanus, being at once high-priest and king, διάδημα περίφετο πρῶτος, was the first to assume a royal crown (in addition, i.e. to the sacerdotal tiara). And then we read at a later period that when Pompey restored another Hyrcanus to the high-priesthood of which, and of the royalty then attaching thereto, he had been deprived by his brother Aristobulus, τὴν μὲν τοῦ ἔθνους προστασίαν ἐπίτρεψι, διάδημα δὲ φορεῖν ἐκώλυσε, he made over to him the government of his own people, but prevented his wearing a (royal) crown. It is probable, therefore, that the tiara with triple crown described by Josephus, was a combination of the symbols of spiritual and temporal

power, as is the triple crown (see Pl. 33) of the later Roman popes. The triple crown of the Jewish priest-king may have had reference to the three governments (1 Macc. x. 30) of Judea, Samaria, and Galilee.

[14] στλαμὼν χρύσεος. "Band" is the more literal rendering. But St. Jerome was no doubt right in considering the word as being here equivalent to the Latin *lamna*, *a thin plate* of metal.

[15] ἱεροῖς γράμμασι τοῦ θεοῦ τὴν προσηγορίαν ἐπιτετμημένος. The expression is not inconsistent with that which is recorded in Holy Scripture, viz., that the words upon the plate were, "Holiness unto the Lord." (Exod. xxviii. 36.) By ἱερὰ γράμματα are probably meant the older "Samaritan" letters, so called.

difqualifying defect went up to the altar and the Holy Place, having
about them a vefture of fine linen,[16] and abftained carefully from ftrong
wine, out of reverence for the duty they had to perform, that in
nothing they might tranfgrefs while engaged in their holy miniftration. And the high-prieft went up with them, yet not always fo,
but on the feventh days, and on the new moons, and at any national
feftival, or general affembly of the people, of annual obfervance. And
he performed his miniftry, covered from the thighs to the groin with
a girding band; and wearing an inner garment of linen, and over this
a long vefture of blue, circular in form, and furnifhed with a fringe.
To thefe fringes were faftened golden bells, and pomegranates alter-
nating therewith; the bells fignificant of thunder, the pomegranates
of lightning. [Then follows a defcription of the ephod, the breaftplate, and the tiara, much fuch as that already quoted; and he then
adds]:—This drefs he (the high-prieft) was not in the habit of
wearing at other times, but put on one of fimpler character; but
he did wear it on occafions of his entering (ὁπότε εἰσίοι) the moft
Holy Place, which he did once only in each year, and alone, on the
day (of Atonement) when it is cuftomary for all to keep faft unto
God.[17]

---

[16] Ἐπὶ τὸ θυσιαστήριον καὶ τὸν ναὸν ἀνιδόντων
οἱ τῶν ἱερῶν ἄμωμαι βύσσον μὲν ἀμπιχόμενοι.
. . . This drefs being of linen would, in the
nature of things, be white. Compare the
paffage of Philo commented on in note 17.

[17] The ftatement here made, that the high-
prieft wore his "golden veftments" on the
Day of Atonement, is not really inconfiftent
(as has been fuppofed by fome) with the diftinct affertion made by Philo (fee below, p.
8), and confirmed by Lev. xvi. 4, 23. From
both thefe laft we gather that the high-prieft,
before actually entering within the vail on the
Day of Atonement, laid afide his garments of
glory, and entered the Moft Holy Place clad
in white only. What Jofephus here ftates is
perfectly confiftent with this; though all that
he fpeaks of is the fact of thefe garments of
glory being worn on occafion of this particular
day. The fact being, no doubt, that the
high-prieft went into the Holy Place, in his
robes "of glory," and laid them afide, in the
Temple, before entering within the vail.

III.

PHILO JUDÆUS.

OF THE WHITE VESTMENTS WORN ON
THE DAY OF ATONEMENT.

I. LIBER DE SOMNIIS, p. 597.

τὸν μὲν ἀρχιερέα ὁπότε μέλλοι τὰς νόμῳ προστεταγμένας ἐπιτελεῖν λειτουργίας, ὁ ἱερὸς ἐδικαίωσε λόγος ὕδατι καὶ τέφρᾳ περιῤῥαίνεσθαι τὸ πρῶτον εἰς ὑπόμνησιν ἑαυτοῦ, καὶ γὰρ ὁ σοφὸς Ἀβραὰμ ὅτε ἐντυγχάνων ἥει γῆν καὶ σποδὸν εἶναι ἑαυτὸν, ἔπειτ' ἐνδύεσθαι τὸν ποδήρη χιτῶνα καὶ τὸ ποικίλον ὃ κέκληκεν ἐπ' αὐτῷ περιστήθιον, τῶν κατ' οὐρανὸν φωσφόρων ἄστρων ἀπεικόνισμα καὶ μίμημα. Δύο γὰρ ὡς ἔοικεν ἱερὰ θεοῦ· ἓν μὲν ὅδε ὁ κόσμος ἐν ᾧ καὶ ἀρχιερεὺς ὁ πρωτόγονος αὐτοῦ θεῖος λόγος· ἕτερον δὲ λογικὴ ψυχὴ ἧς ἱερεὺς ὁ πρὸς ἀλήθειαν ἄνθρωπος, οὗ μίμημα αἰσθητὸν ὁ τὰς πατρίους εὐχάς τε καὶ θυσίας ἐπιτελῶν ἔστιν, ᾧ τὸ εἰρημένον ἐπιγέγραπται χιτῶνα ἐνδύεσθαι τοῦ παντὸς ἀντιμίμημα ὄντα οὐρανοῦ, ἵνα συνιερουργῇ καὶ ὁ κόσμος ἀνθρώπῳ, καὶ τῷ παντὶ ἄνθρωπος. Δύο μὲν οὖν εἴδη τό τε ῥαντὸν καὶ τὸ ποικίλον τύπων ἔχων ἐπιδέδεικται· τὸ δὲ τρίτον καὶ τελειότατον ὃς ὀνομάζεται διάλευκος αὐτίκα σημανοῦμεν ὅταν εἰς τὰ ἐσώτατα τῶν ἁγίων ὁ αὐτὸς οὗτος ἀρχιερεὺς εἰσίῃ τὴν μὲν ποικίλην ἐσθῆτα ἀπαμφιέσκεται λινῆν δὲ ἑτέραν βύσσου τῆς καθαρωτάτης πεποιημένην ἀναλαμβάνει ἥ δ' ἐστι σύμβολον εὐτονίας αὐγοειδεστάτου φέγγους. Ἀῤῥαγεστέρα γὰρ ἡ ὀθόνη καὶ ἐξ οὐδενὸς τῶν ἀποθνησκόντων γίνεται, καὶ ἔτι λαμπρότατον καὶ φωτοειδέστατον ἔχει μὴ ἀμελῶς καθαρθεῖσα χρῶμα.

The high-prieſt, when about to perform the holy offices by law aſſigned to him, was required by the ſacred word (of God) to ſprinkle himſelf, in the firſt place, with water and aſhes, as a remembrance to him of his own ſelf (for even Abraham, the wiſe, when he was going to make interceſſion, ſpake of himſelf as being duſt and aſhes) and then to put on the long ("tunic") robe, and the ornament of curious work called the breaſtplate, being a copy and image of the light-giving conſtellations that are in heaven. For the Temples of God are, as it ſeemeth, two. One is this, our own world, wherein alfo the Divine Word, God's firft-begotten, is High-prieft; but the other temple is the reafonable foul, whofe Prieft is the true Man, whofe embodied reprefentation is he who duly offers the prayers and facrifices after the manner of our fathers, to whom is given that precept of which I fpake, that he fhould put upon him the robe which is the image of the whole heaven, in order that, in one act of facrifice, the world may join with man, and man with all creation.

We have feen now that two kinds of the types fpoken of above are to be found in the perfon of the high-prieft. We will now fignify the fame truth in refpect of the third and moft perfect (colour) that which is called "throughly white."[18] Whenever that fame high-prieft, of whom we fpake, entereth into the innermoft fanctuary of the Moft Holy Place, he putteth off his variegated garments, and affumeth another vefture of linen, made of byffus, and this ferveth to indicate the intenfity of moft brilliant light. For the cloth thus formed is very hard to rend, neither is the material thereof furnifhed by any creature fubject unto death, and if it be carefully cleanfed, it hath a moft bright and luminous colour.[19]

---

[18] He had been fpeaking of the myftical meaning of the three colours mentioned in Gen. xxx. and xxxi., διάλευκα, i.e. partly white, but capable of meaning ("throughly" or "thoroughly," and fo) "very white;" ποικίλα, variegated; and σποδοειδῆ ῥαντά, "of the colour of afhes (and) fprinkled," or "fpeckled." The play on words to which Philo has recourfe can fcarcely be reproduced in Englifh.

[19] Note here the brilliancy (λαμπρότης, or candor) which ancient writers, both in Eaft and Weft, attribute to veftments of white

linen. Thofe who have obferved the effect produced by white linen, as feen in the bright light of a fouthern climate, will not wonder at fuch expreffions as that of Philo above quoted. With it compare λίνον καθαρὸν καὶ λαμπρόν (Apoc. xv. 6), and again (xix. 8), in fpeaking of the marriage garment worn by the Bride of the Lamb, ἰδόθη αὐτῇ ἵνα περιβάληται βύσσινον καθαρὸν καὶ λαμπρόν. Elfewhere white garments are faid ἀστράπτειν, to gleam as does lightning (Luke, xxiv. 4); or στίλβειν (Mar. ix. 3), to fhine as do the ftars.

c

IV.

HIERONYMUS.

EPISTOLA AD FABIOLAM DE VESTE SACERDOTALI.[20]

[Vol. ii. p. 574.]

Usque hodie in lectione veteris Testamenti super faciem Moysi velamen positum est. Loquitur glorificato vultu, et populus loquentis
gloriam ferre non sustinet. Quum autem conversi fuerimus ad Dominum, auferetur velamen: occidens littera moritur, vivificans spiritus
suscitatur. Dominus enim spiritus est, et lex spiritalis. Unde et
David orabat in Psalmo: *Revela oculos meos: et considerabo mirabilia
de lege tua.* . . . .

Et ne longum faciam (neque enim propositum mihi est nunc de
tabernaculo scribere) veniam ad sacerdotalia vestimenta: et antequam
mysticam scruter intelligentiam, more Judaico, quæ scripta sunt, sim-
pliciter exponam: ut postquam vestitum videris sacerdotem, et oculis
tuis omne ejus patuerit ornamentum, tunc singulorum caussas pariter
exquiramus.

Discamus primum communes sacerdotum vestes atque pontificum.
Lineis feminalibus, quæ usque ad genua et poplites veniunt, verenda
cælantur, et superior pars sub umbilico vehementer astringitur: ut si
quando expediti mactant victimas, tauros et arietes trahunt, portant-
que onera, et in officio ministrandi sunt, etiam si lapsi fuerint, et
femora revelaverint, non pateat quod opertum est. Inde et gradus
altaris prohibentur fieri: ne inferior populus ascendentium verenda
conspiciat: vocaturque lingua Hebræa hoc genus vestimenti MACHNASE
(מכנסי) Græcè περισκελῆ, à nostris feminalia, vel bracæ[21] usque ad genua
pertingentes. Refert Josephus (nam ætate ejus adhuc templum stabat:
et necdum Vespasianus et Titus Jerosolymam subverterant, et erat

---

[20] Written at Bethlehem in the year 396
or 397.
[21] *A nostris feminalia vel bracæ ad genua*

pertingentes." This last is exactly our own
" knee-breeches."

IV.

ST. JEROME

ON THE SACERDOTAL VESTMENTS.[20]

Letter to Fabiola.

In the reading of the Old Teſtament, even to this day, there is a veil upon the face of Moſes. There is a glory upon his face as he ſpeaks, and the people cannot bear to look thereon. But when we have turned unto the Lord the veil ſhall be taken away. Then doth the letter which killeth die, and the ſpirit, which giveth life, is ſtirred up. For the Lord is a Spirit, and ſpiritual, too, is the Law. For which cauſe David prayed in the Pſalm (cxix. 18) "Take thou the veil from mine eyes, and I will conſider the wondrous things of thy law."

[Then after a digreſſion concerning the parts of the various victims reſerved for the uſe of the prieſts under the Levitical law, and a ſtatement of their myſtical ſignification, he proceeds as follows:]

I come now to the ſacerdotal robes (of the Levitical prieſt), and before inquiring into their myſtical meaning, I will ſet down literally, after the manner of the Jews, what is written, that ſo, when you have ſeen the prieſt clad in his robes, and all his adornment has been ſet out before your eyes, we may then inquire likewiſe into the reaſons of each particular.

Let us obſerve, firſt, what were the veſtments common to prieſts and to high-prieſt alike. They have a covering for the thighs made of linen, and reaching down to the knees and the back of the leg, the upper part thereof being tied tightly about the middle of the body, ſo that when lightly clad for the flaying of victims, dragging forwards bulls or rams, carrying burdens, or engaged in other office of miniſtration, there may be no unſeemly expoſure. . . . This kind of veſtment is called in Hebrew, MACHNASE [מכנסי], in Greek περισκελῆ, and in Latin feminalia (thigh-pieces) or bracæ.[21] It is ſaid by Joſephus (and in his day the Temple was yet ſtanding, and Jeruſalem not yet

ipfe de genere facerdotali, multoque plus intelligitur quod oculis videtur, quàm quod aure percipitur) hæc feminalia de byffo retorta ob
fortitudinem folere contexi, et poft quàm incifa fuerint, acu confui.
Non enim poffe in tela hujufcemodi fieri.

Secunda ex lino tunica eft ποδήρης, id eft, talaris, duplici findone,
quam et ipfam Jofephus byffinam vocat, appellaturque CHOTONATH
(כתנת) id eft, χιτών, quod Hebræo fermone in *lineam* vertitur. Hæc
adhæret corpori, et tam arêta eft et ftriêtis manicis, ut nulla omninò
in vefte fit ruga : et ufque ad crura[22] defcendat. Volo pro legentis
facilitate abuti fermone vulgato. Solent militantes habere lineas, quas
camifias[23] vocant, fic aptas membris et aftriêtas corporibus, ut expediti fint vel ad curfum, vel ad prælia, dirigendo jaculo, tenendo
clypeo, enfe vibrando, et quoquumque neceffitas traxerit. Ergo et
facerdotes parati in minifterium Dei, utuntur hac tunica, ut habentes
pulchritudinem veftimentorum, nudorum celeritate difcurrant. [Note 6,
p. 2.]

Tertium genus eft veftimenti, quod illi appellant ABANET (אבנט), nos
cingulum, vel baltheum, vel zonam poffumus dicere. Babylonii novo
vocabulo HEMIAN (המין) vocant. Diverfa vocabula ponimus, ne quis erret in nomine. Hoc cingulum in fimilitudinem pellis colubri, qua exuit
fenectutem, fic in rotundum textum eft, ut marfupium longius putes.
Textum eft autem fubtemine cocci, purpuræ, hiacynthi, et ftamine
byffino, ob decorem et fortitudinem : atque ita polymita arte distinêtum, ut diverfos flores ac gemmas artificis manu non textas, fed
additas arbitreris. Lineam tunicam, de qua fupra diximus, inter umbilicum et peêtus hoc ftringunt baltheo, qui quattuor digitorum habens
latitudinem, et ex una parte ad crura dependens, cum ad facrificia
curfu et expeditione opus eft, in lævum humerum retorquetur.

Quartum genus eft veftimenti, rotundum pileolum, quale piêtum

---

[22] S. Jerome here diftinêtly ftates (what
is contrary to general impreffion) that the
χιτὼν ποδήρης of the Jewifh priefts extended
only *ad crura*, *i.e.* about half-way between
the knee and the ankle. He is probably
right. Though ποδήρης means literally (like
talaris) *reaching to the feet* ; it was probably a
conventional term for *any* of the *longer* tunics
worn on occafions of ftate, whether it aêtually
reached to the feet or no. And it is difficult to underftand how a clofe fitting tunic
that really reached to the feet, and was not

open at the fides, could have allowed of the
aêtive (even violent) exertions that would
fometimes be required of the Levitical priefts.

[23] *Camifia.* S. Ifidore (Orig. xix. 22, 29)
derives the word *a camis*, "*quod in his dormimus
in camis, id eft in ftratis noftris.*" With him
it is a night-fhirt. In S. Jerome's time it
was evidently a term of the *lingua vulgaris*, for
which he offers a fort of apology. From it
are defcended it. Camicia (and Camice "an
alb," to which *camifia* is compared above);
Fr. and Eng. Chemife.

overthrown, and he was himself of the priestly order, and the eye in such matters as this is more to be trusted than the ear) that these *feminalia* were woven of byssus, doubled upon itself for greater strength, and sewn together with a needle when properly cut out; it being impossible to make a garment of this kind in the ordinary way upon a loom.

Next comes a linen tunic, of the kind called ποδήρης, that is, reaching to the feet, made double of the fine linen called *sindon*, or, according to Josephus, of *byssus*, like the last. The name of this is CHOTONATH (*i.e.* χιτών), a word equivalent in Hebrew to the Latin *linea*. This is closely fitted to the body, and is so scanty, and with sleeves so narrow, that there is no fold in this garment. It reaches a little below the knee.[22] For better understanding of what I say I may employ a somewhat common word of our own. Our soldiers, when on service, wear linen garments, which they call "shirts,"[23] fitting so closely, and so fastened about the body, as to leave them free for action, whether in running or in fighting, hurling the javelin, holding the shield, wielding the sword, or whatever else, as need may require. And so the priests, standing prepared for the service of God, wear a tunic such as this, so that while they have their robes of beauty, they may hasten to and fro like men that stand stripped for speed.

The third of the priestly vestments is what the Jews call ABANET, a word which may be rendered girdle, belt, or zone. In Chaldaic it has a different name, HEMIAN. I mention these different names to prevent mistake. This belt is made like the skin of a serpent, wherewith it puts off the decay of old age. And it is woven round so as to resemble a long purse. The warp thereof is of scarlet, purple, and blue; the web of fine flax for beauty and strength. The ornaments thereon are so wrought by the skill of the embroiderer, that the various flowers and gems might well be deemed to have been set there in reality, rather than woven by the hand of the artificer. The linen tunic, already spoken of, is girt into the waist by this belt, which is four fingers broad, and with one part of it pendent below the knee, but is thrown back on to the left shoulder when the more active duties of actual sacrifice so require.

The fourth of the vestments is a small round cap, such as we see on the head of Ulysses, much as though a sphere were to be divided

in Ulyſſe conſpicimus, quaſi ſphæra media ſit diviſa, et pars una ponatur in capite : hoc Græci et noſtri τιάραν, nonnulli galerum vocant,
Hebræi MISNEPHETH (מצנפת) : non habet acumen in ſummo, nec totum
uſque ad comam caput tegit : ſed tertiam partem à fronte inopertam
relinquit : atque ita in occipitio vitta conſtrictum eſt, ut non facilè
labatur ex capite. Eſt autem byſſinum, et ſic fabrè opertum linteolo,
ut nulla acûs veſtigia forinſecus appareant.

His quattuor veſtimentis, id eſt, feminalibus, tunica linea, cingulo
quod purpura, cocco, byſſo, hiacynthoque contexitur, et pileo, de
quo nunc diximus, tam ſacerdotes quàm Pontifices utuntur. Reliqua
quattuor propriè Pontificum ſunt, quorum primum eſt MAIL (מעיל), id
eſt, tunica talaris, tota hiacynthina, ex lateribus ejuſdem coloris aſſutas
habens manicas, et in ſuperiori parte qua collo induitur aperta, quòd
vulgò capitium[21] vocant, oris firmiſſimis ex ſe textis, ne facilè rumpantur. In extrema parte, id eſt, ad pedes, ſeptuaginta duo ſunt tintinnabula, et totidem mala punica, iiſdem contexta coloribus, ut ſuprà
cingulum. Inter duo tintinnabula unum malum eſt : inter duo mala
unum tintinnabulum, ut alterutrum ſibi media ſint : cauſſaque redditur. Idcirco tintinnabula veſti appoſita ſunt, ut quum ingreditur
Pontifex in Sancta Sanctorum, totus vocalis incedat, ſtatim moriturus
ſi hoc non fecerit.

Sextum eſt veſtimentum quod Hebraica lingua dicitur EPHOD (אפד).
Septuaginta ἐπωμίδα, id eſt, ſuperhumerale appellant. Aquila ἐπένδυμα,
nos EPHOD ſuo ponimus nomine. Et ubiquumque in Exodo, ſive
in Levitico ſuperhumerale legitur, ſciamus apud Hebræos EPHOD appellari. Hoc autem eſſe Pontificis veſtimentum, et in quadam Epi
ſtola ſcripſiſſe me memini : et omnis Scriptura teſtatur ſacrum quiddam
eſſe, et ſolis conveniens Pontificibus. Nec ſtatim illud occurrat, quòd
Samuel qui Levita fuit, ſcribitur in regnorum primo libro, habuiſſe
ætatis adhuc parvulæ *ephod bad*, id eſt, *ſuperhumerale lineum :* quum
David quoque ante arcam Domini idem portaſſe referatur. Aliud eſt
enim ex quattuor ſupradictis coloribus, id eſt, hiacyntho, byſſo, cocco,
purpura, et ex auro habere contextum : aliud in ſimilitudinem ſacerdotum ſimplex et lineum. Auri laminæ, id eſt, bracteæ, mira tenuitate tenduntur, ex quibus ſecta fila torquentur, cum ſubtegmine trium
colorum, hiacyntho, cocci, purpuræ, et cum ſtamine byſſino : et efficitur

---

[21] *Capitium,* here the opening of the tunic,
its " head-piece " ſo to ſay. Compare Papias
(apud Ducange), "Capitium, ſummitas tunicæ,
capitis foramen in veſte."

through the centre, and one-half thereof to be put upon the head. This is what in Greek and in Latin is called a tiara, but fometimes alfo *galerus;* in Hebrew, MISNEPHETH. It has no peak at top, nor does it cover the whole head as far as the hair extends, but leaves about a third of the front part of the head uncovered. It is attached by a band (*vitta*) on to the back of the head, fo as not to be liable to fall off. It is made of byffus, and is fo fkilfully finifhed with an outer linen cover that no marks of the needle are to be feen without.

Thefe four veftments, viz. the drawers, the linen tunic, the girdle woven with purple, fcarlet, fine linen, and blue, and the cap juft defcribed, are in ufe by priefts and high-priefts alike. The remaining four belong exclufively to the high-priefts. And thefe of the firft is the MAIL, a full-length tunic, entirely of blue, with fleeves on either fide of the fame colour; and made open at top, where the opening is made for the head,[21] a ftrong edging being attached to the felvage to prevent its tearing. On its lower edge, at the feet, there are feventy-two bells, and as many pomegranates, made in the fame colours as the girdle above defcribed. The bells and the pomegranates alternate one with the other. And a reafon is affigned for the addition of thefe bells, namely, that when the high-prieft enters into the Holy of Holies, there may be a found heard all about him as he goes, feeing that he would incur inftant death were this not done.

The fixth of the veftments is called in Hebrew EPHOD, by the LXX, ἐπωμίς, *i.e. fuperhumerale.* In the verfion of Aquila it is ἐπένδυμα [or "fuperveftment"], with our own writers the original word, ephod, is often retained. And wherever in Exodus or in Leviticus the word *fuperhumerale* is read, this is to be underftood as reprefenting the Hebrew EPHOD. That this veftment belongs exclufively to the high-prieft, I remember to have faid in one of my letters, and all Scripture proves the fame, that this veftment is of a facred nature and fuited for the high-priefts alone. Let it not be objected that, in the firft Book of Kings, we read of Samuel, who was a Levite, having, when yet quite a child, a "linen ephod," EPHOD BAD, for David alfo is faid to have worn a fimilar drefs before the ark. But it is one thing to have an ephod woven in the colours already defcribed (blue, fine linen, fcarlet, purple and gold); another thing to have a fimple linen ephod refembling (in fhape) that

palliolum miræ pulchritudinis, præftringens fulgore oculos in modum
Caracallarum,[25] fed abfque cucullis. Contra pectus nihil contextum
eft, et locus futuro Rationali derelictus. In utroque humero habet
fingulos lapides claufos et aftrictos auro, qui Hebraicè dicuntur soom
(שהם): ab Aquila et Symmacho et Theodotione onychini : à Septuaginta fmaragdi transferuntur: Jofephus, fardonychas vocat, cum Hebræo
Aquilaque confentiens : ut vel colorem lapidum, vel patriam de-
monftraret. Et in fingulis lapidibus fena Patriarcharum nomina funt,
quibus Ifraeliticus populus dividitur. In dextro humero majores filii
Jacob, in lævo minores fcripti funt : ut Pontifex ingrediens Sancta
Sanctorum, nomina populi pro quo rogaturus eft Dominum, portet in
humeris.

Septimum veftimentum eft menfura parvulum, fed cunctis fupradictis facratius. Intende quæfo animum, ut quæ dicuntur, intelligas. Hebraicè vocatur HOSEN (חשן), Græcè autem λόγιον, nos *Rationale* poffumus
appellare, ut ex ipfo ftatim nomine fcias myfticum effe quod dicitur.
Pannus eft brevis ex auro et quattuor textus coloribus, hoc eft, iifdem
quibus et Superhumerale, habens magnitudinem palmi per quadrum,
et duplex, ne facile rumpatur. Intexti funt enim ei duodecim lapides
miræ magnitudinis atque precii per quattuor ordines : ita ut in fingulis
verficulis terni lapides collocentur. In primo ordine fardius, topazius,
fmaragdus ponitur. Symmachus diffentit in fmaragdo, ceraunium pro
eo transferens. In fecundo carbunculus, fapphirus, jafpis. In tertio
lyncurius, achates, amethyftus. In quarto chryfolithus, onychinus,
berillus. Satifque miror cur hiacynthus prætiofiffimus lapis in horum
numero non ponatur : nifi fortè ipfe eft alio nomine lyncurius. Scru-
tans eos qui de lapidum atque gemmarum fcripfere naturis, lyn-
curium invenire non potui.[26] In fingulis lapidibus fecundum ætates
duodecim tribuum fculpta funt nomina. Hos lapides in diademate

---

[25] The *caracalla*, originally a Gaulifh drefs,
was introduced among the Romans by M.
Aurelius Antoninus [Emperor A.D. 210 to
217], furnamed "Caracalla" from his ha-
bitual wearing of it. It was furnifhed with a
hood (*cuculla*), and this is the reafon why
S. Jerome adds here "*fed abfque cucullis.*"
An Emperor having fet the fafhion, it fpeedily
paffed into general ufe. And we find it mentioned from time to time either as a fplendid
drefs (fuch as the context here fhows to be
meant) or as worn in ordinary life, by per-

fons high and low, the name being retained
in reference to its fhape, though in material
and in colour it might vary infinitely. In
the ftory of the martyrdom of St. Alban
given by Bede [Hift. Eccl. lib. i. cap. 6],
we find it worn by a clergyman (*clericus*)
in Britain, and the context there implies that
at that time it was a fomewhat unufual drefs.
This was during the perfecution of Diocletian
at the clofe of the third century.
[26] See Theophraftus περὶ τῶν λίθων, 28, 31,
and Plin. Hift. Nat. lib. xxxvii. c. 4.

of the priests. The gold-leaf used in making this robe is drawn
out to a marvellous thinnefs, and then twifted into feparate threads.
The woof is of three colours,—blue, fcarlet, and purple, and the
web of byffus; and fo a veftment is formed of wondrous beauty,
dazzling the eyes as does our own caracalla,²³ but not furnifhed
with a hood. Upon the breaft there is an open fpace left, affording room for the "Rational," which is there to be. On either
fhoulder there is a fingle ftone, enclofed and fet in gold. Thefe
ftones are in Hebrew called soom, explained as meaning *onyx* by
Aquila, Symmachus, and Theodotion, but by the LXX as *emeralds*.
Jofephus, following the Hebrew and Aquila, calls them *fardonyx*, to
indicate either the colour of the ftones, or, it may be, the place
where they are found. On each of thefe ftones are the names of fix
of the twelve patriarchs, who give their names to the twelve Tribes
of Ifrael. On the right fhoulder are inferibed the elder fons of Jacob,
the younger on the left; in order that the high-prieft, as he enters
the Holy of Holies, may bear upon his fhoulders the names of the
people for the which he is about to entreat the Lord.

The feventh veftment is fmall in fize, but more holy than all
thofe above mentioned. Give me your efpecial attention now, for
the better underftanding of what I fay. It is called in Hebrew
hosen, in Greek λόγιον. We ourfelves may call it the "Rational,"
that the very name may at once point to a myftical meaning. It
is a fmall piece of cloth, woven in gold and four colours, the
fame as the ephod. It is fquare, and of a palm's breadth each
way, and made double for greater ftrength. Into it were faftened
twelve precious ftones of great fize, and very coftly, in four rows,
three ftones to each line. On the top line were a fardine ftone, a
topaz, and an emerald. Symmachus differs as regards the "emerald,"
which he renders "*ceraunius.*" On the fecond line, a carbuncle,
fapphire, and jafper. On the third, lyncurius, agate, and amethyft.
On the fourth, a chryfolite, an onyx, and a beryl. I greatly wonder
that fo precious a ftone as the jacynth has here no place. But perhaps
the lyncurius is but another name for it. I have examined treatifes
on precious ftones and gems, but have found no mention²⁶ of the
lyncurius. On thefe feveral ftones are engraved the names of the
tribes according to the ages of the patriarchs. We read (Ezek.
xxviii.) of thefe ftones on the diadem of the Prince of Tyre, and in
the Revelation of John (Rev. xxi.), where they form the walls of

principis Tyri, et in Apocalypfi Joannis legimus, de quibus ex
ftruitur cœleftis Jerufalem : et fub horum nominibus et fpecie, virtutum vel ordo, vel diverfitas indicatur. Per quattuor Rationalis
angulos, quattuor annuli funt aurei, habentes contra fe in Superhumerali alios quattuor : ut quum appofitum fuerit λόγιον in loco,
quem in Ephod diximus derelictum, anulus veniat contra anulum, et
mutuo fibi vittis copulentur hiacynthinis. Porrò ne magnitudo et
pondus lapidum contexta ftamina rumperet, auro ligati funt atque
conclufi : nec fuffecit hoc ad firmitatem, nifi et catenæ ex auro
fierent, quæ ob pulchritudinem fiftulis aureis tegerentur,[27] haberentque
et in Rationali fuprà duos majores anulos, qui uncinis Superhumeralis
aureis necterentur, et deorfum alios duos : nam poft tergum in
Superhumerali contra pectus et ftomachum, ex utroque latere erant
anuli aurei, qui catenis cum Rationalis inferioribus anulis junge-
bantur : atque ita fiebat, ut aftringeretur et Rationale Superhumerali,
et Superhumerale Rationali, ut una textura contra videntibus puta-
retur.

Octava eft lumina aurea, id eft, sis zaab (זהב ציץ), in qua fcriptum eft nomen Dei Hebraicis quattuor litteris JOD, HE, VAV, HE
(יהוה), quod apud illos ineffabile nuncupatur. Hæc fuper pileolum
lineum commune omnium Sacerdotum, in Pontifice plus additur,
ut in fronte vitta hiacynthina conftringatur, totamque Pontificis pulchritudinem Dei vocabulum coronet et protegat.

Didicimus quæ vel communia cum Sacerdotibus, vel quæ fpecialia
Pontificis veftimenta fint : et fi tanta difficultas fuit in vafis fictilibus,[28]
quanta majeftas erit in thefauro, qui intrinfecus latet ! Dicamus igitur
prius quod ab Hebræis accepimus : et juxta morem noftrum, fpiritua-
lis poftea intelligentiæ vela pandamus. . . . . .

---

[27] In Jofephus σύριγγες. But his defcription here differs fomewhat from that of S.
Jerome. See above, p. 5.

[28] In vafis fictilibus. He alludes, of courfe,
to 2 Cor. iv. 7, where the Vulgate is, "*Habemus autem thefaurum iftum in vafis fictilibus
ut fublimitas fit virtutis Dei et non ex nobis.*"

the heavenly Jerufalem ; and under their names and fpecies are fuggefted the order and diverfe nature of the feveral virtues. Through
the four corners of the Rational are inferted four golden rings, having
four others on the ephod juft oppofite to them ; fo that when the
λέγιον is fitted to the place which I have defcribed as left open in
the ephod, ring may be over againft ring, and be faftened together
with bands of blue. Moreover, the ftones were faftened together
with a fetting of gold, for fear that from their fize and weight the
web to which they are attached fhould give way. Nor would this
have been fufficient fecurity, had not chains of gold been made
(covered, for greater beauty, with fmall cylinders [27] of gold), having
two larger rings on the upper part of the Rational (to be attached
to the golden hooks of the ephod), and two others on the lower
part. For, on the back of the ephod, at a height to correfpond
with the breaft and lower part of the throat, there were golden
rings on either fide, joined by chains to the lower rings of the
Rational ; and fo it was that the Rational was clofely faftened to
the ephod, the ephod to the Rational, in fuch manner as to appear
to the fpectator as if they were all of one piece.

Eighth in order was the plate of gold, SIS ZAAB, on which was
infcribed the name of God in the four Hebrew letters Yod, He,
Vav, He, "The unutterable Name," as they declare it. This is
added in the cafe of the high-prieft over and above the linen cap
common to all the priefts. It is attached to his forehead with a
faftening band of blue. And fo the Divine Name is as a crown
and protection to the whole of that "fair beauty" with which the
high-prieft is clad.

We have now learnt what robes the high-prieft has in common
with the priefts, and what fpecially appropriated to himfelf. And
if we had fo much of difficulty in fpeaking of "earthen veffels" [28]
what majefty fhall there be in the treafure that lies concealed within !
Firft, then, let me fay what I have learnt on this matter from Hebrew authors, and after that, as our wont is, we may fpread open
the fails of fpiritual interpretation.

[Here follows, at fome length, the myftical meaning attributed
by the Jews to all the details already given. The four colours reprefent the four elements—earth, air, fire and water ; the pomegranates and bells mean the thunder and lightning, or elfe the
harmony of all the elements. The ephod, and its two precious

Tetigimus expofitionem Hebraicam, et infinitam fenfuum fylvam alteri tempori refervantes, quædam futuræ domus ftravimus fundamenta.[29] . . . . Legimus in Levitico, juxta præceptum Dei, Moyfen lavifle Aaron et filios ejus : jam tunc purgationem mundi, et rerum omnium, fanctitatem Baptifmi, facramenta fignabant. Non accipiunt veftes, nifi lotis prius fordibus, nec ornantur ad facra, nifi in Chrifto novi homines renafcantur. Vinum enim novum in novis utribus mittitur. Quòd autem Moyfes lavat, legis indicium eft. Habent Moyfen et Prophetas, ipfos audiant. Et ab Adam ufque ad Moyfen omnes peccaverunt. Præceptis Dei lavandi fumus, et quum parati ad indumentum Chrifti tunicas pelliceas depofuerimus,[30] tunc induemur vefte linea, nihil in fefe mortis habente, fed tota candida :[31] ut de baptifmo confurgentes, cingamus lumbos in veritate, et tota priftinorum peccatorum turpitudo celetur. Unde et David : *Beati quorum remiffæ funt iniquitates, et quorum tecta funt peccata.* Poft feminalia et lineam tunicam induimur hiacynthino veftimento,[32] et incipimus de terrenis ad alta confcendere. Hæc ipfa hiacynthina tunica, à Septuaginta ὑποδύτης, id eft, fubucula nominatur, et propriè Pontificis eft, fignificatque rationem fublimium non patere omnibus, fed majoribus

---

[29] *Quædam futuræ domus ftravimus fundamenta ;* i.e. he had prepared the way for his own myftical application.

[30] He takes up here the thought, alluded to as we have feen, by Philo (p. 8), that garments of animal origin (whether of fur or of wool) favour of mortality and corruption. Hence the expreffion of the text is equivalent to the ἀπεκδυσάμενοι τὸν παλαιὸν ἄνθρωπον, "ftripping off the old humanity" of St. Paul (Col. iii. 9).

[31] *Sed tota candida.* On the meaning of *candidus,* fee above note 19. The allufion is here to the white garments worn by the newly baptized.

[32] *Veftimento hiacynthino.* In fpeaking of the Jewifh myftical interpretation of this colour, "*the foundation for his own building,*" he had noticed that to them this "jacynth blue," was fignificant of the fky. Hence what he here fays. So again below, *cidaris et vitta hyacinthina cælum monftrant.*

stones, are the two hemispheres, whereof one is above and the other below the earth. The girdle is the ocean. The rational (or breast-plate) the earth. The general result is described by S. Jerome as being this, that God's high-priest bearing upon his vestments the typical representation of all created things, should show how all creatures stand in need of the mercy of God, and that, in sacrific-ing unto Him, expiation might be for the state of the entire uni-verse, and that he might pray, both by voice and by the dress he bare, not for children, and parents, and kinsmen only, but for all creation.[33] He then proceeds as follows] :—

I have now touched upon the exposition of these things given by the Jews, and while reserving for another opportunity an infinite number of mystical meanings, have laid something of a foundation for the building that is to be.[29] . . . We read in Leviticus that, according to God's commandment, Moses washed Aaron and his sons. So even at that early time there were sacramental acts signifying the purifying of the world and of all created things, and the sanctity of baptism. They receive not their robes till they have washed off the filth of the flesh, nor are they adorned for holy rites, except they be born again as new men in Christ. For new wine is put in new bottles (*utribus — ἄσκοις*). And in that it is Moses who washeth them, this pointeth to the law, "*They have Moses and the prophets, let them hear them,*" and, "*From Adam even unto Moses all sinned.*" It is by God's commandments that we are to be washed clean, and when, being made ready for the garment of Christ, we shall have laid aside our garments made of skins,[30] then shall we be clad in the linen robe which hath in it nothing which is of death, but is wholly bright and pure,[31] that so rising up from our baptism we may gird up our loins with truth and all the deformity of former sins be put out of sight. Whence also David saith, "*Blessed are they whose iniquities are forgiven, and whose sins are covered.*" After the drawers and the linen tunic, we put upon us a vestment of blue,[32] and begin to mount up from things on earth to things above. This very tunic of blue is called by the Seventy ὑποδύτης, that is, "under-garment," and belongs properly to the high-priest; and it signifieth that the meaning of the higher things of God lies not open to all, but only to those somewhat advanced in the Christian life, or who

---

atque perfectis.[34] Hanc habuerunt Moyſes et Aaron et Prophetæ, et
omnes quibus dicitur : *In montem excelſum aſcende tu, qui evangelizas
Sion.* Nec ſufficit nobis priorum ablutio peccatorum, baptiſmi gratia,
doctrina ſecretior, niſi habuerimus et opera. Unde jungitur et Ephod,
id eſt, Superhumerale,[35] quod Rationali copulatur : ut non ſit laxum,
neque diſſolutum, ſed hæreant ſibi invicem et auxilio ſint. Ratio [36] enim
operibus, et opera ratione indigent : ut quod mente percipimus, opere
perpetremus. Duoque lapides in Superhumerali, vel Chriſtum ſignificant et Eccleſiam, duodecim Apoſtolorum, qui ad prædicationem
miſſi ſunt, nomina continentes : vel litteram et ſpiritum, in quibus
continentur legis univerſa myſteria. In dextra ſpiritus, in læva littera
eſt. Per litteras ad verba deſcendimus, per verba venimus ad ſenſum.
Quàm pulcher ordo, et ex ipſo habitu ſacramenta demonſtrans. In
humeris opera ſunt, in pectore ratio.[36] Unde et pectuſculum comedunt
ſacerdotes. Hoc autem Rationale duplex eſt,[37] apertum et abſconditum,
ſimplex et myſticum, duodecim in ſe lapides habens, et quattuor
ordines, quos quattuor puto eſſe virtutes, prudentiam, fortitudinem,
juſtitiam et temperantiam, quæ ſibi hærent invicem : et dum mutuo
miſcentur, duodenarium efficiunt numerum : vel quattuor Evangelia,
quæ in Apocalypſi deſcribuntur plena oculis, et Domini luce radiantia
mundum illuminant. In uno quattuor, et in quattuor ſingula. Unde
ὁήλωσις et ἀλήθεια, id eſt, doctrina et veritas in pectore,[38] Sacerdotis eſt.
Quum enim indutus quis fuerit veſte multiplici, conſequens eſt, veritatem quam corde retinet, ſermone proferre : et ob id in rationali
veritas eſt, id eſt, ſcientia, ut noverit quæ docenda ſint : et mani-
feſtatio atque doctrina, ut poſſit inſtruere alios, quod mente concepit.
Ubi ſunt qui innocentiam Sacerdoti dicunt poſſe ſufficere ?[39] Vetus lex
novæ congruit : idipſum Moyſes quod Apoſtolus. Ille ſacerdotis
ſcientiam ornat in veſtibus : iſte Timotheum et Titum inſtruit diſ-
ciplinis. Sed et ipſe veſtimentorum ordo præcipuus. Legamus Levi-

---

[34] *Majoribus atque perfectis.* *Majoribus* has
reference (as elſewhere to growth in years, ſo
here) to growth in grace. For *perfectus* =
τίλιιος, ' full-grown,' ſee " Eirenika," note 68,
p. 120.

[35] The ſhoulder and arm, he means, are
naturally aſſociated with ideas of *activity*, and
ſo of good works.

[36] *Ratio* (Reaſon and Underſtanding) uſed
in reference to " *Rationale*," the word uſed
throughout for the λόγιον, the " breaſtplate"
of our Engliſh Verſion.

[37] It was made *duplex ne facile rumperetur*,
as he had ſaid above.

[38] To the Romans not the head but the
breaſt (or the *heart*) was the ſeat of the underſtanding. " *Non tu corpus eras ſine pectore.*"
" *Rudis et ſine pectore miles.*"

[39] *i.e.* that it mattereth not greatly that he
have *knowledge.* As to the meaning of *ſacerdos* (biſhop, as well as prieſt), ſee Index
in voc.

have attained unto fulneſs of growth. With this garment were clad Moſes, and Aaron, and the prophets, and all they to whom that word is ſpoken, "*Aſcend up unto the lofty mountain, thou that bringeſt glad tidings to Sion.*" (Iſa. xl. 9.) But the waſhing away of ſins, the grace of baptiſm, the more hidden knowledge, theſe are not ſufficient for us, unleſs we have alſo (good) works, and therefore there is joined to thoſe other veſtments the ephod, that is, the "Superhumeral,"[35] which again is ſo coupled to the ("Rational") breaſtplate, that it may not be looſe nor unattached, but that both may be cloſely joined and be a mutual help each to other. For reaſon[36] needeth works, and works need reaſon; that ſo what we mentally perceive we may by works carry out in act. And the two ſtones upon the ephod ſignify, either Chriſt and the Church (as containing the names of the twelve apoſtles who were ſent to the preaching of the Goſpel), or the letter and the ſpirit, wherein are contained all the myſteries of the law. On the right is the ſpirit; on the left is the letter. Through letters we reach unto words: through words we come to meaning. How beauteous is the order, ſhowing forth ſacramental truths even by the very dreſs of which we ſpeak. On the ſhoulders are (good) works: on the breaſt reaſon. For which cauſe the prieſts have the breaſt (of the ſacrifice) to eat. But this Rational is two-fold,[37] open and yet hidden; ſimple, and yet myſtical; having upon it twelve ſtones, and four rows, which I hold to be four virtues, viz. wiſdom, courage, juſtice, temperance, which are cloſely united one unto the other, and by their mutual conjunction produce a duodecimal number. Or elſe they may be the four Goſpels, which in the Apocalypſe are deſcribed as full of eyes, and which, beaming with the light of the Lord, enlighten the whole world. In one, the four; and in the four each and all the ſeparate parts. And, therefore, ὁήλωσις and ἀλήθεια, "manifeſtation" and "truth," are on the breaſt[38] of the prieſt. For when a man hath been clad in the manifold veſture, it followeth that he expreſs in word the truth which he holdeth in his heart. And therefore in the Rational there is "truth," that is "knowledge," that he may know what is to be taught, and "manifeſtation" and "doctrine" that he may be able to inſtruct others of that which his own reaſon hath comprehended. Where are they that ſay that it ſufficeth for a prieſt[39] that he be of innocent life? The old law agreeth with the new; Moſes was in the one, what the Apoſtle was in the other.

ticum. Non prius Rationale, et fic Superhumerale, fed ante Superhumerale, et deinceps Rationale. *A mandatis tuis*, inquit, *intellexi:*
prius faciamus, et fic doceamus : ne doctrinæ auctoritas caſſis
operibus deſtruatur. Hoc eſt quod in Propheta legimus : *Seminate*
vobis in juſtitia, et metite fructum vitæ : illuminate vobis lumen ſcientiæ.
Primùm feminate in juſtitia, et fructum vitæ æternæ metite : poſtea
vobis ſcientiam vindicate. Nec ſtatim abſoluta perfectio eſt, ſi quis
Superhumerale et Rationale habeat : [40] niſi hæc ipſa inter ſe forti com-
pagine folidentur, et ſibi invicem connexa ſint : ut et operatio rationi
et ratio operibus hæreat : et his præcedentibus, doctrina ſequatur et
veritas.

Lamina aurea rutilat in fronte : nihil enim nobis prodeſt omnium
rerum eruditio, niſi Dei ſcientia coronemur. Lineis induimur, orna-
mur hiacynthinis, facro baltheo cingimur, dantur nobis opera, Rationale in pectore ponitur : accipimus veritatem, profert ſermo doctrinam :
imperfecta ſunt univerſa, niſi tam decoro currui dignus quæratur
auriga, et ſuper creaturas creator inſiſtens, regat ipſe quæ condidit.
Quod olim in lamina monſtrabatur,[41] nunc in ſigno oſtenditur crucis.[42]
Auro legis ſanguis Evangelii pretioſior eſt.[43] Tunc ſignum juxta
Ezechielis vocem gementibus figebatur in fronte : nunc portantes crucem dicimus : *Signatum eſt ſuper nos lumen vultus tui Domine. . . .*[44]

Jam ſermo finitur, et ad ſuperiora retrahor. Tanta debet eſſe

---

[40] "Both ephod and breaſtplate," *i.e.* both good works and knowledge.

[41] *i.e.* "Holineſs unto the Lord." See above, Note 15.

[42] *i.e.* the ſign of the croſs traced *upon the forehead* in baptiſm, putting, as it were, Chriſt's mark thereon, and declaring the newly-baptized to be "Holy unto the Lord."

[43] The ſign of *the croſs* carries our thoughts to the precious blood thereon ſhed, called by St. Paul, τὸ αἷμα τοῦ σταυροῦ.

[44] Quæ ſequuntur *de ſeminalibus apud ipſum requirant eruditi lectores. Virgineis Fabiolæ oculis parum apta videntur.*

For Moſes deviſeth " knowledge " among the veſtments of the prieſts ;
Paul furniſheth Titus and Timothy with " Doctrine." But the
very order of the veſtments is noteworthy. Let us read Leviticus.
It is not, firſt, the rational, and after that the ephod ; but, firſt, the
ephod, and afterward the rational. " *From thy commandments,*" ſaith
one, " *have I got underſtanding.*" (Ps. cxix. 104.) Let *doing* be
firſt in order with us, and ſo let us go on to teaching, left the
authority of our teaching be done away by the worthleſsneſs of
that we work. This is that we read in the Prophet (Hoſ. x. 12),
" *Sow your ſeed in righteouſneſs, and reap the fruit of life ; Kindle ye
for you the light of knowledge.*" Firſt ſow in righteouſneſs, and reap
the fruit of life ; afterward claim knowledge as your own. Yet
fulneſs of Chriſtian growth is not then at once completely attained
when one hath both ephod and breaſtplate ; unleſs theſe two be
firmly compacted one unto the other, and in ſuch wiſe mutually
connected, that both our working of that which is good be cloſe
joined to reaſon, and reaſon cloſe joined to works ; and that, while
theſe lead the way, doctrine and truth follow.

[He then defers further explanation concerning the twelve ſtones
of the breaſtplate, ſaying that his letter is already too long, and adding a few further particulars, he ſays :]

A plate of gold glitters on the forehead, for learning the moſt
univerſal is nothing worth unto us, unleſs we be crowned with the
knowledge of God. We are clothed in linen, we are adorned with
the veſtments of celeſtial blue, we are girt about with the ſacred
belt, works are given unto us, the rational is put upon our breaſt,
we accept the truth, our words bring forth doctrine—all theſe together are imperfect, unleſs for ſo fair an equipage a fitting guide
be found, and the Creator, ſet on high above His creatures, Himſelf direct that which He hath made. What in old times was ſhown
upon the golden plate is now ſet forth in the ſign of the Croſs.
The gold of the law is leſs precious than the Blood of the Goſpel.
In thoſe former times, according to that word of Ezekiel (Ezek.
ix. 4), a mark was put upon the brow of them that mourned ; but
now we that bear the croſs (upon our foreheads) ſay, " The light
of thy countenance, O Lord, is ſigned upon us."

And now my diſcourſe is drawing to a cloſe, and I return to
that of which I was ſpeaking above. Such ſhould be the knowledge

E

scientia et eruditio Pontificis [45] Dei, ut et greffus ejus, et motus, et
univerfa vocalia fint. Veritatem mente concipiat, et toto eam habitu
refonet et ornatu: ut quidquid agit, quidquid loquitur, fit doctrina
populorum. Abfque tintinnabulis enim et diverfis coloribus et gemmis floribufque virtutum, nec Sancta ingredi poteft, nec nomen
Antiftitis [46] poffidere.

---

[45] *Pontificis. Pontifex* is literally a "*bridge-maker*," γιφυρωποιὸς, as the Greek writers fometimes tranflate it. And the following quotation will fuggeft the origin of the term: "The Tiber was the natural highway for the traffic of Latium; and . . . formed from very ancient times the frontier defence of the Latin flock againft their northern neighbours. . . . Rome combined the advantages of a ftrong pofition, and of immediate vicinity to the river; *it commanded both banks of the ftream* down to the mouth. . . . That Rome was indebted accordingly, if not for its origin, at any rate for its importance, to thefe commercial and ftrategical advantages of its pofition, there are many indications to fhow. . . . *Thence arofe the unufual importance of the bridges over the Tiber, and of bridge-building generally,* in the Roman commonwealth. Thence came the galley in the city arms." MÖMMSEN, *Hiftory of Rome,* book i. cap. iv. Bearing in mind how in ancient times all matters of grave import to the ftate were invefted with the fanctions of religion, we fhall not wonder to find the conftruction and care of thefe *bridges* placed under the fuperintendence of that College of Magiftrates (not *priefts* in our fenfe of the word) which from the very beginning of Roman hiftory was fupreme in all matters pertaining to religion. With this body of facerdotal "Bridgemakers," with the firft citizen of the Republic, or, as in later times, an emperor, at their head (as *Pontifex Maximus*), we may compare our own "*Trinity Board,*" with a prince of the blood as "Mafter." [The parallel might be extended, *inexperto fi fas ita dicere,* in refpect of the *Pontificum cœnæ* and the Greenwich banquets.]

The Chriftian ufe of the term is owing mainly to St. Jerome's verfion of the Bible. From the 5th century onwards, the ufe of *Pontifex* as = *facerdos* (Note 61), or bifhop, and of *Pontifex fummus* as = *archbifhop,* or metropolitan, became very common. In earlier writers it is very rare; and in the older Italic verfion we find *facerdos* or *fummus facerdos* where St. Jerome (*writing at Rome*) fpeaks of *Pontifex,* or *Pontifex fummus.* [For the term *Pontifex Maximus,* which has a fpecial meaning of its own, fee Index of Notes.]

and the learning of one chief[45] in holy miniſtry to God, as that his walk and movement, and everything about him ſhall be vocal to the ears of men. With his mind let him embrace the truth, and in all his habit and adornment cauſe it to ſound forth to others; that whatſoever he doeth, whatſoever he ſpeaketh, may be for inſtruction unto all men. For without the bells, and the divers colours, and the gems, and the flowers of divers virtues, he can neither enter the Holy of Holies, nor make his own the name of one chief[46] among God's ſervants.

---

[46] *Antiſtes* (*ante-ſtes* — compare the Greek πϱο-στάτης), properly one *in foremoſt place*, and hence occaſionally uſed by claſſical writers of heathen prieſts (*ſacrorum antiſtes*, Cic. and Juv. *antiſtes Jovis* Nep. and the fem. *antiſtita*

Phœbi, Ov.) and frequently in Chriſtian literature of biſhops. Hence, in later Latin, the forms *antiſtitium* = *ſacerdotium*, and *antiſtitari* = *epiſcopum agere*.

V.

S. JEROME.

EPISTLE TO MARCELLA CONCERNING THE EPHOD WORN BY SAMUEL.

[WRITTEN AT ROME, A.D. 384.]

[WISHING to explain how it was that, while the "ephod" or *fuperhumerale* is properly a garment of the high-prieſt alone, we yet read of Samuel, and of the prieſts at Nob, wearing an ephod, and of David, in one place, doing likewiſe, he ſays that theſe ephods were of *linen* only, and *white*.]

" *Propterea autem Samuel et octoginta quinque viri facerdotes ephod lineum portaſſe referuntur, quoniam facerdos magnus folus habebat licentiam ephod non-lineo veſtiendi, verum, ut Scriptura commemorat, auro, hyacintho, purpura, cocco, byſſoque, contexto. Cæteri habebant ephod non illa varietate diſtinctum et duodecim lapidibus ornatum, qui in humero utroque reſidebant : ſed lineum et ſimplex et toto candore puriſſimum.*"

" The reaſon why Samuel, and the eighty-five prieſts are ſaid to have worn an ephod *of linen*, is this, that the high-prieſt alone had the right to wear an ephod made, not of linen, but, as the Scripture records, made of gold, and blue, and purple, and ſcarlet, and fine linen. All the reſt had an ephod,[17] not varied in colour like to this, nor ornamented with the twelve ſtones of the breaſtplate, but of linen and unadorned, and moſt pure in the perfection of i brilliant whiteneſs."

---

[17] This difficulty about the ephod of David and of Samuel has often been noticed by modern writers. The ſolution of the difficulty is, no doubt, that which S. Jerome (as, nearer our own times, Lightfoot) ſuggeſts, viz. that the term ephod was originally a *general* term for an upper garment of a peculiar ſhape : *the* ephod, peculiar to the high-prieſt, being diſtinguiſhed from other ephods by its material, colour, and infignia.

VI.

S. JEROME.

ON EZEKIEL XLIV.

[Vol. iii. 1028, fqq.]

[He is commenting on the words that occur ver. 17, fqq. : which are as follows :

" *When they enter the gates of the inner court, they shall be clothed with garments of linen : and nothing that is of wool shall come upon them when they minister at the gates of the inner court, and further within. Bands of linen shall be upon their heads,*[18] *and they shall have linen drawers upon their loins ; they shall not gird themselves with that which causeth sweat.*[49] *And when they go forth out of the outer court unto the people they shall put off the garments*[50] *wherein they had ministered, and shall replace them in the treasuries of the sanctuary, and shall put on other garments, and they shall not sanctify the people with their ministering garments. But their heads they shall not shave, nor yet let their hair grow long ; but they shall poll their heads ; neither shall any priest drink wine when he is about to enter into the inner court.*"

Upon this he comments as follows :]

In the first place, I must explain the words here recorded. Among other precepts given by the Word of the Lord to the priests this is one, that at the very gates of the inner court they shall put

---

[48] S. Jerome here gives as an alternative rendering, " *They shall have linen caps* (cidares) *upon their heads.*"

[49] Here, too, as an alternative rendering (for *in sudore*) *violenter.*

[50] *Stolas* in the text. In the LXX. στολὴ is used either (α) as a generic term for the entire vesture of the priest, confidered as a whole, or (β) (generally in the plural στολαὶ) of particular vestments spoken of as portions of that whole. And this double use of στολὴ

is reproduced, in the use of *stola*, first in the Latin versions, and secondly in the early Christian writers. From the usage here noticed, two others require to be distinguished : (γ) the *classical* use, according to which *stola* was particularly used of the long robe, edged with the *instita*, characteristic of the Roman matron ; and (δ) the *later Christian usage*, discussed in the Introduction, according to which *stola*, like our own " stole," is the equivalent of *orarium.*

on garments, that is, facred robes, of linen, and ufe no under garments of wool, either in the gates of the inner court, or yet farther
within, that is in the Holy and the Moft Holy Place ; and, again, that
bands, or caps of linen, be on their heads, and linen drawers upon
their loins. . . . And as he had once already prefcribed what
veftments were to be worn by the priefts when engaged in their
miniftries within, he now again enjoins that when they go forth they
fhall put off their former veftments in the treafuries or fide-chambers
of the Holy Place, and put on others ; left by retaining the holy garments they fhould fanctify the people who ftand without, who have
not as yet been fanctified, nor made themfelves ready for the fanctifi-
cation of the Temple, fo as to be Nazarites unto the Lord. [51] By all
this we learn that we, too, ought not to enter into the Holy of
Holies in our every-day garments, juft fuch as we pleafe, when they
have become defiled from the ufe of ordinary life, but with a clean
confcience, and in clean garments, hold in our hands the Sacraments
of the Lord.[51]   As for what follows, " *Their heads they fhall not fhave,
nor fuffer their locks to grow long, but polling they fhall poll their
heads,*" by this it is clearly fhown that *we* ought not to have fhaven
heads like the priefts and worfhippers of Ifis and Serapis, nor
yet, on the other hand, to wear long, flowing hair, which is for the
luxurious only, for barbarians or men of the fword ; but in fuch
wife that the feemly habit of priefts may be fet forth in our very
outward features. But in place of what I have quoted, the LXX.
fay, " *Their heads they fhall not fhave, and their hair they fhall not
clofely poll, but a covering fhall they have upon their heads.*" And
according to this we learn that we are not to make a baldnefs
upon our heads with a razor, nor to cut the hair of the head fo
clofely[52] that we fhall look as though we were fhaved, but to let the
hair grow long enough to cover the fkin. Or it may be fimply
that priefts ought always to put a covering on their heads, according
to that line of Virgil, " *With purple amice covered o'er, veil thou thy
locks.*" But this is a forced interpretation. But wine is not to be
drunk by priefts and Levites, and this not only in the time of their

---

[51] The original is as follows : *Per quæ dif-
cimus non quotidianis et quibuslibet pro ufu vitæ
communis pollutis veftibus, nos ingreffi debere in
Sancta Sanctorum, fed munda confcientia et mundis veftibus tenere Domini facramenta.*

[52] Note this paffage as proving clearly that
in St. Jerome's time, " the tonfure " was, a
Rome, at any rate, unknown as a mark of
the Chriftian prieft.

miniſtration, but even (beforehand) when they are about to enter into the Holy of Holies, left the mind become oppreſſed, and the ſenſes dulled. Hence that of the Apoſtle,—"*It is good,*" ſaith he, "*not to drink wine nor to eat fleſh.*" And in another place : "*And wine, wherein is exceſs.*" "*For the people did eat, and drink, and roſe up to play.*" (1 Cor. x. 7.) And for that of his allowing Timothy to drink a little wine, he ſhowed plainly why he allowed this. "*For thy ſtomach's ſake,*" he ſays, "*and for thine often infirmities.*" Garments of linen are uſed by the Egyptian prieſts, not only inſide their temples, but without alſo. ⁵¹ Moreover, the religion that is of God has one dreſs for holy miniſtry, another for the uſage of common life.⁵³ Drawers (of linen) are rightly put on, that ſeemlineſs and propriety may be maintained, left when they aſcend the ſteps of the altar (Exod. xx. 26), and haſten to and fro in the work of their miniſtry there be any unſeemly expoſure. Heathen ſuperſtition has its ſhaven heads. But as far as my knowledge goes, I do not think that any heathen abſtains from wine.

The ſpiritual meaning of all this will be ſeen by what follows. That there are garments holy and ſpiritual the Apoſtle himſelf teaches us, ſaying, "*Put ye on*" ("clothe yourſelves with ") "*the Lord Jeſus Chriſt.*" And elſewhere, "*Put ye on bowels of mercy, of goodneſs, of humility, of gentleneſs, of patience.*" And again, "*Having ſtripped off the old man, together with his deeds, and having put on the new man which is renewed unto (fulneſs of) knowledge after the likeneſs of the Creator.*" [He then quotes 1 Cor. xv. 54, ſaying that this, too, appears to him to have a ſimilar reference.] As to the prieſtly veſtments there is a full account in Exodus, and I myſelf once wrote a book on the ſubject, to which and the interpretation there given the enquiring reader may be referred. For the ſubject is too wide a one to be embraced within the compaſs of a ſhort diſcourſe. Theſe veſtments we make for ourſelves by our own exertion, even ſuch a garment (*tunicam*) as the Lord had, and which could not be rent.

---

⁵¹ The original is as follows: *Porro religio divina alterum habitum habet in miniſterio, alterum in uſu vitaque communi.* It is doubtful whether, by *religio divina*, St. Jerome refers to Jewiſh or to Chriſtian obſervances. The reference to the *feminalia linea* that immediately follows ſeems to ſhow that *Sirmondus* (quoted later in this work) was right in ſuppoſing him to ſpeak here of *Jewiſh* obſervances. Moſt writers on ritual, *quoting the paſſage without its context,* have aſſumed the exaſt contrary, as though there were no doubt at all about the matter. [As a matter of controverſy it matters little which of the two be really referred to, or whether both, as I believe.]

And these vestments we put on when we come to the knowledge
of the secret and hidden things of God, and have that spirit that
searcheth even the deep and profound things of God, things not to
be set forth before the people, nor brought before the eyes of them
that are not sanctified, nor made ready for the holiness of the Lord ;
left haply if they hear things beyond their capacity, they be unable
to endure the greatness of such knowledge, and be choked, as it
were, with this " strong meat," whereas they had need still to be
fed with milk. . . . As for that which follows, " *Bands (vittæ)*
or caps (cidares) of linen shall be on their heads," this, I think,
points to the festive crown of grace, of which it is written (Prov.
iv. 9), " A crown[34] of grace shall be set on thine head." Nor
need we find difficulty in those words of the Apostle concerning the
covering, or the leaving bare, the head. "*A woman,*" he saith, " *ought*
to have a covering upon her head because of the angels. For if a woman
will not be thus covered, then let her cut close her hair. But if it be a
shame unto a woman that her hair be close cut or shorn, then let her
cover (her head). For the man ought not to cover his head, seeing he
is the image and glory of God. But the woman is the glory of the
man (or " of her husband.") For if it be not proper for men to
cover the head, it might be thought inconsistent with this that the
priests are here bidden to cover their heads with caps or bonnets.
But if we read somewhat more carefully, the words that preceded
will solve the difficulty of those now before us. For it is said above,
" *When they minister in the gates of the inner court and yet farther*
within " (*i.e.* in the Holy Place.) For if we enter in to the Holy
Place and stand before the face of the Lord, we ought to cover our
heads :[35] " *For in the sight of the Lord shall no flesh living be justified.*"
(Ps. cxlii. 2.) And, " *Even from a child man's heart is set upon*

---

[34] *Coronam enim gratiarum suscipiet tuus vertex.* It is hardly necessary, probably, to point out that our modern word " crown," is generally suggestive (in the English version of the Bible, for example) of an entirely different idea to that suggested to classical readers by *corona*, or by the corresponding Greek word στέφανος. In classical, and in early Christian usage, these words are expressive of the *chaplet* (of whatever materials) worn by persons of all classes on festive occasions, worn by priests (and priestesses) in honour of particular deities, by victors in the circus or the like, or by triumphant soldiers. The distinctive word for the crown of royalty is διάδημα (*diadema*). But it may be well to mention that in *later* Christian writers, as we shall see as we proceed, the word *corona* is occasionally used, as our own " crown," with reference to insignia of royalty.

[35] " We ought to cover our heads," *i.e.* in self-abasement, as conscious of our own *unworthiness*, of which he proceeds to speak.

wickednefs." (Gen. viii. 21.) Then, laftly, we wear inwardly a vefture about our loins, left, in the prefence of God, aught of unfeemlinefs appear, belonging to a polluted confcience, or to that which pertaineth unto married life. With fuch under-garments the Saviour would have His Apoftles girt when He faith, " *Let your loins be girded, and burning lights be in your hands.*" (Luke, xii. 35.) And the Apoftle faith unto the faithful, " *Stand, therefore, having your loins girt about in truth.*" (Eph. vi. 14.) And to the followers of Chrift doth that apply which is written concerning Chrift Himfelf, " *Righteoufnefs fhall be the girdle of his loins, and with the truth fhall his fides be clothed.*" (Ifa. xi. 5.) And with this girdle that is here fpoken of, he that is holy, and hath attained unto the height (*culmen*) of all virtue, doth not bind himfelf " violently."[56]

---

[56] See above, note 49.

VII.

S. JEROME.

WHITE GARMENTS WORN IN OFFICES OF CHRISTIAN MINISTRATION.

ADVERSUS PELAGIANOS, LIB. I. VOL. IV. p. 502.

[AFTER fpeaking of the pretences made by the Pelagians to fome-thing approaching to a direct revelation of Divine Truth, he adds] :—

"*Nec hoc fufficit, fed repente mutaris in Stoicum, et de Zenonis nobis tonas fupercilio, Chriftianum illius debere effe patientiæ ut fi quis fua auferre voluerit gratanter amittat. Nonne nobis fatis eft patienter perdere quod habemus, nifi violento atque raptori agamus gratias, et cum cunctis benedictionibus profequamur? Docet Evangelium ei qui nobifcum velit iudicio contendere, et per lites ac jurgia auferre tunicam, etiam pallium effe concedendum: non præcipit ut agamus gratias, et læti noftra per-damus. Hoc dico, non quod aliquid fceleris in hac fententia fit, fed quod ubique ὑπερβολικῶς mediocria tranfeas et magna fceleris. Unde ad-jungis gloriam veftium et ornamentorum Deo effe contrariam. Quæ funt, rogo, inimicitiæ contra Deum fi tunicam habuero mundiorem:[57] fi Epifcopus, Prefbyter, et Diaconus, et reliquus ordo Ecclefiafticus, in adminiftratione facrificiorum candida vefte procefferint? Cavete Clerici, cavete Monachi: viduæ et virgines periclitamini, nifi fordidas vos atque pannofas vulgus afpexerit. Taceo de hominibus fæculi quibus aperte bellum indicitur, et inimicitiæ contra Deum fi preciofis atque nitentibus utantur exuviis.*"

"Even this does not content you. You turn ftoic of a fudden, and thunder againft us with all the fternnefs of a Zeno, and declare that a Chriftian fhould be fo patient as to rejoice in lofing whatfoever any man may choofe to take from him. Is it not enough, then, for us to fubmi

---

[57] *Mundiorem. Mundus* as applied to cloth-ing has a primary reference to cleanlinefs, but is often ufed with a fecondary implication of the feemly beauty that belongs to garments bright and pure. So Livy fpeaks of a *cultus jufto mundior* — an over-elegance of perfonal attire.

patiently to lofs of what is ours, unlefs we thank him who with violence has robbed us, and follow him with every expreffion of bleffing? The Gofpel teaches, it is true, that to one who would contend with us at law, and rob us of our under garment we fhould give up our outer garment alfo, but it bids us not exprefs gratitude to the wrongdoer, and fhow gladnefs at the lofs of our goods. I mention this, not as though there were anything criminal in your holding fuch an opinion, but becaufe in everything alike you are actuated by the fame fpirit of exaggeration, and without thought or regard for any moderate courfe, are ever aiming at great things. Hence you go on to fay that all fplendour of drefs or ornament is offenfive unto God. But I would fain know what offence there would be againft God in my wearing a fomewhat handfome[57] tunic; *or if, in the adminiftration of the Holy Things, Bifhop, Prieft, and Deacon, and the other officers of the Church, come forward dreffed in white garments.* Beware ye that are of the Clergy, beware ye Monks: and you too, widows and virgins, are in peril, unlefs you appear in public in fqualid habit and in rags. I fay nothing of men of the world, againft whom war is thus openly proclaimed, and who are accufed as enemies of God if they wear coftly or fplendid garments."

VIII.

HEGESIPPVS.[58]

LINEN VESTMENTS SAID TO HAVE BEEN WORN BY JAMES THE BROTHER OF THE LORD.

APUD S. HIERONYMUM, IN CATALOGO SCRIPT. ECCLES.

JACOBUS qui appellatur frater Domini, cognomento Juſtus, ut non-nulli exiſtimant Joſeph ex alia uxore, ut autem mihi videtur Mariæ fororis matris Domini, cujus Johannes in libro ſuo meminit, filius, poſt paſſionem Domini ſtatim ab Apoſtolis Ierofolymorum Epiſcopus ordinatus, unam tantum ſcripſit epiſtolam, quæ de ſeptem Catholicis eſt, quæ et ipſa ab alio quodam ſub nomine ejus edita aſſeritur : licet paullatim tempore præcedente obtinuerit auctoritatem. Hegeſippus, vicinus Apoſtolicorum temporum, in quinto commentariorum libro de Jacobo narrans ait : *Suſcepit eccleſiam Ieroſolymorum poſt Apoſtolos frater Domini Jacobus, cognomento Juſtus. Multi ſiquidem Jacobi vocabantur. Hic de utero matris ſanctus fuit, vinum et ſiceram non bibit, carnem nullam comedit, nunquam attonſus eſt nec unctus unguento, nec uſus balneo. Huic ſoli licitum erat ingredi Sancta Sanctorum. Siquidem veſtibus lineis non utebatur ſed lineis, ſoluſque ingrediebatur Templum, et flexis genibus pro populo deprecabatur : intantum ut camelorum duritiem traxiſſe ejus genua crederentur.*

"The government of the Church of Jeruſalem was committed, after the Apoſtles, to James, the brother of the Lord, ſurnamed 'The Juſt,' there being many then who bore the name of James. He was holy from his mother's womb : he drank neither wine nor ſtrong drink, ate no fleſh-meat, never cut cloſe the hair of his head, nor anointed himſelf with unguents, nor uſed the bath. To him alone was it allowable to enter the Holy of Holies, ſeeing that he wore garments made, not of wool, but of linen ; and he was wont to enter

---

[58] Hegeſippus, a Jew converted to Chriſtianity, died *circa* A.D. 180. Only fragments of his works have been preſerved.

the Temple alone, and on bended knees to entreat God on behalf of His people ; infomuch that men believed that his knees had grown hard, even as are the knees of a camel."[50]

---

[50] In judging of the hiftorical references to be drawn from this ftatement we muft remember, firft, that we have not the *ipfiffima verba* of Hegefippus, but a Latin tranflation of his words by S. Jerome. We cannot, therefore, now tell whether the *Sanƈta Sanƈtorum* of S. Jerome reprefents τὰ ἅγια fimply (which *might* mean only "the Sanƈtuary," as a fomewhat vague defignation), or ἅγια ἁγίων, which could only mean "The Moft Holy Place," entered once in the year by the high-prieft alone.

And fo again of that "*Templum ingrediebatur*," we cannot now fay whether the original fpoke of τὸν ναὸν, or of τὸ ἱερόν. The former would imply the actual building (made up of "the Holy" and "the Moft Holy" Place). The latter term includes the whole facred enclofure, with its many fubordinate buildings.

However this be, it would be contrary to all hiftorical probability that St. James, the head of the Chriftian Church at Jerufalem, and not of Levitical defcent, fhould have been allowed, as a literal matter of faƈt, to enter the "Holy of Holies" of the Jewifh temple. The real explanation of this, as of fome other fimilar paffages which will be quoted, I believe to be this,— that fome early writers, who were themfelves thoroughly converfant with the fignificance of the infignia of priefthood and of royalty among the Jews, ufed, occafionally, expreffions in fpeaking of Apoftles and others, which would be φανᾶντα ευνιτοῖσι, fuggeftive of important truths to men as well informed as themfelves, but which could only lead to error if taken as literal ftatements of hiftorical faƈt. Compare the paffage from Epiphanius, quoted below, p. 40, and Note 62 upon that paffage.

IX.

POLYCRATES,[60] OF EPHESVS.

OF THE GOLDEN PLATE WORN BY ST. JOHN.

APUD EUSEBIUM. HIST. ECCL. V. 24.

EUSEBIUS is fpeaking of the difpute between Victor, Bifhop of Rome, and certain Eaftern Bifhops, concerning the proper time of the Eafter Feftival. As to this the traditionary ufage of the Churches in Afia Minor differed from that of other Churches. And Polycrates of Ephefus, who held firft place among the Bifhops of Afia Minor, wrote as follows " to Bifhop Victor and the Roman Church ":—

. . . Ἡμεῖς οὖν ἀραδιούργητον ἄγομεν τὴν ἡμέραν, μήτε προστίθεντες μήτε ἀφαιρούμενοι. Καὶ γὰρ κατὰ τὴν Ἀσίαν μεγάλα στοιχεῖα κεκοίμηται ἅτινα ἀναστήσεται τῇ ἡμέρᾳ τῆς παρουσίας τοῦ Κυρίου ἐν ᾗ ἔρχεται μετὰ δόξης ἐξ οὐρανῶν, καὶ ἀναστήσει πάντας τοὺς ἁγίους, Φίλιππον τῶν δώδεκα ἀποστόλων ὃς κεκοίμηται ἐν Ἱεραπόλει, καὶ δύο θυγάτερες αὐτοῦ γεγηρακυῖαι παρθένοι. Καὶ ἡ ἑτέρα αὐτοῦ θυγάτηρ ἐν Ἁγίῳ Πνεύματι πολιτευσαμένη ἐν Ἐφέσῳ ἀναπαύεται, ἔτι δὲ καὶ ὁ Ἰωάννης ὁ ἐπὶ τὸ στῆθος τοῦ Κυρίου ἀναπεσὼν ὃς ἐγενήθη ἱερεὺς τὸ πέταλον πεφορεκὼς καὶ μάρτυς καὶ διδάσκαλος, οὗτος ἐν Ἐφέσῳ κεκοίμηται.

[Then follows an enumeration of other bifhops of renown and martyrs whom Polycrates alleges as having all adhered to the fame tradition in this matter.]

" For our own part we obferve the day with fcrupulous exactnefs, neither adding nor taking away. In Afia great luminaries of the Church have been gathered to their reft, who fhall rife again in the day of the Lord's coming, when He cometh with glory from heaven, and fhall raife up all the faints, fuch as were Philip, one of the twelve, who now is at reft in Hierapolis; and his two daughters

---

[60] As Polycrates was contemporary with Irenæus of Gaul and Victor of Rome (*fed.* A.D. 192 to A.D. 202), the date of this letter is determined to the clofe of the fecond century.

who waxed old in virgin eftate, while his other daughter, after a Chriftian life in the Holy Spirit, refteth now in Ephefus. Yea moreover, John alfo, he that reclined on the Lord's breaft, *and became a prieft* [61] *wearing the golden plate,* [62] and a Witnefs, and a Teacher, he, I fay, now fleepeth in Ephefus."

---

[61] As the terms *iεgιὸς* and *Sacerdos* are ufed in a great variety of meanings in ecclefiaftical writers, and as the ambiguity thence arifing will frequently come under notice in the courfe of thefe extracts, it may be well here briefly to enumerate thofe meanings, and to defignate each by a feparate (Greek) letter for facility of reference. The two words then (which may be regarded as equivalent) are ufed,—

α. Of the Jewifh high-prieft. [So *ὸ iεgιὸς* not unfrequently in LXX.]

β. Of Levitical priefts of the fecond order.

γ. Of the Levitical priefts generally, fo as to include both the high-prieft and the priefts of the fecond order.

δ. Of our Lord Jefus Chrift. [So in Heb. v. 6; vii. 21; x. 21.]

ε. Of Chriftian bifhops.

ϛ. Of Chriftian prefbyters, or priefts.

ζ. Of thofe who in Chrift's Church minifter in holy things unto God, whether bifhops or prefbyters.

What is here briefly ftated will be fhown more at length with regard to *Sacerdos* in a fubfequent note (See Index *in voc.*), in the extract from Pope Celeftine's Letter to the Bifhops of Gaul. [I fhall refer, whenever neceffary, to the various modifications of meaning above enumerated, by the number of the Note prefixed to the various letters. Thus 62 *α* will indicate a reference to the Jewifh high-prieft, 62 *ε* to Chriftian bifhops, and fo for the reft. But it muft be underftood that it is *only by context* that we can determine which of the above meanings was prefent to the mind of the writer in any given paffage. And my references therefore are only to be regarded as expreffions of *opinion* founded upon ftudy of fuch context.]

[62] I quote both the context and the words of the original text, that the reader may judge for himfelf what is their true meaning. The word *iεgιὸς* by itfelf is ambiguous, and may mean either a high-prieft or a prieft of the fecond order, as context may fuggeft. But, as the diftinctive mark of a high-prieft was the *τίταλος*, or plate of gold, marking his fupreme authority, or "royal priefthood," Polycrates ufes here the defcriptive expreffion, "a prieft that had worn the *τίταλον*" (much as ecclefiaftical hiftorians fpeak of a "mitred abbot"), in order to bring out the fact on which he was then concerned to infift, viz., *the fupreme Apoftolic authority* of St. John, whofe office in the Chriftian Church was to bear rule in fpiritual things over the fpiritual Ifrael, even as the high-prieft of old over Ifrael after the flefh. For this laft compare the paffage from Epiphanius that follows (p. 40.) I may obferve that the explanation above given will at once account for the very peculiar ufe of the participle of the *præfens perfectum*, *πεφορεκώς*. The proper connotation of that participle is (fee *Eirenica*, Notes 49, 52, and 61) that of a *ftate* or *condition* refulting from a paft act. And this idea (flightly modified by the peculiarities of this exceptional context) is exactly coincident with the explanation above fuggefted.

λ.

EPIPHANIVS.[1]

BISHOP OF SALAMIS, A.D. 367 TO A.D. 403.

ADV. HÆS. LIB. I. CAP. 29.

[THE writer has been fpeaking of the prophecies concerning One who fhould "*fit on the throne of David.*" Thefe prophecies, he adds, muft needs have their fulfilment, feeing that no declaration of Holy Scripture faileth of accomplifhment. He proceeds as follows] :—

By the "throne of David," and by the "fitting as a king," is meant the office of priefthood in God's Holy Church, which is a rank at once of royalty and of fupreme priefthood, together conjoined of Chrift, which He hath beftowed upon His holy Church, removing and placing in that His Church the throne of David, which abideth for ever. . . . . Now, when the feat of kingly power had thus been transferred in Chrift to the Church, the royal dignity was likewife transferred from the family of that Judah that was after the flefh, and from the Jerufalem that once was. And now the throne is fet in God's Holy Church, and that for ever, having two titles to this dignity, in refpect of kingfhip the one, in refpect of fupreme priefthood the other. It is a throne of royalty firft, by inheritance from Chrift Jefus our Lord : and this after two manners, becaufe of His being of the feed of David the king, by natural defcent, and as being what indeed He is, a greater King, from all eternity, in refpect of His Godhead. It is a throne, too, of priefthood, becaufe he is himfelf a high-prieft, and firft in rank in a line of high-priefts, feeing that James (called the brother of the Lord, and apoftle) was ftraight-

---

[1] Epiphanius, furnamed ὁ πεντάγλωσσος, as being acquainted with five languages, was born in Paleftine *of Jewifh parents.* He was chofen bifhop of the Metropolitan See of Conftantia (formerly *Salamis*) in Crete, A.D. 367. The paffage here given is quoted, or rather referred to, by St. Jerome in his "Catalogus Illuftrium Virorum."

way eftablifhed as bifhop, and he again was, by birth, the eldeft fon of Jofeph, but, in regard of rank, was called brother of the Lord, becaufe of their affociation one with the other.

For this James was a fon of Jofeph, begotten of Jofeph's (firft) wife, not of Mary (the mother of the Lord), as I have already often faid, and clearly proved. Moreover, we find that he was of the feed of David, as being Jofeph's fon, and became a Nazarene. For he was Jofeph's firft-born and confecrated unto God. Befide this, I find that he exercifed prieftly office,[64] after the manner of the ancient priefthood, and for this reafon was allowed to enter the Holy of Holies once in every year, as the law according to Scripture bade the high-priefts do. For fo many before me have recorded of him, fuch as were Eufebius, Clement, and others. Moreover, it was allowable for him to wear the golden plate upon his head, as is teftified by the afore-mentioned truftworthy writers.[65]

---

[64] The original is as follows: Ἔτι δὲ καὶ ἱερατεύσαντα αὐτὸν κατὰ τὴν παλαιὰν ἱερωσύνην εὕρομεν, διὸ καὶ κρίτω αὐτῷ ἅπαξ τοῦ ἐνιαυτοῦ εἰς τὰ ἅγια τῶν ἁγίων εἰσιέναι, ὡς τοῖς ἀρχιερεῦσιν ἐπίλοιπεν ὁ νόμος κατὰ τὸ γιγραμμένον. οὕτω γὰρ ἱστόρισαν πολλοὶ πρὸ ἡμῶν περὶ αὐτοῦ Εὐσίβιος τι καὶ Κλέμης καὶ ἄλλοι. Ἀλλὰ καὶ τὸ πίταλον ἐπὶ τῆς κεφαλῆς ἐξὸν αὐτῷ φορεῖν καθὼς οἱ προειρημένοι ἀξιόπιστοι ἄνδρες ἐν τοῖς ὑπ' αὐτῶν ὑπομνηματισμοῖς ἐμαρτύρησαν. In referring to "Eufebius," he no doubt has in view the letter of Bifhop Polycrates preferved by Eufebius, and quoted above, p. 38.

[65] It will be feen that the general fcope of this paffage is to prove the applicability to our Lord of the prophecies concerning One who fhould *fit on the throne of David for ever.* This was fo, he argues, in refpect both of the Kingfhip of Chrift, and in refpect of His Prieft-hood. And all that he fays of James is brought in by way of fhowing how the fact of *his relationfhip,* as half-brother in the eye of the law, *to our Lord,* pointed him out as having a claim, as neareft of kin, to prefide (*reign,* as it were) over the Church at Jerufalem immediately after our Lord Himfelf had afcended into heaven. His argument is bafed upon the fact (familiar to him as originally a Jew) that the offices both of the high-prieft and of the *Rofh Abboth,* or head of the Sanhedrim (= the Greek πατριάρχης), were regarded by the Jews as hereditary, and paffing, therefore, in default of direct heirs *to the neareft of kin.*

XI.

THEODORET.[66]

THE SACRED ROBE SENT BY CONSTANTINE TO MACARIUS OF JERUSALEM.

[ECCLES. HIST. LIB. II. CAP. XXIII.]

.Κωνστάντιος γὰρ ἀπὸ τῆς ἑσπέρας ἐπανελθὼν ἐν ταύτῃ διέτριβε. Πολλὰ δὲ τῶν συνεληλυθότων ἐπὶ τοῦ βασιλέως (ὁ Ἀκάκιος) κατηγοράσας καὶ σύστημα πονηρῶν ἀνθρώπων ἀποκαλέσας ἐσ᾽ ὀλέθρῳ καὶ λύμῃ τῶν ἐκκλησιῶν συγκρο- τούμενον, τὸν βασιλέως ἄνηψε θυμόν. Οὐχ ἥκιστα δὲ αὐτὸν χαλεπῆναι πεποίηκεν ἃ κατὰ τοῦ Κυρίλλου συντέθεικε. Τὴν γὰρ ἱερὰν στολὴν ἣν ὁ πανεύφημος Κων- σταντῖνος ὁ βασιλεὺς τῶν Ἱεροσολύμων ἐκκλησίαν γεραίρων δεδώκει τῷ Μακαρίῳ τῷ τῆς πόλεως ἐκείνης ἀρχιερεῖ, ἵνα ταύτην περιβαλλόμενος τὴν τοῦ θείου βαπτίσ- ματος ἐπιτελῇ λειτουργίαν, ἐκ χρυσῶν δὲ αὕτη κατεσκεύαστο νημάτων, πεπρακέναι τὸν Κύριλλον ἔφη, καὶ ταύτην τινὰ τῶν ἐπὶ τῆς θυμέλης λογιζομένων πριάμενον περιβαλέσθαι μὲν, ὀρχούμενον δὲ πεσεῖν καὶ συνθλιβῆναι καὶ θανάτῳ παραδοθῆναι.

"Constantius, after his return from the West, continued for some time in this city (Constantinople). Acacius brought many accusa- tions to the Emperor against the bishops who had assembled at Seleucia, abusing them as a pack of mischievous men got together for the ruin and destruction of the Churches, and so excited him to anger against them. What more than all excited his indignation was the charge which Acacius devised against Cyril (Bishop of Jerusalem). The Emperor Constantine, of famous memory, as a mark of honour to the Church at Jerusalem, had sent to Macarius, then bishop of that city, a sacred robe, made of threads of gold, which he should put upon him when performing the office of holy baptism. This robe Acacius

---

[66] Theodoret, born at Antioch, circa A.D. 393, studied under Theodore of Mopsuestia and S. Chrysostom; became Bishop of Cyrus in Syria, A.D. 420; died A.D. 457.

declared had been fold by Cyril, and that a ftage-dancer had bought it and put it on, but that, in dancing, he fell and received injuries which proved fatal."[67]

---

[67] I have quoted the above paffage, becaufe the fact of a "facred veftment" being given to Macarius of Jerufalem is one which is often referred to by writers on ecclefiaftical veftments. What really follows from the above paffage is that Conftantine thought that a fplendid robe of fome kind might properly be worn by a patriarch at the Office of Holy Baptifm. What was the nature of the robe does not appear. But it is evident that whether the ftory of Cyril's having fold it be true or no, it was one of which, with at leaft a fhow of probability, it could be faid that it had been purchafed by a ftage-dancer, and by him worn in public exhibitions. As to the *apoftolic* origin of the fo-called "facerdotal veftments," the ftory proves nothing at all, but if anything, goes to prove their imperial and fecular origin.

XII

ST. AUGUSTINE [18] OF HIPPO.

ON THE LEVITICAL VESTMENTS.

Quæstiones in Heptateuchum, Lib. ii. Cap. cxxix.

In this chapter he has occasion to notice the dress of the high-priest as a whole, and also special portions of it, as the λόγιον, or *rationale*, and the *lamina aurea*. In all these he sees a mystical reference to Christ or to sacraments of the Church, but does not even in the slightest way allude to any corresponding vestments worn in offices of Christian ministry. The concluding words of the chapter are the following :—

Quod autem præfiguratum est in sancto sanctorum, ut super arcam quæ Legem habebat esset propitiatorium, ubi Dei misericordia significari intelligenda est, qua propitius fit eorum peccatis qui Legem non implent ; hoc mihi videtur etiam in ipsa veste sacerdotis [20] significari : nam et ipsa quid aliud quam Ecclesiæ sacramenta significat ? Quod in λογίῳ, id est Rationali, in pectore sacerdotis [21] posito, judicia constituit, in lamina vero sanctificationem et ablationem peccatorum : tanquam Rationale sit in pectore simile arcæ in qua Lex erat, et lamina illa in fronte similis propitiatorio quod super arcam erat, et ut utrobique servaretur quod scriptum est, *Superexultat misericordia judicio.* (Jac. ii. 13.)

---

[18] Bishop of Hippo, 365 ; died A.D. 450.
[20] *Sacerdos* throughout this passage is used, as the previous context shows, of the Jewish high-priest. See above Note 61 a.

XIII.

POPE CELESTINE.[70]

ON EPISCOPAL DRESS.

[THE letter from which extracts are here given, will be found in Labbé's "Concilia," vol. ii. p. 1618. It is addressed "To all the Bishops of the Provinces of Vienna and Narbonne."]

"We have been informed that certain priests[71] of the Lord are devoting themselves rather to superstitious observances in dress than to purity of thought and of faith. But it is not to be wondered at that the customs of the Church should be broken by men who have not grown up in the Church, but coming in by another way, have introduced with them into the Church what had been theirs in another[72] mode of life. By dressing in a *pallium*[73] and wearing a girdle[74] round their loins, they think to fulfil the truth of Scripture, not in the spirit but in the letter. But if the precepts to which they refer were for this end given, that after this strange fashion they should be observed, why are not the precepts which follow observed in like manner, and so 'burning lights' held in the hands as well as 'a staff?' The words they quote have a mystical meaning of their own, and to men of understanding are so clear as to be observed according to a more fitting interpretation. For by the girding up of the loins is signified Chastity, and by the staff Pastoral Rule, and by 'burning lights' the brightness of good works, concerning which it is said (Matt. v. 16), 'Let your works shine.' But supposing it so to be, that men dwelling in remote districts, and far from others, wear this dress, out of custom rather than of reason, yet whence such a dress in the Churches of Gaul? And why is the custom, observed for so many years, and by such great bishops, to be discarded for another garb? We should be distinguished from the common folk, and from the rest, by our learning, not by our gar-

---

[70] Bishop of Rome from November, 423, to April, 432.

ments; by our mode of life, not by what we wear; by purity of thought, not by peculiarities of drefs. For if we begin to affect innovations, we fhall tread under foot the traditions of our fathers, only to make room for worthlefs fuperftitions. We ought not, therefore, to attract to objects fuch as thefe the untrained minds of the faithful. It is teaching they require, not mockeries like thefe. Nor is it an impofing appearance to the eye that is needed, but precepts to be inftilled into the mind."

The original is as follows :—

Didicimus quofdam Domini facerdotes [71] *fuperftitiofo potius cultui infervire quam mentis vel fidei puritati. Sed non mirum fi contra ecclefiafticum morem faciunt qui in ecclefia non creverunt, fed alio venientes itinere fecum hæc in ecclefiam quæ in alia converfatione* [72] *habuerant, intulerunt. Amicti pallio,* [73] *et lumbos præcincti,* [74] *credunt fe fcripturæ fidem non per*

---

[71] *Sacerdotes Domini.* I have tranflated the word *Sacerdos* by prieft for want of a better word. In point of fact, however, this term, when employed in a Chriftian fenfe, is in early writers ufed far more frequently of bifhops than of priefts,—not unfrequently of bifhops and priefts inclufively—and is feldom if ever ufed as the diftinctive appellation of the fecond order of the Chriftian miniftry.

St. Gregory *always* ufes *Sacerdos* as the equivalent of *epifcopus, facerdotium* of *Epifcopatus.* So St. Gregory of Tours (De Gloria Epifc. cap. cx. p. 989), Venerable Bede, and others. Honorius of Autun (apud Ducange *in voc.*), lib. i. cap. 182; and Rhabanus Maurus de Inftit. Cleric. cap. 5, p. 314; recognife the properly inclufive ufe of the term. *Sacerdos autem vocari poteft five epifcopus fit five prefbyter.* In a letter of John of Ravenna to St. Gregory the Great, and in paffages of Innocent III., quoted below, we fhall come upon one or two inftances in which it is clear from the context that *Sacerdos* is ufed as a defignation of a prefbyter. Compare Note 61.

[72] *In alia converfatione.* He means, probably, " while living under *monaftic* rule," (fee the next Note). Several inftances are alluded to in early writers of monks who retained their monaftic habit after promotion to epifcopal dignity. A well-known inftance is that of Fulgentius, Bifhop of Rufpa. *Orario quidem ficut omnes epifcopi nullatenus utebatur.*

Pellices cingulo tanquam monachus utebatur. . . . . Cafulam pretiofam vel fuperbi coloris nec monachos fuos habere permifit, nec ipfe habuit. Subtus cafulam nigello vel lactineo pallio circumdatus inceffit. Quando temperies aeris invitabat folo pallio intra monafterium eft coopertus. Nec depofito faltem cingulo fomnum petivit. In qua tunica dormiebat in eadem facrificabat. [Ferrandus Diaconus apud Thomaffinum.]

[73] *Amicti pallio.* By *pallium* is here meant the coarfe outer garment traditionally affociated in idea with the prophets of the old covenant, and adopted in early Chriftian times by hermits and monks (fee next Note), and by others living a life of fimilar aufterity. The word *pallium* occurs in a great variety of meanings in early writers. Several of thefe will come before us in the courfe of this work, and will be noticed in the order of their occurrence.

[74] With this mention of *pallium* and *cingulum* as characteriftic of a monaftic drefs, compare Salvianus (apud Thomaffinum) ad Eccles.Cathol. lib. iv. Addreffing a monk of unworthy character, he fays: *Licet religionem* (*i.e.* monaftic life) *veftibus fimules, licet fidem cingulo afferas, licet fanctitatem pallio mentiaris,* etc. The mention of a *pelliceum cingulum* (ζώνη δερματίνη) in the paffage quoted in Note 72 is an indication that the drefs of John the Baptift was taken as a type by the earlier monks. So S. Germanus (quoted later in this volume) more diftinctly implies.

*fpiritum fed per literam completuros. Nam fi ad hoc ifta præcepta funt
ut taliter fervarentur, cur non fiunt pariter quæ fequuntur, ut* lucernæ
ardentes in manibus *una cum* BACULO *teneantur? Habent fuum ifta
myfterium, et intelligentibus ita clara funt ut ea magis qua decet figni-
ficatione ferventur. Nam in lumborum præcinctione caftitas, in baculo
regimen paftorale, in lucernis ardentibus boni fulgor operis, de quo dicitur,*
Opera veftra luceant, *indicantur. Habeant tamen iftum forfitan cultum,
morem potius quam rationem fequentes, qui in remotioribus habitant locis,
et procul a ceteris degunt. Unde hic habitus in ecclefiis Gallicanis, ut
tot annorum tantorumque pontificum in alterum habitum confuetudo ver-
tatur? Difcernendi a plebe vel ceteris fumus doctrina non vefte, converfatione non habitu, mentis puritate non cultu. Nam fi ftudere incipiamus
novitati, traditum nobis a patribus ordinem calcabimus ut locum fuper-
vacuis fuperftitionibus faciamus. Rudes ergo fidelium mentes ad talia non
debemus inducere. Docendi enim potius funt quam illudendi. Nec im-
ponendum eft eorum oculis, fed mentibus infundenda præcepta funt.*

XIV.

JACOBUS SIRMONDUS.[75]

ON THE ORIGIN OF ECCLESIASTICAL VESTMENTS.

(FROM HIS ANNOTATIONS ON THE LETTER ABOVE QUOTED.)

[HAVING quoted a bifhop of Rome I may be allowed here to add
the comment of a learned Jefuit, Jacobus Sirmondus. He writes as
follows :—]

Taxat Cæleftinus epifcopos quofdam qui novo et infueto habitus
genere uterentur : docetque difcerni ab aliis debere clericos non vefte
fed vita et moribus. Sunt qui habitum interpretentur quo incedebant :

---

[75] He was born A.D. 1559 ; was made Confeffor to Louis XIII. in 1637 ; and died, at a
great age, 1651.

alii ut Dionyſius Exiguus, quo miniſtrabant.   *Quod non debeant*, inquit,
ſacerdotes aut clerici amiƈti pallio et præcinƈti lumbos in ecclesia miniſtrare.
Sed res eodem relabitur.   Nam primis ecclesiæ ſæculis clerici quas
in vita communi veſtes uſurpabant, iiſdem etiam in ſacris utebantur,
ſed mundioribus et optimis, id eſt, ut Hieronymus exponit in caput
xliv. Ezechielis, *non quotidianis et quibuslibet pro uſu vitæ communi pollutis,*
ſed mundis.   Quod idem aliis verbis ſignificat lib. i. contra Pelagianos,
Pelagium exagitans.   [*Here he quotes the paſſage already given,*
p. 34].   Candidam enim veſtem dicit Albam, quæ in uſu tum erat
more Romano, eamque nitidam et lautiorem, qualis prenſantium magiſ-
tratum, qui candidati propterea vocabantur.   Et color igitur et forma
veſtium eadem principio fuit ecclesiaſticis et reliquis.   Sed cum formam
alii poſtea mutaſſent, ecclesia prudenti consilio priſtinam in ſacris retinuit: et ornatum licet preciumque ad venerationem veſtibus ſacris
adjecerit, formam tamen non mutavit; ita ut Romanas veſtes nunc
etiam referant, Alba tunicam, caſula togam, nisi quod caſula ſeu planeta
ancisis proavorum noſtrorum memoria lateribus a togæ amplitudine
abire cæpit.   Et quia vetus hæc forma non perinde in quotidianis
clericorum veſtibus, ut in ſacris, retenta eſt, ex eo faƈtum ut nunc in
Ecclesia quod de veteri lege ad Ezechielem obſervarat S. Hieronymus,
religio divina alterum habitum habeat in miniſterio, alterum in uſu vitaque
communi.   Quod ipſum quoque accidit in lingua Latina, qua Divina
officia celebramus.   Nam cum ea quondam in uſu publico paſſim
eſſet ſub imperio Romano, eademque ſacrorum in ecclesia vox eſſet,
quæ populi; populus linguam, ut ſolet, poſtea mutavit, ecclesia Latinam
merito retinuit.

XV.

ISIDORE OF PELUSIUM.[16]

OF THE LINEN STOLE AND THE WOOLLEN OMOPHORION.

Epist. Lib. i. Cap. 136.

Ἑρμίνῳ Κόμητι.[17]

"Ὅσον αὐτὸς ἄπληστος εἶ πρὸς τὴν μάθησιν τοσοῦτον ἐγὼ πρόθυμος πρὸς τὴν ὄχλωσιν, μόνον εἰ θεὸς δῷ ταῖς εὐχαῖς σου τὴν εὕρεσιν ἄνωθεν.

Ἡ ὀθόνη[18] μεθ' ἧς λειτουργοῦσιν ἐν τοῖς ἁγίοις, οἱ διάκονοι τὴν τοῦ Κυρίου ἀναμιμνήσκει ταπείνωσιν, νίψαντος τοὺς πόδας τῶν μαθητῶν καὶ ἐκμάξαντος. Τὸ δὲ τοῦ ἐπισκόπου ὠμοφόριον ἐξ ἐρίας ὂν ἀλλ' οὐ λίνου τὴν τοῦ προβάτου δορὰν σημαίνει ὅπερ πλανηθὲν ζητήσας ὁ Κύριος ἐπὶ τῶν οἰκείων ὤμων ἀνέλαβεν. Ὁ γὰρ ἐπίσκοπος εἰς τύπον ὢν τοῦ Χριστοῦ τὸ ἔργον ἐκείνου πληροῖ, καὶ δείκνυσι πᾶσι διὰ τοῦ σχήματος ὅτι μιμητής ἐστι τοῦ ἀγαθοῦ καὶ μεγάλου ποιμένος ὁ τὰς ἀσθενείας φέρειν τοῦ ποιμνίου προβεβλημένος. Καὶ πρόσχες ἀκριβῶς. Ἡνίκα γὰρ αὐτὸς ὁ ἀληθινὸς ποιμὴν παραγίνεται διὰ τῆς τῶν εὐαγγελίων τῶν προσκυνητῶν ἀναπτύξεως,[19] καὶ ὑπανίσταται καὶ ἀποτίθεται τὸ σχῆμα τῆς μιμήσεως ὁ ἐπίσκοπος, αὐτὸν δηλῶν παρεῖναι τὸν Κύριον, τὸν τῆς ποιμαντικῆς ἡγεμόνα, καὶ θεὸν, καὶ δεσπότην.

To Count Herminus.

" As thou art ever unwearied in learning, fo am I ever ready to teach, if only God, in anfwer to thy prayers, grant me from above the finding of that thou feekeft.

---

[16] *Ifidorus, gente Ægyptius, ortu forfan Alexandrinus, et Chryfoftomi difcipulus, claruit circ. ann.* 412. *Vitam egit monafticam circa Pelufium, ex feptem Nili oftiis maximum.* Cave, Hift. Lit. vol. i. p. 390.

[17] Κόμης. One of the many Latin words (*comes*) which under the Empire were adopted into Greek, and thence again, in many cafes, into the Eaftern languages, with which that Greek was brought in contact. It is here ufed probably of the governor of a province, in which fenfe *comes* is often ufed by the later Latin writers.

[18] ἡ ὀθόνη. Taken by itfelf this word might imply a linen veftment of any kind, whether fhiped like a maniple, or like a ftole. But there is no trace of the maniple in the Eaftern Church, and there is little doubt but that the veftment here fpoken of refembled the Latin *orarium*,—our own "ftole." So St.

H

" The linen veftment [78] with which the deacons minifter in the Holy Place, is a memorial of the humility of our Lord, in wafhing, and wiping dry, the feet of the difciples. But that which the bifhop weareth on his fhoulders, made not of linen but of wool, fignifieth the fleece of the fheep, for which, when it had wandered away, the Lord fought, and took it up on his own fhoulders. For the bifhop, being a type of Chrift, fulfilleth Chrift's work, and by the habit he wears fetteth forth unto all that he who is fet to bear the infirmities of the flock is a follower of the good and great Shepherd. And this do thou note carefully. For when, by the unrolling [79] of the adorable Gofpels, the true Shepherd Himfelf cometh nigh, the bifhop rifeth up to do Him honour, and layeth afide the habit of His femblance, fhowing that the Lord Himfelf is prefent, who is the chief Shepherd, and God, and Ruler over all."

Chryfoftom (or rather a fermon that bears his name), in the fermon on the Prodigal Son, fpeaks of the deacons as μιμούμενοι τὰς τῶν ἀγγέλων πτέρυγας ταῖς λιπταῖς ὀθόναις ταῖς ἐπὶ τῶν ἀριστερῶν ὤμων κειμέναις, " prefenting the femblance of angels' wings in the light veſtments of linen which refted on their left ſhoulders." And with this agrees the reference made to the fame ὀθόνη by S. Germanus

of Conftantinople (quoted later in this volume).

[79] ἀναπτύξως—unrolling, and fo opening. To St. Ifidore, writing early in the 5th century, the Gofpels were probably ftill actually *volumina*, "rolls," as we fee them reprefented in the picture which forms the frontifpiece to the prefent work. Comp. Luke, iv. 17, ἀναπτύξας τὸ βιβλίον.

XVI.

INCERTI AUCTORIS HOMILIA DE UNO LEGISLATORE S. CHRYSOSTOMI NOMINE INSCRIPTA.[80]

THE LEVITICAL VESTMENTS.

[THE writer is enlarging on thofe words of David, ὁ Κύριος ἐβασίλευσεν (Ps. xcvi. 1), and on the parallel expreffion (Ps. xcii. 1), ὁ Κύριος ἐβασί- λευσεν· εὐπρέπειαν ἐνδύσατο. Commenting on thefe laft words, " He clothed Himfelf with beauty," he proceeds as follows] :—

We men clothe ourfelves outwardly with raiment, in order that we may hide whatever is unfeemly in our nature. But for what end fhould God cover over His incorporeal nature, replete as it is with light, or rather itfelf the radiant fource of light? But in truth He fpeaketh here of the body of Chrift as itfelf the garment wherewith He is clothed. "*The Lord is King: He hath put on beauteous apparel.*" By this beauty of which David fpeaks he meaneth the body of Chrift's flefh. For beauteous this was, having nothing of the uglinefs of fin. *For He did no fin, neither was guile found in His mouth.* "The Lord hath clothed Himfelf with power: yea, He hath girded Himfelf about." Seeing that a girdle is the ornament of kings,[81] and ferveth as an indication of a king and of a judge, therefore doth he here fet

---

[80] Photius, writing in the 9th century, and at Conftantinople, fpeaks of this fermon as one of the genuine works of S. Chryfoftom. Moft modern critics, however (Bifhop Pear- fon is the only notable exception), regard it as the work of another and later author. The Benedictine editors follow Ufher in afcribing it to the age of Juftinian, or about the middle of the 6th century. See Montfaucon's Pre- face, Chryfoftomi Opera, tom. vi. p. 469.

[81] ἐπειδὴ τὸν βασιλέα ζώνη κοσμεῖ. In the Byzantine reprefentations of royal perfonages, the embroidered girdle, of confiderable width, and ftudded with jewels, forms one of the moft confpicuous ornaments. See, for ex-

ample, the figures of the Emperor Michael, and of the Emprefs Theodora, given by Du- frefne in his *Differtatio de Imperatorum Conftan- tinopolitanorum Nummis* (appended to the Glof- fary), pl. vi. This reference by S. Germanus of the *girdle* of our Lord to royal, rather than to prieftly, infignia, is to be accounted for by the fact that the girdle was not, till after the 8th century (at the earlieft) recognifed as part of the ornament of the drefs of Chriftian miniftry, feeing that if anything of the kind was worn, it was for convenience not for fhow, and did not appear. In the Levitical drefs, on the other hand, it was the moft marked ornament of the ordinary facerdotal coftume.

Him forth as both reigning and judging. For Esaias saith: "*There
shall come forth a rod*[82] *out of the root of Jesse, and a flower shall spring
therefrom, and the Spirit of God shall rest upon Him; and with righteous-
ness shall His loins be girded, and with truth His sides be clothed.*"
(Isa. xi. 1, 2, 5.)

This vesture of Christ, I mean His flesh, was worn after a hidden
manner, and in image, by the high-priest under the law. And mark
now with attention how the shadows served as interpreters of the
Truth, how the types gave their light before the fuller light of the
Gospel. I speak now with reserve, and accommodate my words as
far as may be, to simple and unlearned hearers, that they be not carried to and fro with uncertainties of doctrine.

The high-priest, then, when he entered into the Holy of Holies,
put upon him a ποδήρης (a garment, that is, that hung down from the
head to the feet) together with ephod,[83] girdle, drawers, golden plate,
tiara,[84] or priestly cap,[85] the Rational upon his breast, and all that the

---

[82] ῥάβδος. In this word which according
to context may mean either (α) the young
shoot of a tree, or (β) among many other
secondary meanings, a *sceptre*, the writer sees
a prophecy of Christ's royalty, as in the words
δικαιοσύνη and ἀλήθεια which follow, he finds
symbolised His office as a Judge.

[83] ἐπωμίδα. Following the LXX.

[84] Τιάρα [also τιάρας, τιάρης, τιήρης], a
Persian word, and Persian head-dress. So
S. Chrysostom speaks of it, *Homil.* 17, in
Acta: καθάπερ οἱ Πέρσαι τὴν τιάραν περι-
λόντες, καὶ τὰς ἀναξυρίδας καὶ τὰ ὑποδέ-
ματα τὰ βαρβαρικὰ, τὴν ἄλλην στολὴν τὴν
ἡμῖν ἐπιχώριον ὑπελθόντες, καὶ κειράμενοι χρῷ
κρύπτουσι τῇ σχήματι τὸν πόλεμον. "As
the Persians, by taking off their tiara, their
trousers and foreign shoes, and assuming the
dress commonly worn by ourselves, and shav-
ing the skin, conceal under this outward semblance the war they bear in their hearts."
But a tiara of a peculiar shape, *with an up-
right peak*, was the distinctive mark of Persian kings. So Æschylus speaks of it, *Pers.*
662, where the Chorus implore Darius to re-
appear on earth, βασιλείου τιάρας φάλαρον
τιφυόντων. Comp. Aristoph. *Aves.* 487. And
of ecclesiastical writers, St. Jerome uses the
word of the high cap (shaped like a "Cap
of Liberty") which was then regarded as the
characteristic mark of "men of the East."

[On Ezech. cap. xxiii. and on Dan. cap. iii.]
*Tiara genus pileoli quo Persarum Chaldæorumque
genus utitur.* So again St. Isidore, Hisp. *Orig.*
lib. xix. cap. xxx. *Imperatores Romani, et reges
quidam gentium, aureis coronis utuntur. Persæ
tiaras gerunt, sed reges rectas, satrapæ incurvas.
Reperta autem tiara a Semiramide Assyriorum
regina. Quod genus ornamenti exinde usque hodie
gens ipsa retinet.* And Photius (9th century),
κυρβασία, τιάραν ἢ οἱ μὲν βασιλεῖς ὀρθὴ ἐχρῶντο,
οἱ δὲ στρατηγοὶ ἐπικεκλιμένῃ. As for this
contrast of form compare Xen. *Anab.* ii. 5,
23, where Tissaphernes is represented as saying, τὴν ἐπὶ τῇ κεφαλῇ τιάραν βασιλεῖ μόνῳ
ἔξεστιν ὀρθὴν ἔχειν. The use of the term as a
designation for the *regnum*, or crown of
royalty, worn by the later popes, is, as may be
supposed, of very late date indeed.

[85] τιάραν, τουτέστι κιδάριον. Two things
are here to be remarked. First the mere fact
that the preacher should find it necessary to
explain the LXX. word τιάρα by κιδάριον,
affords of itself a strong presumption that no
tiara, nor anything corresponding thereto in
shape, could, in his time, have been generally
known as the characteristic decoration of
Christian bishops (compare below, Note 89).
And secondly as to the word κιδάριον itself.
[The *var. lect.* κυρβασίαν must be regarded as
an explanatory gloss, substituting a comparatively
common word for one which in literary Greek

Scripture there fetteth forth, and which yourfelves may fee. In [86] all this that which outwardly is fafhioned is one—other is that which thereby is to be underftood. For God delighteth not in blue, and purple, and fcarlet, and fine linen. That for which God looketh is purity of heart. But in the embodiment of thefe colours He fetteth before us, as in a picture, the femblance of the divers virtues. For if God did indeed find pleafure in thofe veftments of glory, why did He not clothe Mofes therewith before that he clothed Aaron? But Mofes was himfelf without that vefture, and yet clothed therewith the priefts. Mofes was not wafhed with water, and yet did he wafh *them*. He was not anointed with oil, yet did he anoint them. He wore not a prieftly veftment, yet he put that veftment on the priefts; that thou thereby mighteft learn that to him that is perfect [87] virtue fufficeth for all adornment.

But let us fet the prieft before us, from the head downwards. For the very name of what he putteth upon him is matter of doubt and queftion, and has been rendered by another word in Greek. To begin then with the head. What was firft? "Tiara," or what, is the name it bears? And why [88] is that which he weareth fafhioned as a tiara? Becaufe the high-prieft was head of the people, and there was need that one who was made head of all, fhould himfelf have power fet upon his head. For abfolute and arbitrary power is not to be endured, but if it have the fymbol of fupreme power fet upon it, then is it made fubject unto law. Therefore it is commanded that the head of the prieft be not bare but covered, in order that he who is head of the people may learn that he too hath a Head (in heaven). For [89] this caufe in the church alfo, in the ordaining of priefts (61 ε), the

---

is very rare, and confined to very late writers.] It is properly an adjective, with the meaning "pertaining to the Corybantes," or priefts of Cybele, and hence ufed of a cap, or bonnet of peculiar fhape, fuch as they wore. *In Graeci tate, quae dicitur, vulgari, κορυβάντιον nihil aliud fignificat quam κυρβασία (a Perfian cap, or tiara).* Lobeck on Soph. *Ajax.* p. 374, Note.

[86] Ἄλλα μὶν τὰ σχήματα, ἄλλα δὲ τὰ νοήματα. Οὐ γὰρ πάντως Θεὸς ἀσπάσεται ὑακίνθι καὶ πορφύρα καὶ κόκκῳ καὶ βύσσῳ· Θεὸς γὰρ ψυχῶν ἀτιμῶ καθαρότητι· ἀλλ' ἐν ταῖς σωματικαῖς ἄντοι διαγράφει τῶν ἀρετῶν τὴν εἰκόνα. Εἰ γὰρ ἀληθῶς ταῖς στολαῖς ἐκτ-

ταις ταῖς ἐνδόξοις ἐκτπαύετο διὰ τί πρὸ τοῦ Ἀαρὼν τὸν Μωυσῆν οὐκ ἐνέδυσεν.

[87] ἵνα μάθῃς ὅτι τῷ τελείῳ ἀρκεῖ ἡ ἀρετὴ πρὸς κόσμον. For the meaning of τέλειος compare Note 34. The word feems here to be ufed of the perfection of the Gofpel as compared with the imperfect and typical character of the law.

[88] The original text feems to be corrupt. As no queftion of importance is involved, I need not enter into the hiftory of the conjecturally amended text tranflated as above.

[89] διὰ τοῦτο καὶ ἐν τῇ ἐκκλησίᾳ ἐν ταῖς χειροτονίαις τῶν ἱερέων τὸ εὐαγγέλιον τοῦ Χριστοῦ ἐπὶ κεφαλῆς τίθεται, ἵνα μάθῃ ὁ χειροτ-

gofpel of Chrift is laid upon their heads, that he who is ordained
may learn that he then receiveth the true tiara of the Gofpel; and
may learn this alfo, that though he be head of all, yet doth he act in
fubjection to God's laws; though he be ruler of all, yet is he too
under rule to the law; though in all things a fetter forth of the Word,
yet himfelf to that Word in fubjection. Therefore faid one, a worthy
man of the former times, Ignatius by name, of high renown as bifhop
and as martyr, when writing to a certain prieft,[90] " *Without thy will let
nought be done: but thyfelf do nought without the will of God.*" We
fee then that to one who is chief in prieftly miniftry to God the
Gofpels (laid upon his head) are a fign that he is under authority.
For this caufe Paul fpeaketh concerning a woman having her head
covered, " *The woman ought to have wherewith to cover her head,*" this
covering being the fymbol of authority. The tiara then was the fign
of authority; and fo, too, was the golden plate, whereon was infcribed
that which is written in God's Word, the Name of God being thereon
engraved, and fhowing this firft, that the Name of God is none other
than the power of God.

After the prieftly cap and the golden plate, there are two emeralds
on the fhoulders of the high-prieft, having upon them the names of
fix tribes on the one fide, and of the other fix on the other fide.
Herein is a fign of what, in the prieft, fhould be fet forth to view.
And the emerald is affigned unto him, as having a twofold beauty;
in refpect of its colour, pale, yet lovely to look upon, and in refpect
of its purity, like in power to a mirror. And as a prieft fhould
exercife himfelf in all holy abftinence, and in his life be as a mirror
unto men, therefore doth God will that the high-prieft fhould bear
the fymbol of virtue upon his fhoulders. Yet why upon the fhoulders?
As the name of God is fet upon his head, fo is joint[91] fet upon

---

νούμενος ὅτι τὴν ἀληθινὴν τοῦ εὐαγγελίου τιάραν
λαμβάνει· καὶ ἵνα μάθῃ ὅτι εἰ καὶ πάντων ἐστὶ
κεφαλὴ ἀλλ' ὑπὸ τούτους πράττει τοὺς νόμους,
κ. τ. λ. Thomaffinus, referring to this paffage,
fays, and with good reafon: *Inde non inepte
colligeret quis fimpliciffima tunc fuiffe pontificum
capitis indumenta.* He might have faid yet
more, that from this paffage compared with that
of S. Germanus, (quoted later in this volume)
to which alfo he refers, it fcarcely admits of
doubt, that no epifcopal infignia correfponding
to the tiara of the high-prieft were known at

Conftantinople in the 6th century, or even at
the beginning of the 8th.

[90] ἱερεὺς is here ufed in reference to a
Chriftian *bifhop* (it is the letter to Polycrates
that is here quoted). Compare Note 61.

[91] The two precious ftones here fpoken of
ferved the purpofe of a *clafp.* Hence apparently the allufion in the text: ἱττώδὲ οἱ οὐ
θεοῦ ὥσπερ ἐπὶ τῆς κεφαλῆς, τὸ ἄρθρον ἐπὶ τοῦ
ἄρθρου. The explanation is unfatisfactory, but
I have no better to fuggeft.

joint. And once more, why upon the fhoulders? Becaufe the fhoulders are fignificant of activity,[92] feeing that to them doth active power belong. . . . Upon the breaft of the prieft was worn the oracle, or. breaftplate, containing the twelve graven ftones,—fardius, topaz, emerald, carbuncle, fapphire, jafper, jacynth, agate, amethyft, chryfolith, beryl, onyx. Among thefe twelve ftones were diftributed the names of the twelve tribes. And here, too, is a faying hard to be underftood. Above, upon the fhoulders, the ftones were of one kind, and bearing but one name, as emeralds. But lower down upon the breaft the ftones are thus diverfe. What doth this mean? Seeing that human nature, of which we had our birth, is one, but that by diverfities of will we are divided, therefore is one of thefe fymbols affigned unto the will, the other to that nature which is common to man. By the Name of God, then, was fignified active virtue, the elements whereof are reafon and truth.

On the lower border of the prieft's (61 α) robe, is the fringe[93] thereof, whereon are flowers and pomegranates, with golden fruits and bells. And what meant thefe in the vefture of the prieft (61 α)? Shall we deem that God found pleafure in thefe flowers? Was it of His defire that the prieft fhould be clothed round about with flowers that are of earth (61 α)? Not fo. But in this outward habit of the prieft (61 α) He fetteth forth the image of all virtues. Above, upon the head, the Name of God; upon the breaft, the Oracle; below, flowers and fruits, even the righteous habits of Chriftian virtues, fuch as are merciful kindnefs, juftice, brotherly love.[94]

---

[92] ἐπειδὴ πραξέως ἐστι σημεῖον. 'Η γὰρ πρακτικὴ δύναμις ἐν τοῖς ὤμοις ἥρτηται. Compare Note 35.

[93] λῶμα, as in the LXX.

[94] It will be feen on perufal of the paffage above given that its language throughout is fuch as none could with any probability be fuppofed to ufe, who deemed that the drefs worn in offices of holy miniftry by himfelf and by other Chriftian bifhops or priefts, had been modelled of fet purpofe, by apoftolic, or by later ecclefiaftical, authority, upon the type of the Levitical veftments. See more particularly the paffages quoted in Notes 86, 87, and 89.

XVII.

DIVUS GREGORIUS PAPA.[96]

ON THE LEVITICAL VESTMENTS AND INSIGNIA.

EXPOSITIO MORALIS IN BEATUM JOB, LIB. XXVIII. CAP. VI.

[COMMENTING on the words, *Ubi eras quando ponebam fundamenta terræ* (Job, xxxviii. 4), he writes as follows :]—

" *In Scriptura facra quid aliud fundamenta quam prædicatores accipimus? Quos dum primos Dominus in fanĉta Ecclefia pofuit, tota in eis fequentis fabricæ ftruĉtura furrexit. Unde et Sacerdos cum taber-naculum ingreditur duodecim lapides portare in peĉtore jubetur : quia vide-licet femetipfum pro nobis facrificium offerens Pontifex nofter, dum fortes in ipfo exordio prædicatores exhibuit, duodecim lapides fub capite in prima fui corporis parte portavit. Sanĉti itaque Apoftoli et pro prima oftenfione ornamenti lapides funt in peĉtore, et pro prima foliditate ædificii in folo fundamenta. Unde David Propheta cum fanĉtam Ecclefiam in fub-limibus Apoftolorum mentibus poni ædificarique confpiceret, fundamenta ejus, inquit, in montibus fanĉtis. (Ps. lxxxvi.) Cum vero in facro eloquio non fundamenta fed fingulari numero fundamentum dicitur, nullus alius nifi ipfe Dominus defignatur, per cujus divinitatis potentiam nutantia infirmitatis noftræ corda folidantur. De quo et Paulus ait :* Fundamen-tum aliud nemo poteft ponere præter id quod pofitum eft Chriftus Jefus. *Ipfe quippe fundamentum fundamentorum eft : quia et origo eft inchoantium et conftantia robuftorum.*" [96]

" By ' foundations ' in the Holy Scripture, we are to underftand thofe preachers of God's Word (the Apoftles) who were fet fore-moft in the Church by the Lord, and on whom, therefore, was built up the whole ftruĉture of the fpiritual Building that followed. And

---

[96] St. Gregory the Great, Bifhop of Rome from A.D. 590 to 604.

this is the reafon that the high-prieft, when he enters the Tabernacle, is bidden to wear the twelve ftones (of the 'Rationale') on his breaft, becaufe our own High-prieft, in fetting forth at the very firft mighty preachers of His Word, carried, as it were, twelve ftones, in fubjection to the Head, in the forefront of His own Body. And fo the Holy Apoftles are both ftones upon the breaft, in accordance with that firft fetting forth of ornament, and in refpect of the firft folid grounding of 'the Building' are as foundation-ftones laid in the ground. Hence that word of Prophet David as he beheld the holy Church being founded and built up upon the exalted minds of the Apoftles, '*Her foundations,*' faith he, '*are upon the holy mountains.*' But when in the Divine Word we hear fpeak not of 'foundations,' as of many, but of 'the foundation' as of one only, then is none other intended but the Lord alone, by the power of whofe divine nature fteadfaftnefs is given to the tottering heart of human infirmity. Of Him fpeaketh Paul when he faith, 'Other foundation can no man lay fave that which is already laid, even Chrift Jefus.' For He is the Foundation of all foundations, feeing that He is both the beginning of Life to them that begin, and the fuftaining ftrength of them that are ftrong."[96]

---

[96] This paffage is quoted as a ftrong evidence (to fay the leaft) that to St. Gregory nothing was known in the drefs of Chriftian Bifhops that correfponded to the Rational of the Jewifh high-prieft; and that the idea of any fuch correfpondence being intended never occurred to him. He neither cafts about to find any fuch correfpondence, nor thinks it neceffary to account for there being none. Compare his own words (quoted below, p. 61), *Veftimenta facerdotis quid aliud quam recta opera debemus accipere?* "By the veftments of the high-prieft what are we to underftand but righteous works?"

XVIII.

DIVUS GREGORIUS PAPA.

SYMBOLISM OF THE HIGH-PRIEST'S BREASTPLATE.

PASTORALIS CURA, PARS SECUNDA (TOM. I. p. 1185), CAP. II.

[IN this chapter he is fpeaking of the purity of thought which becometh them who take upon them the charge of "*carrying living
veffels* [97] *into the Temple of Eternity.*" He proceeds as follows :]—

*Hinc divina voce præcipitur ut in Aaron pectore rationale judicii
vittis ligantibus imprimatur : quatenus facerdotale cor nequaquam cogitationes fluxæ poffideant, fed ratio fola conftringat : ne indiscretum quid vel
inutile cogitet, qui ad exemplum aliis conftitutus ex gravitate vitæ femper
debet oftendere quantam in pectore rationem portet. In quo etiam rationali
vigilanter adjungitur ut duodecim nomina patriarcharum defcribantur.
Afcriptos etenim patres femper in pectore ferre, eft antiquorum vitam fine
intermiffione cogitare. [Plura et fimilia in eandem fere fententiam fequuntur.]* [98]

"Hence it is that by the voice of God that precept is given that
on the breaft of Aaron the (breaftplate) Rational of Judgment fhould
be clofely faftened with attaching bands, forafmuch as it would not be
meet that the heart of the prieft fhould be occupied by loofe imagina-
tions, but by reafon alone be conftrained : that nothing indifcreet nor
mifchievous may fill the mind of one, who, fet as he is for an enfample
unto others, ought to fhow plainly how much of reafon he beareth on
his breaft. And of this Rational this, too, is carefully enjoined, that
the twelve names of the Patriarchs be thereon infcribed. For by the
continual bearing of the fathers graven upon the breaft, is meant the
remembering without ceafing the lives of them that are of the former
times." [*Here follows much more to the fame effect, in general, though
not verbal, accordance with the comment of S. Jerome already quoted.*] [98]

---

[97] In allufion to the words of Ifaiah, lii. 11,
Mundamini qui fertis vafa Domini.

[98] To this paffage the fame remark applir,
as to the laft quoted. See Note 96.

XIX.

DIVUS GREGORIUS PAPA.

OF THE EPHOD OR SUPERHUMERAL.

Pastoralis Cura, Pars ii. Cap. iii. p. 1187.

[He is urging upon the Paſtor that he ſhould ever lead the way in all good work, that ſo the Flock, guided at once by the voice of their Shepherd, and by his good life, may make their onward way by example rather than by precept only. In illuſtration he refers[99] to the ſetting apart (by Levitical law) of the right ſhoulder and the breaſt[100] of the offerings as the prieſt's portion. He purſues his thought in theſe words :—]

" *Unde ſupernæ quoque vocis imperio in utroque humero ſacerdos vela-mine ſuperhumeralis aſtringitur :*[101] *ut contra adverſa ac proſpera virtutum ſemper ornamento muniatur: quatenus juxta vocem Pauli, Per arma juſtitiæ a dextris ſiniſtriſque gradiens, cum ad ſola quæ anteriora ſunt nititur, in nullo delectationis infimæ latere flectatur. Non hunc proſpera elevent, non adverſa perturbent, non blanda uſque ad voluptatem demulceant, non aſpera uſque ad deſperationem premant: ut dum nullis paſſionibus intentionem mentis humiliat, quanta in utroque humero ſuperhumeralis pulchritudine tegatur oſtendat. Quod recte ſuperhumerale ex auro, hya-cintho, purpura, bis tincto cocco, et tota fieri byſſo, præcipitur, ut quanta ſacerdos*[102] *clareſcere virtutum diverſitate debeat, demonſtretur. In ſacer-dotis*[102] *quippe habitu ante omnia aurum fulget, ut in eo intellectus ſapientiæ principaliter emicet. Cui hyacinthus, qui aerio colore*[103] *reſplendet, adjun-gitur: ut per omne quod intelligendo penetrat non ad favores intimos ſed ad amorem cæleſtium ſurgat; ne, dum incautus ſuis laudibus capitur, ipſo*

---

[99] So S. Jerome previouſly, Epiſtle to Fabiola.

[100] Compare Note 37, above.

[101] *Velamine ſuperhumeralis aſtringitur.* [*Super-humeralis* is here a " genitive of appoſition."] " He hath the covering of the ephod *faſtened cloſely about him* on either ſhoulder." The alluſion is to the marked contraſt between the *cloſe-fitting* garb of the Levitical prieſt (ſpecially noticeable in the ephod), as com-pared with the more flowing veſtments of

Chriſtian miniſtry. See above Note 6, p. 2. In that Note the words quoted from the original text of Joſephus ſhould be read as follows: στριγγραμμένος τῷ σώματι, καὶ τὰς χειρίδας περὶ τοῖς βραχίοσιν κατιοφιγμένος.

[102] *Sacerdos* is here the high-prieſt. Com-pare Note 61 a.

[103] *Hyacinthus aerio colore.* See above, Note 33, p. 22.

*etiam veritatis intellectu vacuetur. Auro quoque et hyacintho purpura per-
miscetur : ut videlicet sacerdotale* (61 ζ) *cor, cum summa quæ prædicat
sperat, in semetipso suggestiones vitiorum reprimat, easque velut regia
potestate contradicat : quatenus nobilitatem semper intimæ regenerationis
aspiciat, et cælestis regni sibi habitum* [104] *moribus defendat. De hac
quippe nobilitate spiritus per Petrum dicitur :* Vos autem genus electum,
regale sacerdotium . . . . *Auro autem, hyacintho, byssò ac purpurâ, bis
tinctus coccus adjungitur, ut ante interni Judicis oculos omnia virtutum
bona ex charitate decorentur : et cuncta quæ coram hominibus rutilant,
hæc in conspectu occulti Arbitri flamma intimi amoris accendat. Quæ
scilicet charitas, quia Deum simul et proximum diligit, quasi ex duplici
tinctura fulgescit. Qui igitur sic ad Authoris speciem anhelat ut proximorum curam negligat : vel sic proximorum curam exsequitur ut a divino
amore torpescat : quia unum horum quodlibet negligit in superhumeralis
ornamento habere coccum bis tinctum nescit. Sed cum mens ad præcepta
charitatis tenditur, restat proculdubio ut per abstinentiam caro maceretur.
Unde et bis tincto cocco byssus adjungitur. De terra enim byssus nitenti
specie oritur.* [105] *Et quid per byssum nisi candens decore munditiæ corporalis
castitas designatur ? Quæ videlicet byssus torta pulchritudine superhumeralis innectitur : quia tunc castimonia ad perfectum munditiæ candorem ducitur cum per abstinentiam* [106] *caro fatigatur. Cumque inter virtutes
cæteras etiam afflictæ carnis meritum proficit, quasi in diversa superhumeralis specie byssus torta candescit.* [107]

---

[104] *Cælestis regni habitum,*—the dress of celes-
tial royalty (*regni* = kingship rather than *kingdom*), i.e. the dress proper to one who is a partaker of that " royal priesthood " of which the
text goes on to speak.

[105] *Byssus nitenti specie—candens,* &c. For the
word *byssus* see Note 5, p. 2 ; and for the
brilliant whiteness (*candor*) here attributed to it,
compare Note 19, p. 9.

[106] The *maceratio carnis per abstinentiam* is
here spoken of as specially typified by the *byssus*
of the high-priest's ephod. The reason of this
will be made clear by the following quotation.
*Sicut byssus vel linum candorem, quem ex natura
non habet, multis tunsionibus attritum par artem
acquirit, sic et hominis caro munditiam quam non
obtinet per naturam, multis castigationibus macerata
sortitur per gratiam.* Innocentius III. Myste-
riorum Missæ, lib. i. cap. li.

[107] I have thought it unnecessary to translate
the above passage at length. It is sufficient to

observe upon its general character. It will be
seen that throughout a spiritual antitype (not
an actual one) is traced, between the literal
vestments of the Levitical and the spiritual
clothing of the Christian priesthood. The
divers colours of the high-priest's ephod are
intended to teach *with what variety of virtues*
he should be adorned who serves in holy ministry to God. The gold is significant of the
"understanding of wisdom " (because of its
exceeding *preciousness;* he was thinking probably of Job, xxviii. 15–19). The *blue,* of
heavenly (Note 33) aspiration. The *purple*
of the "power as of a king " wherewith the
Christian priest should crush the power of evil
thought within his heart. The scarlet is typical of charity, kindled, as he suggests, as into
fire, by the flame of holy love. The linen,
fine and white, of the subduing (Note 106) of
the flesh by Christian abstinence.

XX.

DIVUS GREGORIUS PAPA.

OF THE BELLS UPON THE TUNIC OF THE EPHOD; AND OF THE LEVITICAL VESTMENTS IN GENERAL.

Pastoralis Cura, Pars ii. Cap. iv. p. 1189.

[The Christian pastor should know both how with discretion to keep silence, and, to the profit of them that hear, *to speak*. In this regard he must be prepared boldly to rebuke if need be. He then proceeds:—]

Clavis quippe apertionis sermo correptionis est: quia increpatio culpam detegit, quam sæpe nescit ipse etiam qui perpetravit. Hinc Paulus ait (Tit. i. 9) : Ut potens sit exhortari in doctrina sana, et eos qui contradicunt redarguere. . . . . *Hinc per Esaiam Dominus admonet dicens :* Clama, ne cesses, quasi tuba exalta vocem tuam. *Præconis quippe officium suscipit quisquis ad sacerdotium accedit : ut ante adventum Judicis qui terribiliter sequitur ipse scilicet clamando gradiatur. Sacerdos ergo si prædicationis est nescius quam clamoris vocem daturus est præco mutus ? Hinc est enim quod super pastores primos in linguarum specie Spiritus Sanctus insedit : quia nimirum quos repleverit de Se, protinus loquentes facit. Hinc Moysi præcipitur ut tabernaculum Sacerdos ingrediens tintinnabulis ambiatur, ut videlicet voces prædicationis habeat, ne superni Spectatoris judicium ex silentio offendat. Scriptum quippe est* (Exod. xxviii. 35) : Ut audiatur sonitus quando ingreditur sanctuarium in conspectu Domini, et non moriatur. *Sacerdos namque ingrediens vel egrediens moritur, si de eo sonitus non audiatur : quia iram contra se occulti Judicis exigit, si sine sonitu prædicationis incedit. Aptè autem tintinnabula vestimentis illius describuntur inserta. Vestimenta etenim sacerdotis quid aliud quam recta opera debemus accipere ? Propheta attestante qui ait*

(Ps. cxxxii. 9) : Sacerdotes tui induantur juftitiam. *Veftimentis itaque illius tintinnabula inhærent, ut vitæ viam cum linguæ fonitu ipfa quoque bona opera clament facerdotis.*[108]

---

[108] In this paffage again, as in thofe already quoted, the "bells" of the older facerdotal drefs, and the veftments in general, receive a purely fpiritual interpretation as referred to Chriftian priefthood. The "bells" are the voice of him who in God's Name is both "apt to teach," and "bold to rebuke." And the veftments are good works, the "clothing of righteoufnefs" which becometh the priefts of the Lord.

XXI.

DIVUS GREGORIUS PAPA.

THE USE OF THE PALLIUM, A MATTER OF ROMAN PRIVILEGE.

Epistolarum ex Registro Divi Gregorii Lib. iv. Ep. 2.

[Childebert, king of the Franks, had written to St. Gregory requeſt-
ing that the *Pallium*, and Vicarial authority from the ſee of Rome
(*vices Apoſtolicæ ſedis*), might be conferred on Vigilius, Biſhop of
Arles. In writing to Vigilius, and announcing his aſſent to this, St.
Gregory ſpeaks of the ſending of this *pallium* as an ' ancient cuſtom.' [109]]

Quod vero in eis (ſc. epiſtolis) juxta antiquum [110] *morem, uſum pallii ac
vices ſedis apoſtolicæ poſtulaſti, abſit ne aut tranſitoriæ poteſtatis culmen,
aut exterioris cultus ornamentum, in vicibus noſtris ac palliis quæſiſſe te
ſuſpicer. Sed quia cunctis liquet unde in Galliarum regionibus fides ſancta
prodierit,* [111] *cum priſcam conſuetudinem apoſtolicæ ſedis fraternitas veſtra*

---

[109] See Epiſt. Lib. iv. liii. in which St.
Gregory writes to Childebert himſelf on the
ſame ſubject.

[110] St. Gregory here ſtates that for Biſhops of
Arles to receive the privilege of the Roman
Pallium, and vicarial authority, was in accordance with "ancient cuſtom," or (as the context rather ſuggeſts) with "the cuſtom obſerved in former times." The *Pallium* here
ſpoken of is the *Pallium* worn by archbiſhops.
In St. Gregory's time this had already aſſumed
that later form, in which (with ſlight modifications only) it has ever ſince been retained.
That is to ſay, inſtead of being ſhaped like a
modern ſtole, as in the pictures of XVSTVS
PP. ROM., photographed in this volume, it
preſented in front the appearance of the Engliſh
letter Y, and was all but identical with the

ώμοφόριον of the Greek Church, already deſcribed (p. 49) by S. Iſidore of Peluſium.
    As for the "cuſtom of former times" to
which St. Gregory refers, full information will
be found in *Thomaſſinus, De Beneficiis*, part ii.
lib. ii. cap. liv., where the whole queſtion of
the Roman *Pallium* is treated with mnch learning and conſiderable candour : and further particulars of importance in Gieſeler's Eccl. Hiſt.
vol. i. p. 446.
    [111] St. Gregory, in ſaying this, implies, of
courſe, that the Churches of Gaul owed their
Chriſtianity to the Roman Church. It is probable, though not certain, that he was miſtaken
in ſo thinking, and that thoſe Churches were
by their firſt origin connected with the
Churches of Aſia Minor, of which Epheſus
was the primatial ſee. [See Palmer's Pri-

repetit, quid aliud quam bona suboles ad sinum matris ecclesiæ recurrit? [110]

" As for the requeſt you have made, in accordance with ancient cuſtom, in your letters addreſſed to me, that you may be allowed to uſe the *Pallium*, and be made Vicar of the Apoſtolic See, I will not for a moment fear that in making this requeſt you have had regard to any exaltation of temporary power, or to the increaſe of outward adornment. As it is clear to all men from what ſource [111] the Holy Faith ſpread in the regions of Gaul, when you aſk, as your Brotherhood now does, for the renewal of the cuſtomary privilege beſtowed of old by the Apoſtolic See, what is this but the return of a goodly offspring to the boſom of the mother Church?" [112]

---

mitive Liturgies, p. 155, 299.] However this may be, it is noteworthy that St. Gregory here gives as a reaſon why the Gallic Churches ſhould ſubmit to the patriarchal authority of the See of Rome, that from Rome they had originally received the knowledge of Chriſtian truth. He ſays not a word of it being the duty of *every* Church to ſubmit itſelf to the See of Rome as having, by Divine right, a Headſhip over the univerſal Church of Chriſt.

[112] This letter will ſerve as an example of a great number of others occurring in St. Gregory's epiſtles, relating to this (then, as now) vexed queſtion of the Papal Pallium. See lib. iv. 53, 54. 55, 56; lib. v. ep. 7, 8, 18, 33; lib. vii. ep. 11; lib. x. ep. 55.

XXII.

DIVUS GREGORIUS PAPA.

THE USE OF THE *MAPPULA* REGARDED AT ROME
AS A MATTER OF PAPAL PRIVILEGE,
NOT OF GENERAL RIGHT.

Epistola Joannis Episcopi (Ravennatis) ad Gregorium Papam
de usu Pallii et diversis ornatibus [tom. 2. p. 1055]
Lib. x. Ep. 55.

*Quod de mappulis a presbyteris et diaconis meis præsumptum Apostolatus
vester scripsit, vere fateor, tædet me aliquid exinde commemorare, cum per
se veritas, quæ apud dominum meum sola prævalet, ipsa sufficiat. Nam cum
hoc minoribus circa urbem* [113] *constitutis ecclesiis licitum sit, poterit etiam
apostolatus mei domini, si venerabilem clerum primæ Apostolicæ sedis suæ
requirere dignatur, modis omnibus invenire, quia quoties ad episcopatus
ordinationem, seu responsi, sacerdotes vel levitæ Ravennatis Ecclesiæ
Romam venerunt, quod omnes in oculis sanctissimorum decessorum vestrorum
cum mappulis sine reprehensione aliqua procedebant. Quare etiam eo
tempore quod (leg. quo) istic a prædecessore vestro peccator ordinatus sum,
cuncti presbyteri et diaconi mei in obsequium Domini Papæ mecum pro-
cedentes usi sunt.*

----

[113] By *urbem* is of courfe meant Rome.

K

XXIII.

DIVUS GREGORIUS PAPA.

Lib. ii. Ep. liv. (*apud Labbé Conc.* tom. v. p. 1127) ad Joannem
Episcopum Ravennatem.

[After a long and fevere reproof of the mode in which the bifhop
had prefumed to wear the *pallium*, on other days, and in other places,
than was ufual, he adds the following concerning the *mappula*, or
maniple] : —

Illud autem quod pro utendis a clero veftro mappulis fcripfiftis, a noftris
eft clericis fortiter obviatum, dicentibus nulli hoc unquam alii cuilibet
ecclefiæ conceffum fuiffe : nec Ravennates clericos illic vel in Romana
civitate tale aliquid cum fua confcientia præfumpfiffe : nec fi tentatum
effet ex furtiva ufurpatione fibi præjudicium generari. Sed etiamfi in
qualibet ecclefia hoc præfumptum fuerit, afferunt emendandum, quod non
conceffione Romani Pontificis fed fola furreptione præfumitur. Sed nos
fervantes honorem fraternitatis tuæ, licet contra voluntatem antedicti cleri
noftri, tamen primis diaconibus veftris, quos nobis quidam teftificati funt
etiam ante eis ufos fuiffe, in obfequio duntaxat tuo mappulis uti permit-
timus : alio autem tempore vel alias perfonas hoc agere vehementiffime pro-
hibemus.

XXIV.

DIVUS GREGORIUS PAPA.

THE PRIVILEGE OF WEARING A DALMATIC, GRANTED TO AREGIUS, BISHOP OF GAP, AND TO HIS ARCHDEACON.

EPIST. EX REGISTRO, LIB. VII. TOM. II. p. 924.

[AFTER writing at fome length upon other fubjects, he proceeds as follows] : —

Præterea communis filius Petrus diaconus nobis innotuit quod fraternitas veftra, tempore quo hic fuit, popofcerit ut fibi et archidiacono fuo utendi dalmaticis licentiam præberemus. Sed quia ita hominum fuorum infirmitate compulfus feftinanter abfceffit, ut nec ipfe mæror incumbens diu, ut dignum erat, et res defiderata pofcebat, fineret imminere : et nos in multis implicitos ut Ecclefiafticæ rationis confideratio novum hoc inconfulte et fubito non permitteret indulgere : idcirco poftulatæ rei prolongatus effectus eft. Nunc vero charitatis tuæ bona revocantes ad animum, hujus authoritatis noftræ ferie, petita concedimus, atque te et archidiaconum tuum Dalmaticarum ufu decorandos effe conceffimus, eafdemque Dalmaticas, dilectiffimo filio noftro Cyriaco Abbate deferente, tranfmifimus.

XXV.

S. ISIDORE OF SEVILLE.

OF THE INSIGNIA OF CHRISTIAN PRIESTHOOD.

[IN the fecond book of the *De Officiis Ecclefiafticis*, St. Ifidore [114] treats at length of the various orders of the Chriftian miniftry. The following paffages ferve to indicate what in his time were regarded as the characteriftic infignia of the clergy] :

CAP. VII.

Quod detonfo capite fuperius, inferius circali corona relinquitur, facer-dotium regnumque ecclefiæ in eis exiftimo figurari. Tiara enim apud veteres conftituebatur in capite facerdotum. Hæc ex byffo confecta, rotunda erat quafi fphera media; et hoc fignificatur in parte capitis tonfa. Corona autem, latitudo aurei eft circuli quæ regum capita cingit. Utrumque igitur fignum exprimitur in capite clericorum, ut impleatur etiam quadam corporis fimilitudine quod fcriptum eft, Petro apoftolo præ-docente, Vos eftis genus electum, regale facerdotium.

"The cutting off the hair from the upper part of the head, and leaving it in the form of a crown, lower down, is in my judgment a figurative fetting forth of the priefthood and royalty of the Church. For with God's ancient people it was cuftomary to place a tiara on the heads of priefts. This 'tiara' was made of byffus, and was round like a fphere, divided in twain; and this it is which is fignified by the part of the head which is fhorn. But the chaplet of hair reprefents the broad circlet of gold which encompaffes the heads of kings. Each of thefe emblems therefore is expreffed on the heads of the clergy, fo as by outward fimilitude to fet forth that which is written, in the teaching of the apoftle Peter, *Ye are a chofen generation, a royal priefthood.*

---

[114] S. Ifidore was born at Carthagena about the year 560 A.D., and died A.D. 636.

CAP. V.

THE PASTORAL STAFF AND EPISCOPAL RING.

*Huic (sc. Episcopo) dum consecratur datur baculus ut ejus indicio sub-
ditam plebem vel regat, vel corrigat, vel infirmitates infirmorum sustineat.
Datur et anulus propter signum pontificalis honoris, vel signaculum secre-
torum. Nam multa sunt quæ carnalium minusque intelligentium sensibus
occultantes sacerdotes quasi sub signaculo abscondunt, ne indignis quibusque
sacramenta Dei aperiantur.*

"To the bishop at the time of his consecration is given a staff,
that, as this sign suggests, he may both rule and correct the people
committed to his care, and support the infirmities of such as are weak.
A ring likewise is given him, for the signifying of pontifical dignity,
or to be as it were a seal for guarding of things secret. For many
things there are which they who minister unto God keep concealed
from the knowledge of carnal men and wanting in wise understanding,
lest divine mysteries be laid open to such as are unworthy."

CAP. VIII.

OF THE WHITE MINISTERING DRESS WORN
BY DEACONS.

*Propterea Altari albis induti assistunt ut cælestem vitam habeant, candi-
dique ad hostias et immaculati accedant, mundi scilicet corpore et pudore
incorrupti.*

"The reason why they" (the deacons [115] of whom he is speaking)
"assist at the altar clad in white garments is this, that a heavenly [116]
life may be theirs, and that bright and pure, and without stain, they
may approach unto the holy offerings, being clean in body and in
chastenefs undefiled."

---

[115] In Cap. vii, when speaking of the second
order of the Christian ministry, S. Isidore says
nothing of any distinctive dress or insignia
specially characteristic of the Presbyter. But
I cannot forbear quoting the following expression of half-humorous severity, which he
lets fall in passing. "Presbyters," he says,
"are so called not from any reference to the
decrepitude of old age, but because of the
wisdom which is proper to fulness of years.
"But this being so," he adds, "one cannot but
wonder why it is that fools are ordained."
Quod si ita est, mirum cur insipientes ordinentur.

[116] His thought is of the bright white garments in which angels are described as clad.

XXVI.

ST. ISIDORE OF SEVILLE.

ON THE VESTMENTS OF LEVITICAL PRIESTHOOD.

[In Cap. v. of the fame book that has been quoted above, viz. *De Eccles. Off.* Lib. ii., St. Isidore treats of priesthood in general, and has occasion to speak of the vestments worn by Aaron and by his sons. He writes as follows] : —

Veniamus nunc ad sacratissimos ordines clericorum, eorumque originem demonstremus, quod est sacerdotii fundamentum vel quo authore pontificalis ordo adolevit in seculo. Initium quidem sacerdotii Aaron fuit, quanquam et Melchisedech prior obtulerit sacrificium, et post hunc Abraham, Isaac et Jacob. Sed isti spontanea voluntate, non sacerdotali authoritate, ista fecerunt. Cæterum Aaron primus in lege sacerdotale nomen accepit, primusque pontificali stola indutus victimas obtulit, jubente Domino ac loquente ad Moysem, Accipe, inquit, Aaron et filios ejus, et adplicabis ad ostium Tabernaculi Testimonii : cumque laveris patrem cum filiis indues Aaron vestimentis suis, id est Linea et Tunica et Superhumerali et Rationali, quod constringes balteo, et pones tiaram, et oleum unctionis fundes super caput ejus, atque hoc ritu consecrabitur. Filios quoque illius adplicabis et indues tunicis lineis, cingesque balteo, Aaron scilicet et liberos ejus, et impones eis mitras eruntque sacerdotes mei lege perpetua. *Quo loco contemplari oportet Aaron summum sacerdotem id est episcopum fuisse. Nam filios ejus presbyterorum figuram præmonstrasse. Fuerunt enim filii Aaron et ipsi sacerdotes quibus merito adstare debuissent Levitæ, sicut summo sacerdoti. Sed hoc fuit inter summum sacerdotem Aaron et filios ejusdem Aaron, qui et ipsi sacerdotes fuerunt, quod Aaron super tunicam accipiebat poderem stolam* [17] *sanctam, coronam auream,*

---

[17] It will be seen from the above that the "holy robe" of Aaron was in St. Isidore's judgment something distinct from the white tunic common to Aaron himself and to his sons. And though the mode in which he enumerates the vestments and insignia leaves it open to doubt, whether by 'Stola' he means the vesture of the high-priest taken as a whole, or one particular portion of it, the latter seems on the whole more probable; and if so, the "Tunic of Blue" must be the vestment to which he refers.

mitram et zonam auream et Superhumerale, et cætera quæ supra memorata sunt. Filii autem Aaron cincti tantummodo et tiarati [118] *ita adstabant sacrificio Dei.*

---

[118] Note here, that with St. Isidore, the word *corona* (note 54, p. 32) is used in speaking of the distinctive decoration added to the *mitra* of the high-priest, while the sons of Aaron are spoken of as *tiarati*, wearing a "*tiara.*" But the same word *tiara* had pre-viously been used (in quoting from Exodus) of the cap, or linen mitre, worn by the high-priest. [See note 84, p. 52, as to the meaning of "*Tiara.*" The passage there quoted from the *De Originibus* of St. Isidore will illustrate his usage of *corona* here.]

XXVII.

ST. ISIDORE OF SEVILLE.

ENUMERATION OF THE VESTMENTS OF LEVITICAL PRIESTHOOD.

DE ORIGINIBUS, LIB. XIX. CAP. XXI.

[HE enters in this part of his treatise on the subject of dress in general ; and after a few introductory lines as to the original invention of the textile arts, he commences with the "eight kinds of sacerdotal vestments mentioned in the law."]

Octo sunt in lege genera sacerdotalium [119] *vestimentorum.* Poderis *est tunica sacerdotalis linea, corpori astricta,*[120] *usque ad pedes descendens. Unde et nuncupatur, πόδας enim Græci pedes dicunt. Hæc vulgo camisia* [121] *vocatur.* Abaneth *cingulum sacerdotale rotundum polimita arte ex cocco purpura hyacinthoque contextum, ita ut flores atque gemmæ in eo videantur esse distinctæ.* Pileum *est ex bysso* [122] *rotundum quasi sphæra media, caput tegens sacerdotale, et in occipitio vitta constrictum. Hoc Græci et nostri tiaram* [123] *vel galeam* [124] *vocant.*

Machil *quæ est tunica talaris, tota hyacinthina, habens ad pedes* LXXII *tintinnabula ; totidemque intermixta ac dependentia punica mala.*

Ephod *quod Latine interpretatur superindumentum. Erat enim pal-*

---

[119] He uses the term, inclusively, of both high priest, and priest of the second order. Compare note 61.

[120] On this closeness of fit here noticed, see above, note 6, p. 2.

[121] He follows St. Jerome in comparing the *tunica talaris* of the Levitical priest to the *camisia* of ordinary life in his own time. See note 23, p. 13.

[122] On the word *Byssus* (βύσσος) see note 5, p. 2. The word was never so naturalised in the Latin language as to pass into common use. St. Isidore speaks of it as a term whose real meaning was doubtful. "*Byssus candida confecta ex quodam genere lini grossioris. Sunt et qui genus quoddam lini byssum esse existiment.*" Etym. lib. xix. cap. xxii.

[123] For the word *Tiara*, see note 84, p. 52.

[124] Of several various readings which are here found (due to the ignorance of copyists when classical terms are concerned), the true one is probably *galerum*. This was a word specially used of the sacerdotal cap of heathen priesthood (see Index *in voc.*). At a later time the scarlet hat, assigned to the Roman cardinals by Innocent IV. (at the Council of Lyons, A.D. 1244), was known as *galerus rubeus.* See Dufresne Glossar. *in voc.*

lium [125] *fuperhumerale ex quattuor coloribus et auro contextum, habens in utroque humero lapides duos fmaragdinos auro conclufos, in quibus fculpta erant nomina patriarcharum.*

Logicon *quod Latine dicitur rationale, pannus duplex, auro et quattuor textus coloribus, habens magnitudinem palmi per quadrum, cui intexti erant quattuor* [126] *pretiofiffimi lapides. Hic pannus fuper humerale* [l.eg. *fuperhumerali*] *contra pectus Pontificis annectebatur.*

Petalum *aurea lamina in fronte Pontificis, quæ nomen Dei tetragrammatum Hebraicis literis habebat fcriptum.*

Batin (fic) *five feminalia, id eft bracæ lineæ ufque ad genua pertingentes, quibus verecunda facerdotis velabantur.*

[Having thus enumerated the veftments of Levitical priefthood, he goes on to defcribe briefly every other known garment belonging either to male or to female drefs. Interfperfed among fuch terms as *Toga, Chlamys, Sagum, Mantum, Prætexta,* we find the following] : —

PALLIUM.

Pallium [127] *eft quo adminiftrantium fcapulæ conteguntur, ut dum miniftrant expeditius difcurrant.*[128] Plautus : Si quid facturus es appende in humeris pallium, et pergat quantum valet tuorum pedum pernicitas. *Dictum autem pallium a pellibus, quia prius fuper indumenta pellicea veteres induebantur, quafi pellea, five a palla per diminutionem.*

PENULA.

Penula eft pallium [129] *cum fimbriis longis.*

---

[125] *Pallium.* St. Ifidore generally ufes this word as a generic term, nearly equal to our own "garment," requiring fome fpecial defcription to indicate any fpecial article of drefs. Thus the *paludamentum* is defcribed as *infigne pallium Imperatorum* ; the *penula* as *pallium cum fimbriis longis* ; the *lacerna* as *pallium fimbriatum quo olim foli milites utebantur.* So again of the *prætexta puerilis,* the *penula,* and many others. A more fpecific ufe of the word will be noticed below. See note 127.

[126] We can hardly fuppofe that this miftake of *four* for *twelve* is due to St. Ifidore. Probably the eye of the copyift was caught, or his memory mifled, by the *quattuor,* which had juft preceded, in fpeaking of the colours.

[127] The *Pallium* here noticed is the Greek ἱμάτιον, the outer garment or wrapper, worn occafionally at leaft by perfons of all conditions of life, as already noticed in the Introduction

(fee Index *in voc.*) It correfponded in general ufe to the Roman *toga,* but in the earlier Roman language (that of republican times) was as diftinctly fuggeftive of a Greek coftume as the *toga* of that of Rome.

[128] St. Ifidore has been led into error by this particular paffage of Plautus. The *pallium* in itfelf was no more fuited for vigorous exertion than the *toga* or the *penula.* And it is precifely for this reafon that in this paffage of Plautus (Captiv. Act. iv. Sc. 1) Ergafilus, the Parafite, fays, *eodem pacto ut comici fervi folent conjiciam in collum pallium, primo ex me hanc rem ut audiat, i.e.* he will gather his cloak about his fhoulders *to enable him to run the fafter.* But fo to carry the *pallium* was the exception, not, as St. Ifidore feems to think, the rule.

[129] On this generic ufe of *pallium* fee above, note 125.

OF THE CASULA.

Casula [130] *est vestis cucullata, dicta per diminutionem a casa, quod totum hominem tegat, quasi minor casa.   Unde et cuculla quasi minor cella.   Sic et Græce planetas dictos volunt, quia oris errantibus evagantur.   Unde et stellæ planetæ, id est vagæ suo errore motuque discurrunt.*

OF THE DALMATIC.

[Throughout this portion of his Treatise St. Isidore gives but one slight intimation of any vestment which he regards as belonging to offices of Christian ministry.   He is describing various modifications of the *tunic,* and amongst others mentions the Dalmatic.]

Dalmatica [131] *vestis primum in Dalmatia, provincia Græciæ, texta est, tunica sacerdotalis candida, cum clavis ex purpura.*

[130] This definition of the *casula,* or "chasuble" is quoted by almost all writers on ritual, ancient and modern.   But as far as I have observed, none have noticed a remarkable confirmation of the derivation here assigned being really correct.   From another passage of St. Isidore (De Off. Eccl. lib. v.) it is clear that in his time, at least, the word *casula* was really used in the sense of a *hut,* or "*minor casa.*" He is speaking of Elias and Elisha, and other such, and says, *habitabant in solitudine, urbibusque relictis faciebant sibi casulas prope fluenta Jordanis.*

[131] For further particulars of this vestment see Index *in voc.* It is evident that by *sacerdotalis* reference is here made not to Jewish or to heathen, but to Christian *sacerdotes.* [Compare note 71.]   From very early times (those of S. Silvester according to Roman tradition) the Dalmatic had been adopted as a ministering vestment of the Church at Rome. And to this Roman usage St. Isidore probably makes reference in this passage.   But it is open to question, as far as this passage is concerned, whether by *sacerdotalis* is meant episcopal, or in a more general sense, *sacerdotal.* Compare note 71, p. 46.

XXVIII.

ACTS OF THE FOURTH COUNCIL OF TOLEDO.

HELD UNDER THE PRESIDENCY OF ST. ISIDORE OF SEVILLE, A.D. 633.

[THE acts of this Council are throughout of great interest, in their bearing upon questions of ecclesiastical antiquity. The sections of special interest to the question now under discussion are the following]:—

INSIGNIA OF CHRISTIAN MINISTRY.

§ XXVIII. *Episcopus, presbyter, aut diaconus, si a gradu suo injuste dejectus in secunda synodo innocens reperiatur, non potest esse quod fuerat nisi gradus amissos recipiat coram altario de manu episcopi; [si episcopus]* [132] *orarium, annulum et baculum : si presbyter, orarium et planetam : si diaconus, orarium et albam : si subdiaconus, patenam et calicem : sic et reliqui gradus ea in reparationem sui recipiant quæ eum ordinarentur perceperunt.*

"If a bishop, presbyter, or deacon, be unjustly deposed, and in a subsequent synod be found innocent, he cannot be what he had previously been, unless he receive again the rank he had lost from the hand of a bishop, before the altar. If he have been a bishop, he must receive *orarium (i.e.* stole), ring, and staff; if a presbyter, *orarium* and *planeta (i.e.* chasuble); if a deacon, *orarium* and alb; if a subdeacon, paten and chalice; and so the other minor orders are to receive, with a view to their restoration, what at the time of ordination they originally received."

§ XL. *Orariis duobus nec episcopo quidem licet, nec presbytero uti, quanto*

---

[132] The words *si episcopus*, are not in the present text, though evidently required by the context. The word EPI (*i.e. episcopi*) just be- | fore would easily be confused in translation with the EPS here required.

*magis diacono qui minifter eorum eft. Unum igitur orarium oportet
Levitam geftare in finiftro humero, propter quod orat, id eft prædicat:* [133]
*dextram autem partem oportet habere liberam ut expeditus ad minifterium
facerdotale difcurrat. Caveat igitur amodo Levita gemino uti orario, fed
uno tantum et puro nec ullis coloribus aut auro ornato.*

" Not even a bifhop, or a prefbyter, is allowed to wear two *oraria*
(ftoles), how much lefs a deacon who is their attendant minifter. The
deacon therefore muft wear one *orarium*, as befits his office, and
that on the left fhoulder. But the right fide fhould remain free, fo
that he may haften to and fro in duties of facerdotal fervice. The
[" Levite "] deacon therefore, from this time forth, muft not wear
his *orarium* double. He fhould wear but one, and that plain, not
decked out with any colours, nor with gold."

§ XLI. *Omnes clerici vel lectores, ficut Levitæ et facerdotes, detonfo
fuperius toto capite inferius folam circuli coronam relinquant: non ficut
hucufque in Galliciæ partibus facere lectores videntur, qui prolixis ut
laici comis in folo capitis apice modicum circulum tondent. Ritus enim
ifte in Hifpania hucufque hæreticorum fuit. Unde oportet ut pro ampu-
tando ecclefiæ fcandalo hoc fignum dedecoris auferatur, et una fit tonfura,
vel habitus, ficut totius Hifpaniæ eft ufus. Qui autem hoc non cuftodierit
fidei catholicæ reus erit.*

" All clerks, or Readers, as well as Levites and priefts, are to cut off
the hair from the whole of the upper part of the head, and leave only
a circular band of hair beneath ; not as hitherto in parts of Gallicia
appears to have been done by Readers, who, wearing their hair long
like laymen, cut a fcanty circle only on the very top of the head.
For in Spain this fafhion has been confined hitherto to heretics. To
remove therefore all occafion of offence in the Church, this mark of
unfeemlinefs muft be done away, and one mode of tonfure, and

---

[133] *Propter quod erat id eft prædicat.* St.
Ifidore was a ftudent of Etymology, as his xx.
books *De Originibus* teftify. But with him,
as with other ancient writers, whether Greek
or Latin, etymology is a weak point. To
underftand what he means here the reader
muft bear in mind that he ufes *orat* with reference to its (probable) root meaning " fpeaks; "
and that *prædicare* here does not mean " *preach* "

in the modern fenfe of the word, but like
κηρύσσειν, " *to make proclamation.*" He alludes
to the office of the deacon in " uttering aloud "
the various directions to the people which
occur in the courfe of the Liturgy, and more
particularly perhaps to the duty, often affigned
to a deacon of reading (" *Apoftolum* ") the
Epiftle, or the Gofpel, of the day.

of drefs, prevail, in accordance with the ufage of the whole of Spain. To difregard this will be an offence againft the Catholic faith."

It is evident from thefe canons that in Spain, at the beginning of the 7th century, the "orarium," or ftole, was worn both by bifhops and prefbyters, and by deacons, though, by the latter, in a diftinctive manner, on the left fhoulder only. Alfo that the ftaff and ring were regarded as fpecial infignia of a bifhop; the *planeta* as the proper veftment of a Prefbyter; and the Alb, or white tunic, of a Deacon.

XXIX.

VENERABLE BEDE.[134]

ON THE LEVITICAL VESTMENTS.

OUR countryman Bede, writing early in the eighth century, in his treatife *De Tabernaculo* (lib. iii. cap. ii. fqq.), enters at confiderable length upon the fubject of the veftments of the Aaronic priefthood. He lays[135] it down as a general principle that the ordination and the drefs of the Levitical priefthood is in this wife properly applicable to the priefthood of the Chriftian Church, that the outward fplendour which in the former times fhone brightly in an ornate vefture, fhall now, fpiritually underftood, be inwardly confpicuous in the hearts of them who ferve in holy miniftry to God. And in the acts of them who minifter, there fhould be an outward glory alfo,—a glory beyond what is feen in the good works of the faithful generally. He adds,[136] that what is written in Holy Scripture, concerning Aaron, and the veftments of Levitical priefthood, may be underftood primarily in reference to our Lord; but that it becomes us rather to confider therein what pertaineth to our own godly converfation in Him, and alfo what hath regard to correction of life and manners.

In accordance with this general view is the meaning which he attributes to the feveral veftments which he proceeds to enumerate. Thefe are

---

[134] Bede was born (probably) in the year 673 A.D., and died A.D. 735.

[135] Cap. ii. The original is as follows, *Defcripta foffura tabernaculi confequenter facerdotes qui in eo miniftrent ordinantur. Quorum quidem ordinatio et habitus recte ecclefiæ facerdotibus congruit ita ut omne quod illie in ornatu veftium clarum extrinfecus fulgebat hoc intellectum* fpiritualiter in ipfis facerdotum noftrorum mentibus altum intus emineat, hoc in eorum actibus præ cæteris fidelium meritis foris gloriofum clarefcat.

[136] *Ibid. in fin. Hæc quidem ita principaliter de Domino poffunt accipi; fed nos magis in eis quæ ad fignificantiam noftram in Domino piæ converfationis pertineant, quæque ad correctionem noftrorum refpiciant morum, decet intueri.*

1. The Superhumeral or Ephod.

This being fo worn as to cover *the fhoulders*, he regards [cap. iv.] it as typical of the labour [137] of good works, of "the eafy yoke, and light burden," fpoken of by our Lord.

2. The "Rational," or Breastplate.

This is interpreted [cap. v.] of the purity of heart and thought which befitteth one higheft in holy miniftry to God. And whereas *Doctrina et Veritas,*—doctrine and truth,—were to be inferibed either literally or facramentally upon that "breaftplate," this was (fo he writes) for this end, that it might the more clearly appear that this ornament was not only a part of the actual vefture of the older High Prieft, but was alfo an announcement beforehand of evangelic truth, having reference either to our Lord Himfelf, or to His Apoftles, or indeed to all who proclaim before men the fame grace and the fame truth as they.

3. The Tunic of Blue.

He fays that this outer tunic of the high-prieft's drefs was of full length, reaching to the feet, like to the inner tunic of linen. He adds, that to be clothed in a tunic of blue, even to the feet, is to perfevere in good works even to our life's end.

4. The Plate of Gold.

The golden plate upon the forehead of the high-prieft is fignificant of the affurance of our "profeffion," which we bear upon our brow, faying each one in the words of the apoftle, "*God forbid that I fhould glory, fave in the crofs of our Lord Jefus Chrift.*" [138]

5. The Inner Tunic of Linen.

By linen, or byffus, is meant (fo all, he fays, agree) Chriftian continence, and bodily chaftity. And Chriftian priefts (61 ζ) may then be faid to have the clofe fitting linen veftment, or tunic, of

---

[137] Compare note 35, p. 22.
[138] Compare St. Jerome quoted above, p. 24,

Quod olim in lamina monftrabatur, nunc in figno oftenditur crucis.

byffus, when they maintain in full vigour the life of continence to
which they have devoted themfelves.

6. OF THE "TIARA," OR PRIESTLY CAP.

"The Tiara, which was alfo called 'cidaris' and 'mitra,' was at
once a covering and an ornament to the head of the High Prieft;
that by this he might be admonifhed, that all the fenfes" (having their
feat *in the head*) "fhould be ever confecrated to God." He goes on
to fay that after comparing the accounts given in Holy Scripture, and
in Jofephus, much remains ftill uncertain as to the material and the
colour of thefe caps or mitres, and of the *coronulæ* or encircling bands,
whether of linen or of gold, by which they were encompaffed. But
their figurative meaning, he thinks, is fuch as this. "Prieftly caps
(*mitræ*) and encircling bands of linen, are worn by Chriftian priefts
(*facerdotes*, 61 ζ), who fo maintain, in the beauty of chaftity, both
Sight, Hearing, Tafte, Smell, and Touch, as that they may hope in
requital thereof to receive from God that crown of life which He hath
promifed to fuch as love Him."

7. OF THE PRIEST'S GIRDLE.

Whereas, by the wearing of a linen tunic is fignified the dedicating
the whole body to the bright purity of a chafte life, fo may Chriftian
priefts (61 ζ) be faid to encompafs this tunic with a girdle, when with
fuch vigilance and circumfpection they guard their purity as that
they fhall not through felf-fatisfaction become inactive in good works.

8. ON THE LINEN DRAWERS.

Thefe, which are to be worn, as he remarks, both by Aaron and
by the other priefts, he confiders as defignating *illam caftimoniæ por-
tionem quæ ab appetitu copulæ conjugalis cohibet, fine qua nemo vel
facerdotium fufcipere vel ad altaris poteft minifterium confecrari, id eft, fi
non aut virgo permanferit aut contractæ uxoriæ conjunctionis fœdera
folverit.*[139]

---

[139] The original paffage, which I have ab-
breviated as above, is of very great length. In
it Bede follows, and that profeffedly, "the
Fathers;" for fo, even in Bede's time, St.
Jerome and St. Auguftine and other fuch
Doctores Ecclefiæ, were ftyled. Like them, he
affigns throughout a figurative meaning to the
Levitical veftments, without alluding in any
way to any literal veftments, proper to Chriftian priefthood, which had been modelled
upon thofe defcribed in Exodus and Leviticus.

9. THE UNDER GIRDLE OF THE HIGH PRIEST.

Before quitting the fubject, he obferves that whereas eight veftments are mentioned in Exodus as proper to the high-prieft, a ninth
feems to be added in Leviticus, viz., a belt (*baltheus*), with which the
linen tunic was girt in before the putting on of the tunic of blue.
But this belt or girdle he feems to confider as a figurative expreffion
only, not as anything actually worn (cap. ix. *in fin.*).

XXX.

GERMANUS
PATRIARCHA CONSTANTINOPOLITANUS.[140]

THE TONSURE, THE CHRISTIAN VESTMENTS, AND
THE DRESS OF MONKS.

Μυστικὴ Θεωρία, p. 206.

Τὸ ξύρισμα τῆς κεφαλῆς τοῦ ἱερέως, καὶ τὸ γυροειδὲς αὐτοῦ τμῆμα τὸ μέσον τῶν τριχῶν, ἀντὶ τοῦ ἀκανθίνου στεφάνου ὅπερ ὁ Χριστὸς ἐφόρεσεν. Ὁ ἐν τῇ κεφαλῇ τοῦ ἱερέως περικείμενος διπλοῦς στέφανος ἐκ τῆς τῶν τριχῶν σημειώσεως εἰκονίζει τὴν τοῦ ἀποστόλου Πέτρου τιμίαν κάραν, ἥν, ἐν τῷ τοῦ Κυρίου καὶ διδασκάλου κηρύγματι ἀποσταλεὶς, καὶ κερεὶς ὑπὸ τῶν ἀπειθούντων τῷ λόγῳ, ὡς ἐμπαιζόμενος ὑπ' αὐτῶν, ταύτην ὁ διδάσκαλος Χριστὸς εὐλόγησε, καὶ ἐποίησε τὴν ἀτιμίαν τιμὴν, καὶ τὴν χλεύην εἰς δόξαν, καὶ ἔθηκεν ἐπὶ τὴν κεφαλὴν αὐτοῦ στέφανον, οὐκ ἐκ λίθων τιμίων, ἀλλὰ τῷ λίθῳ καὶ τῇ πέτρᾳ τῆς πίστεως αὐτοῦ ἐκλάμπουσαν, ὑπὲρ χρυσίον καὶ τοπάζιον καὶ λίθους τιμίους. Κορυφὴ γὰρ κεκαλλωπισμένη καὶ στέφανος τοῦ δωδεκαλίθου, οἱ ἀπόστολοί εἰσι· πέτρα δὲ ὁ παναγιώτατος ἀπόστολος ὑπάρχει ἀρχιεράρχης τοῦ Χριστοῦ.

Ἡ στολὴ[141] τοῦ ἱερέως ὑπάρχει κατὰ τὸν ποδήρη Ἀαρὼν, τουτέστιν ἱμάτιον ὅ ἐστιν ἱερατικὸν ἔνδυμα, τὸ μέχρι τῶν ποδῶν, τὸ τιμιώτατον. Ἔστι δὲ πυρσοειδὲς κατὰ τὸν προφήτην τὸν λέγοντα· ὁ ποιῶν τοὺς ἀγγέλους αὐτοῦ πνεύματα καὶ τοὺς λειτουργοὺς αὐτοῦ πυρὸς φλόγα. Καὶ πάλιν· τίς οὗτος ὁ παραγινόμενος ἐξ Ἐδώμ; Ἐδὼμ γὰρ ἑρμηνεύεται γήϊνος, ἢ ἐκλεκτὸς, ἢ κόκκινος. Εἶτα ἐπάγει· Ἐρύθημα ἱματίων αὐτοῦ ἐξ ἀμπέλου Βοσόρ. Διὰ τί σου ἐρυθρὰ τὰ ἱμάτια, καὶ τὰ ἐνδύματά σου ὡς ἀπὸ πατητοῦ ληνοῦ; ἐμφαίνοιτο τὴν βαφεῖσαν τοῦ Χριστοῦ στολὴν τῆς σαρκὸς ἐν αἵμασιν, ἐν τῷ ἀχράντῳ αὐτοῦ σταυρῷ. Πάλιν δὲ ὅτι καὶ

[140] It is matter of queſtion among critics to which of the two patriarchs named Germanus this treatiſe ſhould be referred. Of theſe two one was appointed to the See of Conſtantinople in the year 715 A.D., and was afterwards depoſed by the Emperor Leo. The other Germanus was made patriarch of Conſtantinople A.D. 1222, but reſided at Nicæa, the metropolitan city being then in the hands of the Latins. De La Bigne and other editors aſſign the work to the older Germanus, who lived in the eighth century. A comparison of the preſent paſſage with that from the pſeudo-Chryſoſtom given above,

XXX.

S. GERMANUS[140] OF CONSTANTINOPLE.

THE TONSURE, THE CHRISTIAN VESTMENTS, AND THE DRESS OF MONKS.

RERUM ECCLESIASTICARUM THEORIA, p. 135.

THE tonfure of the prieft's head, and the circle cut away in the midſt of the hair, is in place of the crown of thorns worn by Chriſt. The double circlet, marked out by the hair of the head, ſets forth in ſemblance the honoured head of apoftle Peter, which, when he was ſent forth to preach the Gofpel of His Lord and Maſter, was ſhorn in mockery by them that were difobedient to the word. But the head that was ſo ſhorn Chriſt did blefs, and made difhonour to be unto him for honour, and mockery to be to him for glory; and ſet upon his head a crown, not made of coſtly ſtones, but radiant with light from the ſtone and rock of His faith, above the brightnefs of gold and topaz and precious ſtones. For the adorned head, and the coronal of twelve ſtones, are the apoftles; and by the rock is meant the moſt holy apoftle, chief in the hierarchy of Chriſt.

The veſture[141] of the prieft accordeth with the long tunic (ποδήρη;) of Aaron, being an outer garment worn by priefts, reaching down to the feet, and of higheſt honour. The colour thereof is as of fire, according to the word of the prophet, "*Who maketh his angels ſpirits, and his miniſters a flaming fire.*" And again, "*Who is this that cometh from Edom?*" For this word "Edom" is by interpretation either "earthy," or "elect," or "ſcarlet in colour." And then he addeth, "*The rednefs of his garments is of the vineyard of Bofor. Why are thy garments red, and thy veſture as from the treading out of the*

---

[140] p. 51, and that from patriarch Symeon of Theffalonica later in this volume, will, I think, confirm their judgment.

[141] ἡ ϛολή. By the word ϛολή here uſed, we are to underſtand not the "ſtole" technically ſo called (this is a weſtern uſage of "ſtole," dating from the eighth century), but what was in the Eaſt regarded as the characteriſtic veſtment of Chriſtian prieſthood, viz. the φιλώνιον (ſee note 143), of which he ſays that it reſembles the "long tunic" of Aaron in reſpect of its defcending even to the feet. [On ϛολή and ſtola, ſee further remarks in note 50.]

κοκκίνην χλαμύδα [142] ἐφόρεσιν ἐν τῷ πάθει ὁ Χριστός, ἐμφαίνουσιν οἱ ἀρχιερεῖς ποίου ἀρχιερέως εἰσὶν ὑπασπισταί. Τὸ δὲ ἀπεζωσμένοις τοὺς ἱερεῖς περιπατεῖν φιλώνιος, [143] δείκνυσιν ὅτι καὶ ὁ Χριστὸς ἐν τῷ σταυρῷ ἀπερχόμενος οὕτως ἦν βαστάζων τὸν σταυρὸν αὐτοῦ. Ἐν ταῖς ἄνω λαμπρότησι τῶν νοερῶν οὐρανίων λειτουργῶν, προφητῶν καὶ ἱεραρχῶν, εἰσὶ πρεσβύτεροι εἴκοσι τέσσαρες, καὶ διάκονοι ἑπτά· οἱ μὲν πρεσβύτεροι κατὰ μίμησιν τῶν Σεραφικῶν δυνάμεων εἰσι, ταῖς μὲν στολαῖς δικὴν πτερύγων κατακεκαλυμμένοι, ταῖς δὲ δυσὶ πτέρυξι τῶν χειλέων τὸν ὕμνον βοῶντες, καὶ κατέχοντες τὸν θεῖον καὶ νοητὸν ἄνθρακα Χριστὸν ἐν τῷ θυσιαστηρίῳ τῇ λαβίδι τῆς χειρὸς φανερῶς φέροντες.

Οἱ δὲ διάκονοι εἰς τύπον τῶν ἀγγελικῶν δυνάμεων ταῖς λεπταῖς τῶν λεπτῶν ὡραίων [144] πτέρυξιν, ὡς λειτουργικὰ πνεύματα εἰς διακονίαν ἀποστελλόμενα περιτρέχουσι.

Πρῶτον μὲν τὸ στιχάριον, [145] λευκὸν ὄν, τῆς θεότητος τὴν αἴγλην ἐμφαίνει, καὶ τοῦ ἱερέως τὴν λαμπρὰν πολιτείαν. Τὰ λωρία [146] τοῦ στιχαρίου εἰσι, τὰ ἐν τῇ χειρί, ἐμφαίνοντα τὸν δεσμὸν τοῦ Χριστοῦ· δήσαντες γὰρ αὐτὸν ἀπήγαγον πρὸς Καιάφαν τὸν ἀρχιερέα καὶ τὸν Πιλᾶτον. Τὰ λωρία τὰ εἰς τὰ πλάγια εἰσὶ τὸ αἷμα τὸ ῥεῦσαν ἐκ τῆς πλευρᾶς τοῦ Χριστοῦ ἐν τῷ σταυρῷ.

Τὸ περιτραχήλιόν ἐστι τὸ φακιώλιον, [147] μεθ' οὗ ἐπεφέρετο ἀπὸ τοῦ ἀρχιερέως δεδεμένος, καὶ συρόμενος ἐπὶ τὸ πρόσθεν ἐπὶ τῇ τραχήλῳ ὁ Χριστός, ἐν τῷ πάθει αὐτοῦ ἀπερχόμενος. Τὸ δὲ τοῦ ἐπιτραχηλίου δεξιὸν μέρος σήμενι ὁ κάλαμος ὃν ἔδωκαν ἐμπαίζοντες τῇ δεξιᾷ τοῦ Χριστοῦ. Τὸ δὲ τοῦ ἐξ εὐωνύμου μέρους ἡ τοῦ σταυροῦ βασταγὴ ἐπὶ τῶν ὤμων αὐτοῦ.

Ἡ δὲ ζώνη ἣν περιζώννυται σήμενι ἡ εὐπρέπεια ἣν ὁ Χριστὸς βασιλεύσας εὐπρεπῆ περιεζώσατο δύναμιν τῆς θεότητος.

Τὸ δὲ φιλώνιον ἐμφαίνει τὴν ἀπὸ κοκκίνου πορφύραν, ἥνπερ τῷ Ἰησοῦ ἐμπαίζοντες οἱ ἀσεβεῖς ἐφόρεσαν. Ἔστι δὲ καὶ ἡ στολὴ τοῦ βαπτίσματος.

Τὸ ὠμοφόριόν [148] ἐστι τοῦ ἀρχιερέως κατὰ τὴν στολὴν τοῦ Ἀαρὼν ἥνπερ ἐφόρουν

---

[142] Κοκκίνην χλαμύδα. He refers to Matt. xxviii. 28. The χλαμύς of the Greeks answered to the *sagum* (note 5, p. iv.) or *paludamentum* of the Romans, among whom, however, the word *chlamys* itself was naturalised. It was a short cloak, sometimes used by travellers, but in nine cases out of ten spoken of as part of a soldier's dress, and for this reason occasionally also of an emperor's, who was (as his name *Imperator* implies) a king regarded in the character of commander-in-chief. In shape it was not unlike the cavalry cloak worn in our own army.

[143] φιλώνιον is a later form (note 152) of *φαινόλης*, of which *pænula* is the Latin equivalent.

[144] Ὡράριον, equal to *orarium*, one of the many Latin words which the later Greek naturalised. Compare notes 146, 147, and 151. As an ecclesiastical term, it appears only to be used of the *deacon's* "stole," as we now call it, not as in Latin of the corresponding vestment (*ἐπιτραχήλιον*) worn by priests. But a passage of Symeon of Thessalonica (De Sacris Ordinationibus, p. 145) seems clearly to show that *the same vestment* which was called *ὠράριον*, as worn on one shoulder by the deacon (and probably also when named simply as an ecclesiastical vestment), became an *ἐπιτραχήλιον* or *περιτραχήλιον*, when worn round the neck, and pendent from it, by a priest. See the passage in Dufresne *in voc.* ἐπιτραχήλιον.

[145] Τὸ στιχάριον λευκὸν ὄν. This στιχάριον of the Greeks corresponds to the *tunica alba* (or "alba" simply) of the Western Church.

grape?" By this is signified the vesture of Christ's flesh, dyed red with blood on His immaculate crofs. And again, becaufe in His paffion Christ was clothed with a fcarlet robe,[142] in this too do His chief priests fhow what manner of High-priest He is under whom they ferve.

Then for that of the priests walking with Phelonion [143] unconfined by any girdle, this fhoweth how that Christ alfo, when about to depart this life upon the crofs, did after the like manner bear His crofs. Amid the fupernal glories of the unfeen heavenly miniftry, prophets and hierarchs, there are four and twenty elders (or "prefbyters"), and feven deacons. The elders have the femblance of the feraphic powers, and with their robes they cover themfelves as with wings; and with the two wings of their lips they lift up the voice of praife, and upon the altar they lay hold upon Him who is the divine and fpiritual Coal, even Christ, bearing Him openly in the forceps of the hand. But the deacons, figuring forth the angelic hofts, with the light wings of their light ftoles,[144] hafte onward, as miniftering fpirits fent forth for the fervice of men.

And firft the "fticharion,"[145] being white, fignifieth the fplendour of Godhead, and the bright purity of life which becometh Christian priests. The ftripes [146] of the fticharion upon the wriftband of the fleeve, are fignificant of the bands wherewith Christ was bound; for they bound Him and led Him away to Caiaphas the high-priest, and to Pilate. The ftripes acrofs the robe itfelf fignify the blood which flowed from Christ's fide upon the crofs. The Peritrachelion is the band [147] wherewith He was taken bound from the palace of the high-priest, and dragged on by the neck, at the time of His paffion. By the right fide of the Epitrachelion is fhowed the reed which they put in mockery into the right hand of Christ. And by the left part thereof the bearing of the crofs upon His fhoulders.

The girdle, wherewith the priest girdeth himfelf about, fignifieth the beauty wherewith Christ, entering upon His kingdom, did gird Himfelf withal, even the beauteous majefty of Godhead.

In the Phenolion we may fee the fcarlet robe which thofe ungodly ones, in mockery of Jefus, did put upon Him. And this ferveth alfo as the robe of baptifm.

The Omophorion [148] belongeth to one chief in priestly miniftry to

---

[146] λώριον. An adaptation, in a late Greek form, of the Latin *lorum*.

[147] φακιώλιον (*aliter* φακιόλιον), probably a Byzantine corruption from *fafciola*. Compare note 152 below.

[148] Affuming that περιτίθεται is rightly read here, the word can grammatically apply only to οἱ ἐν ὑμῖν ἀρχιερεῖς. But there is no part of the Aaronic veftments which by any ftretch of imagination could be defcribed as "*put*

οἱ ἐν νόμῳ ἀρχιερεῖς, σουδαρίοις μακροῖς τὸν εὐώνυμον ὦμον περιτίθεντες, κατὰ τὸν ζύγον τῶν ἐντολῶν τοῦ Χριστοῦ. Τὸ δὲ ὠμοφόριον ὃ περιβέβληται ὁ ἐπίσκοπος δηλοῖ τὴν τοῦ προβάτου δορὰν, ὅπερ πλανώμενον [149] εὑρὼν ὁ Κύριος ἐπὶ τῶν ὤμων αὐτοῦ ἀνέλαβε καὶ σὺν τοῖς μὴ πεπλανημένοις ἠρίθμησεν. Ἔχει δὲ καὶ σταυροὺς, διὰ τὸ καὶ τὸν Χριστὸν ἐπὶ τοῦ ὤμου βαστάσαι τὸν σταυρὸν αὐτοῦ. Ἔτι δὲ καὶ οἱ θέλοντες κατὰ Χριστὸν ζῆν ἐπὶ τῶν ὤμων αἴρουσι τὸν σταυρὸν αὐτοῦ ὅ ἐστιν ἡ κακοπάθεια· σύμβολον γὰρ κακοπαθείας ὁ σταυρός.

Τὸ μοναχικὸν σχῆμά ἐστι κατὰ μίμησιν τοῦ ἐρημοπολίτου καὶ Βαπτιστοῦ Ἰωάννου· ὅτι τὸ ἔνδυμα αὐτοῦ ἦν ἐκ τριχῶν καμήλου καὶ ζώνη δερματίνη περὶ τὴν ὀσφὺν αὐτοῦ. Τὸ δὲ κείρεσθαι τὴν κάραν ὁλοτελῶς κατὰ μίμησιν τοῦ ἁγίου ἀποστόλου Ἰακώβου τοῦ ἀδελφοθέου, καὶ Παύλου τοῦ ἀποστόλου καὶ τῶν λοιπῶν. Τὰ δὲ ἀναβόλαιά [150] ἐστι κατὰ τὰ ἀναβόλαια ἅπερ ἐφόρουν ἱμάτια. Τὰ δὲ κουκούλλια [151] κατὰ τὸν λέγοντα ἀπόστολον ὅτι ἐσταύρωται [152] μοι ὁ κόσμος, κἀγὼ τῷ κόσμῳ.

Τὸ δὲ μανδύον [153] ἔμφαινον διὰ τῆς ἀπολελυμένης ἁπλώσεως τὴν πτερωτικὴν [deeſt ταχύτητα vel ſimile aliquid] τῆς τῶν ἀγγέλων μιμήσεως· καθότι ἀγγελικὸν σχῆμα λέγεται.

Ἡ δὲ ὀθόνη [154] μεθ᾽ ἧς λειτουργοῦσιν οἱ διάκονοι δηλοῖ τὴν τοῦ Χριστοῦ ταπείνωσιν, ἣν ἐνεδείξατο ἐν τῷ νιπτῆρι. Τὸ δὲ ἐγχείριον τὸ ἐπὶ τῆς ζώνης ἐστι τὸ ἀπόμαξαν τὰς χεῖρας αὐτοῦ λέντιον. Καὶ πέφυκε τὸ ἐγχείριον ἔχειν ἐπὶ τῆς ζώνης ἀντίτυπον τοῦ ἀπομάξαντος τὰς χεῖρας καὶ τοῦ Ἀθῶς εἰμι ἐπιφωνήσαντος.

---

about the left shoulder with long bands or kerchiefs." I believe therefore that there is some corruption of the text here, or elſe ſome forgetfulnneſs of ſtrict grammatical conſtruction. Reference ſeems to be made to the way in which the Chriſtian ὠμοφέριον was doubled back over the left ſhoulder, and hung down the back, while the other end hung pendent (like the extremity of the archiepiſcopal *pallium*) in front.

[149] Theſe words are taken all but *verbatim* from S. Iſidore of Peluſium, quoted above, p. 49.

[150] Τὰ ἀναβόλαια. The diminutive ἀναβολάιον appears in Latin as *anabaladium*, which again was corrupted into *ombologium*. This laſt is deſcribed by Latin writers (ſee Ducange *in*

voc.) ſometimes as covering *the head*, ſometimes as covering the *ſhoulders*. He ſeems to intimate that the ἀναβόλαια here ſpoken of correſpond with the older *pallium* (note 73.) One end of this was really ἀναβαλλόμενον "thrown up" over the left ſhoulder.

[151] Τὰ κουκούλλια. Another imported Latin word. It is the Latin *cucullus*, our own "cowl," which in mediæval writers appears as *cuculla*. As early as St. Jerome's time this "cowl" is ſpoken of as worn by monks.

[152] He alludes no doubt to the croſs upon the cowl of Eaſtern Biſhops (worn alſo by the σταυροφόρος or privileged clergy of the Cathedral Church at Conſtantinople) which was ſo placed as to appear upon the forehead, when the cowl was worn upon the head. A ſimilar

God, like to that robe of Aaron which the high-priests wore under the law, putting it about the left shoulder with long bands of linen, even as the yoke of Christ's commandments.

But the Omophorion,[119] wherewith bishops are clad, signifieth the fleece of the sheep which the Lord found wandering, and took it upon His shoulders, and numbered it among them that had not wandered. And this hath crosses marked upon it, because that Christ also bare the cross upon His shoulders. And they that desire to live after Christ's example, they too take up His cross, even the endurance of hardship. For the cross is the symbol of His endurance.

The monastic habit is after the manner of that dweller in the desert, John the Baptist; for his raiment was of camel's hair, and a leathern girdle was about his loins.

They that shave the whole head do it in imitation of the holy apostle James, the "brother of God," and of apostle Paul, and of the rest. And the "anabolæa"[150] are after the manner of the outer garments which they were wont to wear. The Cowls[151] are in accordance with that of the apostle, who saith, "*The world is crucified*[152] *unto me, and I unto the world.*"

The cape,[153] open as it is and simple, is a symbol of the winged speed of angels, and is spoken of commonly as belonging to the dress of angels.

But the vestment of linen [154] wherewith the deacons minister at the altar, is in sign of the humility of Christ which He showed in respect of the Bason (when He washed the disciples' feet). And the napkin upon their girdle is the towel wherewith He dried His hands. And this carrying of a napkin upon the girdle is in antitype of him who wiped his hands and cried, "I am innocent."

---

cowl is to be seen on the head of BENE-
DICTVS I PAPA ET MONACHVS, in a
drawing (unedited as far as I know) in the
collection at Windsor.

[153] Τὸ μανδίον. Again, a neuter form, sub-
stituted for the older forms μανδύας and
μανδύη. This constant obliteration (*following
upon confusion*) of the older distinctions of
gender is in the later Greek, as in debased
Latin, a natural result of barbarous deteriora-

tion. The word μανδύας is somewhat vaguely
used, sometimes of a garment nearly resembling the Latin *pænula*, sometimes of a kind
of cape, shaped much like a *sagum* (note 5,
p. iv.) See Ferrarius, De Re Vest. Pars ii.
Lib. i. cap. ii. The cloak here described is
probably the ordinary walking dress of the
clergy in the East.

[154] These words are quoted verbatim from
S. Isidore of Pelusium (*supra*, p. 49).

XXXI.

RABANVS MAVRVS.[155]

DE INSTITUTIONE CLERICORUM.[156]

LIB. I. CAP. 7. THE ALB THE CHARACTERISTIC DRESS OF A DEACON.
POPE SYLVESTER'S ORDINANCES.

Levitæ . . . proptcrea altari albis induti affiftunt, ut hinc admoniti cæleftem vitam habeant, candidique ad hoftias et immaculati accedant. Quos primus fecit Sylvefter Papa, tricefimus quartus pontifex in Romana ecclefia poft Petrum, Dalmaticis uti, et conftituit ut pallio [157] linoftimo eorum læva tegeretur, ficut in geftis pontificalibus continetur.

CAP. 14. THE SACERDOTAL HABIT OF THE 9TH CENTURY
COMPARED WITH THE VESTMENTS OF LEVITICAL PRIESTHOOD.

De vefte ergo facerdotali moderna ad antiquum veteris teftamenti habitum comparationem facientes, fecundum maiorum fenfum, quid myftice fignificet, profequamur.

CAP. 15. OF THE SUPERHUMERAL OR EPHOD.

Primum ergo eorum [158] indumentum eft Ephod Bad, quod interpre-

---

[155] Rabanus (furnamed "Maurus" by his tutor Alcuin), waa born A.D. 785, and in 810 was fet at the head of the fchool attached to the monaftery of Fulda. He was made Abbot of Fulda in 822, and in 847 became Archbifhop of Mayence.

[156] This treatife dates from the year 819 A.D.

[157] This expreffion has caufed difficulty owing to the diverfity of meanings in which the word *pallium* occurs (fee note 125). The pallium (cloth) of linen woof (*linoftimum*) which was to cover *the left hand* of the Roman deacon, is in all probability the *mappula*,

which we find the Roman clergy claiming as exclufively their own in the time of St. Gregory. (Cap. fupra, pp. 65 and 66.)

[158] By *eorum* are evidently meant the Levitical priefts. And as Rabanus feems to have known of no actual veftment in ufe by Chriftian priefts which would anfwer to the Ephod Bad, he follows the older writers in giving to this a fpiritual application. The ephod being a covering to the *fhoulders* has reference, he fays, to the activity in good *works* (note 35, p. 22) of one who is to be fet over God's people in the Church.

tatur fuperhumerale lineum, quod fignificat munditiam bonorum operum. Hinc bene in lege, cum Dominus de vefte facerdotali Moifen inftituit, primum de Superhumerali faciendo præcepit, quia quifquis ad facerdotium magifteriumque populi Dei promovendus eft, primum ejus debent opera cognofci, ut dum hoc, quod foris omnibus patet, inrepræhenfibile patuerit, convenienter ex tempore et integritas cordis ejus, et fidei fynceritas fcrutetur.

CAP. 16. OF THE Ποδήρης, OR LONG TUNIC.

Secundum eft linea tunica, quæ Græce ποδήρης, Latine talaris dicitur, eo quod ad talos ufque defcendat. Hanc Jofephus byffinam vocat, cujus fignificatio myftica inpromptu eft. Cum enim conftet, lino vel byffo continentiam et caftitatem fignificari, ftrictam[101] habent lineam facerdotes,[159] cum propofitum continentiæ non enerviter, fed ftudiofe confervant. Hæc ad talos ufque defcendit, quia ufque ad finem vitæ hujus bonis operibus infiftere debet facerdos, præcipiente ac promittente Domino, *Efto fidelis ufque ad mortem, et dabo tibi coronam vitæ.*

CAP. 17. OF THE GIRDLE.

Tertium veftimentum eft cingulum five balteum, quo utuntur ne tunica ipfa defluat, et greffum impediat. Hoc nimirum cuftodiam mentis fignificat. Qui enim tunica talari indutus abfque cingulo incedit, defluit tunica, ac relicto corpore, ventis et frigoribus intrandi fpatium tribuit : quin et præpeditis greffibus, incedendi ufum retardat, vel etiam calcantibus fe, caufa efficitur ruinæ. Ergo lineas induunt facerdotes, ut caftitatem habeant : accinguntur balteis, ne ipfa caftitas fit remiffa et negligens, ne vento elationis animum perflandi aditum impendat, ne crefcente iniquitate refrigefcere faciat charitatem ipforum, ne bonorum greffus operum[160] jactantia fuæ præfumptionis impediat, ne præpedito virtutum curfu ipfa etiam terreftris concupifcentiæ fordibus polluta vilefcat, et ad ultimum, Authorem fuum ad ruinam fuperbiendo impellat.

---

[159] *Sacerdotes.* On the comprehenfive meaning of this term fee note 61, p. 39.

[160] *Bonorum greffus operum,* "the fteps of good works," *i.e.* the "walk" of the Chriftian man in all good works for God.

Cap. 18. Of the Mappula, or Phanon.

Quartum vero, mappula five mantile, facerdotis indumentum eft, quod vulgo phanonem [161] vocant, quod ob hoc eorum tunc manibus tenetur, quando Miffæ officium agitur, ut paratos ad minifterium menfæ Domini populus confpiciat. Mappæ ergo convivii et epularum adpofitarum linteamina funt, unde diminutivum mappula, ficut et mantilia, nunc pro operiendis menfis funt : quæ, ut nomen ipforum indicat, olim tergendis manibus præbebantur. Oportet ergo facerdotes et miniftros altaris mappulas manibus tenere, quorum officium eft divina facramenta conficere, ut cum devotione mentis opus fpontaneum concordet, digne exerceatur officium, quod pie divino eft munere collatum.

Cap. 19. Of the Orarium, which some call "Stole."

Quintum quoque eft quod orarium dicitur, licet hoc quidam ftolam vocent. Hoc enim genere veftis folummodo eis perfonis uti eft conceffum, quibus prædicandi [162] officium eft delegatum. Bene etiam oratoribus Chrifti orarium habere convenit, quia cum indumentum eorum officio proprio concinat, et ipfi fedulo ad verbi minifterium cohortentur, et plebs ipfis commiffa, indicium falutare confpiciens, ad meditationem legis concurrere ferventius admonetur. Apte ergo orarium collum [163] fimul et pectus tegit facerdotis, ut inde inftruatur, quod quicquid ore proferat, tractatu fummæ rationis attendat, ut illud apoftoli femper in eo impleatur quod dicit (1 Cor. xiv. 15): *Orabo fpiritu, orabo et mente : pfallam fpiritu, pfallam et mente* ; et iterum (2 Cor. vi.): *Os noftrum ad vos, ó Corinthii, cor noftrum dilatatum eft.* Ne forte fi improvife et irrationabiliter loquatur, damnum patiatur, Salomone atteftante, qui ait (Prov. xvi.): *Cor fapientis erudiet os ejus, et labiis illius addet gratiam.* Item (Prov. xxi.), *Qui cuftodit os fuum, cuftodit animam fuam : qui inconfideratus eft ad loquendum, fentiet mala.*

---

[161] *Phanon,* alfo written *Fanon.* Comp. Alcuinus (quoted later in this book), *Sudarium, quod ad tergendum fudorem in manu geftari mos eft, quod ufitato nomine Fanonem vocamus.*

[162] *Prædicandi officium.* See p. 76, note 133.

[163] *Collum . . pectus . . ore . . rationis.* He connects the *neck* with the *voice* (comp. Amalarius De Eccl. Off. cap. 17, quoted p. 96), and the *breaft* (fee note 38, p. 22) with *reafon.*

CAP. 20. OF THE DALMATIC.[164]

Sextum namque eſt quod Dalmatica a Dalmatia Græciæ provincia, in qua primum texta eſt, nuncupatur. Hæc veſtis in modum eſt crucis faɛta,[165] et paſſionis Domini indicium eſt. Habet quoque et purpureos tramites ipſa tunica, a ſummo uſque ad ima, ante ac retro deſcendens [*Leg.* deſcendentes], necnon et per utramque manicam : ut admoneatur miniſter Domini per habitus ſui ſpeciem, cujus muneris particeps eſt, ut cum per myſticam oblationem paſſionis Dominicæ commemorationem agit, ipſe in eo fiat hoſtia Deo acceptabilis.

CAP. 21. OF THE CASULA, OR CHASUBLE.[166]

Septimum ſacerdotale indumentum eſt, quod caſulam vocant ; diɛta eſt autem per diminutionem a caſa, eo quod totum hominem tegat, quaſi minor caſa : hanc Græci planetam nominant. Hæc ſupremum omnium indumentorum eſt, et cætera omnia interius per ſuum munimen tegit et ſervat. Hanc ergo veſtem poſſumus intelligere charitatem quæ cunɛtis virtutibus ſupereminet, et earum decorem ſuo tutamine protegit et illuſtrat. Nec enim ullus jam erit virtutum ſplendor, ſi non eas charitatis irradiaverit fulgor, quod oſtendit Apoſtolus, dicens (1 Cor. xiii): *Si linguis hominum loquar et angelorum, charitatem autem non habeam, faɛtus ſum ſicut æs ſonans, aut cymbalum tinniens : Et ſi habuero prophetiam, et noverim myſteria omnia, et omnem ſcientiam : et ſi habuero omnem fidem, ita ut montes transferam, charitatem autem non habuero, nihil mihi prodeſt. Charitas patiens eſt, benigna eſt : Charitas non æmulatur, non agit perperam, non inflatur, non eſt ambitioſa, non quærit quæ ſua ſunt, non irritatur, non cogitat malum, non gaudet ſuper iniquitate, congaudet autem veritati. Omnia ſuffert, omnia credit, omnia ſperat, omnia ſuſtinet. Charitas nunquam excidit*, et reliqua. Sine hac, nec ſacerdos ipſe ad altare adpropinquare debet, nec munus offerre, nec preces fundere. Unde veritas ipſa dicit (Matt. vi.): *Si offers munus tuum ad altare, et ibi recordatus fueris, quia frater tuus habet aliquid adverſum te,*

---

[164] Comp. note 131, p. 74 and the letter of S. Gregory quoted p. 67.

[165] *In modum crucis.* He alludes to the appearance preſented by this veſtment when the

ſleeves are ſtretched out on either ſide, as in the figures of " *Orantes.*"

[166] Comp. note 130, p. 74.

relinque ibi munus tuum ante altare, et vade prius reconciliari fratri tuo, et tune veniens offeres munus tuum. Et item (Mar. xi.): *Cum stabitis ad orandum, dimittite si quid habetis adversum aliquem,* et reliqua. De hoc itaque fpiritali virtutum indumento, Apoftolus ad Coloffenfes ita fcripfit (Col. iii.): *Induite,* inquit, *vos ficut electi Dei, fancti et dilecti, viscera misericordiæ, benignitatem, humilitatem, modeftiam, patientiam,* et cætera: Et de charitatis eminentia paulo poft fubjunxit, dicens: *Super omnia autem hæc charitatem habentes, quod eft vinculum perfectionis.*

CAP. 22. OF THE SANDALS.

Induunt quoque facerdotes pedes fandaliis five foleis, quod genus calceamenti evangelica authoritate eis eft conceffum, ut Marci evangelium teftatur (Mar. vi.): quia hoc calceamentum myfticam fignificationem habet, ut pes neque tectus fit, neque nudus ad terram, id eft, ut nec occultetur evangelium, nec terrenis commodis innitatur. Nam fcriptum eft in Apoftolo (Eph. vi.): *Et calceati pedes in præparatione evangelii pacis.* Sicut ergo fandalia partem pedis tegunt, partem inopertam relinquunt: ita et evangelii doctores partim evangelium operire, partimque aperire debent: ita videlicet, ut fidelis et devotus fufficientem habeat doctrinam, et infidelis et contemptor non inveniat blafphemandi materiam. Admonet etiam et nos hoc genus calceamenti, ut carni noftræ et corpori in neceffitatibus confulamus, non in libidinis lafciviam defluamus, de quibus utrifque nos divina lex inftruit. Scriptum eft enim (Ifa. lviii.), *Carnem tuam ne defpexeris;* et item (Rom. xiii.): *Carnis curam ne feceritis in concupifcentiis.*

CAP. 23. THE PALLIUM OF AN ARCHBISHOP.

Super hæc autem omnia fummo pontifici [167] (qui Archiepifcopus vocatur) propter Apoftolicam [168] vicem pallii honor decernitur, quod genus indumenti crucis fignaculum purpureo colore exprimit, ut ipfo indutus pontifex, a tergo et pectore crucem habeat, fuaque mente pie

---

[167] *Summo Pontifici.* Note that with Raban *Pontifex Summus,* means not "the Pope," but an Archbifhop. See above note 45, p. 26.

[168] *Apoftolicam vicem.* He means either "Apoftolic Office," *i.e.* office of higheft authority in the Church, or (and this, I think more probable) "reprefentation of the Apoftolic See," *i.e.* of Rome. For the phrafe *vices Apoftolicæ fedis,* fee above p. 63.

et digne de paffione redemptoris cogitet, ac populo, pro quo dominum deprecatur, redemptionis fuæ fignaculum demonftret. Condecet quoque bene, ut ipfa Apoftolica dignitas Apoftolicum virum faciat, ut plena devotione, fano fermone, et digna operatione poffit dicere cum Apoftolo (Gal. vi.): *Mihi autem abfit gloriari nifi in cruce Domini noftri Jefu Chrifti, per quem mihi mundus crucifixus eft, et ego mundo.* Hæc quæque de habitu facerdotali ad fenfum fecundum modulum ingenioli [169] noftri breviter diximus, non præjudicantes his, qui congruentius et dignius de eadem re poffint fcribere et plenius difputare. [170]

---

[169] *Ingenioli noftri,* &c. This is evidently the expreffion of one who felt that he had not confined himfelf to the traditional teaching "of the Fathers" concerning the fpiritual fignificance of the older Levitical veftments (as typifying Chriftian virtues), but had advanced fomething of a new theory of his own on a fubject which he evidently fuppofes that others befide himfelf are likely to difcufs.

[170] The paffage above given is of fpecial importance to this inquiry, as in the idea here fuggefted of a correfpondence between the feven "facerdotal veftments" of Chriftian miniftry, and the feven veftments of "the law," we have probably the very earlieft example of an attempt being made to draw out in detail a comparifon between the two. Raban himfelf appears to have been confcious how few were in his time the points of refemblance. But the hint which he here throws out was foon improved upon by others, as we fhall fee in the paffages which follow.

XXXII.

AMALARIUS METENSIS.[171]

OF THE VESTMENTS OF CHRISTIAN PRIESTHOOD.

[DE ECCL. OFF. LIB. II. CAP. 15–26.]

CAP. 15. OF CLERICAL VESTMENTS IN GENERAL.

PRIMO notandum eft, ita effe clericorum habitum conftitutum in ecclefiafticis officiis, ut in omnibus Chriftiano populo poffit præbere exemplum bonæ converfationis. Quod quodammodo fignificat Hieronymus in libro [176] de vefte facerdotali ad Fabiolam : *Legimus,* inquiens, *in Levitico, juxta præceptum Dei Moifen laviffe Aaron et filios ejus. Jam tunc purgationem mundi et rerum omnium fanctitatem baptifmi facramenta fignabant. Non accipiunt veftes, nifi loti prius fordibus : nec coronantur ad facra, nifi in Chrifto novi homines renafcantur.* Ex his verbis intelligimus, veftes facerdotales ad converfationem populi Chriftiani pertinere.

CAP. 16. SACRED VESTMENTS RESERVED FOR HOLY USE ALONE.

Stephanus [173] natione Romanus ex patre Iobio, ut legitur in geftis episcopalibus, conftituit facerdotibus Levitifque veftes facratas in ufu quotidiano non uti in ecclefia. Tale quid Dominus per Ezechielem loquitur : *Hæc funt gazophylacia fancta, in quibus veftiuntur facerdotes, qui appropinquant ante Dominum in fancta fanctorum.* Et paulo poft : *Cum autem ingreffi fuerint facerdotes, non egredientur de fanctis in atrium exterius, et ibi reponent veftimenta fua, in quibus miniftrant, quia fancta*

---

[171] Amalarius is firft heard of as a deacon at Metz, then (A.D. 825) as a bifhop fent on a miffion from the Council of Paris to the Emperor Lewis ; and, laftly, as fent on a miffion from the Emperor to Pope Gregory IV. This treatife dates from about the year 824 A.D. Some editors have attributed it to a contem-

porary archbifhop, Amalarius Fortunatus, of Treves.

[172] See above p. 10, fqq. The words quoted by Amalarius will be found at p. 20.

[173] Stephanus I. fed. 253–257 A.D. The reference to Ezechiel which follows is to cap. xliv. See above p. 29, fqq.

funt, veſtienturque veſtimentis aliis, et ſic procedent ad populum. Et
iterum : *Cumque ingrediuntur portas atrii interioris, veſtibus lineis in-
duentur, nec aſcendat ſuper eos quicquam laneum, quando miniſtrant in
portis atrii interioris et intrinſecus.* Et poſt pauca : *Cumque egredientur
atrium exterius ad populum, exuent ſe veſtibus ſuis, in quibus miniſtra-
verant, et reponent ea in gazophylacia ſanctuarii, et veſtient ſe veſtimentis aliis.* Quamvis hæc ſpiritaliter intelligere debeamus, tamen admoniti ſumus a ſupra memorato apoſtolico,[174] ut mutationem veſtimenti
juxta literam compleamus. Nobis enim qui ſpiritu ſumus renati, ante
oculos bonum eſt frequentare quod in mentem tranſeat. Per lineam
veſtem, qua tantummodo utimur in ſanctis, intelligimus ſubtilem
orationem, exutam ab omni carnali cogitatione ante Dominum. Lo-
cutio vero ad populum alia debet eſſe, tamque groſſa, ut intelligi valeat
a populo. Unde et Hieronymus in libro[175] decimotertio ſuper Ezechielem : *Et quia ſemel præceperat quibus veſtibus uti deberent ſacerdotes
quando intrinſecus in miniſteriis ſunt, rurſum jubet ut egredientes, in
gazophylaciis ſive in exedris ſanctorum ſe exuant priſtinis veſtibus, et
induantur aliis, ne ſi ſanctas veſtes habuerint, ſanctificent populum foris
poſitum, qui necdum fuerit ſanctificatus, nec ſe præparaverit in ſancti-
ficatione templi, ut ſit Domini Nazaræus.* *Per quæ diſcimus, non quotidianis et quibuſlibet pro uſu vitæ communis pollutis veſtibus nos ingredi
debere in ſancta ſanctorum : ſed munda conſcientia et mundis veſtibus
tenere Domini ſacramenta.* *Porro religio divina*[176] *alterum habitum
habet in miniſterio, alterum in uſu vitaque communi.* Namque et hic ex
verbis Hieronymi admoniti ſumus mutationem veſtimenti. Sequitur
ejuſdem in eodem : *Hæc veſtimenta proprio nobis labore conficimus, quæ
texta ſunt deſuper, qualem et Dominus habebat tunicam, quæ ſcindi non
poteſt : quibus induimur, quando ſecreta Domini et arcana cognoſcimus,
et habemus ſpiritum qui ſcrutatur etiam alta et profunda Dei, quæ non
ſunt monſtranda vulgo, nec proferenda ad populum, qui non eſt ſanctificatus,
nec Dei ſanctitudini præparatus : ne ſi majora ſe audierint, majeſtatem
ſcientiæ ferre non poſſint : et quaſi ſolido ſuffocentur cibo, qui adhuc lacte
infantiæ nutriendi ſunt.*[177] Inter regulas ſacræ ſcripturæ ſeptem hæc
una ex illis conſtat, ut a litera tranſeamus ad ſpiritum, et a ſpiritu
ad literam : Ac ideo non abhorret a vero, quamvis de laneo veſtimento
accipiamus ſecundum ſpiritum, ſi ſecundum literam perfecerimus mu-

[174] *Apoſtolico, i.e.* by Stephanus, Biſhop of the "Apoſtolic See."
[175] See above p. 30.
[176] See note 53, p. 31.
[177] For the myſtical reference attributed to woollen garments ſee note 30, p. 30.

tationem veſtimenti, quod et ſecundum literam et ſecundum ſpiritum
rite poſſumus intelligere.

CAP. 17. OF THE AMICE.

Amiǎus[178] eſt primum veſtimentum noſtrum, quo collum undique
cingimus. In collo eſt namque vox, ideoque per collum loquendi uſus
exprimitur. Per amiǎum intelligimus[179] cuſtodiam vocis, de qua Pſalmiſta dicebat: *Dixi, cuſtodiam vias meas, ut non delinquam in lingua
mea: poſui ori meo cuſtodiam.* Et in alio Pſalmo: *Pone, Domine,
cuſtodiam ori meo.* Amiǎus ideo dicitur, quia circumjicitur. In iſto
primo veſtimento admonetur caſtigatio vocis.[179]

CAP. 18. OF THE ALB.

Poſtea camiſiam induimus, quam Albam vocamus, de qua Hieronymus in epiſtola memorata de veſte ſacerdotali ad Fabiolam: *Secunda ex
lino tunica, eſt poderis, id eſt, talaris,* et in ſequentibus, *Hæc adhæret
corpori, et ita arǎa eſt et ſtriǎis manicis, ut nulla omnino in veſte
ſit ruga, et uſque ad crura deſcendat. Volo pro legentis facilitate, abuti
ſermone vulgato: Solent militantes habere lineas, quas camiſias vocant
ſic aptas membris et adſtriǎas corporibus, ut expediti ſint vel ad curſum,
vel ad ·prælia, dirigendo jaculo, tenendo clypeo, enſe librando, et quocunque neceſſitas traxerit. Ergo et ſacerdotes parati in miniſterio Dei
utantur hac tunica, ut habentes pulchritudinem veſtimentorum nudorum
celeritate diſcurrant.* In eo diſtat veſtimentum illud a noſtro, quod
illud ſtriǎum eſt, noſtrum vero largum. Etenim hi, qui, in veteri
teſtamento ſpiritu ſervitutis erant adſtriǎi, de quo dicebat Paulus:

---

[178] The amice was in ſhape (when opened
out ſquare) and in primitive uſe, nearly the
counterpart of our modern "white neckcloth." But inſtead of being folded ſeveral
times upon itſelf, it ſeems to have been either
kept open or doubled but once. Hence it
covered both neck and ſhoulders, and ſerved
to keep the outer garment from actual contact
with the ſkin. This mode of wearing it is
ſtill preſerved in Roman uſe. See Rock's
Hierurgia, vol. ii. p. 612, with the plate ad-
joining. But the thought of making this
neckcloth a *helmet* alſo [by holding it for a
few moments *upon the head,* ſee Rock, *loc.
cit.*] was an invention to which Amalarius and
his contemporaries were not prepared. We
ſhall find this, however, in a later author
quoted in this work. See the Index *in voc.*
Amictus.

[179] *Caſtigatio vocis.* See above note 163,
p. 90.

Non enim accepistis spiritum servitutis in timore. Nos vero quia
Filius liberavit, liberi sumus ; non accepimus spiritum servitutis in timore,
sed spiritum adoptionis filiorum. Ac ideo sic illorum strictum,[180] nostrum
largum, propter libertatem qua Christus nos liberavit. Quia primum
vestimentum diximus esse castigationem vocis, videamus si secundum habeat [181] aliquam castigationem corporis. Dicit Beda [182] in
libro de Tabernaculo ; *Hæc etenim linea, manus ac brachia debet
stringere sacerdotis, ne quid nisi utile faciant : pectus, ne quid inane
cogitet : ventrem, ne delicias ultra modum appetendo, deum se gulosis facere
præsumat : subjecta ventri membra, ne lasciviendo totam sacerdotalis habitus pulchritudinem corrumpant : genua, ne ab orationis instantia torpeant :
tibias et pedes, ne ad malum currant.* Induatur ergo sacerdos primo linea
stricta, ut et corpus ab iniquis operibus, et a pravis cogitationibus mentem
compescat. Quod ibi significat strictura vestimenti, hoc apud nos lini [183]
castigatio. Quia usque ad pedes Beda provenit disserendo de lineis
vestibus, congruum est, ut nosmetipsos absolvamus de sandaliis, sive ut
alio nomine campobis,[184] qui supersunt in pedibus. Sandalia subtus
cooperiunt pedem, desuper nudum relinquunt, de quibus dicit idem,
qui supra, in tractatu super Marcum : *Marcus dicendo calceari eos
sandaliis, vel soleis, aliquid hoc calceamentum mysticæ significationis habere
admonet, ut pes neque tectus sit, neque nudus ad terram, id est, nec occultetur evangelium, nec terrenis commodis innitatur.* Sicut per linum,
quo pedes vestiuntur, castigatio pedum significatur, ita per sandalia pro-
fectus ad prædicandum.

CAP. 19. OF THE CHASUBLE.

Casulam, quæ est generale indumentum sacrorum ducum,[185] ante
cæteras vestes quæ sequuntur, præponimus. In illis quæ supra præ-

---

[180] For the reason why the Levitical vestments were thus "closely fitted" to the body,
see note 6, p. 2.

[181] *Videamus si habeat.* To this the same
remark will apply that was made above, note
169, p. 93.

[182] The quotation is from the *De Tabernaculo,* lib. iii. cap. 8. See note above, p. 78,
sqq.

[183] *Lini castigatio.* See note 106, p. 60.

[184] *Campobis.* The true reading is probably
campagis. The *Campago* was a kind of shoe
worn at one time by Roman Senators only
(Albertus Rubenius *De Re Vest.* lib. ii. cap. 5),
and subsequently reserved as a special privilege
to the Roman clergy (Divi Gregor. Epist.
lib. vii. epist. 28).

[185] The term *sacri duces* seems to be here
used nearly as οἱ ἡγούμενοι in H.S. as a
general term for the two higher orders of the
ministry.

tulimus, castigatio corporis a vitiis designatur, excepto in sandaliis. In sequentibus vero opera justitiæ demonstrabuntur. Dicit Beda in libro memorato de Tabernaculo : *Vestes sanctæ Aaron, quas illi fecit Moises, opera sunt justitiæ et sanctitatis.* Casula vero, quæ pertinet generaliter ad omnes clericos, debet significare opera quæ pertineant ad omnes : hæc enim sunt fames, sitis, vigiliæ, nuditas, lectio, psalmodia, oratio, labor operandi, doctrina, silentium, et cætera hujusmodi. In istis enim nullus sacrorum Dux negligens debet esse. Quando istis operibus vestitur, casula indutus est. Hæc in aperto sunt, et tam ad minores gradus pertinent, quam ad supremos. Casula dupla est post tergum inter humeros, et ante pectus. Per humeros opera exprimuntur. In eis duplex sit vestimentum, quia sic debemus bona opera foris proximis ostendere, ut eadem intus coram Domino integra servemus. In pectore duplex, quia in eo utrunque debet esse, et doctrina et veritas : veritas interius, doctrina ad homines. Hæc duo duplicia sint conjuncta, quia tunc bene ministratur, cum opus et ratio in unum conveniunt. Opus ad humeros, ratio ad pectus.[106]

CAP. 20. OF THE STOLE.

Stolam [107] accipit diaconus, quando ordinatur ab episcopo. Ipsa enim semper utitur in opere ministerii. Per stolam designatur onus leve ac suave, de quo Dominus dicit : *Tollite jugum meum super vos, jugum enim meum suave est, et onus meum leve.* Per jugum evangelium intelligimus, de quo dicit Hieronymus in commentariis Matthæi : *Quomodo levius lege evangelium, cum in lege homicidium, in evangelio ira damnetur?* Et paulo post : *In lege multa præcepta sunt, quæ Apostolus non posse compleri plenissime docet. In lege opera requiruntur, quæ qui fecerit, vivet in eis : In evangelio voluntas requiritur, quæ si etiam effectum non habuerit, tamen præmium non amittet.* In eo quod stola ad genua tendit, quæ solent curvari causa humilitatis, hoc intelligimus, quod Dominus dicit : *Discite a me, quia mitis sum et humilis corde.* Sciat se diaconus in stola superposita collo, ministrum evangelii esse, non præpositum. Evangelium CHRISTUS est.

---

[106] *Opus ad humeros,* note 35, p. 22; *ratio ad pectus,* note 38, p. 22.

[107] The word *stola* here appears to the exclusion of the older word *orarium.* The vestment here meant closely resembled in shape the stole still worn in the Western Church. See the Plates dating from the 9th century among the Illustrations of this volume.

CAP. 21. OF THE DALMATIC.

Dalmatica a Silveſtro Papa inſtituta eſt. Per Dalmaticam intelligimus religionem fanctam immaculatam, quæ eſt apud Deum et Patrem, ut viſitentur pupilli et viduæ in tribulationibus eorum, et viſitatores immaculatos ſe cuſtodiant ab hoc ſeculo. Ipſa Dalmatica duas coccineas lineas habet retro, ſimiliterque in anteriori parte : quia vetus teſtamentum et novum rutilant dilectione [188] Dei et proximi. Immaculatum eſſe, ad Deum pertinet : viſitare fratres, ad proximum. Per colorem coccineum opera miſericordiæ, quæ ex charitate fiunt in pupillis et viduis, intelligimus : per candorem, viſitatorum munditia deſignatur. Ipſa eſt enim veſtis, de qua dicitur in pſalmo quadrageſimo quarto : *Adſtitit regina a dextris tuis in veſtitu deaurato, circundata varietate.* Unde Auguſtinus in eodem pſalmo : *In veſte iſta varietas ſit, ſciſſura non ſit. Ecce varietatem intelleximus de diverſitate linguarum, et veſtem intelleximus propter unitatem.* Et in ſequentibus, *Circumamicta varietate. Pulchritudo intrinſecus. In fimbriis autem aureis, varietas linguarum, doctrinæ decus.* Fimbriæ, quæ procedunt de Dalmatica, verba ſunt ejus prædicatoris, cujus religio ſancta et immaculata eſt. Sicut verba ab aura aeris raptantur, ita fimbriæ ſpiramine venti. Profert Paulus candidas fimbrias circa manus ad utilitatem gentium, quando dicit, *Magis autem laboret operando manibus ſuis quod bonum eſt, ut habeat unde tribuat neceſſitatem patienti.* Quod Paulus prædicavit, opere complevit, dicens ad Corinthios de ſe : *In tribulationibus, in laboribus.* Quod ita Ambroſius in eadem epiſtola : *Laborare non deſtitit manibus ſuis, ne cui gravis eſſet.* Fert fimbrias candidas in latere, quando dicit : *Caſtigo corpus meum, et in ſervitutem redigo ;* et in alio loco : *In caſtitate, hoc eſt, caſtitate corporis, et in vigiliis.* Qui hanc cuſtodit, immaculatum ſe cuſtodit ab hoc ſeculo. Fert coccineas circa humeros et pectora, quando dicit : *In charitate non ficta.* Ficta charitas eſt, quæ dimittit viduas et pupillos in tribulatione, et ſubvenit in proſperitate. Quæ fimbriæ ante ſunt et retro, quia mandatum dilectionis et in veteri teſtamento, et in novo, manet. Unde Johannes : *Chariſſimi, non mandatum novum ſcribo vobis, ſed mandatum vetus, quod habuiſtis ab initio. Mandatum vetus, eſt verbum quod audiſtis. Iterum mandatum novum ſcribo vobis.* Quod ita Beda : *Eadem charitas*

---

[188] *Rutilant dilectione.* On the aſſociation of red colour with the idea of charity, ſee above, p. 60, where St. Gregory ſays that the *bis tinctus coccus* of the Levitical high-prieſt is typical of charity (note 107 *in fin.*).

*et mandatum vetus est, quod ab initio commendata: et mandatum novum,
quia tenebris ejectis desiderium novæ lucis infundit.* Aliquæ Dalmaticæ
habent viginti octo fimbrias ante et retro. Ubi est octies repetitus
septiformis spiritus propter genera hominum quos replet, ut laudent
Deum, hoc est, reges terræ, et omnes populi, principes et judices,
juvenes et virgines, senes et juniores: et aliquæ triginta et triginta,
singulæ lineæ altrinsecus quindecim ; quia charitas et in veteri testamento
et in novo quindecim ramos ex se producit. Quisquis studet prodesse
fratribus in adversitate et in prosperitate, iste habet fimbrias coccineas
in utroque humero. Hæ duæ fortunæ signantur per sinistrum et dextrum humerum. Quindecim ramos charitatis enumerat: *Patiens
est, benigna est: non æmulatur, non agit perperam, non inflatur, non
est ambitiosa, non quærit quæ sua sunt, non irritatur, non cogitat
malum, non gaudet super iniquitate, congaudet autem veritati. Omnia suffert, omnia credit, omnia sperat, omnia sustinet.* Linea quæ
in medio est, est quasi stipes charitatis. Quod enim significant
lineæ sive fimbriæ in dextro humero sive sinistro, hoc significant in
anteriori parte hominis, quæ pertinet ad novum testamentum. Sinistrum latus habet fimbrias, quia actualis vita solicita est, et turbatur
erga plurima : at dextrum latus non habet, quia contemplativa vita
quieta est. Per ipsam figuratur regina, quæ stat a dextris. Ipsa est
una Columba ; perfecta et proxima stat a dextris, et nihil in se sinistrum
habet. Largitas brachiorum, largitatem et hilaritatem datoris demon-
strat. Diaconus qui non est indutus Dalmatica, casula legit circumcinctus,[189] ut expedite possit ministrare : vel quia suum est ire ad comitatum propter instantes necessitates. Ipsa habet pertusas subtus alas,
quoniam Christum vult imitari, qui lancea perfossus est in latere, et
vult ut nos sequamur ejus vestigia, quod significat pertusus in latere.

CAP. 22. OF THE UPPER TUNIC WORN OVER THE ALB.

Sicut in camisia [190] designatur castigatio corporis, ita in tunica
virtutes intimæ, quæ ad solos sublimes pertinent, de qua Hieronymus
in epistola ad Fabiolam : *Hæc ipsa hyacinthina tunica, subucula nominatur, et proprie pontificis est, significatque rationem sublimium non patere*

---

[189] It is not easy to give a meaning to these
words which will be in accordance with what
we know from other sources, and from Amalarius himself, to have been the characteristic
dress of the deacon. The meaning, probably,

is this, that a deacon, *if* not dressed in a Dalmatic, wears a Chasuble, but gathered into the
waist by a girdle.

[190] For the word *camisia* see note 23, p. 13.

omnibus sed majoribus atque perfectis.[191] Ipsa est interior, ipsaque designat virtutes animæ, quæ non multis cognitæ sunt, et quas semper debet habere perfectas. Unde Beda in tractatu super Lucam : *Quis etenim nesciat viscera misericordiæ, benignitatem, humilitatem, patientiam, modestiam, castitatem, fidem, spem et his similia, sine ulla temporum intercapedine a fidelibus esse servanda ?* Ipsa non cingitur, sed camisia. Quæ ita est fabrefacta, ut non impediat cursum nostrum ad ministrationem, quoniam memoratæ virtutes liberum nobis iter præbent ad contemplationem Dei. Camisia cingulo continentiæ constringitur, præcipiente Domino : *Sint lumbi vestri præcincti,* ut per duas virtutes, id est, obedientiam Domini, et naturalem disputationem,[192] constringatur omnis voluptas. Hæc sunt vestimenta de quibus scribitur in parabolis Salomonis, *Fortitudo et decor indumentum ejus.* Et in superioribus, *Et cingulum tradidit Chananæo.* Si quis voluerit uti duabus tunicis, ostendet se esse diaconum et sacerdotem, sive [193] ut octo sint vestimenta secundum numerum vestimentorum summi pontificis Aaron, cujus vestimenta narrantur fuisse circa caput et corpus usque ad pedes. De vestimento pedum et manuum reticetur. Ad illius normam, ut dixi, habet summus pontifex noster [194] a capite usque ad pedes octo vestimenta. Primum est amictus, secundum camisia, tertium cingulum, quartum stola, quintum et sextum duæ tunicæ, septimum casula, octavum pallium. Porro vestimentum pedum potius pertinet ad nostros pontifices, quam ad Aaron. Dicitur nostris pontificibus : *Euntes, docete omnes gentes :* Aaron tantum in Judæa versabatur. Sudarium in manu, potius ad nostros quam ad Aaron : quoniam major munditia est in novo testamento, quam esset in veteri : et illa bona habemus, quæ illi habuerunt, et plura per Jesum Christum Dominum nostrum. Sacerdos in suo officio non se exuit casula, quia præcipiente Domino per Moisen non debet exire de sanctis, sicut scriptum est : *Nec egredientur de sanctis.* Ubi intelligi datur, debere eum jugiter in continentia et abstinentia manere.

---

[191] See the passage from S. Jerome at p. 20. The words are quoted *verbatim,* with the exception of the three or four which refer to the LXX usage of ὑπεδύσης. The omission somewhat changes the sense of the original text.

[192] *Naturalem disputationem.* He probably means " contending against natural inclination " (the lusts of the flesh.)

[193] *Sive ut octo . . . reticetur.* I must confess that I am unable to follow exactly the thought of the writer in this passage. Two thoughts, however, we may trace. First he

hints that the two tunics may in some cases be adopted in order to accommodate the number of the Christian vestments to those of the tabernacle. And again, that in order to preserve this correspondence we must say nothing of what was worn on the hands and the feet of Christian priests.

[194] By the words *summus pontifex noster* we are probably to understand the *pontifex summus* (or chief Pontiff) " *of us Christians,*" in other words, an archbishop. Compare what he says below of *nostros pontifices.* [For the word *pontifex,* see note 45, p. 26.] See also note 167, p. 92.

Cap. 23. The Pallium worn by Archbishops.

Pallium archiepifcoporum fuper omnia indumenta eft, ut lamina in fronte folius pontificis.[195]   Illo difcernitur archiepifcopus a cæteris epifcopis.   Pallium fignificat torquem, quem folebant legitime certantes accipere.   Quo dono admonentur cæteri ad legitimum certamen.   Quod habet duas lineas[196] a fummo ufque deorfum ante et retro.   Significat enim fummæ doctrinæ decorem per difciplinam mandatorum Domini acceptabilem.   Circulus circa collum, difciplina eft Domini circa fermonem prædicatoris ; ut non fit alter fermo prædicationis, et aliud opus, dicente Paulo, *Nemini dantes ullam offenfionem, ut non vituperetur minifterium noftrum.*   Quod ita Ambrofius in tractatu epiftolæ ad Corinthios : *Vituperatur enim minifterium ipforum, fi ea quæ verbis docebant, operibus fuis, ut fierent, exempla non darent.*   Mandata Veteris Teftamenti, a principio Genefeos ufque finem, in humerali linea operando et docendo portet pontifex : in pectorali Novi, a primitiva ecclefia ufque in finem.   De torque dicebat Salomon in parabolis, *Ut addatur gratia capiti tuo, et torques collo tuo.*   Quod ita Beda in eodem : *Mos apud veteres fuit, ut legitime certantes, coronam in capite, torquem in collo, acciperent.   Et nobis ergo fi difciplinam Conditoris noftri, fi gratiæ matris fcita, cuftodimus, major inde virtutum fpiritalium claritas augetur.   Additur gratia capiti, cum charitas quæ principale mentis ornabat, ardentius inflammatur.   Additur et collo torques, cum fulgore perfectæ operationis fermo prædicationis, qui per collum procedit, confirmatur : ac ne contemni ab auditoribus debeat, indeficienti virtutum connexione docetur.   Sed et his qui Mofaicæ legis decreta Domino veniente fervabant, addita eft gratia novi teftamenti cum fpe regni cæleftis, cujus fplendor eximius ad exemplum coronæ vel torquis, nullo unquam fine claudetur.*

[195] *Pontifex* is here the Jewish high-prieft. Amalarius implies that as the high-prieft was diftinguifhed from other priefts by the golden plate upon his brow, fo are archbifhops diftinguifhed from other bifhops by the wearing of the *pallium*.

[196] The two lines (behind and in front) here fpoken of, and the *torques*, or collar, are evidently a defcription of fuch a later *pallium* (fee note 110, p. 63) as may be feen figured in the reprefentation of Egbertus, Archbifhop of Treves, and in the Mofaic pictures of the popes of the 12th century, given in this volume. He fays the bifhop is to bear upon the fhoulder-line (fee no.c 35) the precepts of the old covenant of *works;* on the pectoral-line (*i.e.* the part of the pallium which hangs down in front) thofe of the new covenant, "from the firft beginnings of the Church unto the end."

CAP. 24. OF THE SUDARIUM OR MANIPLE.

Sudario folemus tergere pituitam oculorum et narium atque fuper-fluam falivam decurrentem per labia. Ac ideo fudarium fignificat ifto in loco ftudium mundandæ cogitationis, quo naturales et velut ingenitas noftras delectationes ftudemus tergere. Sive propter effufionem lachry-marum tergendam fertur fudarium, ut in martyrologio Bedæ legitur, quod pater nofter Arfenius propter redundationem lachrymarum ter-gendam, fudarium femper in finu vel in manu habuerit. In manu finiftra portatur, ut oftendatur in temporali vita tædium nos pati fuper-flui humoris, hoc eft, carnalis delectationis. Et iterum : Sudarium ad hoc portamus, ut eo detergamus fudorem qui fit ex labore proprii corporis, quod legimus ufitatum fuiffe circa corpus Chrifti. Unde legitur,[197] *Et fudarium quod fuit fuper caput ejus.* Sudor tædium noftro corpori eft. Si non effet tædium, non toties tergeretur. Habet ali-quoties mens tædium, dicente pfalmifta : *Dormitavit anima mea præ tædio.* Tædium in anima, quafi fudor in corpore. Tædium animi aliquoties folet fieri ex confcientia peccatorum, aliquoties ex acciden-tibus, ut eft omne flagellum quod patitur ab alieno corpore : aliquoties ex infirmitate proprii corporis, quæ infirmitas aliquoties folet accidere ex peccatis. Quando tædium ex infirmitate peccatorum frontem con-fcientiæ noftræ tegit, habeamus fudarium ex lino caftigatum et mundum, qualia funt verba David prophetæ : *Cor mundum crea in me Deus, & fpiritum rectum innova in vifceribus mei.* Et fi fuerit infirmitas ex approbatione,[198] ficut in Iob, dicamus quod dixit : *Sicut Domino placuit, ita factum eft : fit nomen Domini benedictum.* Munda cogitatio in David fuit, quando dixit, *Cor mundum crea in me Deus :* mundaque in Iob, quando dixit, *Sicut Domino placuit, ita factum eft.* Sic et nos, quando tædio aliquo afficimur, ne majore triftitia abforbeamur, in con-folationem noftri quafi quoddam fudarium exempla prædicta fanctorum patrum ad corroborandam patientiam, ad detergendum tædium fuma-mus. Per fudarium intelligimus mundos affectus et pios in labore.[199]

---

[197] *Sudarium, &c.* He alludes (but with a ftrange mifapplication of the original paffage) to John, xx. 7, where there is mention of "the napkin" (Gr. σουδάριον) that was laid upon the face of our Lord after His death.

[198] *Ex approbatione :* i.e. fent as a trial of our faith.

[199] *In labore.* In time of trouble or of toil.

CAP. 25. OF THE SANDALS WORN BY BISHOPS, PRIESTS, ETC.

Varietas fandaliorum, varietatem miniftrorum pingit. Epifcopi et facerdotis pene unum eft officium; at quia nomine et honore difcernuntur, difcernuntur etiam varietate fandaliorum, ut vifibus noftris error auferatur, qui poteft intereffe propter fimilitudinem officii. Epifcopus habet ligaturam in fuis fandaliis, quam non habet prefbyter. Epifcopi eft huc illueque difcurrere per parochiam [600] ad regendam plebem : ne forte cadant fandalia de pedibus, ligata funt. Ex eo poteft fciri, quantum neceffe fit ei firmare greffus mentis, qui in turbis populorum verfatur. Prefbyter qui domi [601] hoftias immolat, fecurius incedit. Diaconus quia diffimilis eft epifcopo ab officio, non eft neceffe ut habeat diffimilia fandalia ; et ipfe ligaturam habet, quia fuum eft ire ad comitatum. Subdiaconus quia in adjutorio eft diacono et pene in eodem officio, neceffe eft ut habeat diffimilia fandalia, ne forte æftimetur diaconus. Myftice, quia fandalia prædicatoris curfum fignant, folea, quæ fubtus eft, admonet prædicatorem, ut non fe implicet terrenis negociis. Lingua de albo corio, quæ fubtus calcaneum [602] eft, monftrat, debere effe eandem feparationem innocentem et fine dolo, ut poffit de eo dici, *Ecce vere Ifraelita, in quo dolus non eft.* Non fit talis, quales pfeudo-apoftoli errant, qui prædicabant per invidiam et contentionem. Lingua quæ inde furgit, et eft feparata à corio fandaliorum, linguam eorum monftrat, qui prædicatori bonum teftimonium debent proferre, de quibus dicebat Paulus : *Oportet et cum teftimonium bonum habere ab his qui foris funt.* Hi funt in inferiore parte, et funt quodammodo feparati à converfatione fpiritalium. Lingua fuperior, fpiritalium lingua eft, qui prædicatorem introducunt in opus prædicationis. Hæc requiruntur in pofteriore vita prædicatoris. At intrinfecus de albo corio circundata funt fandalia : Ita oportet effe prædicatoris intentionem candidam coram Deo ex pura confcientia : extrinfecus vero nigrum ap-

---

[600] *Parochiam, i.e.* his diocefe. Such was the primitive meaning of the word παροικία in ecclefiaftical Greek (fee Bingham, vol. iii. p. 37), and thence of *parochia* in Latin. The word was ufed, according to its proper meaning, to fignify the "neighbourhood," *i.e.* the neighbouring diftrict which had its centre in any particular town,—fuch town forming the capital, fo to fpeak, both for civil and for ecclefiaftical purpofes. Our own "counties," each with its "county town," would perhaps be the neareft approach to fuch a παροικία, though as a rule our counties are very much larger than the ancient ecclefiaftical παροικους

[601] *Domi.* Not "at home" in the fenfe of in his "own houfe," but *domi* "ftaying at home," *i.e.* ftaying in the town wherein he dwelt, and in whofe Church *heftias immolabat,* to adopt the language of Amalarius.

[602] *Calcaneum,* probably the "tread" of the foot, to ufe a fhoemaker's phrafe. It is a word of the *lingua vulgaris,* and furvives, as moft of fuch words do, in the prefent language of Italy. [*Calcagno,* the heel.]

paret, quoniam videtur prædicatorum vita deſpecta à ſecularibus propter multitudinem preſſurarum præſentis mundi.   Superior pars ſandaliorum per quam pes intrat, multis filis confuta eſt, ut non diſſol-
vantur duo coria.   In initio enim debet ſtudere prædicator pluribus
virtutibus atque ſententiis ſcripturarum, ut opera forinſeca cum his quæ
intrinſecus nitent coram Deo, non disjungantur.   Lingua ſandaliorum
quæ ſuper pedem eſt, linguam prædicatoris poteſt figurare.   Linea opere
ſutoris facta, præcedens à lingua ſandalii uſque ad finem ejus, evangelicam perfectionem : lineæ præcedentes ex utraque parte, legem et
prophetias, quæ in evangelio recapitulantur.   Etenim ipſæ recapitulatæ
ſunt ad medianam lineam, quæ uſque ad finem currit.   Ligatura myſterium incarnationis Chriſti : quæ incarnatio in aliquibus aperta eſt humanis
ſenſibus humano more, ſicuti eſt poni in præſepio, pannis involvi, et
cætera.   Et aliter : Dicit Dominus in evangelio : *Quodcunque ſupurero-*
gaveris, ego cum rediero, reddam tibi.   Diſponit Dominus his qui evangelium prædicarent, de evangelio vivere : ſupererogavit Paulus, quia
ſine ſumptu expoſuit evangelium, operabatur manibus ſuis victus ſibi
neceſſaria.   Opus Pauli quod ſupererogavit evangelio, poſſumus intelligere
corrigias ſupererogatas ſandaliis, quæ manibus huc illucque ducuntur
ut ligentur.   Firmo greſſu it prædicator, qui nulli oneroſus eſt.

   Breviter deſideramus recapitulare omnem ornatum clericorum.
Caput clerici mens eſt.   In ſuperiore parte diſco opertum, ubi eſt imago
Dei, in inferiore parte circundatum capillis, quaſi aliquibus cogitationibus de præſenti neceſſitate.   Amictus eſt caſtigatio vocis, Alba
cæterorum inferiorum ſenſuum, præſidente magiſtra ratione, interius
per diſciplinam continentiæ conſtringente, quaſi quodam cingulo, voluptatem carnis.   Calceamenti linea, prohibitio pedum ad malum
feſtinando.   Sandalia ornatus, iter prædicatoris, quia cæleſtia non debet abſcondere, neque terrenis inhiare.   Secunda tunica, opera mentis
ſunt : caſula, opera corporis pia.   Stola, jugum Chriſti, quod eſt
evangelium.   Dalmatica diaconi et ſui miniſtri, quæ eſt itineri [203]
habilis, cura proximorum eſt.   Sudarium, piæ et mundæ cogitationes,
quibus detergimus moleſtias animi ex infirmitate corporis.   Pallium
archiepiſcoporum, torques devotiſſimæ prædicationis et in veteri teſtamento, et in novo.

---

[203] *Dalmatica . . . quæ eſt itineri habilis.*
By a dalmatic "ſuitable for travel," he means
a ſhort dalmatic, not reaching lower than the
knee.   This ſhortened dalmatic, aſſigned to
deacon and ſubdeacon (*ſui miniſtri*) is ſuggeſtive, he ſays, of the activity which they
ſhould diſplay in work of charitable relief (*cura*
proximorum).   This will be explained by what
has been ſaid in the Introduction, of the various
forms of the tunic anciently in uſe.

XXXIII.

WALAFRIDUS STRABO.[204]

Cap. 24. DE VASIS ET VESTIBUS SACRIS.

De Rebus Ecclesiasticis.

Vasa quoque, quibus præcipue noftra Sacramenta imponuntur et confecrantur. Calices funt et Patenæ. Calix dicitur à Græco nomine κάλιξ.[205] Patena à patendo, quod patula fit. Ampulla, quafi parum [206] ampla. Zepherinus[207] Ro. Pontifex xvi patenis vitreis Miffas celebrare conftituit. Tum deinde Urbanus[208] xviii Papa, omnia minifteria facrata fecit argentea, et patenas 25. In hoc ficut et in reliquis cultibus, magis et magis per incrementa temporum decus fuccrevit Ecclefiæ. Bonifacius[209] martyr et Epifcopus interrogatus, Si liceret in vafis ligneis facramenta conficere, refpondit: *Quondam facerdotes aurei ligneis calicibus utebantur: nunc e contra, lignei facerdotes aureis utuntur calicibus.* Sylvefter[210] Papa conftituit, Sacrificium altaris non in ferico, non in panno tincto celebrari, nifi tantum lineo e terra[211] procreato: ficut corpus Domini Jefu Chrifti in findone munda fepultum eft. Veftes etiam facerdotales per incrementa ad eum, qui nunc habetur, auctæ funt ornatum. Nam primis temporibus communi indumento veftiti, Miffas agebant, ficut et hactenus quidam Orienta-

---

[204] Walafrid was of German birth, and a pupil of Rabanus Maurus (fee note 155) at Fulda. At a later period he became Dean of St. Gall, and in 842 A.D. was made Abbot of Refenau (*Augiæ Majoris*) in the diocefe of Conftance. The text is that of Hittorpius.

[205] Mifprinted in Hittorpius κύλιξ.

[206] His etymology is at fault here. The word is probably *amb-olla* or *ambi-olla*. The old Latin *ampulla* was a jar, or bottle, which from its full fwelling fhape came to be ufed metaphorically of anything that was over

big or its place [*Projicit ampullas et fefquipedalia verba:* Hor.]. This later ufe is illuftrated by the verb *ampullari*, to be pompous or bombaftic, and the *It.* ampollofità, "bombaft." Compare the Fr. Ampoulé, bombaftic. The *It.* Ampolletta, Fr. Ampoulette, an "hour-glafs," have preferved the original fignification of the word.

[207] Zephyrinus *fed.* 202-218.

[208] Urbanus *fed.* 223-230.

[209] Our countryman Winifrid was born at *Crificdunum* (Crediton) in Devon, A.D. 670.

XXXIII.

WALAFRID STRABO.[204]

Cap. 24. OF HOLY VESSELS AND VESTMENTS.

De Rebus Ecclesiasticis.

THE veffels on which for the moft part our holy oblations (*facramenta*) are placed and confecrated are Chalices and Patens. The Chalice is fo called from the Greek word χάλυξ.[205] The Paten, from *patere*, in reference to its open flat furface. The *Ampulla*, or Flagon, as though from *parum ampla*,[206] in refpect of its fmall fize. Zepherinus,[207] fixteenth Bifhop of Rome, ordered the celebration of maffes on patens, made of glafs. Then again, Urbanus,[208] eighteenth Pope, made of filver all the veffels to be ufed in holy miniftry, and amongft thefe twenty-five patens. In this, as in other matters of outward obfervance, the beauty of the church's ornaments increafed with the increafe of years. Boniface,[209] martyr and bifhop, was once afked whether it were lawful to confecrate the holy elements in veffels of wood. To this he replied, " *Golden priefts, and wooden chalices, fuch was once the rule. Now it is the priefts that are wooden, while the chalices that they ufe are of gold.*" Pope Sylvefter[210] ordained that the facrifice of the altar fhould be celebrated not in filk nor in dreffes of dyed cloth, but only in linen, which is produced from out the earth;[211] even as the body of our Lord

---

When confecrated *epifcopus Germanicum* by Gregory II. in 723, he affumed the name of Bonifacius, by which he has fince been known. A letter of his to Cuthbert, Archbifhop of Canterbury (Spelman, Concil. p. 241), breathes a fimilar fpirit of fevere condemnation againft the increafing luxury in drefs and ornament of the churchmen of his time. " *Supervacuam et Deo odibilem veftimentorum fuperftitionem omni intentione prohibere ftude, quia illa ornamenta veftium, ut illis videtur, quod ab aliis turpitudo dicitur, latiffimis clavis et vermium imaginibus clavata, adventum Antichrifti, ab illo tranf-*

miffa, præcurrunt. Illius calliditate per minif-tros fuos introducere intra clauftra monafteriorum fornicationem et luxuriam clavatorum juvenum, et fæda confortia, et tædium lectionis et orationis, et perditionem animarum. Hæc indumenta nudita-tem animæ fignificantia, figna in fe oftendunt arrogantiæ et fuperbiæ et luxuriæ et vanitatis; de quibus Sapientia dicit : Arrogantiam, et fuper-biam, et viam pravam, et bilinguia detector."

[210] Sylvefter fed. 314-335.

[211] He implies a contraft with the *animæ* origin of woollen garments. See note 30.

lium facere perhibentur. Stephanus [212] autem xxiv conftituit, facerdotes
et Levitas veftibus facratis in ufu quotidiano non uti, nifi in Ecclefia
tantum. [213] Et Sylvefter ordinavit, ut Diaconi dalmaticis in Ecclefia
uterentur, et pallio linoftimo eorum læva tegeretur. [214] Et primo
quidem facerdotes Dalmaticis ante Cafularum ufum induebantur : poftea
vero cum Cafulis uti cœpiffent, Dalmaticas Diaconibus concefferunt.
Ipfos tamen Pontifices eis uti debere, ex eo clarum eft, quod Gregorius
vel alii Romanorum præfules, aliis Epifcopis earum ufum permiferunt,
aliis interdixerunt. Ubi intelligitur non omnibus tunc fuiffe conceffum,
quod nunc pene omnes Epifcopi, et nonnulli prefbyterorum, fibi licere
exiftimant, id eft, ut fub Cafula Dalmatica veftiantur.

Statutum eft autem Concilio Bracarenfi, [215] *Ne facerdos fine orario cele-
bret Miffam.* Addiderunt in veftibus facris alii alia : vel ad imitationem
eorum quibus veteres utebantur facerdotes, vel ad myfticæ fignifica-
tionis expreffionem. Quid enim fingula defignent, quibus utimur
nunc, à prioribus noftris fatis expofitum eft. Numero autem fuo antiquis refpondent : quia ficut ibi tunica fuperhumeralis, linea, [216] fuperhumerale, rationale, balteus, feminalia, tiara et lamina, fic hic dalmatica,
alba, mappula, orarium, cingulum, fandalia, cafula et pallium. Unde
ficut illorum extremo foli Pontifices, fic horum ultimo fummi tantum
paftores utuntur. [217]

---

[212] Stephanus *fed.* 253–257.

[213] Dr. Hefele remarks with truth that
fuch a prohibition implies that the veftments
of Chriftian miniftry were then fuch as *could*
have been worn for other than ecclefiaftical
ufe.—*Liturgifche Gewänder*, p. 153.

[214] *Ut eorum læva pallio linoftimo tegeretur.*
Compare note 157, p 88. The interpretation
there given (as again here) to the fomewhat
obfcure interpretation of the text is fuggefted by the many ancient monuments, in
which the left hand of bifhops, priefts, or
deacons is feen, covered either with the *orarium* or fome other piece of cloth, when holding facred veffels or facred books. We may
not improbably conjecture that this direction
to the Roman deacons had reference, in the
firft inftance, to the care that was neceffary in
the ufe of thofe filver veffels (replacing the
earlier glafs veffels), introduced according to
Roman tradition by Urbanus, rather earlier in
the third century. Hence probably the origin
of that *mappula* (the later maniple), the ufe of
which was claimed (*fupra*, pp. 65, 66) in St.

Gregory's time as an exclufively Roman privilege by the Roman clergy, and only after
long debate allowed, under guarded reftrictions,
to the principal deacons of the Church of
Ravenna. [As to the *privilege* of wearing a
Dalmatic noticed by Walafrid, fee above p.
67.]

[215] The fecond Council of Bracara held A.D.
572.

[216] In Hittorpius punctuated thus, " *Tunica,
fuperhumeralis linea, fuperhumerale,*" &c. So
written it is unintelligible.

[217] Note here that with Walafrid the
"*Amice*" is not reckoned among the veftments
at all, and he has to make up the number
required by adding the *fandals*, which in point
of fact conftitute a remarkable contraft to the
bare-footed miniftrations of the law.

Note alfo that it is clear that no epifcopal
mitre (in the modern fenfe of the word) could
have been in ufe in Walafrid's time, as it is
impoffible to conceive, were it otherwife, that
he fhould have failed to notice the coin-
cidence.

Jesus Chrift was buried in clean linen. And only by succeffive additions did the prieftly garb attain to that degree of ornament which
is now obferved. For in the earlieft times mafs was performed by
men wearing the drefs of ordinary life, as is faid to be done even to
this day by fome in the Eaftern Churches. But Stephanus,[212] twenty-
fourth Pope, directed that priefts and Levites fhould not employ their
facred drefs for ordinary daily ufe, but referve them exclufively for the
Church.[213] By order of Silvefter, deacons were to ufe dalmatics in
the church, and their left hand was to be covered with a *pallium*
(cloth) of linen weft.[214] And in the firft inftance, before chafubles
came into ufe, thofe of the prieftly order wore dalmatics. But afterwards, when they began to wear chafubles, they left the ufe of the dalmatic to deacons. Yet that even pontiffs themfelves ought to wear it,
is clear from this, that Gregory and other Roman primates (*præfules*)
allowed the ufe of the Dalmatic to fome bifhops, forbade it in the cafe
of others. And by this it is evident that in thofe days that was not
matter of general privilege (the wearing I mean of a Dalmatic under
the Chafuble) which now almoft all bifhops and priefts think is permitted them. Then at the Council of Bracara [215] it was prefcribed
that no prieft fhould celebrate mafs without an Orarium (or " ftole ").
Succeffive additions were made in this matter of veftments from time
to time, partly by way of imitating what was worn by the priefts
of the old Covenant, partly for the expreffion of a myftical meaning.
What is fignified by each of the veftments worn in our own day,
thofe who have preceded me have fufficiently fhown. But in refpect
of their number they correfpond with the veftments of the old law.
For whereas then there were the tunic of the ephod, the tunic of
linen,[216] fuperhumeral (or ephod), breaftplate, girdle, drawers, tiara, and
frontlet, fo have we now dalmatic, alb, maniple, ftole, girdle, fandals,
chafuble, and pallium. And as the laft named of thofe older veftments
was worn only by high-priefts, fo is the laft of thefe Chriftian veftments
worn only by chief paftors.[217]

XXXIV.

ALBINUS FLACCUS ALCUINUS.[218]

THE PRIESTLY VESTMENTS OF THE LAW AND OF THE GOSPEL.

LIBER DE DIVINIS OFFICIIS.

NUNC dicendum de fingulis veftibus, quibus facerdotes vel reliqui ordines in veteri teftamento utebantur. Erant autem octo fpecies veftium facerdotalium, id eft, tunica linea ftricta, tunica hyacinthina, fuperhumerale, rationale, cidaris, balteum, lamina aurea in fronte pontificis, et feminalia linea. His omnibus pontifex tempore facrificii induebatur: cæteris vero, minoris gradus facerdotibus, folis quatuor licebat uti, id eft, tunica linea ftricta, cidari, balteo, et feminalibus. Reliqua vero quatuor tantum fummi pontificis erant.

Nunc de fingulis explanemus. Tunica linea, veftis erat interior, quam camifiam dicimus vel fupparum. Hæc ftricta dicitur, quoniam adhærebat corpori, et ita erat ftrictis manicis,[219] ut nulla ei omnino ruga ineffet. Sicut folent milites habere tunicas lineas fic aptas membris, ut expediti fint dirigendo jaculo, tendendo clypeum, librando gladium, qualem et Joab habuiffe legitur ftrictam ad menfuram habitus corporis fui: pro qua nunc facerdotes vel clerici albas habent. Tunica tota hyacinthina exterior, nullumque alium colorem recipiens, ufque ad pedes defcendens, ficut et linea, unde et utraque græce podéris, id eft, talaris vocabatur, habens fimilitudinem malorum granatorum aure-

---

[218] This treatife was by the earlier editors affigned, without fufpicion, to Alcuin, our countryman, pupil of Bede, who died A.D. 804. But there is a general agreement now in affigning it to a much later date. Thus Cave (Hift. Lit. tom. i. p. 638): *Alcuini non effe* (De Divinis Officiis Liber) *et poft annum 1000 fcriptum effe, certo certius conftat.* And Dr. Hefele, in referring to the work, writes to

the fame effect: " *in dem Werke . . . . das früher Alkuin zugefchrieben, aber neuern Unterfuchungen gemäfz erft in 10ten oder 11ten Jahrhundert verfafzt wurde.*"—Liturg. Gewänd. p. 156. [The text is that of Hittorpius, p. 74 *fqq.*]

[219] *Stricta . . . ftrictis manicis, &c.* See note 6, p. 2.

orum, et tintinnabula aurea. Erat autem fine manicis ad colobiorum [200] fimilitudinem, et ideo unde manus educerentur, aperta erat. Pro tunica hyacinthina noftri pontifices primo colobiis utebantur. Eft autem colobium veftis fine manicis.

Hæ duæ veftes, id eft, tunica byffina ftricta, et tunica hyacinthina, balteo adftrictæ erant, quód erat cinguli genus ex byffo retorta, hyacintho, purpura ac vermiculo,[201] opere plumari,[202] in fimilitudinem pellis colubri, latitudinis quatuor digitorum. Pro balteo nunc zonarum, quas Romanas appellant, ufus receptus eft. Superhumerale,[203] quod Hebraice ephod dicitur, fic vocatum, quod humeros obnuberet: cujus contextus de omnibus coloribus erat, magnitudinis cubitalis, id eft, ufque ad cingulum pertingens, amplectens omnem locum pectoris, et ad manus ejiciendas hincinde apertum. Cui veftimento locus vacuus dimittebatur in medio pectore, magnitudine palmi, ubi inferebatur rationale, quod Hebraice dicitur effin, et Græce logion. Habebat autem fuperhumerale in utroque humero fingulos lapides onychinos, et in fingulis lapidibus erant fculpta fingula duodecim patriarcharum nomina. Habent etiam nunc miniftri ecclefiæ Chrifti fuperhumerale, quod amictum [204] vocamus, quando ad altare miniftrant. Rationale [205] opere polymito factum erat, juxta texturam fuperhumeralis, id eft, eifdem coloribus factum erat, quadrangulum, habens menfuram palmi in longitudinem et latitudinem. Erant in eo quatuor ordines lapidum, terni per fingulos verfus diftributi: fculpti erant fingulis duodecim patriarcharum nominibus. Erant autem catenulæ aureæ, et uncini aurei: necnon et aurei annuli, tam in quatuor fummitatibus rationalis, quam et in fummitatibus fuperhumeralis, quæ catenulæ inferebantur, jungebantque rationale et fuperhumerale fuperius, inferius vero vittis hyacinthinis fibi nectebantur. Pro rationali nunc fummi pontifices,[206] quos archiepifcopos dicimus, pallio [207] utuntur, quod à fancta Romana fede,

[200] *Colobium,* i.e. a tunic without fleeves.

[201] *Vermiculus* [whence the Fr. Vermeil, Eng. Vermilion] the equivalent of *coccus,* or fcarlet.

[202] *Opere plumari,* i.e. embroidery.

[203] *Superhumerale* . . . . *ephod.* See above pp. 4. 14.

[204] *Amictum.* See above, note 178, p. 96.

[205] *Rationale.* See p. 22, note 36.

[206] *Summi pontifices.* Note 45, p. 26. Alcuin himfelf gives a good and pious (but unhiftorical) derivation of the word in this fame treatife (p. 73), *Pontifex,* he fays, *quaſi pontem faciens; eo quod pontem, id eft, viam aliis præbere*

debeat, *verbo et exemplo, unde homines tranſeant ad vitam cœleſtem.* He probably was not at all aware of the claſſical ufage of the word.

[207] *Pro rationali* . . . *pallio utuntur.* For the *pallium* here fpoken of fee note 196, p. 102. Anything lefs like the "rational" or breaft-jewel of the Jewifh high-prieft, with its twelve precious ftones, than the pallium of an archbifhop, it would be difficult to conceive. But fuch comparifons were not too violent for writers of the tenth or eleventh century. And thefe, I regret to add, have not been without their followers in the nineteenth.

Apostolico [226] dante, suscipiunt. Tiara [227] erat vestis, pileolum videlicet rotundum, quasi sphæra media sic divisa, ut et pars una ponatur in capite, ita ut medii verticis medietatem non excedat, habens vittas, quæ convolutæ sæpius connectuntur, ne facile dilabantur. Et hoc quidem minorum erat sacerdotum : Summus autem Pontifex præter pileum habebat coronam auream, triplicemque, super quam à media fronte surgebat quasi calamus quidam aureus, similis herbæ, quæ hebraice acano, græce autem hios, [229] quæ apud nos latine cidaris. Per circulum vero habebat flores, similes flori plantaginis, ab occipitio usque ad utrunque tempus. In fronte vero erat locus patens, ubi inserebatur lamina aurea, quæ quatuor literis nomen Dei habebat scriptum.

Hujuscemodi vestis non habetur in Romana ecclesia, vel in nostris regionibus. Non enim moris est, ut pileati divina mysteria celebrent. Apud græcos autem hoc dicitur, qui pileos, id est, cuphias [230] gestant in capite dum affistunt altaribus. Lamina aurea in fronte pontificis, in qua sanctum Domino sive sanctum Domini sculptum habebatur, ornamentum erat cæteris sacratius indumentis. Sanctum autem Domino, quod ibi sculptum erat nomen sanctum et venerabile Dei, quod per quatuor literas scribebatur, יהוה scilicet, iod, he, vau, heth ; et dicebatur ineffabile, non quod dici non possit, sed quia nec definiri et compræhendi sensu ullius creaturæ, ut digne Deo aliquid dici possit. Ligabatur autem vitta hyacinthina super tiaram, ut totam pontificalis ornatus pulchritudinem Dei vocabulum coronaret ac protegeret. Neque hanc ornamenti speciem Christi accepit ab illis ecclesia. Octavum, id est, novissimum ornamentum seminalia linea, quibus operiebant carnem turpitudinis suæ, ab renibus usque ad femina sive (ut usitatius) femora, cum ad sacrificium accedebant. Hujusmodi habitus ita notus est in nostris regionibus, ut ex eo Gallia bracata cognominata sit.

Compræhensum breviter, quibus vestibus ornarentur sacerdotes et ministri templi Dei, Mosaicæ legis temporibus, quas ad instar illorum, revelata evangelii gratia, suscepit Ecclesia. Sunt tamen alia quæ apud illos non habebantur, ut stola, [231] sandalia, et sudarium, [232] quod ad tergen-

---

[226] *Apostolico*, i.e. the " pope," Bishop of the Apostolic See. For the word *tiara*, which follows, see note 84, p. 52.

[229] *Hios.* He refers to the word ὑοσκύαμος, or *Hyoscyamus.* The Latin *cidaris* has nothing whatever to do with this plant, but, like the Greek κίδαρις, which it represents, is the proper designation of a *royal* (or of a high-priest's) tiara.

[230] *Cuphias.* The Greek κουφία or σκουφία,

a skull-cap, a word noticed by Eustathius, on Iliad x, and of not unfrequent occurrence in Byzantine Greek. But it is nowhere used by any classical writer, as far as I am aware.

[231] *Stola.* Here used absolutely for the older word *orarium.* It is of the "stole" as we understand the word, that he is speaking. Compare note 187, p. 98.

[232] *Sudarium.* See above, p. 103, and note 197.

dum fudorem in manu geftari mos eft, quod ufitato nomine fanonem vocamus.[233]

Verum quia illo tempore figuris omnia et ænigmatibus obumbrabantur, convenit, ut quid illa veftimenta myftice fignificaverint, quove nomine nunc fpecialiter in ecclefia venerantur, non verbatim, fed capitulatim oftendamus. Veftimenta illa, quæ in fanctis officiis portanda erant, typus erant fanctarum virtutum, unde et fancta dicebantur. Ad hæc facienda non tam diverfa, quam fpeciofæ fpecies fumebantur, aurum videlicet, quod eft fplendor fapientiæ divinæ, cui jungebatur hyacinthus,[234] qui eft color aerius, cælefte videlicet defiderium. Purpura apponebatur, quæ fanguinis imitatur colorem, ut per duo genera martyrii noverint fe exercendos electi, id eft, fi neceffe fit, non dubitent mori pro Chrifto, et pacis tempore in feipfis appetitus occidant, mortificantes membra fua cum vitiis et concupifcentiis. Coccus[235] bis tinctus, Dei et proximi dilectionem indicat efficaciter tenendam. Byffus geminam caftitatem, corporis fcilicet et animæ, fignificat: unde de vere vidua dicit Apoftolus, *Ut fit fancta corpore et fpiritu.* His ornamentis debet Chrifti pontifex refulgere, his coloribus exornari. Tunica linea, et byffina ftricta, mortificationem[236] carnis pretendit. Byffum enim vel linum, multiplici elaboratum contufione, et naturæ fubtilitate deductum ac textum, in veftem proficit. Sic nullus Chrifto ornari poterit, nifi caftigatis et mortificatis omnibus carnis paffionibus: unde et bene ftricta dicitur. Strictum enim, caftum dicimus: e contra lafcivum, diffolutum vocamus. Tunica tota hyacinthina, quæ aerio refulgebat[237] colore, cæleftem defignat converfationem: quæ tota erat hyacinthina, quia facerdos nihil debet curare terrenum: nemo enim, ait Apoftolus, militans Deo, implicat fe negociis fecularibus, ut ei placeat, cui fe probavit. Balteus five cingulum, quo tunica hæc cum interiore, id eft, linea, cingebatur, continentiam infinuat, quæ mater eft et cuftos pudicitiæ, qua maxime ornari pontifices condecet: hanc, qui ingratus eft Deo, perdit, ficut Job de talibus dicit: *Balteum regum diffolvit, et*

---

[233] *Fanon.* This word is fuppofed to be connected with the German *fahne*, meaning a piece of cloth (of wool or of linen), and hence, according to the various ufes to which fuch a piece of cloth may be applied, a banner or enfign; a clerical veftment; a " corporal."

[234] *Hyacinthus . . . color aerius.* See note 32, p. 10.

[235] *Coccus . . . dilectionem indicat.* See note 188.

[236] Compare note 106, p. 60.

[237] *Refulgebat . . erat . . . cingebatur . . . induebatur, &c.* From the ufe of thefe tenfes of paft time it is clear that throughout this portion of the treatife the author is fpeaking of the fpiritual fignificance of the Levitical veftments, not of thofe worn in Chriftian miniftry. It is not till fomewhat later (fee below p. 115) that he goes on to fpeak of thefe laft.

præcingit fune renes eorum. Regum enim, id eſt, ſanctorum ſacerdotum, balteum, hoc eſt, pudicam continentiam diſſolvit, id eſt, diſſolvi permittit, cum de ſuis virtutibus extolli cœperint : et præcingit fune aſperæ pœnitentiæ renes eorum, ut incipiant ſuis caſibus ingemiſcere, qui aliorum lapſibus debuerant auxilio ſubvenire.

Superhumerale, quod Hebraice ephod dicitur, obedientiam mandatorum Dei ſignificat, quo induebatur ſacerdos, ut meminerit præcepta Dei ſtrenue quaſi onus humeris impoſitum debere portare. Quod vero nomina patriarcharum inter ſacrificia et in humeris, ſicut et in pectore, portabat, monetur per hoc ſacerdos, ut priorum patrum fidem et exempla ſequatur,[238] ut fidelium, qui ſunt filii apoſtolorum, in ſuis orationibus meminerit, et ut ipſis eadem exempla ſequenda proponat.

Rationale, quod erat in fronte [239] pontificis, deſignat, quia paſtor ſapientia et doctrina debet præditus eſſe. Nam et ideo rationale judicii dicitur, quia debet rector eccleſiæ ſubtili ſemper examinatione bona malaque diſcernere, et quid vel quibus, quando et qualiter conveniat, ſtudioſe cogitare. Hoc enim quod dicitur, *Pones in rationale judicii doctrinam et veritatem,* ut videlicet habeat ſcientiam ſcripturarum, quo poſſit alios docere, et contradicentes arguere. Quadrangulum erat, propter quatuor Evangeliorum doctrinam : duplex, propter ſcientiæ et operis firmitatem. Menſura palmi, quod eſt digitorum extenſio, deſignat diſcretionem in perſeverantia bonorum operum.

Quatuor ordines lapidum, qui erant in rationali, nominibus patriarcharum inſculpti, quatuor exprimunt principales virtutes, prudentiam, temperantiam, fortitudinem, juſtitiam. Terni in unoquoque lapides, fidem ſanctæ Trinitatis, ſive fidem, ſpem, et charitatem, demonſtrant. Quæ omnia in pectore pontificis neceſſario eſſe debere, hujus ornamenti, id eſt, rationalis ſpecie præmonetur. Tiara, quæ et cidaris et mitra vocatur, et contegebat et ornabat caput pontificis, admonet eum omnes ſenſus capitis Deo conſecrare debere, ne vel oculi pateant ad videndum vanitatem, vel cæteri ſenſus, qui in capite vigent, iniquitati conſentiant, et per illos intromiſſa delectatio inceſtet animi ſanctitatem. Lamina aurea, divinæ majeſtatis atque potentiæ figura eſt, quæ in fronte pontificis deportabatur, quia illa ineffabilis Deitatis potentia cunctis, quæ creavit, ſupereminet : et idcirco, quaſi cuncta

---

[238] *Ut priorum patrum fidem et exemplum ſequatur* . . . So St. Gregory, quoted at p. 58.

[239] *Rationale . . . in fronte.* By "frons" is here meant not the "brow" or "forehead," but the "front." Compare the expreſſion uſed by St. Gregory (*ſup.* p. 56) *in prima ſui corporis parte.*

fanctificans, eximiam fibi fedem in fronte, hoc eft, in mentis princi-
palitate conftituit.

Quatuor literæ in lamina fcriptæ, quatuor funt cornua crucis, totum
mundum complectentis. Cruci enim Chrifti in omni creatura apex [240]
conceditur, qua omnium fidelium frontes fignantur.

Quod lamina femper in fronte pontificis effe videbatur, oftendit,
quia dignitatem, quam prætendit in habitu, exercere femper debet in
opere, ut Domini placitum femper habere, et fubditorum vota Domino
idoneus fit femper offerre. Feminalia, quibus pudenda loca corporis
tegebantur, continentiam a concubitu defignant, quæ magnopere omnibus gradibus obfervanda præcipitur. Unde dicitur, *ad velandam turpitudinem.* Turpe eft enim, facerdotem nota lafciviæ ætatis infamari,
quem convenit velut in arce caftimoniæ, ab omnibus fufpici et vene-
rari.

Quod vero feminalia ipfi fibi imponant, cætera Moifes : defignat,
unumquemque fe à carnali concupifcentia refrenare debere. Deinde
virtutibus fibi fubditos, quafi Moifem miniftrum templi veftibus, ex-
ornare.

OF THE VESTMENTS OF CHRISTIAN PRIESTHOOD.

1. THE SANDALS.

Sandaliæ dicuntur foleæ. Eft autem genus calceamenti, quo induuntur miniftri Ecclefiæ, fubterius quidem folea muniens pedes à
terra, fuperius vero, nil operimenti habens, patet : quo juffi funt Apoftoli à Domino indui. Significat autem, miniftrum verbi Dei non
debere terrenis incumbere, fed potius cæleftibus inhiare, et prædicationem fuam nulli occultare.

2. THE SUPERHUMERAL.

Poft fandalias in Ecclefiæ veftimentis fequitur Superhumerale,[241]
quod fit ex lino puriffimo. Per linum quod ex terra fumitur, et per
multos labores ad candorem ducitur, defignatur corpus humanum,
quod ex terra conftat. Sicut ergo linum per multos labores ad can-

---

[240] *Apex.* The higheft point of anything, and fo " the place of higheft honour."

[241] *Superhumerale.* He means the " amice " (*amictus*) as he had faid above, p. 111, *fuper-humerale quod amictum vocamus.*

dorem perducitur, ita corpus humanum multis calamitatibus attritum, candidum et purum esse debet ab omni sorde peccatorum.

3. The Alb.

Postea sequitur podéris, quæ vulgo Alba dicitur. Significat autem perseverantiam in bona actione. Hinc Joseph inter fratres suos, talarem tunicam habuisse describitur. Tunica usque ad talum, est opus bonum usque ad consummationem. In talo enim finis est corporis. Ille ergo bene inchoat, qui rectitudinem boni operis usque ad finem debitæ perducit actionis. Qui enim perseverarit usque in finem, hic salvus erit.

4. The Girdle.

Deinde sequitur Zona, quæ cingulum dicitur, qua restringitur podéris, ne laxe per pedes diffluat. Per quam designatur discretio omnium virtutum: virtutes enim sine discretione, non virtutes, sed vitia sunt: nam virtutes in quodam meditullio sunt constitutæ.

5. The Stole.

Sequitur orarium. Orarium, id est, stola, dicitur eo quod oratoribus, id est, prædicatoribus concedatur. Admonet illum, qui illo induitur, ut memor sit, sub jugo Christi, quod leve et suave est, esse se constitutum.

6. The Dalmatic.

Dalmatica quæ sequitur, ob hoc dicitur, eo quod in Dalmatia sit reperta. Usus autem Dalmaticarum à B. Silvestro Papa institutus est: nam antea colobiis utebantur. Colobium vero est vestis sine manicis. Significat autem in eo quod est sine manicis, unumquemque fidelem exercitatum esse debere ad bona opera exercenda. Cum ergo nuditas brachiorum culparetur, ut diximus, à B. Silvestro Dalmaticarum repertus est usus. Est autem vestimentum in modum crucis, monens, indutorem suum crucifixum esse debere mundo, juxta Apostolum, *Mihi mundus crucifixus est, et ego mundo.* Habet etiam in sinistra parte sui fimbrias. Per sinistram partem præsens vita figu-

ratur, quæ diverſis curis abundat : quæ curæ ſignificantur per fimbrias ſiniſtræ partis. Per dexteram quæ fimbriis caret, futura vita
exprimitur, in qua nullæ curæ ſolicitant animas ſanctorum. Incon-
ſutilis etiam eſt, quia in Eccleſia vel in corde uniuſcujuſque
fidelis, nulla debet eſſe ſciſſura, ſed indiſciſſa fidei integritas. Siniſtrum
latus habet fimbrias, quia actualis vita ſolicita eſt, et turbatur erga
plurima. At dexterum latus non habet, quia contemplativa vita nihil
in ſe habet ſiniſtrum. Largitas [242] brachiorum, largitatem et hilaritatem
datoris ſignificat. Diaconus qui non eſt indutus Dalmatica, Caſula
circumcinctus legit, ut expedite poſſit miniſtrare, vel quia ipſius eſt ire
ad comitatum propter inſtantes neceſſitates.

7. The Maniple.

Mappula quæ ſiniſtra parte geſtatur, qua pituitam oculorum et
narium detergimus, præſentem vitam deſignat, in qua ſuperfluos humores patimur.

8. The Chasuble.

Caſula quæ ſuper omnia indumenta ponitur, ſignificat charitatem,
quæ alias virtutes excellit. De qua Apoſtolus, commemoratis quibuſdam virtutibus, ait : *Major autem horum eſt charitas.*

9. The Pallium.

Pallium Archiepiſcoporum ſuper omnia indumenta eſt, ut lamina
in fronte pontificis. Pallium nihil eſt aliud, niſi diſcretio inter Archi-
epiſcopum et ejus ſuffraganeos. Pallium ſignificat torquem, quem
ſolebant legitime certantes accipere. Hoc etiam erat lamina illa, ut
dixi, quam ſummus pontifex circa tempora ferebat, in qua ſcriptum
erat nomen Dei Tetragrammaton, id eſt, quatuor literarum, יהוה, Jod,
He, Vau, et Heth. Eſt autem interpretatio, Jod, principium, He iſte,
Vau vita, et Heth paſſio, id eſt, iſte eſt principium paſſionis vitæ. Paſſi
igitur ſunt multi ante Chriſtum, ſed nemo eorum per ſuam paſſionem
hominibus vitam attulit : Chriſtus vero, cujus ſanguis in cruce fuſus

---

[242] All that follows from here to the end | writers, quoted in this volume, eſpecially (ſee
of the chapter is a kind of *cento* from earlier | notes 243, 244) from Amalarius.

eſt pro totius mundi redemptione, humano generi attulit vitam. Secundum alium doctorem, Jod principium, He iſte, Vau et Heth vita interpretatur. Quod ita poteſt conjungi, Iſte eſt principium et vita Chriſtus. Vocabatur autem hoc nomen ſanctum Domini, quod interpretatur ineffabile, non quod non fari, ſed quod diffiniri, ut eſt, minime poſſit.

Stephanus natione Romanus ex patre Jobio, ut legitur in geſtis Pontificalibus, conſtituit ſacerdotibus Levitiſque veſtes ſacras in uſu quotidiano non uti niſi in Eccleſia. Hinc Hieronymus in libro 14. ſuper Ezechielem, *Porro religio alterum habitum habet in miniſterio, alterum in uſu vitaque communi.* Sudario ſolemus tergere pituitam oculorum et narium, atque ſuperfluam ſalivam decurrentem per labia : ſignificat ſtudium mundanæ [Leg. mundandæ] cogitationis. In manu ſiniſtra portatur, ut oſtendatur in temporali vita tædium nos pati ſuperflui humoris. Varietas [243] Sandaliorum, varietatem ſignificat miniſteriorum. Epiſcopi et ſacerdotis pene unum officium eſt. At quia nomine et honore, diſcernuntur etiam et varietate ſandaliorum, ut viſibus noſtris error auferatur. Epiſcopus habet ligaturam in ſuis ſandaliis, quam non habet Preſbyter. Epiſcopi eſt huc illucque diſcurrere per parochiam : ne forte cadant ſandalia de pedibus, ligata ſunt. Preſbyter qui domi hoſtias immolat, ſublimius [244] incedit. Diaconus quia diſſimilis eſt epiſcopo in ſuo officio, non eſt neceſſe ut habeat diſſimilia ſandalia : et ipſe ligaturam habet, quia ſuum eſt ire ad comitatum. Subdiaconus qui in adjutorio Diaconi eſt, et pene in eodem officio, neceſſe eſt ut habeat diſſimilia ſandalia, ne forte Diaconus æſtimetur. Sandalia ſignificant, quia prædicator neque cæleſtia debet abſcondere, neque terrenis inhiare.

---

[243] What is here ſaid of the ſandals is identical, almoſt to a word, with a paſſage of Amalarius already quoted (p. 104). See note *in loc.*

[244] *Sublimius.* This is ſcarcely intelligible. In the parallel paſſage of Amalarius (p. 104) we find *ſecurius,* "more careleſſly," " with leſs of precaution " (*i.e.* without this *ligatura*). And this probably is the true reading here. A ſimilar compariſon ſupplies the correction, *mundandæ* for *mundanæ,* given above. Probably alſo in line 16 above, *diſcernuntur* ſhould be read twice, as in the parallel paſſage.

XXXV.

B. IVO CARNOTENSIS.[245]

DE ECCLESIASTICIS SACRAMENTIS ET OFFICIIS SERMONES.

SERMO IN SYNODO DE SIGNIFICATIONIBUS INDUMENTORUM SACERDOTALIUM.

QUIA fanctitas minifterii fanctitatem expetit miniftrorum, quales ad facerdotium promoveri debeant perfonæ, in fuperiori fermone breviter ex Apoftolica inftitutione commemoravimus, fed in quo habitu ordinari vel ad altare accedere debeant, illi fermoni non inferuimus. De indumentis ergo facerdotalibus, vel de pontificalibus, diligenter confiderandum eft, quid in moribus facerdotum fignificet illa varietas veftium, quid fulgor auri, quid nitor gemmarum : [246] cum nihil ibi debeat effe ratione carens, fed forma fanctitatis et omnium imago virtutum. Sicut enim bona domus in ipfo veftibulo agnofcitur, fic Chrifti facerdos cultu facrarum veftium oftendit exterius, qualis apud fe effe debeat interius. Ifte autem facrarum veftium ritus, per Moifem fumpfit exordium : quamvis Chriftiana religio, plus intenta rebus quam figuris, facerdotes fuos non omnibus illis veteribus induit ornamentis.

§ 2. THE LEVITICAL VESTMENTS AND INSIGNIA.

Infpiciamus ergo prius veterum ornamenta pontificum, vel quo ordine illis utebantur, vel cum ordinarentur, vel cum thymiama oblaturi fancta fanctorum ingrederentur. Deinde noftra cum illorum indumentis conferentes, quid fimile, quid diffimile inter fe habeant, et quomodo etiam in rebus fignificatis conveniant, attendamus. Duo

---

[245] St. Ivo (or Yvo) was born at Beauvais, and was a pupil of Lanfranc, then Prior of Bec. We firft hear of him as Abbot of S. Quintin, in his native town, and afterwards as Bifhop of Chartres (*Carnota*). He died A.D. 1115. See Cave, H. L. vol. ii. p. 160. The text is that of Hittorpius. But the division of the text into fections is that of the prefent editor.

[246] Note that at this period (clofe of eleventh century) gold and jewels are fpoken of as decorations of Chriftian veftments, for it is of thefe laft, evidently, not of Jewifh veftments, that St. Ivo here fpeaks.

enim Cherubin propitiatorium adfpiciunt, quia facramenta utriufque teftamenti ad divinæ propitiationis fidem intendunt ; quæ in facerdotio veteri fub multiplici eft facrificiorum velamine adumbrata, in novo autem teftamento per unum verum perfectumque eft facrificium completa.   In ornamentis itaque utrorumque facerdotum et fublimitas facerdotii commendatur, et facerdotum cafta dignitas fignificatur, quatenus[247] per exteriorem habitum difcant, quales intra fe debeant effe, qui vices illius veri fummique Pontificis gerunt, in quo fuit omnis plenitudo virtutum, quam profitentur exteriora ornamenta membrorum.

Sed jam ad id, quod propofuimus, veniamus : et primum, qualiter Moifes Aaron et filios ejus, Domino jubente, ornaverit, et poftea induerit, videamus.   Sic enim legitur in Levitico (Lev. viii.) : *Et fecit Moifes, ficut præcepit ei Dominus : et convocavit fynagogam ad januam tabernaculi teftimonii, et applicuit Moifes Aaron fratrem fuum et filios ejus, et lavit eos aqua, et veftivit eum tunica, et præcinxit eum zona, et veftivit eum tunica interiore, et impofuit ei fuperhumerale, et cinxit eum fecundum facturam humeralis, et impofuit fuper eum logion, et fuper logion manifeftationem et veritatem, et impofuit fuper caput ejus mitram, et pofuit fuper mitram ante faciem ejus laminam auream, in qua fcriptum erat nomen Domini.*

Notandus eft ordo verborum.   Licet enim de conftituendo pontifice præcepiffet Dominus, et elegiffet, tamen vocatur Synagoga. Idcirco enim requiritur præfentia populi in eligendo facerdote, ut fciant omnes, quia qui doctior eft ex omni populo, qui omni virtute præftantior, hic eligi debet ad facerdotium, et hoc cum confenfu Ecclefiæ, ne qua poftea retractatio, ne quis fcrupulus remaneat, fed omnium teftimonio commendetur, fecundum Apoftolum (1 Tit. iii.) : *Oportet epifcopum bonum habere teftimonium ab his qui foris funt.* Ita plebis teftimonio approbatos primo lavat, poftea induit. Moifes quippe in hoc facto typum legis gerit, qui ordinandos facerdotes prius lavat, antequam induat.   Nifi enim quis prius fuerit per legis obfervationem probatus, non eft ad facerdotium promovendus.

§ 3. First, the Long Tunic of Linen.

Ita vero probatus, induitur tunica, quæ apud eos byffina eft, apud nos linea. Byffus enim eft genus lini candidiffimi, et ad fummum

---

[247] *Quatenus* in mediæval writers is nearly equivalent to our own " to the end that."

candorem multa vexatione [248] et ablutione perductum. Significat autem perfectam carnis munditiam, fecundum illud quod in Apocalypfi legitur (Apoc. xix.) : *Byffus funt juftificationes fanctorum.* Hanc munditiam caro facerdotis ex fe non habet, ficut nec linum ex fe eft candidum, fed ficut dictum eft, multis caftigationibus et ablutionibus redditur candidum, ut aptum fiat indumentis pontificum. Forma eft facerdotalis munditiæ, ut fecundum Apoftolum (1 Cor. ix.), facerdotes carnem fuam caftigent, et in fervitutem redigant : et præeunte gratia, habeant per induftriam, quod non potuerunt habere per naturam. Hæc veftis Græce ποδήρης, id eft, talaris, appellatur, quia a collo ufque ad talos extenditur : et ita eft arcta, [249] et membris corporis contemperata, ut fua forma teftificetur, facerdotem nihil habere diffolutum, nihil remiffum, fed ad omne opus bonum effe expeditum.

§ 4. Second and Third, the Girdle and the Linen Drawers.

Hæc eadem veftis circa renes zona fortius adftringitur, ut caftitas facerdotis nullo incentivorum æftu diffolvatur. Quod bene fignificatur in quatuor coloribus, quibus zona illa variata erat, byffo, purpura, hyacintho, et cocco : quibus coloribus quatuor elementa fignificantur : [250] quorum complexione natura conftat humana, quorum diftemperantia fluxus carnis generat, nifi medicinali cohibeatur continentia. Talium enim conjectores [251] naturarum, per byffum, quia de terra oritur, terram ; per purpuram, quia fanguine cochlearum marinarum tingitur, aquam ; per hyacinthum, quia colorem fereni aeris imitatur, aërem ; per coccum, qui colore flammeo rutilat, fignificari ignem voluerunt. Quorum, ut dictum eft, exuberantia in renibus maxime fuperfluos humores, pravi humores illicitos motus, generant ; qui nifi freno parfimoniæ reprimantur, caftitatis dignitas in eis facili impulfu periclitatur. Ubi autem major eft pugna, major eft adhibenda cuftodia. Inde eft, quod inter indumenta pontificalia [252] adhuc circa renes applicantur linea feminalia,

---

[248] *Multa vexatione, &c.* Compare note 106, p. 60.

[249] *Ita eft arcta, &c.* It is of the Levitical veftment that he is here fpeaking, and here (as throughout) he follows clofely in the fteps of S. Jerome. See the paffage quoted in p. 12, *fup.* and compare note 6, p. 2.

[250] *Quatuor elementa.* This fymbolifm is fpoken of by St. Jerome as having been learnt

by himfelf *ab Hebræis. Vid. fup.* p. 19, *in fin.*

[251] *Conjectores, i e.* Interpreters.

[252] *Pontificalia.* This muft refer to the Levitical pontifex (note 45, p. 26), or high-prieft, for he fays a few lines below, "*feminalibus non utuntur novi facerdotii pontifices :*" and this being fo, *adhuc* muft be underftood as meaning "furthermore."

R

non tam ad velandam carnis turpitudinem, quæ jam ſolitis operta
eſt veſtimentis, quam propter ſignum caſtitatis conſervandæ.   Unde
et Apoſtolus dicit (1 Cor. xii.) : *Honeſta noſtra nullius egent :*
Quæ autem inhoneſta ſunt, his abundantiorem honorem circundamus.
Feminalibus non utuntur novi ſacerdotii pontifices, quibus eſt in-
juncta ſervandæ caſtitatis quotidiana neceſſitas, ſicut eſt quotidie
offerendi conceſſa poteſtas : cum pontifices umbræ ſervientes, expleta
vice ſua, feminalia ſua ſolverent, tempore vicis ſuæ tamen ea induerent.
Reliqua duo, poderis et zona, veteribus et novis ſacerdotibus fiunt
indumenta communia :   quamvis zona noſtrorum ſacerdotum non ſit
quatuor intexta coloribus, aut propter penuriam materiarum, aut
propter abſentiam artificum : undecunque tamen ſit, et hæc et illa
unum gerunt temperantiæ typum.

§ 5. Fourth, the Tunic of Blue.

Sequitur quartum indumentum, tunica interior vel hyacinthina, qua
et in veteri et in novo teſtamento ſoli utuntur pontifices.   Duabus enim
tunicis merito induitur pontifex, quia debet de theſauro ſuo proferre
nova et vetera, *i.e.* legem intelligere ſecundum literam, quemadmodum
ante adventum Chriſti obſervabatur, et ſecundum ſpiritum, quemadmodum poſt adventum Chriſti intelligitur.   Unde et ſecunda tunica,
interior appellatur, vel hyacinthina, cujus color cæli ſerenitatem imitatur : ut per hoc intelligatur, quia pontifex plus debet de cæleſtibus
cogitare, quam de terrenis.   Rectus quippe ordo eſt, ut primum ſtudea-
mus munditiæ carnis, per quam veniamus ad munditiam cordis, quæ nos
provehat ad intellectum divinitatis, juxta illud (Matt. v.) : *Beati mundo*
corde, quoniam ipſi Deum videbunt.

§ 6. Fifth, the Superhumeral, or Ephod.[53]

Quinta veſtis eſt ſuperhumerale quæ Hebraice vocatur ephot.   Hæc
veſtis, ſacerdotalis ſimul et pontificalis apud nos eſt : apud Hebræos

---

[53] By the "ſuperhumeral" common to
prieſts and biſhops he means the "amice."
Compare Hugo de S. Victor (quoted later in
this volume), *amictus ſuper humeros, quod nos*
ſuperhumerale dicere poſſumus. The amice (a
ſquare piece of linen, ſee note 178, p. 96)
has this in common with the Levitical ephod
(*ſuperhumerale* of the Vulgate, ἐπωμίς apud
LXX) that a portion of it lay upon the ſhoulders. But in all other reſpects the amice and
the ephod are as utterly unlike as two garments well could be ; the latter being a cloſe-
fitting coat, ſhaped as may be ſeen in the
picture of the Jewiſh high-prieſt among the
illuſtrations of this volume. [Even Dr. Bock
admits the entire abſence of any reſemblance
between the two. Vol. ii. p. 20.]

vero, tantum pontificalis, et apud eos eisdem est variata coloribus, quibus et zona pontificalis, de qua dicitur in ordinatione pontificis : *Et circuncinxit eum (de Moise loquens) secundum facturam humeralis.* Humeri quippe fortes sunt ad agenda opera, et portanda onera, quæ ex circunductione humeralis, suis ligaturis constringuntur, quia pontificem et innocentia et operibus justitiæ oportet esse constrictum, ut in eo nihil inveniatur dissolutum, nihil remissum. Quod vero significant varii colores in zona, idem significant in superhumerali : quia quicquid de terrenis operamur, sive in largitione, sive in restrictione temporalium, totum sumimus ex contemperantia quatuor elementorum. Unde est quod quaternarius decies ductus, surgat in quadragenarium, quia elementorum quatuor abundantia legitime dispensata, quod significat denarius, ad verum perducit jubileum, qui exhibitione acquiritur bonorum operum. Quadragenarius enim numerus partibus suis denominatis quinquagenarium facit. Quo numero in lege supradictus jubileus (Lev. xxv.), *i.e.* remissionis annus exprimitur, veram præfigurans libertatem, quam qui adeptus fuerit, nullam timebit ulterius servitutem. Huic bonorum operum significationi concinit, quod in humerali duobus preciosis lapidibus insculpta erant nomina duodecim patriarcharum, sex in uno, et sex in altero : quorum alter superpositus erat dextro humero, alter sinistro. Nihil horum vacat a mysterio. Senarius enim, propter sui perfectionem, opera justitiæ significat : Nomina patriarcharum memoriam sanctorum, quam semper in exemplum bonorum operum habere debemus a dextris et a sinistris, id est, in prosperis et in adversis, significant. Et ideo illa nomina in lapidibus scribuntur : quia quod in lapide sculpitur, vix aut nunquam inde aboletur. Nec illud vacat a mysterio, quod pontifex cingitur secundum facturam superhumeralis, quia secundum opera sua unicuique retribuetur. Quod autem nostrorum pontificum superhumerale non est tot coloribus intextum, nec est tam preciosis gemmis redimitum, nihil refert, cum Christiana religio veritati serviens, compendiosis figuris idem intelligi faciat, quod vetus observantia sumptuosis.

§ 7. Sixth, the Rational or " Breastplate."

Postquam pontificis [254] verenda velata sunt suis indumentis, postquam

---

[254] *Pontificis, i.e.* the Levitical high-priest, but not without a reference to those Christian *pontifices* or bishops (note 45) to whom the right of wearing a " Rational " (see note 256) was conceded.

cæleftia jam cœpit meditari, poftquam juftitiæ operibus ornatus eft, poftquam utroque cingulo, ut in omnibus fortiter et perfeveranter ftaret, confirmatus eft, imponitur Rationale pectori pontificis, quod Græce logion dicitur, per quod fapientia, quæ in ratione confiftit, indicatur. Imponitur Rationali manifeftatio et veritas.[255]   Manifeftatio ideo, quia non fufficit pontifici habere fapientiam, nifi etiam poffit manifeftare quæ novit, et reddere rationem de ea, quæ in nobis eft, fide et fpe. Veritas vero, quia non debet pontifex de fuo corde prophetare, fed ea tantum quæ veritas habet, manifeftare.   Sunt autem adinvicem concatenata Rationale et Humerale : quia cohærere fibi invicem debent ratio et opera : ut quod mentis ratione concepimus, opere impleamus. Et notandus eft ordo rerum : quia non prius Rationale, quam Humerale : quia non prius fapientia, quam opera : fed prius opera, deinde fapientia.   Unde habetur in pfalmo (Pfa. cxviii.) : *A mandatis tuis intellexi :* et de Domino Jefu dicitur (Act. i.), *Quæ Jefus cœpit facere et docere.*   Deinde non prius manifeftatio, quam Rationale : quia nemo docere debet quæ non novit.   Huic ordini concordat propheta cum dicit (Ofe. x.) : *Seminate vobis ad juftitiam, et metite fructum vitæ, et illuminate vobis lumen fcientiæ.*   In hoc pectoris ornamento duodecim lapides inferti erant, xii. patriarcharum nomina in fe fculpta habentes : quia fanctorum patrum exempla pontifex femper debet habere in memoria, et fecundum ea moderari facta fua. In duodenario autem numero lapidum, poteft fignificari apoftolica doctrina : quia et ipfi lapides, per quatuor ordines funt diftributi, et terni et terni in fingulis angulis Rationalis pofiti.   Quod Apoftolicæ doctrinæ bene congruit, quæ fidem Trinitatis per quatuor evangelia in omni parte mundi prædicavit.   Hic ornatus folius erat pontificis, ficut et nunc [256] eft apud eos, quibus eo uti conceffum eft, propter diftantiam majorum et minorum facerdotum.

---

[255] *Manifeftatio et veritas.*   This is the literal rendering of the δήλωσις καὶ ἀλήθεια of the LXX. St. Jerome (quoted at p. 22) tranflates them by " *doctrina et veritas.*"   Our own tranflators have preferred the original Hebrew words Urim and Thummim, of which " light and perfection " would probably be the neareft tranflation.   See Smith's Dict. of the Bible *in voc.*

[256] *Sicut et nunc eft, &c.*   By the Rational " conceded " to certain among Chriftian bifhops he means probably the Roman pallium, worn by Weftern archbifhops under privilege of the Roman See.   In this comparifon he follows the reputed Alcuin.   See note 227, p. 111. Amalarius, on the other hand, regards this " pallium " as correfponding in fignificance to the " golden plate " of the high-prieft.   See note 195, p. 102.   [Dr. Bock thinks that the Rational here fpoken of was an actual jewel made in imitation of the Jewifh Rational.   This is not impoffible.   See Liturg. Gewünder, vol. i. p. 388, *fqq*; and compare Honorius Auguft. Gemma Animæ. lib. i. cap. ccxiii. *et ibi notata.*]

§ 8. Seventh and Eighth, the "Mitra" and the Golden
Plate.

Ita ornato pontifice,[257] fuperponitur capiti ejus mitra, quæ alio
nomine cidaris vel tiara vocatur, quæ regnum quinque fenfuum,[258] quo
præminere pontifex debet, intelligitur.   In capite enim ufus habetur
omnium corporalium fenfuum : quod cum bene regitur, caput viri, id
eft, Chriftus decenter ornatur.   Et quia caput Chrifti Deus eft,
Lamina aurea fuperponitur, cui infculptum eft nomen Dei, quod
Hebræi vocant ineffabile (1 Cor. ii.) : ut per hoc intelligatur, Deum
ficut omnium conditorem, ita effe rectorem : et ad honorem et gloriam
ejus effe referendum, quicquid a Domini facerdotibus bene fuerit dif-
penfatum.   Hæc indumenta, octo effe debere conftituit Moifes in
Exodo : fed in Levitico de eifdem indumentis tractans, de octavo, id
eft, fœminalibus, tacuit.   Unde Hieronymus in epiftola ad Fabiolam,
fcribit : Ubi refertur quomodo Moifes Aaron fratrem fuum veftimentis
pontificalibus induerit, de folis feminalibus nihil dicitur, hac, arbitror,
caufa : quia ad genitalia noftra et verenda lex non mifit manum, quia
ipfi fecretiora noftra confeffione digna tegere debemus et velare, et con-
fcientiam puritatis Deo judici fervare.   De cæteris vero virtutibus,
fortitudine, juftitia, humilitate, manfuetudine, liberalitate, poffunt et alii
judicare : pudicitiam fola novit confcientia, et humani oculi certi hujus
rei effe judices non poffunt, abfque his, qui paffim in morem brutorum
animalium in libidinem feruntur.   Unde Apoftolus (1 Cor. vii.) : *De
virginibus autem præceptum Domini non habeo.*   Et in Evangelio cum
Dominus de eunuchis voluntariis et non voluntariis ageret, addidit in
fine (Matt. xix.) : *Qui poteft capere, capiat.*   Tanquam diceretur : Feminalibus ego vos non veftio, nec impono alicui neceffitatem.   Qui
vult facerdos effe, ipfe fe veftiat, ipfe fe caftitate muniat.   Igitur
ipfi affumamus feminalia, ipfi noftra verecunda operiamus, non quæ-
ramus alienos oculos : ita tegantur genitalia, ut cum intramus fancta
fanctorum, nulla appareat turpitudo, ne moriamur.

---

[257] *Pontifice.*   Here again the Levitical
high-prieft, as is clear from what he fays of
the "*lamina aurea*" put upon his head, compared with what he fays below (§ 9) when
fpeaking of Chriftian priefts and bifhops, "*nulli
autem lamina aurea.*"

[258] *Regnum quinque fenfuum.*   Compare Venerable Bede, quoted above, p. 80 (§ 6).

§ 9. Distinctions in the Use of these Vestments.

Notandum vero est, quod minoribus sacerdotibus neque duplex tunica datur, neque humerale, neque rationale, neque lamina aurea, sed tantum poderis, et mitra, et zona, qua stringatur tunica byssina. Funguntur tamen sacerdotio, sed non illa sublimitate, qua funguntur, qui omnibus octo indumentis decorantur. Novi quoque testamenti sacerdotes non omnibus illis utuntur indumentis, quia nec duabus utuntur tunicis, nec rationali, præter solos pontifices: nulli autem lamina aurea, quia sicut dicit B. Hieronymus in supramemorata epistola, *quod olim in lamina monstrabatur, nunc in signo crucis ostenditur. Auro enim legis, sanguis evangelii preciosior est.* [*Supra*, p. 24, note 41.]

§ 10. Vestments of Christian Priesthood.

Utuntur autem tunica linea, quæ poderis dicitur, vel talaris, quæ omnium figurat castigationem membrorum, et zona quæ tunicam stringit, quæ dissolutam et remissam prohibet esse castitatem. Utuntur et superhumerali,[259] per quod exiguntur opera justitiæ a sacerdote, quia non sufficit temperantia, et a malo abstinentia, quæ superioribus duobus indumentis figurabatur, nisi opera justitiæ et misericordiæ subsequantur. Unde et in Psalmo dicitur (Pf. xxxiii.; 1 Pet. iii.): *Define a malo, et fac bonum.* Unde ipsum humerale poderi adstringitur. Utuntur et stola, quæ alio nomine orarium vocatur: qua vetus sacerdotium non utebatur. Hoc tanquam jugum bobus arantibus vel triturantibus collo juxta humeros superponitur, ut illud evangelicum ab eis impleatur (Matt. xi.): *Tollite jugum meum super vos, et discite a me, quia mitis sum et humilis corde: Jugum enim meum suave est, et onus meum leve.* Hæc a collo per anteriora descendens, dextrum latus ornat et sinistrum, ut doceat sacerdotem, per arma justitiæ a dextris et a sinistris, id est, in prosperis et adversis, debere esse munitum: quod ad fortitudinem pertinet, sine qua cæteræ virtutes facile expugnantur, et minime coronantur.[260] Unde dicit Apostolus (Heb. x.): *Patientia vobis neces-*

---

259 *Utuntur et superhumerali.* See above, note 253.

260 *Minime coronantur, i.e.* win not the vic-

tor's crown (compare note 54, p. 32), which the Lord bestoweth on them that are faithful unto the end.

faria eft, ut reportetis repromiſſiones : et in evangelio Dominus (Matt. x. ; xxiv.): *Qui perſeveraverit uſque in finem, hic ſalvus erit.* Inde eft quod ftola cum zona poderis quibufdam nexibus colligatur : quia virtutes virtutibus adjuvantur, ne aliquo tentationis impulfu moveantur. His omnibus indumentis fuperponitur cafula,[261] quæ alio nomine planeta vocatur : quæ quia communis eft veftis, charitatem fignificat (1 Cor. xii.), quæ univerfis virtutibus fuperponitur : quia cæteræ virtutes nihil fine ea utile operantur. Unde dicit Apoftolus (1 Cor. xii.): *Et adhuc excellentiorem viam docebo vos. Aemulamini chari-tatem.* Et quam inutiles abfque ea fint cæteræ virtutes, fubfequenter approbatur, cum præcipuas virtutes, fcientiam fcilicet linguarum, dif-tributionem rerum propriarum, ipfum quoque martyrium, fine ea nihil effe confirmat. Et ideo prudentiæ ponitur loco, quia plenitudo legis eft dilectio. Et quia mentibus bene compofitis, et divino cultui man-cipatis, frequenter fubrepit acedia,[262] oportet ut ad eam frequenter detergendam diligens adhibeatur vigilantia, qua ab oculis cordis emer-gens talis fæpe mundetur pituita. Unde in finiftra manu ponitur quæ-dam mappula, quæ fæpe fluentem oculorum pituitam tergat, et ocu-lorum lippitudinem removeat. Hæc quippe ornamenta, ut dictum eft, non funt ipfæ virtutes, fed virtutum infignia, quibus tanquam fcripturis admonentur utentes, quid debeant appetere, quid vitare, et ad quem finem fua facta dirigere. Adjiciendum eft fupradictis, quia Levitæ fuo modo utuntur fupramemoratis indumentis : idem fignificantibus, quod fignificant in prefbyteris. Utuntur Levitæ Dalmatica, quæ propter fui latitudinem curam proximorum fignificat, quod fignificabat in prefbyteris cafula : quia utrorunque iftorum miniftrorum, ad implendam dilectionem, eadem debet effe cuftodia.

§ 11. Special Vestments Worn by Bishops and Cardinals.

Utuntur epifcopi et cardinales prefbyteri fandaliis, quæ calceamenta funt prædicatorum. Habent autem ad terram foleam integram, ne pes tangat terram : fupra vero conftat ex corio, quibufdam locis per-tufo : [263] quia evangelium non debet terrenis commodis inniti, nec omnia evangelica facramenta omnibus revelari, nec omnibus abfcondi. Unde

---

[261] *Cafula . . . charitatem fignificat.* Compare Rabanus Maurus (Cap. 21) quoted above at p. 91.

[262] *Acedia.* An imported Greek word, ἀκηδία, for the older ἀκηδία, "careleffnefs."
[263] See Bock Liturg. Gewünder, vol. ii. p. 12.

et Dominus diſcipulis ita dicebat (Matt. xiii.) : *Vobis datum eſt nóſſe myſterium regni Dei : cæteris autem in parabolis, ut videntes non videant, et audientes non intelligant.* Hanc ſandaliorum ſignificationem propheta intelligebat, quando dicebat (Eſa. lii. ; Rom. x.) : *Quam ſpecioſi pedes annunciantium pacem, evangelizantium bona.*

Antequam induantur ſandaliis, veſtiuntur caligis byſſinis vel lineis, uſque ad genua protenſis, et ibi bene conſtrictis : per quas ſignificatur, quia debent rectos greſſus facere pedibus ſuis : et genua debilia, id eſt, negligentiis reſoluta, roborare, et ſic ad prædicandum evangelium feſtinare.

§ 12. Unction of Hands and of Head in Ordination.

Unguntur præterea manus [264] preſbyteris et epiſcopis, ut cognoſcant ſe in virtute ſancti ſpiritus hoc ſacramento gratiam conſecrandi accipere, et opera miſericordiæ erga omnes pro viribus exercere debere. Epiſcopo vero ſpecialiter caput ungitur, ut intelligat ſe eſſe illius vicarium, de quo dicitur in Pſalmo (Pſ. xliv.) : *Unxit te Deus, Deus tuus, oleo lætitiæ præ conſortibus tuis.* Accipiunt hac unctione claves regni cælorum, ut quæcunque ligaverint ſuper terram, ſint ligata et in cælis (Matt. xviii.) : et quæcunque ſolverint ſuper terram, ſint ſoluta et in cælo : et quorum peccata detinuerint, ſint detenta, et quorum peccata dimiſerint, ſint dimiſſa (Joan. xx.)

§ 13. Practical Exhortation.

His ita de ornatu ſacerdotali et pontificali breviter prælibatis, admonendi eſtis, ut ſicut ſacramenta profunda audiſtis, ſic ea ſtudeatis et corde intelligere, et opere implere. Non enim auditores legis juſti ſunt apud Deum, ſed factores. Poteſt enim unuſquiſque veſtrum intra ſe regale habere ſacerdotium et ſacerdotales ornatus, ſi quem abluerit et mundum fecerit legis obſervatio, et ſi gratia baptiſmi et unctio chriſmatis illibata permanſerit, et ſi indutus duplicibus indumentis, literæ ſcilicet et ſpiritus, fuerit ; et ſi in his fortiter accingatur, ut ſit caſtus

---

[264] *Unguntur manus.* This ceremony is repreſented in the illuſtrations from the Pontifical of Biſhop Landulfus, given in this volume.

mente et corpore ; fi etiam fuperhumerali operum juftificetur, fi ftola
fortitudinis a dextris et a finiftris muniatur, fi plenitudine fcientiæ,
quam planeta fignificat, cumuletur : poteft, inquam, ita ornatus intra
Dei templum, quod ipfe eft, verum habere facerdotium. Qui autem
nec facris veftibus induti, nec honeftis moribus ornati, ad altare Dei
accedere præfumpferint, ficut filii Aaron, Nadab et Abihu, igne alieno,
quem offerebant ante Dominum, confumpti funt (Lev. x.) ; ita ifti non
divina ordinatione, fed fua præfumptione facerdotium fibi ufurpantes,
cum his, qui ad regales nuptias fine vefte nuptiali intraverunt (Matt.
xxii.), æternis ignibus funt cruciandi. Unde dicitur in Levitico (Lev.
xvi.) : *Et dixit Dominus ad Moifem : Loquere ad Aaron fratrem
tuum, ne intret omni hora in fanɗa interiora, ut non moriatur.* Unde
oftenditur, quod fi inordinate intraret fanɗa fanɗorum, non preparatus,
non indutus facerdotalibus indumentis, non propitiato fibi prius Deo,
morietur : et merito, tanquam qui non fecerit ea, quæ oportet fieri,
antequam accedatur ad altare Dei. Ad omnes enim nos pertinet, nos
omnes inftruit lex Dei, ut fciamus quod debeamus accedere ad altare
Dei, et offerre, fcilicet ut deponamus veftimenta fordida, id eft, carnis
immunditiam, pravitatem morum, inquinamenta libidinum. Unde et
in eodem Levitico, cum enumeraffet Dominus veftes, quibus induen-
dus erat Aaron et filii ejus, adjunxit (Exod. xxviii.) : *Veſties his omnibus
fratrem tuum, et filios ejus cum eo, et cunɗorum confecrabis manus,
fanɗificabifque illos, ut facerdotio fungantur mihi.* Sequitur : *Et utentur
eis Aaron et filii ejus, quando ingredientur teſtimonii tabernaculum,
quando appropinquabunt ad altare, ut miniſtrent in fanɗuario, ne in-
iquitatis rei moriantur.* Ex his omnibus colligitur, quanta fit dignitas
facerdotalis minifterii, et quanta effe debeat fanɗitas miniftrorum : [265]

---

[265] It will be feen by the paffage above
quoted, that St. Ivo, writing at the clofe of
the eleventh century, enumerates the following as the veftments of Chriftian miniftry :—1.
Linen Tunic. 2. Girdle. 3. Superhumeral (*i.e.*
Amice). 4. Stole. 5. Chafuble (or " Planeta ").
6. Maniple. He mentions alfo the dalmatic
as worn by deacons in place of the Chafuble
proper to priefts. The veftments worn by
bifhops only, are the fecond tunic (§ 9),
and (by fome at leaft among them, note 256)
the Rational, whether the pallium of archbifhops, or a Jewel worn on the Breaft. Bifhops
were diftinguifhed alfo by fandals of a peculiar
fhape, and by bufkins (*caligæ*) made of linen.

It will be obferved that while he mentions
the " Mitra," or linen cap of the Levitical
prieft, he is filent as to any fimilar ornament
among the Chriftian veftments. The truth
feems to be that in the eleventh century the
" Mitra " had been already introduced as a
diftinɗive veftment at Rome (Hefele, pp. 230,
231), and through Rome to particular churches
in Germany and elfewhere. But it was not
in St. Ivo's time regarded as one of the ac-
knowledged veftments of Chriftian miniftry.
Of the " golden plate " he fays diftinɗly that
it was nowhere worn, " *nulli lamina aurea* "
(§ 9).

quam qui habuerit, facerdotii merito non carebit.   Qui vero non habuerit, et facerdotii officium ufurpaverit, merito cum fupra memoratis
præfumptoribus interibit.   Multa de facerdotii dignitate, multa de indumentorum facerdotalium myftica pulchritudine, vitantes prolixitatem
fermonis, præterivimus : hoc intendentes, quia ad ædificationem morum, et ad utilitatem audientium ifta fufficiunt.

XXXVI.

HUGO A SANCTO VICTORE.[366]

THE SACERDOTAL VESTMENTS OF CHRISTIAN MINISTRY.

SERMO XIV. [TOM. II. p. 222].

[HE preaches on the words of Pf. cxxxi. "Let thy priefts (*facerdotes*) be clothed with righteoufnefs." He is addreffing his brethren of the clergy only.]

Oportet, fratres cariffimi, ut nos qui in domo Dei facerdotio fungimur, dignam facerdotis juftitiam ducamus, et honeftis in officio veftibus induamur, immo virtutes quæ per veftes facerdotales defignantur, exerceamus. Quid namque prodeft ornari veftibus, nifi ornemur virtutibus? Certe fi videremus facerdotem fine facerdotalibus veftimentis miffam celebrare, fine alba, fine ftola, fine infula, multum miraremur, et cum horrore nimio monftrum tale deteftaremur. Si ergo deteftandus effet qui accederet ad altare fine veftibus, quam deteftandus quam horrendus eft qui accedere præfumit cum vitiis et fine virtutibus? Quantum diftat inter vas quodlibet et cibum, tantum diftat inter fignificans et fignificatum. Veftes fignificant, virtutes fignificantur. Veftes foris coram populo decorant, virtutes intus coram Domino miniftrum commendant. Sicut igitur non audemus accedere ad altare fine veftibus, fic non præfumamus accedere fine virtutibus.

Videamus denique quæ funt iftæ veftes, et quæ per eas fignificentur virtutes. Sunt ergo veftimenta, interior linea, exterior fcilicet alba, amictus fuper humeros, quod nos fuperhumerale dicere poffumus, zona, ftola, manipula, infula. Ante omnia debet facerdos quotidiana veftimenta deponere, deinde manus abluere, et fic candida veftimenta fumere. Depofitio quotidianorum veftimentorum fignificat veteris hominis depofitionem; ablutio manuum, criminum confeffionem; affumptio novorum veftimentorum virtutum exercitationem.

---

[366] Born. 1096, died 1140, A.D. He was Abbot of the Monaftery of St. Victor, near Paris. The text which I have followed is that of Hittorpius.

Linea interior interius eft, exterior exterius. Ifta eft in occulto, illa in manifefto. Ifta latet, illa patet. Propterea interior fignificat munditiam cordis, exterior munditiam corporis.

Superhumerale quod fupra humeros ponitur, ubi onera folent imponi, tolerantiam præfentium fignificat laborum, quæ nobis neceffaria eft fi veri facerdotes volumus effe. Unde de illis qui eam perdiderunt fcriptum eft (Eccl. xi.): *Væ his qui perdiderunt fuflinentiam.* Et Dominus de laude patientiæ in evangelio ait: *In patientia veftra poffidebitis animas veftras* (Luc. xxi.). Suftineamus ergo, fratres, quicquid nobis acciderit adverfum, ut ficut bona fufcepimus de manu Domini, ita et mala fuftineamus.

Zona, quæ lumbos circumdat, et veftimenta conftringit ne diffluant, virtutem continentiæ infinuat, quæ fluxam luxuriæ noftræ lafciviam refrenat.

Stola, quæ collo imponitur, jugum fuave Domini exprimit, de quo Dominus in Evangelio ait (Matt. xi.): *Jugum enim meum fuave eft, et onus meum leve.*

Sequitur manipula, quæ in brachio finiftro dependet, quæ nihil aliud denotat facramenti nifi quod pro cautela ibi ponitur, ne facerdos aliquid in officio fuo incaute et negligenter agat, fed omnia diligenter, ficut qui in confpectu Domini et fanctorum Angelorum confiftit, perficiat. Significat ergo cautelam, per quam cavenda cavemus, et facienda facimus.

His omnibus minifter Domini indutus, his omnibus adornatus, nondum eft aptus officio facerdotali, nec illud implere præfumit, nifi feptimum, quod infula ²⁰⁷ dicitur, cæteris addatur et fuperimponatur. Iftud veftimentum excellentius eft cæteris, eminetque univerfis. Quam igitur virtutem per hoc fignificari dicimus nifi charitatem, de qua dicit Apoftolus, *Adhuc vobis excellentiorem viam demonftramus. Si linguis hominum loquar et angelorum, &c.*, quæ bene novit fraternitas veftra. Qui cum alia dona fpiritualia et virtutes demonftraffet, tandem de charitate intulit dicens, *Si linguis &c.* O beata virtus, Charitas; et beatus folus qui in ipfa ufque in finem perfeverat. Qui ergo cum aliis virtutibus charitatem habet, facerdos eft. Et qui etiam alias fine ifta habet, facerdos non eft.

---

²⁰⁷ *Infula.* This is one of the few early inftances of the ufe of this word to defignate one of the Chriftian veftments. It here means not a covering for the head (which would be in accordance with the claffical ufage of the word), but a chafuble. See below, note 268 *in fin.*

Habeamus igitur, fi veri facerdotes volumus effe, quod effe debemus. Habeamus interiorem lineam per munditiam cordis, exteriorem per munditiam corporis; Superhumerale per patientiam : zonam, per continentiam ; ftolam, per obedientiam ; manipulum (*fic*), per cautelam ; infulam ᶜᶜᵇ per charitatem fraternam. His etenim omnibus armati fanctè et relligiofe perficiemus holocauftum Domini, et dicetur de nobis quod fcriptum eft, *Vos eftis genus electum, regale facerdotium.* Tales fuerunt fancti quorum hodie follennia celebramus. Tales, fratres chariffimi, effe ftudeamus, ut et nos induamur juftitiam, et facti cum ipfis participes meritorum, fieri mereamur focii præmiorum. Quod per merita et interceffionem eorum nobis præftare dignetur, qui vivit et regnat.

ᶜᶜᵇ In this paffage, written fome thirty years after that of St. Ivo laft quoted, the enumeration of the Chriftian veftments correfponds nearly with his, with one apparent exception. He fpeaks of the two tunics, of the amice (which, he fays, may alfo be called "fuperhumeral") of girdle, ftole, maniple, but the laft of the veftments, that which is "more excellent than the reft," which is "added to and fuperimpofed" upon thofe firft mentioned, which is typical of charity, is with St. Hugo not "*cafula,*" but "*infula.*" The whole context of this paffage points plainly to the conclufion that *infula* is here only another name for the chafuble. Such an interpretation is not in accordance with the claffical ufage of the term, but another paffage of the fame writer is conclufive as to his meaning. *Cafula, quæ alio nomine Planeta vel Infula dicitur.* [*Speculum Eccl.* lib. i. cap. 6, apud Dufrefne.]

XXXVII.

HONORIUS AUGUSTODUNENSIS.[269]

SACRED VESTMENTS AND INSIGNIA.

GEMMA ANIMÆ, LIB. I. CAP. 89.

ORIGIN OF THE VESTMENTS.

APOSTOLI et eorum fucceffores in quotidianis veftibus et ligneis[270] calicibus miffam celebraverunt: fed Clemens, tradente Petro Apoftolo, ufum facrarum veftium ex Lege fumpfit: et Stephanus Papa in facris veftibus miffas celebrari conftituit.

LIB. I. CAP. 193. OF THE CLERICAL TONSURE.

Tonfura clericorum initium fumpfit ab ufu Nazaræorum. Hi ex juffu legis crines fuos radebant, et in facrificium Domino incendebant. Nazaræi autem dicuntur *fancti*. Unde Apoftoli ad exemplum eorum miniftros Ecclefiæ docuerunt fe ob fignum tondere, quo recordarentur fe Domino in fanctitate fervire debere. Chriftus rex et facerdos fecit nos fibi et facerdotes et reges. Pars capitis rafa eft fignum facer-dotale: pars crinibus comata fignum regale. Sacerdotes quippe legis tiaram, id eft, pileolum ex byffo in modum mediæ fphæræ rotundum, in capite portabant: reges aureas coronas geftabant. Ergo rafa pars capitis tiaram, circulus crinium refert coronam.[271]

---

[269] Very little is known concerning this writer, as will appear from the following. "Hiftoire de la Vie d'Honoré. Le titre de cet article énonce prefque tout ce que nous favons de certain fur la perfonne d'Honoré." *Hift. Lit. de la France,* tom. xii. p. 165. "Honorius haud diu poft annum 1152 obiiffe videtur, quod facile conjicias de fcriptore qui jam inter annos 1122 et 1125 fe floruiffe et majorem partem librorum fuorum edidiffe difertis verbis affirmat." Wilman, *apud Patrol.* tom. clxxii. p. 13. Ed. *Migne.*

[270] This probably refers to the fame tradition as that implied in the faying of St. Boniface, quoted at p. 207. See note 209.

[271] In this Honorius follows clofely upon S. Ifidore of Seville, De Off. Ecc. vii. quoted at p. 68.

LIB. I. CAP. 198. WHITE GARMENTS, WHY WORN. AND WHY SEVEN IN NUMBER.

Veftes facræ a veteri Lege funt affumptæ. Ideo autem miniftri Chrifti vel Ecclefiæ in albis veftibus miniftrant, quia angeli,[272] æterni Regis miniftri, in albis apparebant. Per albas itaque veftes admonentur ut Angelos Dei Miniftros per caftitatis munditiam in Chrifti fervitio imitentur. Veftes vero, quibus corpus exterius decoratur, funt virtutes, quibus interior homo perornatur. Septem autem veftes facerdotibus afcribuntur, qui et feptem ordinibus infigniti nofcuntur, quatenus per feptiformem Spiritum feptem virtutibus refplendeant, quibus cum Angelis in minifterium Chrifti ornati procedant.

CAP. 201.

[*After defcribing the preparatory wafhing of the hands, and combing of the hair, with the fpiritual fignificance of each act, in* capp. 199, 200, *he proceeds as follows*]:

THE AMICE.

Hinc Humerale,[271] quod in Lege Ephot, apud nos Amictus dicitur, fibi imponit; et illo caput et collum et humeros (unde et Humerale dicitur) cooperit, et in pectore copulatum duabus vittis ad mammillas cingit. Per Humerale, quod capiti imponitur, fpes cæleftium intelligitur. . . . Hæc veftis eft candida. . . .

CAP. 202. THE ALB.

Dehinc Alba induitur, quæ in Lege tunica linea vel talaris, apud Græcos podis (*leg.* poderis) dicitur. Per hanc caftitas defignatur, qua tota vita facerdotis decoratur. Hæc defcendit ufque ad talos, quia ufque in finem vitæ debet in caftimonia perfeverare facerdos. . . . Hæc veftis albedine candet, quia fanctitas coram Deo inter Angelos fplendet.

---

[272] Compare S. Ifidore *Hifp. De Off. Ecc.* viii. *fupra*, p. 69.

[271] For this identification of the " Amice " with the Levitical Ephod or Superhumeral, compare note 253, p. 122.

CAP. 203. THE GIRDLE.

Ex hinc Cingulo cingitur, quod in Lege Balteus, apud Græcos Zona dicitur. Per cingulum (quod circa lumbos præcingitur, et, Alba ne diffluat et greſſum impediat, aſtringitur), mentis cuſtodia, vel conſcientia, accipitur, qua luxuria reſtringitur. . . .

CAP. 204. THE STOLE, OR ORARIUM.

Deinde circumdat collum ſuum Stola, quæ et Orarium dicitur, per quam obedientia Evangelii intelligitur. . . . Cap. 205. Per Stolam quoque innocentia exprimitur. . . . Hac patriarchæ ante Legem utebantur, et primogenita dicebantur. Erat autem veſtis ſacerdotalis quam majores natu cum benedictione patris, ut Jacob ab Iſaac, induebant, et victimas Deo, ut pontifices, offerebant. Unde dicitur, *Vende mihi primogenita tua* (Gen. xxv. 31). Et iterum "*ſtola Eſau.*" Stola dicitur miſſa; [574] erat enim veſtis candida pertingens ad veſtigia, ſed poſtquam cæpit portari Alba, mutata eſt, ut hodie cernitur Stola. [575]

CAP. 206. THE UNDER-GIRDLE.

Exhinc Subcingulum, quod perizoma vel Subcinctorium [575a] dicitur, circa pudenda duplex ſuſpenditur. Per hoc eleemoſynarum ſtudium accipitur, quo confuſio peccatorum contegitur. Hoc duplicatur quia primum animæ ſuæ miſereri peccata devitando, deinde proximo neceſſaria impendendo, cuilibet imperatur.

CAP. 207. THE CHASUBLE.

Deinde Caſula [576] omnibus indumentis ſupponitur (*Leg.* ſuperponitur),

---

[574] *Stola dicitur miſſa.* I can only ſuppoſe theſe words as ſaying that the word "*ſtola*" means "ſent;" and as having reference to the Greek origin of the word, viz. στολή, which again is a paronym of στέλλειν, "to ſend." Honorius, like moſt of his contemporaries, was liable to make miſtakes when dealing with Greek words.

[575] This paſſage is ſomewhat obſcurely worded, but its meaning appears to be this. By the word "ſtola" he thinks was meant originally a full robe (as in fact was the *ſtola matronalis* of claſſical times), not a narrow border-like veſtment ſuch as was called "*ſtola*" in his own time. And the change from the primitive "robe" to the later "ſtola" was made, he thinks, when the "alb" or white tunic became the recogniſed dreſs of Chriſtian miniſtry.

[575a] *Subcinctorium.* On this word ſee note in the extracts from Innocent III. which follow.

[576] Here again he follows S. Iſidore. See note 130, p. 74.

per quam charitas intelligitur, quæ omnibus virtutibus eminentior creditur. Cafula autem quafi parva cafa [277] dicitur : quia ficut a cafa totus homo tegitur, ita charitas totum corpus virtutum complectitur. Hæc veftis et Planeta (quod error fonat) vocatur, eo quod errabundus limbus ejus utrinque in brachia fublevatur. [*He then dwells on the myftical meaning implied in the fact that the Chafuble is gathered in two folds on the breaft, and in three upon the arms.*]

CAP. 208. THE FANON, [278] OR MANIPLE.

Ad extremum facerdos fanonem in finiftrum brachium ponit, quæ et mappula et fudarium vocatur, per quod olim fudor et narium fordes extergebantur. Per hoc pœnitentia intelligitur, quia quotidiani exceffus labes extergitur.

CAP. 209. THE SEVEN VESTMENTS WORN BY BISHOPS ONLY.

Epifcopus eifdem feptem veftibus induitur, infuper et aliis feptem redimitur, fcilicet Sandaliis, Dalmatica, Rationali, Mitra, Chirothecis, Annulo, Baculo.

CAP. 210. THE SANDALS.

[*He fets forth the various myfteries to be found in the various parts of the Sandal, in the upper and lower leather, the black and the white leather, the ftrings, and the feams. He ends all by faying*] : Legis facerdotes habebant Femoralia, quibus turpitudinem tegebant : Ecclefiæ facerdotes fandalia portant, quia etiam aliis munditiam prædicant.

CAP. 211. THE DALMATIC.

Dalmatica a Dalmatia provincia eft dicta, in qua primum eft inventa. Hæc a Domini inconfutili tunica, et Apoftolorum colobio, eft mutuata. Colobium autem erat cucullata veftis, fine manicis,

---

[277] See note 130, p. 74.
[278] *Fanon.* See note 161, p. 90 ; and note 233, p. 113.

T

ficut adhuc videmus in monachorum cucullis [279] vel nautarum tunicis. Quod collobium a S. Sylveſtro [280] in Dalmaticam eſt verſum; et additis manicis infra ſacrificium portari inſtituta. Quæ ideo ad Miſſam a pontifice portatur, ubi paſſio Chriſti celebratur, quia in modum crucis [281] formatur. Hæc veſtis eſt candida.   . . Hujus veſtis manicæ ſunt noſtræ Gallinæ [282] alæ.

CAP. 213. THE "RATIONAL" WORN BY BISHOPS.

Rationale [283] a Lege eſt ſumptum, quod ex auro, hyacintho, purpura, unius palmi menſura erat factum. Huic Doctrina [284] et Veritas, ac duodecim precioſi lapides contexti, nominaque filiorum Iſrael inſculpta erant, et hoc Pontifex in pectore ob recordationem populi portabat. Hoc in noſtris veſtibus præfert (*Leg.* præfertur) per ornatum qui auro et gemmis ſummis Caſulis in pectore affigitur. Monet autem pontificem ratione vigere, auro ſapientiæ, [285] hyacintho [286] ſpiritualis intelligentiæ, purpura patientiæ, in Chriſtum, qui cælum palma [287] menſurat, tendere debere, Doctrina [288] et Veritate radiare, gemmis virtutum coruſcare, duodecim Apoſtolos ſanctitate imitari, totius populi in ſacrificio recordari.

CAP. 214. THE EPISCOPAL CAP, OR MITRE. [289]

Mitra quoque Pontificis [note 45, *in fin.*] eſt ſumpta ex uſu Legis.

---

[279] *Cuculla.* Compare note 151, p. 86.

[280] Compare note 210, p. 107.

[281] Compare note 165, p. 91.

[282] I am unable to explain this alluſion. The words ſeem to point to ſome provincial uſe of the term "*Gallinæ alæ*," as a deſignation for ſleeves of a particular ſhape. [In the following chapter, which for brevity's ſake I have omitted, Honorius ſets forth the myſtical ſymboliſm of the Dalmatic.]

[283] It is clear from what follows that in the time that Honorius wrote, the uſe of a breaſt-plate, in imitation of the Levitical "breaſt-plate" or "rational," had in ſome dioceſes been introduced. It is alſo evident that in the time of the reputed Alcuin no ſuch jewel was known to be in uſe. See note 227, p. 111. The paſſage of St. Ivo quoted at p. 124, and commented on in note 256, leaves

it doubtful whether he knew of any ſuch ornament or no.

[284] See note 255, p. 124.

[285] *Auro ſapientiæ.* For this ſymboliſm compare St. Gregory the Great, quoted at p. 59. See note 107.

[286] *Hyacintho . . . intelligentiæ.* This ſymboliſm has its origin in the words of St. Jerome, quoted at p. 20, *in fin.* See note 30.

[287] *Qui cælum palma, etc.* Theſe words have reference, probably, to what he had ſaid of the rational of the high-prieſt having *unius palmi menſuram.*

[288] Compare note 255, p. 124.

[289] Here for the firſt time [note 265, p. 129] we meet with mention of a mitra *as one of the veſtments of Chriſtian miniſtry.* It is ſtill a cap made of linen only, as far as from this paſſage we can judge.

Hæc ex byſſo conficitur, et Tiara [note 84, p. 52], Ydaros,[290] Infula,[290a] Pileum, dicitur. . . . Mitra ex byſſo facta, multo labore ad candorem perducta [note 106, p. 60], caput pontificis exornat. . .

CAP. 215. THE GLOVES, AND THEIR SYMBOLISM.

Chirothecarum uſus ab epiſtolis[290b] (*Leg.* apoſtolis) eſt traditus. Per manus enim operationes, per chirothecas deſignantur earum occultationes. Sicut enim aliquando manus chirothecis velantur, aliquando exactis chirothecis denudantur, ſic opera bona interdum propter arrogantiam declinandam celantur, interdum propter ædificationem proximis manifeſtantur. Chirothecæ induuntur cum hoc impletur : *Cavete ne juſtitiam veſtram faciatis coram hominibus ut videamini ab iis* (Matt. vi). Rurſus extrahuntur cum hoc impletur : *Luceat lux veſtra coram hominibus ut videant opera veſtra bona, et glorificent Patrem veſtrum, qui in cælis eſt* (ib. v.). Chirothecæ ſunt inconſutiles, quia actiones pontificis debent rectæ fidei eſſe concordes.

CAP. 216. THE EPISCOPAL RING.

Annuli uſus ex Evangelio acceptus creditur, ubi ſaginati vituli conviva prima ſtola veſtitur, annulo inſignitur (Luc. xv.). Olim ſolebant reges litteras cum annulo ſignare : cum hoc ſoliti erant et nobiles quique ſponſas ſubarrhare. Fertur quod Prometheus quidam ſapiens primus annulum ferreum ob inſigne amoris fecerit, et in eo adamantem lapidem poſuerit ; quia videlicet ſicut ferrum domat omnia, ita amor vincit omnia : et ſicut adamas eſt infrangibilis, ita amor eſt inſuperabilis. Quem enim in illo digito portari conſtituit, in quo venam ut cordis deprehendit, unde et annularis nomen accepit. Poſtmodum vero aurei ſunt pro ferreis inſtituti, et gemmis pro adamante inſigniti : quia ſicut aurum cuncta metalla præcellit, ita dilectio univerſa bona

---

[290] *Ydaros. Sic libri impreſſi.* This may have originated in *cydaris*, for the more correct *cidaris*, which is probably the true reading here.

[290a] *Infula.* Here clearly uſed in the ſenſe which in liturgical writers it ſtill retains, that of an epiſcopal cap, or mitre. Compare note 268, p. 153, where *infula* is uſed as the equivalent of *caſula.*

[290b] There can be little doubt that Honorius wrote "apoſtolis." The text (Migne's) which I have here followed ſuggeſts the reading "epiſcopis." But this reading is contrary to ſenſe ; the other makes good ſenſe but bad hiſtory, and is therefore probably the true one.

excellit : et ficut aurum gemma decoratur, ita amor dilectione perornatur. Pontifex ergo annulum portat, ut fe fponfum ecclefiæ agnofcat,
ac pro illa animam, fi neceffe fuerit, ficut Chriftus, ponat, myfteria
fcripturæ a perfidis figillet, fecreta ecclefiæ refignet.

CAP. 217. THE PASTORAL STAFF.

Baculus ex auctoritate Legis et Evangelii affumitur, qui et "virga
paftoralis," et "capuita," et "ferula," et "pedum" dicitur. Moyfes
quoque, dum oves pavit, virgam manu geftavit. Hanc ex præcepto
Domini in Ægyptum pergens fecum portavit, hoftes fignis per eam
factis terruit, qui velut lupi oves Domini tranfgulabant. Gregem
Domini de Ægypto per mare Rubrum hac virga eduxit: paftum de
cælo, potum de petra, hac produxit; ad terram lac et mel fluentem,
velut ad pafcua, hac virga induxit. Nihil autem hæc virga fuit quam
baculus paftoralis, cum quo gregem utpote paftor minavit (*fic*). Hic
baculus apud auctores "pedum" vocatur, eo quòd pedes animalium
illo retineantur. Eft enim lignum recurvum quo paftores retrahunt
pedes gregum. Cap. 218. In Evangelio quoque Dominus apoftolis
præcepit ut in prædicatione nihil præter virgam tollerent (Marc. vi.;
Luc. ix.). Et quia epifcopi paftores gregis Dominici funt, ut Moyfes
et apoftoli fuerunt, ideo baculum in cuftodia præferunt. Per baculum,
quo infirmi fuftentantur, auctoritas doctrinæ defignatur. Per virgam,
qua improbi emendantur, poteftas regiminis figuratur. Baculum ergo
pontifices portant, ut infirmos in fide per doctrinam erigant: virgam
bajulant, ut per poteftatem inquietos corrigant: quæ virga vel baculus
eft recurvus, ut aberrantes a grege docendo ad pœnitentiam trahat; in
extremo eft acutus, ut rebelles excommunicando retrudat, hæreticos
velut lupos ab ovili Chrifti poteftative exterreat. Cap. 219. Hic baculus ex offe et ligno efficitur, quæ cryftallina vel deaurata fphærula
conjunguntur. In fupremo capite infignitur; in extremo, ferro acuitur.
. . . Per durum os, duritia Legis; per lignum, manfuetudo
ecclefiæ, infinuatur; per gemmam fphærulæ, divinitas Chrifti. . . .
Cap. 220. In fphærula eft fcriptum, HOMO, quatenus fe hominem
memoretur. Juxta ferrum eft fcriptum PARCE, ut fubjectis in difciplina parcat, quatenus ipfe a fummo Paftore gratiam inveniat. Unde

et ferrum debet esse retusum, quia judicium sacerdotis per clementiam debet esse delibutum.[291]

CAP. 221 AND 222. OF THE PALLIUM AND CROZIER.

His Insignibus Archiepiscopus fulget. Insuper et Pallio pollet, ut se Christi Passionem [292] populo praeferre demonstret. In duabus quippe lineis Pallii, ante et retro, est purpureum sanctae crucis signaculum. . . . . Crux ante archiepiscopum portatur, quatenus Christum crucifixum sequi admoneatur. Pallium [293] vero pro aurea lamina est institutum, in qua summus Pontifex in Lege Dei nomen Tetragrammaton, id est quattuor literas, in fronte sua praeferebat inscriptum. Quattuor quippe literae illius Nominis, quattuor cornua crucis praemonstrabant, sicut nunc Pallium crucis modum repraesentat. Et quia haec lamina aurea cum forma Crucis in fronte Pontificis portabatur, ideo preciosa Crux frontibus Christianorum chrismate impressa portatur. Pallium autem a solo Apostolico [294] datur, quia haec dignitas a Romano [294] Pontifice jure datur. Quos enim Apostoli provinciis praefecerunt, Archiepiscopi; quos illi paganis praetulerunt, Episcopi, dicebantur; et Apostolorum successores Patriarchae, Petri vero successor " Apostolicus " [294] nominabatur. Huic collata est potestas ab ecclesia archiepiscopos per provincias constituere, quod per Pallii largitionem accipitur. (Cap. 223.) Patriarchae quoque et Apostolicus [294] Pallio utuntur, qui eodem officio praediti esse noscuntur.[295]

CAP. 230. THE DEACON'S DALMATIC, STOLE, AND CHASUBLE.

Diacono . . . Dalmaticae usus conceditur . . . Huic

---

[291] In the four chapters (or rather sections) occupied in the original by this subject of the " staff," I have omitted a good deal which was of no importance to the present work. Here, as in other parts of this work, any omission of this kind is indicated by a dotted line. For a further account of the staff and its symbolism, see the extracts from Innocent III. which follow.

[292] *Pallium . . . Passionem.* This symbolism refers to the purple crosses upon the archiepiscopal pallium.

[293] *Pallium pro lamina.* So Alcuinus quoted at p. 117.

[294] *Apostolicus.* See note 174, p. 95.

[295] From subsequent chapters of this treatise we learn that in Honorius' time the minor orders (below the subdeacon) wore three sacred vestments (*superhumerale, tunica talaris, balteus:* see Cap 226), and the subdeacon five, viz. the three last mentioned and in addition to them, the *subtile, quod et stricta tunica,* and the *sudarium* or maniple, see Cap. 229. And here, too (Cap. 227), we meet with mention of the *cappa* as the proper vestment of the cantores. ['Cappa propria est vestis cantorum, quae pro tunica hyacinthina Legis mutuata est.']

ftola in finiftro humero ponitur, et trans fcapulas ad dextrum latus re-
flectitur, quatenus jugo Chrifti activam vitam fubdat, et per pii laboris
exercitium ad contemplativam perficiat.   Cap. 231. Cum Diaconus
cafulam [296] portat tunc prædicatores fignificat.   . .

Cap. 235. Vestments, why Loose and Large.

Clericorum   . . .   veftis eft laxa, quia clericalis vita debet effe
in eleemofynis et bonis operibus larga.[296 a]

---

[296] With this mention of the chafuble as occafionally worn by deacons, compare note 189, p. 100, and Innocentius III. *Myft. Miff.* lib. i. cap. 5. From the latter we learn that on faft-days the deacon wore a chafuble gathered up in folds (*complicata*) on his left fhoulder.

[296 a] In the paffage of Honorius above quoted we find proof of a confiderable development of the Chriftian veftments here for the firft time (as far as I am aware) formally recognifed. The fubdeacon has now [note 295] five diftinct veftments, the yet inferior orders three; the deacon (as we may gather by inference) fix; the prieft (Cap. 198, p. 135 *fup.*) feven; the bifhop fourteen (Cap. 209, p. 137). St. Hugo, laft quoted, fpeaks only of the prieft's veftments, thofe peculiar to bifhops not being then in queftion, apparently. But St. Ivo [note 265, p. 129], fpeaks of but fix veftments worn by priefts, and of three others (fecond tunic, *caligæ*, and fandals) worn by bifhops; fome of whom, however, are fpoken of as wearing a rational [note 256], and, if archbifhops, a pallium. I may add that the word *infula*, has now (note 290 a) acquired its later technical meaning of a mitre; that the mitre itfelf is now for the firft time fpoken of as one of the diftinctive epifcopal veftments (note 289), and that the gloves (which had been worn for convenience, efpecially in Gaul and Germany, from very remote times) are alfo now raifed to the fame dignity.

XXXVIII.

INNOCENTIUS III. PAPA.[297]

VESTMENTS OF THE LAW AND OF THE GOSPEL.

De Sacro [298] Altaris Mysterio, Lib. i.

[In the 9th chapter of this Treatise the Author had spoken of the points of resemblance, and those of difference, in the offices of Bishop and of Presbyter. In the 10th and following chapters he pursues this subject in its application to the distinctions of ministering dress. He writes as follows]:

The Six Vestments Worn by Presbyters.

Hæc autem communitas et specialitas poteftatum inter Epifcopos et Prefbyteros ipfo numero communium et fpecialium veftium defignatur. Sex autem funt indumenta communia Epifcopis et Prefbyteris: videlicet Amiêtus, Alba, Cingulum, Stola, Manipulus et Planeta.[299] Quia nimirum fex funt in quibus communis Epifcoporum et Prefbyterorum poteftas confiftit, videlicet catechizare, baptizare, prædicare, conficere,[300] folvere et ligare.

The Nine Vestments Worn by Bishops only.

Novem autem funt ornamenta Pontificum fpecialia: videlicet, Ca-

---

[297] "Innocentius III. natione Campanus, patria Anagninus . . . a Clemente III. in cardinalium album cooptatus. Anno 1198 die 8 Januarii Pontifex Romanus eleêtus eft, annos natus 37. . . Anno 1215 generale Concilium Lateranum celebravit, in quo monftrofum Tranfubftantiationis figmentum inter fidei articulos repofuit."—*Cave, Hift. Lit.* vol.ii.

[298] The text is that of the *Opera D. Inno-*

centii Pont. Max., publifhed at Cologne in 1552.

[299] He ufes here the older name for the veftment, commonly known as the cafula or "chafuble."

[300] *Conficere.* The word ordinarily ufed by Weftern writers with the meaning "to confecrate" the holy elements, chrifm, etc.

ligæ, Sandalia, Succinctorium,[301] Tunica, Dalmatica, Mitra et Chirothecæ, Annulus et Baculus.   Quia munia novem funt in quibus fpe-
cialis Epifcoporum poteftas confiftit, videlicet clericos ordinare,
Virgines benedicere, Pontifices confecrare, manus imponere, Bafilicas
dedicare, degradandos deponere, fynodos celebrare, Chrifma conficere
[Note 300], veftes et vafa confecrare.

The Pallium, by whom Worn.

Pallium autem Metropolitanorum et Primatum et Patriarcharum
eft proprium, ut fcilicet per illud a cæteris Epifcopis difcernantur, et
privilegiatam obtineant dignitatem.   Hoc ergo tam in novo quam in
veteri teftamento legitur conftitutum ut Pontifices præter communes
veftes habeant fpeciales.   Sed ibi erant quattuor communes et quattuor
fpeciales, hic autem fex funt communes, novem autem fpeciales.   Id
enim myftica ratio poftulabat.   Nam illæ datæ funt carnalibus et
mundanis : hæ autem datæ funt fpiritualibus et perfectis.   Quaternarius enim convenit carni propter quattuor humores, et Mundo
propter quattuor elementa.   Senarius autem perfectis, quia numerus
eft perfectus, qui redditur fuis partibus aggregatis.[302]   Unde fexto die
perfecit Deus cælum et terram et omnem ornatum eorum.   Novena-
rius fpiritualibus, quia novem funt ordines qui fecundum prophetam per
IX fpecies lapidum defignantur.   Quindecim ergo funt ornamenta
pontificis [note 45, p. 26] quindecim gradus virtutum ipfo numero
defignantia, quos per quindecim Cantica graduum Pfalmifta diftinxit.
Veftes enim facerdotales virtutes fignificant, quibus debent facerdotes
ornari, fecundum illud propheticum : *Sacerdotes tui induantur juftitia,
et fancti tui exultent.*

[*In the chapters immediately following* (Cap. 11 to 32), *the Writer
defcribes in detail the Levitical Veftments, and ftates what he believes to
be their myftical fignificance.   This done, he proceeds to fpeak of the
Veftments of Chriftian Miniftry, explaining their fymbolifm under two
afpects, firft in refpect of Chrift the true High-prieft, and fecondly in
refpect of thofe who are members of Chrift here on earth.*]

---

301 *Succinctorium.*   Compare note 313, p.
153 and Durandus there quoted.

300 Durandus, who transfers much of this
treatife word for word into his own pages, and
this about a "perfect number" amongst the reft,

adds by way of explanation, "*Nam cum unum
duo et tres dicuntur, fenarius numerus impletur :
vel quia in tribus partibus dividitur, id eft, in
fexta tertia et dimidia, videlicet in uno, duobus, et
tribus.*"—*Rat. D. O. Lib. iii.*

CAP. 33. CHRISTIAN VESTMENTS GENERALLY.

Veſtes autem evangelici ſacerdotis aliud deſignant in Capite aliud figurant in Membris. Nam et Caput et Membra ſacerdotis nomine nuncupantur. Ad Caput enim dicit Pſalmographus : *Tu es ſacerdos in æternum ſecundum ordinem Melchiſedech.* Ad Membra vero dicit Apoſtolus : *Vos eſtis genus electum, regale ſacerdotium, gens ſancta, populus acquiſitionis.* Prius ergo exponenda ſunt earum myſteria juxta quod Capiti congruunt, ac demum ſecundum quod Membris conveniunt.

CAP. 35. OF THE VESTMENTS IN RESPECT OF CHRIST.

Pontifex ergo Altaris officio Capitis ſui Chriſti, cujus membrum eſt, repræſentans perſonam, dum pedibus aſſumit ſandalia, illud incarnationis Dominicæ inſinuat calceamentum de quo Dominus inquit in Pſalmo : *In Idumæam extendam calceamentum meum,* id eſt, in gentibus notam faciam incarnationem meam. Venit enim ad nos calceata Divinitas, ut pro nobis Dei filius ſacerdotio fungeretur. Per ligulas quibus ipſa pedibus ſandalia conſtringuntur illud idem accipimus quod per corrigiam calceamenti Joannes Baptiſta ſignificavit, cum ait : *Cujus non ſum dignus corrigiam calceamenti ſolvere.* Unionem ergo ineffabilem, copulamque indiſſolubilem, quibus Verbi Divinitas ſe carni noſtræ conjunxit, per ſandaliorum corrigias intelligimus. Mediantibus vero caligis pedes ſandaliis conjunguntur, quoniam anima mediante carni Divinitas eſt unita. Sicut enim pes corpus ſuſtentat, ita Divinitas mundum gubernat. Unde ait Pſalmiſta : *Adorate ſcabellum pedum ejus, quoniam ſanctum eſt* (Pſ. xcviii.).

CAP. 35. THE AMICE.

Amictus autem, quo ſacerdos caput[303] ſuum obnubit, illud ſignificat quod in Apocalypſi deſcribitur, Angelum Dei fortem deſcendiſſe de cælo amictum nube (Rev. x.). Et in Eſaia : *Ecce Dominus*

---

[303] *Amictus quo caput obnubit.* He alludes, apparently, to the mode of putting on the amice referred to in note 178, p. 96. Hence, too, the alluſion in Durandus : *Amictus, pro galea, caput contegit.—Rat. Div. Off.* Cap. i. And more to the ſame effect in Cap. 2.

afcendet fuper nubem candidam. Veniens autem ad falvationem mundi Dei Filius, magni confilii Angelus, amictus eft nube dum divinitatem abfcondit in carne. Nam caput viri Chriftus, caput Chrifti Deus. Hoc ergo carnis latibulum amictus facerdotis fignificat. Quod per illam fyndonem expreffius defignatur, qua fummus Pontifex [304] caput obducit. Et pulchre quidem quod per calceamentum pedum hoc ipfum per amictum capitis defignatur, quia divinitas in carne latuit et per carnem innotuit. Nam cum notus effet in Judæa Deus, et in Ifrael magnum nomen ejus, in Idumæam extendit calceamentum fuum, et ante confpectum gentium revelavit juftitiam fuam.

Cap. 36. The Alb.

Alba lineum veftimentum longiffime diftans a tunicis pelliceis quæ de mortuis animalibus [Note 30, p. 20] fiunt, quibus Adam veftitus eft poft peccatum, novitatem vitæ fignificat, quam Chriftus et habuit et docuit et tribuit in baptifmo, de qua dicit Apoftolus: *Exuite veterem hominem cum actibus fuis, et induite novum hominem qui fecundum Deum creatus eft.* Nam et in transfiguratione refplenduit facies ejus ficut fol, et veftimenta ejus funt facta alba ficut nix. Semper enim veftimenta Chrifti munda fuerunt et candida, quia peccatum non fecit, nec inventus eft dolus in lingua ejus.

Cap. 37. The Girdle.

Zona facerdotalis illud fignificat quod Joannes Apoftolus ait: *Converfus vidi fimilem filio hominis præcinctum ad mamillas zona aurea.* Per zonam auream perfecta Chrifti charitas defignatur: quam dicit

---

[304] By "*fummus Pontifex*" is here meant the Pope, more exactly defcribed as *Romanus Pontifex* in Cap. 53 below, where fee more concerning the "*orale*" which is the *findon* or veftment of fine linen here referred to. The title, *Pontifex Maximus*, which is now the official title of the Bifhop of Rome, nowhere occurs in the writings of Innocent III. himfelf, as far as I have obferved. The heading of Sermo II. "*In confecratione Pontificis Maximi*," fo given in the Cologne edition of 1552, is of courfe an *editorial* heading only, and by other Roman writers (as *e.g.* Floro-vanti), is quoted as *De confecratione fummi Pontificis.* The earlieft medal on which this later title of *Pontifex Maximus* appears, is one of Martin V. [MARTINVS. V. COLVMNA. PONTIFEX MAXIMVS.] *fed.* 1417-1413; the earlieft coin, one of Paul II. (1464-1421), ftruck at Avignon [PAVLVS PP. II. PONT. MAX. A. I.] Thefe are reprefented in a work, now of great rarity, the *Antiquiores Pontificum Romanorum Denarii, ftudio et cura Benedicti Florovantis.* 4to, *Romæ*, 1734. For the earlier hiftory of the word *Pontifex*, fee note 45, p. 26.

Apostolus supereminentem scientiæ charitatem Christi, ferventem in corde, radiantem in opere. Cujus succinctorium [305] illud significat quod Esaias de Christo loquens prædixit (Esa. xi.) : *Erit justitia cingulum lumborum ejus, et fides cinctorium renum ejus.* (Pf. l.) : *Nam justus Dominus, et justitias dilexit, æquitatem vidit vultus ejus.* (Pf. cxliv.) : *Fidelis Dominus in omnibus verbis suis, et sanctus in omnibus operibus suis.* Duæ summitates illius duæ sunt partes naturalis justitiæ, quam Christus et fecit et docuit : *Quod tibi vis non fieri, alteri ne feceris ; sed quæcunque vultis ut faciant vobis homines, et vos facite illis.*

CAP. 38. THE STOLE.

Stola, quæ super amictum collo sacerdotis incumbit, obedientiam et servitutem significat, quam Dominus omnium propter salutem servorum subivit (Phil. ii.) : *Nam cum in forma Dei esset non rapinam arbitratus est esse se æqualem Deo. Exinanivit enim seipsum, formam servi accipiens, factus obediens usque ad mortem, mortem autem Crucis.* Causam quippe mortalitatis nec contraxit origine, nec commisit in opere, quia quod non rapuit hoc exoluit [*fort.* exsolvit]. Dedit enim illi calicem pater, non judex ; amore, non ira ; voluntate, non necessitate ; gratia, non vindicta. Hic est ille Jacob qui parens præcepto patris Isaac, et consilio matris suæ Rebeccæ, servivit Laban, ut Rachael et Lyam duceret in conjugium.

CAP. 39. THE (SECOND) TUNIC.

Tunica poderis, quæ hyacinthini coloris erat in veteri sacerdotio, tintinnabulis et Malis Punicis ab inferiori parte pendentibus, ut Pontifex totus vocalis incederet, cælestem Christi doctrinam insinuat. Cujus notitiam habuerunt homines quibus Deus per prophetam ait (Esa. xl.) : *In montem excelsum ascende tu qui evangelizas Sion.* Præcipue tamen hanc habuit tunicam evangelicæ textrix doctrinæ, Sapientia Dei Jesus Christus, et dedit illam Apostolis suis : *Omnia,* inquit, *quæcunque audivi a Patre meo nota feci vobis.* Hanc ergo significavit illa tunica Domini quam milites scindere noluerunt, eo quod esset inconsutilis, desuper contexta per totum : damnum fore maximum existimantes si qui doctrinam evangelicam hæresibus scindere moliantur.

---

[305] *Succinctorium.* See Cap. 52, quoted below, and note 313, p. 153.

CAP. 40. THE DALMATIC.

Super hanc tunicam Pontifex [note 45] veſtit Dalmaticam, quæ ſui orma latam et largam miſericordiam Chriſti ſignificat, quam ipſe præ cæteris et docuit et impendit. *Eſtote*, inquit, *miſericordes ſicut et pater veſter miſericors eſt.* Beati namque miſericordes quoniam ipſi miſericordiam conſequentur. Judicium vero ſine miſericordia fiet ei qui non facit miſericordiam, quia miſericordia ſuperexultat judicium (Jaſ. ii.) : Ergo dimittite et dimittetur vobis; *ſicque*, inquit, *orabitis : Dimitte nobis debita noſtra ſicut et nos dimittimus debitoribus noſtris.* Hic eſt ergo Samaritanus ille, proximus noſter, qui fecit nobiſcum miſericordiam, ſuperinfundens vulneribus noſtris vinum et oleum. Nam per viſcera miſericordiæ ſuæ viſitavit nos Oriens ex alto. Qui non ex operibus juſtitiæ quæ fecimus nos, ſed ſecundum miſericordiam ſuam ſalvos nos fecit. Qui pro peccatoribus venit ut de peccatis veniam indulgeret. *Miſericordiam*, inquit, *volo, et non ſacrificium.*

CAP. 41. THE GLOVES.

Chirothecæ ſunt hædorum pelliculæ, quas Jacob manibus Rebecca circumdedit, ut piloſæ manus majoris[305a] ſimilitudinem exprimerent. Pellis hædi ſimilitudo peccati quam Rebecca mater, id eſt, Spiritus ſancti gratia, manibus veri Jacob, id eſt, operibus Chriſti circumdedit : ut ſimilitudinem majoris, id eſt, prioris Adæ, Chriſtus exprimeret. Chriſtus enim ſimilitudinem peccati ſine peccato ſuſcepit, ut incarnationis myſterium diabolo celaretur. Nam ad ſimilitudinem peccatorum eſuriit, ſitivit, doluit et expavit, dormivit et laboravit. Unde cum jejunaſſet quadraginta diebus et quadraginta noctibus, ac poſtea eſuriiſſet, accedens ad eum diabolus eum ad ſimilitudinem prioris Adæ tentavit. Sed quibus primum vicerat, eiſdem modis victus eſt a ſecundo.

CAP. 42. THE CHASUBLE.

Caſula vel Planeta magni Sacerdotis eſt univerſalis Eccleſia, de qua dicit Apoſtolus : *Quotquot in Chriſto baptizati eſtis Chriſtum induiſtis.* (Gal. iii.) Hoc eſt illud Aaron veſtimentum cujus in oram deſcendit

---

[305a] *Majoris, i.e.* of the elder brother, viz. Eſau.

unguentum : fed a capite defcendit in barbam, et a barba defcendit in oram. Quoniam de plenitudine Spiritus ejus nos omnes accepimus, primum Apoftoli, poftmodum cæteri. Quod autem caſula, cum integra fit et integra, extenfione manuum in anteriorem et pofteriorem partem quodammodo dividitur, defignat et antiquam ecclefiam, quæ paffionem Chrifti præceffit, et novam, quæ paffionem Chrifti fubfequitur. Nam et qui præibant, et qui fequebantur, clamabant dicentes, *Ofanna filio David. Benedictus qui venit in nomine Domini.*

CAP. 43. THE MANIPLE.

Quod facerdos manipulum portat in læva, defignat quod Chriftus bravium [306] obtinebat in via. Per manipulum [307] enim præmium defignatur, juxta quod legitur (Pſ. cxxv., cxxvi.) : *Venientes autem venient cum exultatione, portantes manipulos fuos.* Per lævam vita præfens accipitur, juxta quod fcriptum eft, *Læva ejus fub capite meo, et dextra illius amplexabitur me.* Chriftus autem fimul fruebatur et merebatur. Fruebatur in patria,[308] merebatur in via. Nam fimul comprehendebat, et ftadium percurrebat : quia fimul erat in patria et in via. *Nemo,* inquit (Joan. iii.), *afcendit in cælum, nifi qui de cælo defcendit, filius hominis qui eft in cælo.*

CAP. 44. THE MITRE.

Mitra Pontificis illud fignificat quod Propheta loquens de Filio dicit ad Patrem (Pſ. viii.) : *Gloria et honore coronafti eum, Domine, et conftituifti eum fuper opera manuum tuarum.* Hoc eft itaque illud Nomen (Phil. ii.) quod eft fuper omne nomen, ut in nomine Jefu omne genu flectatur,

---

[306] *Bravium*, equivalent to βραβεῖον. The prize of one who conquers in the ftadium. *Omnes currunt, fed unus accipit bravium.* 1 Cor. ix. 24. Compare Phi. iii. 14.

[307] *Manipulum.* The primitive meaning of *manipulus* was a handful, and hence various fecondary meanings, as, α. a bundle of hay, or of corn, "a fheaf" (fo in the Pſalm above quoted, and again in Ps. cxxvii., cxxviii). β. a "handful" of men, acting together as one body, and fo a "company" in the military fenfe of the word. [Others connect this with what follows.] γ. Any other "handful," as a cloth held in the hand, in which fenfe *manipulus*, as a later ecclefiaftical term, has taken the place of the older *mappula.* [The military fenfe noticed under β. may have arifen from the ufe of fuch a piece of cloth as a *Pennon.* Compare note 233 as to the meanings of *Fanon.*] I know of no inftance of the word being ufed as equivalent to *præmium*, a meaning which Innocent may perhaps have inferred from this Pſalm which he quotes.

[308] *In patria*, that is, "in heaven."

cælestium terrestrium et infernorum. Nam et in aurea lamina Cydaris Pontificalis sculptum erat nomen Domini Tetragrammaton, cujus mysterium supra prælibavimus. Per Mitram ergo capitis Christi summam illam honorificentiam intelligimus, quæ propter divinitatem debetur humanitati. Nam propter pedem adoratur scabellum. *Adorate*, inquit (Pf. xcviii.), *scabellum pedum ejus, quia sanctum est.*

Cap. 45. The Staff.

Virga Pontificis Christi potestatem significat. De qua dicit Pfalmista (Pf. xliv. 7) : *Virga recta est virga regni tui. Quia dilexisti justitiam et odisti iniquitatem, propterea te unxit Deus, Deus tuus.* Propter quod et alibi dicit : *Reges eos in virga ferrea* (Pf. ii.). Verum potestas Christi non solum virga sed et baculus est ; quia non solum corripit sed et sustentat. Unde Pfalmista (Pf. xxiii.), *Virga tua et baculus tuus, ipsa me consolata sunt.*

Cap. 46. The Episcopal Ring.

Annulus digiti donum Spiritus Sancti significat. Digitus enim articulatus atque distinctus Spiritum Sanctum infinuat, secundum illud (Exod. viii.): *Digitus Dei est hic.* Et alibi : *Si ego in digito Dei ejicio dæmonia, filii vestri in quo ejiciunt?* [309] (Luc. xi.) Annulus aureus et rotundus perfectionem donorum ejus significat, quæ sine menfura Christus accepit, quoniam in eo plenitudo divinitatis habitat corporaliter. Nam qui de cælo venit super omnes est. Cui Deus non dedit Spiritum ad menfuram : *Super quem videris Spiritum*, inquit (Joan. i.), *descendentem et manentem, hic est qui baptizat in Spiritu Sancto.* Nam (Efa. xi.) *requiescit super eum Spiritus sapientiæ et intellectus*, etc. Ipfe vero secundum differentes donationes distribuit : *Alii*, secundum Apoftolum (1 Cor. xii.), *dans sermonem scientiæ, alii gratiam sanitatum, alii operationem virtutum*, etc. Quod et visibilis pontifex imitatur, alios in Ecclesia constituens Sacerdotes, alios Diaconos, alios Subdiaconos, et hujusmodi.

[In Cap. 47 mention is made of the five Pfalms (81, 84, 85, 115,

---

[309] The author evidently quotes from memory, and has taken the beginning of his quotation from one verse (ver. 20), and the conclusion from another (ver. 19).

and 129 of the Vulgate), and of certain Prayers, to be said by the Bishop when about to celebrate Mass. He then (Cap. 48, *sqq.*) proceeds with the subjects of the vestments, and enumerates then anew, declaring the spiritual significance of each in respect of them who are " members of Christ."]

CAP. 48. THE SANDALS AND STOCKINGS.[310]

Inter hæc pedes pontificis, in præparatione evangelii pacis, caligis et sandaliis calceantur, quorum pulchritudinem admirabatur propheta cum diceret, *Quam speciosi pedes evangelizantium pacem, evangelizantium bona.* Sandalia vero de subtus integram habent soleam, desuper autem corium fenestratum,[311] quia gressus prædicatoris debent subtus esse meniti ne polluantur terrenis, secundum illud : *Excutite pulverem de pedibus vestris* (Matt. x.), et sursum aperti, quatenus ad cognoscenda cælestia revelentur, secundum illud propheticum : *Revela oculos meos et considerabo mirabilia de lege tua* (Ps. cxviii.). Quod autem sandalia quibusdam locis aperta, quibusdam clausa sunt, designat quod Evangelica prædicatio nec omnibus revelari, nec omnibus debet abscondi. Sicut scriptum est (Mar. iv.) : *Vobis datum est nosse mysterium regni Dei, cæteris autem in parabolis.* (Matt. vii.) : *Nolite sanctum dare canibus, nec margaritas spargatis ante porcos.* Prius autem caligis induitur usque ad genua protensis, ibique constrictis, quia prædicator pedibus suis rectos facere gressus, et genua debilia roborare, debet. Nam qui fecerit et docuerit, hic magnus vocabitur in regno cælorum.

[*In Cap.* 49 *he notices the washing of the hands which forms part of the preparation. He then proceeds as follows*] :

CAP. 50. THE AMICE.

Lotis itaque manibus assumit Amictum, qui super humeros circum-

---

[310] " Stockings." I have rendered *caligæ* by this term, as more suggestive to English readers than any other word of the real nature of this portion of the episcopal dress. Full details as to their material and ornamentation will be found in Dr. Bock (*L. G.* vol. ii. p. 2, *sqq.*).

[311] *Fenestratum, i.e.* with open spaces here and there. A similar expression (*corii pertuf.*)

was employed (above p. 127) by St. Ivo. Dr. Bock gives a coloured drawing of a shoe such as that here described, taken from the tomb of Archbishop Arnoldus, of Treves (12th century). In the upper leather " sind kleine durchbohrungen (*foramina obtusa*) ersichtlich." *L. G.* vol. ii. p. 14.

quaque diffunditur. Per quem operum fortitudo fignificatur. Humeri quippe [note 35] fortes funt ad opera peragenda, fecundum illud Patriarchæ Jacob (Gen. xlix.) : *Suppofuit humerum ad portandum, et factus eft tributis ferviens.* Duo vateuli quibus ante pectus ligatur fignant intentionem et finem quibus informandum eft opus, ne fiat in fermento malitiæ et nequitiæ, fed in azymis finceritatis et veritatis. Sacerdos enim non debet otiofus exiftere, fed bonis operibus infiftere et infudare, fecundum quod Apoftolus ait ad Timotheum : *Labora ficut bonus miles Jefu Chrifti.*

CAP. 51. THE ALB.

Alba membris corporis convenienter aptata nihil fuperfluum aut diffolutum in vita facerdotis effe debere demonftrat. Hæc ob fpeciem candoris defignat munditiam, fecundum quod legitur (Eccl. ix.) : *Omni tempore veftimenta tua fint candida.* Fit autem de byffo vel de lino. Propter quod fcriptum eft (Apoc. xix.) : *Byffum* [*Leg.* byffinum] *funt juftificationes fanctorum.* Sicut enim byffus vel linum candorem, quem ex natura non habet, multis tunfionibus attritum per artem acquirit, fic et hominis caro munditiam, quam non obtinet per naturam, multis macerationibus caftigata fortitur per gratiam. Unde facerdos, fecundum Apoftolum, caftigat corpus fuum et in fervitutem redigit, ne forte quum aliis prædicaverit ipfe reprobus fiat. Hæc veftis in veteri facerdotio ftricta [note 101] fuiffe defcribitur, propter fpiritum fervitutis in timore. In novo larga eft, propter fpiritum adoptionis in libertate. Quod autem Aurifrigium [312] habet, et gemmata eft in diverfis locis, et variis operibus ad decorem, illud infinuat quod Propheta dicit in Pfalmo (Pf. xliv.) : *Aftitit regina a dextris tuis in veftitu deaurato, circumdata varietate.*

CAP. 52. THE GIRDLE AND UNDER-GIRDLE.

Debet igitur Alba circa lumbos zona præcingi, ut caftitas facerdotis nullis incentivorum ftimulis diffolvatur. Unde : *Sint lumbi veftri præcincti, et lucernæ ardentes in manibus veftris* (Luc. xii.). In lumbis

---

[312] *Aurifrigium,* aliter *aurifrifia,* whence the | attached to the edge, or other portion, of a
Fr. Orfraie, Eng. Orfrey, an ornamented band | veftment.

enim luxuria dominatur. Sic Dominus loquens de diabolo manifeſtat (Job. xl.): *Virtus ejus in lumbis ejus, et fortitudo ejus in umbilico ventris ſui.* Debent ergo lumbi præcingi per continentiam. Debet et ſubcingi[313] per abſtinentiam, quoniam hoc genus dæmonii non ejicitur niſi in oratione et jejunio. Hinc etiam Apoſtolus ait (Eph. vi.): *State ſuccinĉti lumbos in veritate.*

CAP. 53. SPECIAL INSIGNIA OF THE BISHOP OF ROME.

Romanus autem pontifex poſt Albam et Cingulum aſſumit Orale,[314] quod circa caput involvit, et replicat ſuper humeros, legalis Pontificis ordinem ſequens, qui poſt lineam ſtriĉtam et zonam induebatur Ephot, id eſt Superhumerale, cujus locum [Note 253] modo tenet Amiĉtus. Et quia ſigno Crucis[12] auri lamina ceſſit, pro[293] lamina quam Pontifex gerebat in fronte, Pontifex iſte[315] crucem gerit in peĉtore. Nam myſterium, quod in quattuor litteris auri lamina continebat, in quattuor partibus forma crucis explicuit. Juxta quod inquit Apoſtolus (Eph. iii.): *Ut comprehendatis cum omnibus ſanĉtis quæ ſit longitudo et latitudo et ſublimitas et profundum.* Ideoque Romanus Pontifex crucem quandam inſertam cathenulis, a collo ſuſpenſam, ſibi ſtatuit ante peĉtus, ut ſacra-

---

[313] *Subcingere* is to gird "up" (ſuch being frequently the meaning of *ſub* in compoſition). And the ſame girdle may be ſaid both *præcingere*, in reſpeĉt of its girding in the tunic in "front" of which it is faſtened, and *ſubcingere* in reſpeĉt of its uſe in gathering up (with a view to aĉtive exertion) a garment, which, if worn at its full length, would impede all freedom of movement. When, however, the *zona* and the *ſuccinĉtorium* are diſtinguiſhed (as by Innocent himſelf, *ſupra*, pp. 143, 144), it ſeems that by the latter term we muſt underſtand the long ends of the girdle which hung down from the waiſt nearly to the feet. This will explain the language of Durandus (R. D. O. iii. Cap. 4) ſpeaking of the *ſubcingulum* as *double. A ſiniſtro Pontificis latere duplex dependent ſubcingulum.* [None of the modern Liturgical works which I have conſulted notice the word *ſuccinĉtorium.*]

[314] *Orale.* In Ciampini (Vet. Mon. i. p. 239) an engraving is given in which a headdreſs anſwering to this deſcription may be ſeen, on a figure which probably repreſents Celeſtine III (*ſed.* 1191–1198). This pecu-

liar veſtment, retained in the 13th Century by the Roman biſhop only, was probably a relic of thoſe earlier times when the "mitre" was what the name μίτρα originally implied, a "cap" made of linen, of wool, or of ſilk, utterly unlike the modern mitre.

[315] This wearing of a croſs (generally containing relics) as an ornament, attached to the neck by a chain, is ſpoken of here as peculiar to the Biſhop of Rome. In Roman theory it was ſo, but not in faĉt, even in the Weſtern church. Numerous inſtances to the contrary are mentioned by Dr. Bock, who has alſo engraved ſeveral ancient "Peĉtoral Croſſes," as they are called, and among them one ſent as a preſent by Gregory the Great to the Lombard Queen Theodolinda. In the Eaſt theſe ἐναύρεα ἐγκόλπια were worn both as Imperial and as Epiſcopal ornaments. At the Council of Florence, no Weſtern biſhops were allowed to wear their peĉtoral croſſes in preſence of the Pope. The Greeks maintained and exerciſed their right to do ſo. [See Bock, *L. G.* vol. ii. p. 213. *ſqq.*]

X

mentum quod ille tunc præferebat in fronte, hic autem recondat in
pectore: [318] *Nam corde creditur ad justitiam, ore autem confessio fit ad
salutem.*

CAP. 54. THE STOLE.

Post hæc Stolam,[30] quæ alio modo vocatur Orarium, super collum
sibi sacerdos imponit, ut jugum Domini se suscepisse significet; quæ
a collo per anteriora descendens dextrum et sinistrum latus adornat,
quia per arma justitiæ a dextris et a sinistris, id est, in prosperis et
adversis, sacerdos debet esse munitus.   Stola quippe significat sapien-
tiam vel patientiam, de qua scriptum habetur: *Patientia vobis necessaria est ut reportetis promissiones* (Heb. x.).   Et iterum (Luc. xxi.):
In patientia vestra possidebitis animas vestras.   Hinc est ergo quod
Stola cum Zona nexibus quibusdam colligatur, quia virtutes virtutibus
sociantur, ne aliquo tentationis moveantur impulsu.   Debet autem
sacerdos secundum decretum Braccharensis Concilii [316] de uno eodemque orario cervicem pariter et utrumque humerum premens, signum
crucis in pectore suo præparare.   Si quis autem aliter egerit excommunicationi debitæ subjacebit.   Nisi forte quis dixerit hoc decretum
per contrariam Ecclesiæ Romanæ [317] consuetudinem abrogatum.

CAP. 55. THE TUNIC.

Deinde Pontifex induit Tunicam poderem, id est, talarem, signifi-
cantem perseverantiam.   Unde Joseph inter fratres suos talarem tunicam
habuisse describitur.   Cum vero cæteræ virtutes currant in stadio, per-
severantia tamen accipit bravium [Note 306]: quoniam qui perseve-
raverit usque in finem hic salvus erit.   Unde præcipitur (Apoc. ii.):
Esto fidelis usque ad mortem et dabo tibi coronam vitæ.   Habebat autem
hæc vestis in veteri sacerdotio pro fimbriis mala Punica cum tintinnabulis aureis, quorum supra mysterium exposuimus.

CAP. 56. THE DALMATIC.

Super hanc tunicam episcopus vestit Dalmaticam,[131] sic dictam eo
quod in Dalmatia fuit reperta.   Quæ sui forma figurat largitatem, quia

---

[316] The third Council of Bracara (now Braga, in Portugal) held A.D. 572.

[317] Durandus (R. D. O. iii. v.) transfers
the greater part of this chapter almost word
for word into his own pages, but makes one
important change, " *per contrariam* generalis
Ecclesiæ consuetudinem."

largas habet manicas et protenſas. Unde ſecundum Apoſtolum
(1 Tim. iii.) : *Oportet epiſcopum non eſſe turpis lucri cupidum ſed hoſ-
pitalem.* Non ergo habeat manum ad dandum collectam, et ad re-
cipiendum porrectam, ſed illud efficiat quod Propheta ſuadet (Eſa. lviii.) :
*Frange eſurienti panem tuum et egenos vagoſque duc in domum tuam. Quum
videris nudum operi eum, et carnem tuam ne deſpexeris.* Ob hoc forte
ſpecialiter utuntur Diaconi Dalmaticis, quod principaliter electi ſunt
ab apoſtolis ut menſis ex officio miniſtrarent. Debet autem Dalmatica
habere duas lineas coccineas hinc inde, ante et retro, a ſummo uſque
deorſum, ut pontifex habeat honorem charitatis,[317 a] ad Deum et ad
proximum, in proſperis et adverſis, juxta Veteris et Novi Teſtamenti
præceptum, quod eſt : *Diliges Dominum Deum tuum ex toto corde tuo,
et proximum tuum ſicut teipſum.* Unde Joannes : *Chariſſimi non novum
mandatum ſcribo vobis ſed mandatum vetus, quod habuiſtis ab initio.
Atque iterum mandatum novum ſcribo vobis, etc.* (1 Joan. ii.). In
ſiniſtro quoque latere Dalmatica fimbrias habere ſolet, id eſt, ſolicitudines activæ vitæ ſignantes, quas Epiſcopus debet habere pro ſubditis.
Juxta quod dicit apoſtolus (1 Cor. xi.) : *Præter illa quæ extrinſecus
ſunt, inſtantia mea quotidiana, ſolicitudo omnium eccleſiarum.*

Cap. 57. The Gloves.

Quia vero plerique bonum opus, quod faciunt, inani favore cor-
rumpunt, ſtatim Epiſcopus manus operit chirothecis,[290 a] ut neſciat ſiniſtra
ſua quid faciat dextra ſua. Per chirothecam ergo congrua cautela
deſignatur, quæ ſic facit opus in publico quod intentionem continet
in occulto. Nam etſi Dominus dixerit : *Luceat lux veſtra coram hominibus ut videant opera veſtra bona, et glorificent Patrem veſtrum qui in
cælis eſt,* propter quod chirotheca circulum aureum deſuper habet, ipſe
tamen præcepit, *Attendite ne juſtitiam veſtram faciatis coram hominibus,
ut videamini ab iis. Alioquin mercedem non habebitis apud Patrem
veſtrum qui in cælis eſt.*

Cap. 58. The Chasuble.

Poſtremo ſuper omnes veſtes induit Caſulam [130] vel Planetam,[299] quæ
ſignificat Charitatem [Note 261.]. Charitas enim operit multitudinem

---

[317 a] He connects "charity" with the colour
of ſcarlet, as do Alcuin (ſee note 235, p. 113),
and Gregory the Great, quoted at p. 60 (ſee
note 107, *in fin.*).

peccatorum, de qua dicit Apoftolus (1 Cor. xiii.) : *Adhuc excellentiorem viam nobis demonftro. Si linguis hominum loquar et angelorum, chari-tatem autem non habuero, factus fum velut æs fonans et cimbalum tin-niens.* Et hæc eft veftis nuptialis, de qua loquitur Dominus in Evan-gelio : *Amice, quomodo huc intrafti, non habens veftem nuptialem ?* Quod autem Amictus [170] fuper os Planetæ revolvitur, innuit quod omne opus bonum debet ad charitatem referri. Nam finis præcepti Charitas eft, de corde puro, confcientia bona, et fide non ficta. Quod autem extenfione manuum in anteriorem et pofteriorem partem dividitur, fignificat duo brachia charitatis ad Deum fcilicet et ad proximum. *Diliges*, inquit, *Dominum Deum tuum ex toto corde tuo, et proximum ficut teipfum.* In his duobus mandatis pendet tota Lex et Prophetæ. Latitudo Planetæ fignificat latitudinem Charitatis, quæ ufque ad ini-micos extenditur. Unde : *Latum mandatum tuum nimis.*

Cap. 59. The Maniple.

Verum quia mentibus bene compofitis et divino cultui mancipatis fæpe fubrepit acedia [318] quæ quodam torpore reddit animum dor-mientem, dicente Pfalmifta (Ps. cxviii.), *Dormitavit anima mea præ tædio,* in finiftra manu apponitur mappula, quæ Manipulus [307] vel Suda-rium [197] appellatur, qua fudorem mentis abftergat, et foporem cordis ex-cutiat, ut depulfo tædio vel torpore bonis operibus diligenter invigilet. Per manipulum ergo vigilantia defignatur, de qua Dominus ait : *Vigilate quia nefcitis qua hora Dominus vefter venturus fit.* Unde fponfa dicit in Canticis (Can. v.) : *Ego dormio et cor meum vigilat.*

Cap. 60. The Mitre.

Mitra [309a] Pontificis fcientiam utriufque Teftamenti fignificat: nam duo cornua [310a] duo funt Teftamenta, duæ fimbriæ fpiritus et littera. Circulus aureus, qui anteriorem et pofteriorem partem complectitur, indicat quod omnis fcriba doctus in regno cælorum de thefauro fuo nova profert et vetera. Caveat ergo diligenter epifcopus ne prius velit effe magifter quam norit effe difcipulus, ne fi cæcus cæcum duxerit ambo in foveam cadant. Scriptum eft enim in Propheta : *Quia tu fcientiam repulifti ego te repellam, ne facerdotio fungaris mihi.* (Ofe. iv.)

---

[318] In the text before me *accidia*. The true reading is fupplied by a comparifon with St. Ivo Carnotenfis, quoted at p. 127, from whom thefe words are taken *verbatim*. On

acedia fee note 262, *in loc.*
[309a] For details concerning the Mitre, fee Bock, *L. G.* ii. 164.

Cap. 61. The Ring.

Annulus eſt fidei facramentum, in quo Chriſtus ſponſam ſuam fanctam Eccleſiam ſubarravit, ut ipſa de ſe dicere valeat, Annulo ſuo ſubarravit me Dominus meus, id eſt, Chriſtus. Cujus cuſtodes et pæ-dagogi ſunt epiſcopi et prælati, annulum pro ſigno ferentes in teſti-monium. De quibus Sponſa dicit in Canticis : *Invenerunt me vigiles qui cuſtodiunt civitatem.* Hunc annulum dedit pater filio reverteriti, ſecundum illud : *Date annulum in manum ejus* (Luc. xv.).

Cap. 62. The Staff, and why it is not borne by the Bishop of Rome.

Baculus correptionem ſignificat paſtoralem, propter quod a con-fecratore dicitur confecrato : *Accipe baculum paſtoralitatis.* Et de quo dicit apoſtolus (1 Cor. iv.) ; *In virga veniam ad vos.* Quod autem eſt acutus in fine, rectus in medio, retortus in ſummo, defignat quod pontifex debet per eam pungere pigros, regere debiles, colligere vagos. Quod uno carmine verſificator quidam expreſſit : *Collige, ſuſtenta, ſtimula, vaga, morbida, lenta.*

Romanus autem Pontifex paſtorali virga non utitur, pro eo quod beatus Petrus Apoſtolus baculum ſuum[319] miſit Euchario primo Epiſcopo Trevirorum, quem una cum Valerio et Materno ad prædicandum Evangelium genti Teutonicæ deſtinavit. Cui ſucceſſit in epiſcopatu Maternus, qui per baculum fancti Petri de morte fuerat fuſcitatus. Quem baculum uſque hodie cum magna veneratione Trevirenſis ſervat eccleſia.

Cap. 63. The Pallium.

Pallium,[319] quo majores utuntur epiſcopi, ſignificat diſciplinam qua ſe ipſos et ſubditos Archiepiſcopi debent regere. Per hanc acquiritur torques[320] aurea quam legitime certantes accipiunt, de qua dicit Salo-

---

[319] An ancient ſtaff (not, however, by any means of the *moſt* ancient type) was long pre-ferved at Treves, and ſhown as the identical ſtaff here ſpoken of. It is now at Limburg, and is figured by Dr. Bock (vol. ii. Pl. xxx), who out of regard for the traditions aſſociated with it is confiderate enough not to pronounce an opinion as to its real date.

[320] *Torques* (a neck chain) is the term or-dinarily employed to deſcribe the circular por-tion of the Papal Pallium. Hence it is com-pared in this paſſage to a "chain of gold," ſuch as in the Eaſt eſpecially was often be-ſtowed as a mark of ſpecial favour upon thoſe whom kings "delighted to honour."

mon in Parabolis : *Audi, fili mi, disciplinam patris tui, et ne dimittas legem matris tuæ : ut addatur gratia capiti tuo, et torques collo tuo* (Prov. i.). Fit enim pallium de candida lana contextum, habens desuper circulum humeros constringentem, et duas lineas ab utraque parte dependentes ; quattuor autem cruces purpureas, ante et retro, a dextris et a sinistris : sed a sinistris est duplex et simplex a dextris. Hæc omnia moralibus sunt imbuta mysteriis, et divinis gravida sacramentis. Nam ut scriptura testatur (Eccl. i.): *In thesauris sapientiæ significatio disciplinæ.* In lana quippe notatur asperitas, in candore benignitatis (*Leg.* benignitas) designatur. Nam ecclesiastica disciplina contra rebelles et obstinatos severitatem exercet, sed erga pœnitentes et humiles exhibet pietatem.[301] Propter quod de lana non cujuslibet animalis sed ovis tantum efficitur, quæ mansuetum est animal. Unde Propheta : *Tanquam ovis ad occisionem ductus est, et quasi agnus coram tondente is obmutivit, et non operuit os suum.* Hinc est quod illius semivivi vulneribus, quem Samaritanus duxit in stabulum, et vinum adhibet et oleum ; ut per vinum mordeantur vulnera, et per oleum foveantur ; quatenus qui sanandis vulneribus præest in vino morsum severitatis adhibeat, in oleo mollitiem pietatis. Hoc nimirum et per arcam tabernaculi designatur, in qua cum tabulis virga continetur et manna. Quoniam in mente rectoris cum scripturæ scientia debet esse virga districtionis, et manna dulcedinis, ut severitas immoderate non sæviat, et pietas[301] plus quam expedit non indulgeat. Circulus pallii, per quem humeri[35] constringuntur, est timor Domini, per quem opera[35] coercentur, ne vel ad illicita defluant, vel ad superflua relaxentur. Quoniam disciplina sinistram cohibet ab illicitis formidine pœnæ, dexteram vero temperat a superfluis amore justitiæ. Beatus ergo vir qui semper est pavidus. Nam juxta sententiam Sapientis (Eccl. i.): *Timor Domini peccatum repellit, qui vero sine timore existit justificari non poterit.* Hinc est ergo quod Pallium et ante pectus et super humeros frequenter aptatur.[302] Quatuor cruces purpureæ sunt quatuor virtutes politicæ, Justitia, Fortitudo, Prudentia, Temperantia ; quæ, nisi Crucis Christi sanguine purpurentur, frustra sibi virtutis nomen usurpant, et ad veram beatitudinis gloriam non perducunt. Unde Dominus inquit Apostolis

---

[301] *Pietas,* though properly used of the mingled love and reverence of children to parents (and hence of subjects to their prince, or of men to God), is occasionally employed in speaking of the tender love of parents towards their children. Such, nearly, is its implication here, " gentleness."

[302] He alludes to the three pins of gold (*acus* or *spinæ*), by which, as he says below, the pallium was formerly fastened to the chasuble. They are now appended to the pallium by loops of silk. Bock, *L. G.* ii. p. 191.

(Matt. v.) : *Nisi abundaverit justitia vestra plusquam Scribarum et Pharisæorum, non intrabitis in regnum cælorum.* Hæc est purpurea regis tunica tincta [*al.* juncta *al.* vincta] canibus quam Salomon [323] commemorat in Canticis Canticorum. Is ergo qui gloria Pallii decoratur, si cupit esse quod dicitur, in anteriori parte debet habere justitiam, ut reddat unicuique quod suum est ; prudentiam in posteriori, ut caveat quod unicuique nocivum est ; fortitudinem a sinistris, ut eum adversa non deprimant ; temperantiam a dextris, ut eum prospera non extollant. Duæ lineæ, quarum una post dorsum et altera progreditur ante pectus, activam et contemplativam vitam significant. Quas ita debet exercere Prælatus ut exemplo Moyfi (*leg.* Moyfis) nunc in montem afcendat, et ibi philofophetur cum Domino ; nunc ad caftra defcendat, et ibi neceffitatibus immineat populorum ; provifurus attentius ut, quum fæpe fe dederit aliis, interdum fe fibi reftituat ; quatenus et quum (*Leg.* cum) Martha circa frequens fatagat minifterium, et quum (*leg.* cum) Maria verbum audiat Salvatoris. Utraque tamen gravat [324] inferius, quia corpus quod corrumpitur [325] aggravat animam, et deprimit terrena inhabitatio fenfum multa cogitantem. Quapropter et Pallium duplex eft in finiftra fed fimplex in dextra. Quia vita præfens, quæ per finiftram accipitur, multis eft fubjecta moleftiis, fed vita futura quæ per dexteram defignatur in una femper collecta quiete eft. Quod Veritas Ipfa defignavit, cum intulit, *Martha, Martha, folicita es, et turbaris erga plurima. Porro unum eft neceffarium. Maria optimam partem elegit, quæ non auferetur ab ea in æternum.* Pallium duplex eft in finiftro, quatenus ad tolerandas vitæ præfentis moleftias Prælatus fortis exiftat. Simplex in dextra, quatenus ad obtinendam vitæ futuræ quietem toto fufpiret affectu ; juxta verbum Pfalmiftæ, dicentis : *Unam petii a Domino, hanc requiram, ut inhabitem in domo Domini omnibus diebus vitæ meæ.* Tres autem acus [322] quæ pallio infiguntur ante pectus fuper humerum et poft tergum, defignant compaffionem proximi, adminiftrationem officii, diftrictionemque judicii. Quarum prima pungit animum per dolorem, fecunda per laborem, tertia per terrorem. Prima

[323] Cant. vii. 5, *Comæ capitis tui, ficut purpura regis vincta canalibus.*

[324] *Utraque tamen gravat, &c. Utraque* refers directly to *linea*, indirectly to *vita.* And in faying that " both one and the other is burdenfome " (*utraque gravat*), he refers probably to the leaden weight attached to each extremity of the pallium with a view to make it hang properly. For this laft fee Bock, L. G. vol. ii. p. 193.

[325] *Quod corrumpitur, i.e.* which is " fubject to corruption." Compare the ufe of the prefent participle τῶν ἀπολλυμένων (equivalent to " fubject unto death ") in the paffage of Philo, quoted at p. 8.

pungebat Apoftolum cum dicebat : *Quis infirmatur et ego non infirmor ? quis fcandalizatur, et ego non uror ?*   Secunda eft : *Præter illa quæ extrinfecus funt inftantia mea quotidiana, follicitudo omnium ecclefiarum.*   Tertia : *Si juftus vix falvabitur, impius et peccator ubi parebunt ?*   Super dextrum humerum non infigitur acus, quoniam in æterna quiete nullus eft afflictionis aculeus, nullus ftimulus punctionis.   Abfterget enim Deus omnem lacrymam ab oculis fanctorum, et jam non erit amplius neque luctus, nec clamor, fed nec ullus dolor, quoniam priora tranfierunt.   Acus eft aurea, fed inferius eft acuta, et fuperius rotunda, lapidem continens preciofum, quia nimirum bonus paftor propter curam ovium in terris affligitur, fed in cælis æternaliter coronabitur, ubi preciofam illam margaritam habebit, de qua Dominus ait in Evangelio : *Simile eft regnum cælorum homini negociatori quærenti bonas margaritas.   Inventa autem una preciofa margarita, abiit et vendidit omnia quæ habuit, et emit eam.*   Dicitur autem Pallium plenitudo pontificalis officii, quoniam in ipfo et cum ipfo confertur pontificalis officii plenitudo.   Nam antequam Metropolitanus pallio decoretur, non debet clericos ordinare, pontifices confecrare, vel ecclefias dedicare, nec Archiepifcopus appellari.

Cap. 64. Practical Exhortation.

Ifta funt arma quæ Pontifex debet induere contra fpirituales nequitias pugnaturus.   Nam ut inquit apoftolus, *Arma militiæ noftræ non funt carnalia, fed ad deftructionem munitionum potentia Deo* (2 Cor. x.).   De quibus idem Apoftolus in alia dicit Epiftola (Eph. vi.) : *Induite vos armaturam Dei, ut poffitis ftare adverfus infidias diaboli. State ergo fuccincti lumbos veftros in veritate, et induti loricam juftitiæ, et calceati pedes in præparationem Evangelii pacis : in omnibus fumentes fcutum Fidei, quo poffitis omnia tela nequiffimi ignea extinguere : et galeam falutis affumite et gladium Spiritus, quod eft verbum Dei.*   Provideat ergo diligenter epifcopus, et attendat facerdos ftudiofe, ut fignum fine fignificato non ferat, ut veftem fine virtute non portet, ne forte fimilis fit fepulchro deforis dealbato, intus autem omni pleno fpurcitio.   Quifquis autem facris indumentis ornatur et honeftis moribus non induitur, quanto venerabilior apparet hominibus, tanto indignior redditur apud Deum.   Pontificalem itaque gloriam jam honor non commendat veftium, fed fplendor animarum.   Quoniam et illa quæ quondam carnalibus blandiebantur obtutibus ea potius quæ in ipſis erant intelligenda poscebant : ut quicquid illa velamina in fulgore auri, et in nitore gem marum, et in multimoda operis varietate ſignabant, hoc jam in moribus actibuſque clareſcat. Quod et apud veteres reverentiam ipſæ ſignificationum ſpecies obtinent, et apud nos certiora ſint experimenta rerum quam ænigmata figurarum. Tunc enim valles abundant frumento, quum arietes ovium ſunt induti.

CAP. 65. THE FOUR SACRED COLOURS.

Quattuor autem ſunt principales colores, quibus ſecundum proprietates dierum ſacras veſtes eccleſia Romana diſtinguit, Albus, Rubeus, Niger, et Viridis. Nam et in legalibus indumentis quattuor colores fuiſſe leguntur, Byſſus,[326] et Purpura, Hyacinthus, et Coccus. Albis induitur veſtimentis in feſtivitatibus Confeſſorum et Virginum ; Rubeis in ſolemnitatibus Apoſtolorum et Martyrum. Hinc ſponſa dicit in Canticis (cap. 5), *Dilectus meus candidus et rubicundus, electus ex millibus.* Candidus in confeſſoribus et virginibus, rubicundus in martyribus et apoſtolis. Hi et illi ſunt flores roſarum et lilia convallium. Albis igitur indumentis utendum eſt in feſtivitatibus Confeſſorum et Virginum propter integritatem et innocentiam. *Nam candidi facti ſunt Nazaræi ejus, et ambulant ſemper cum eo in albis. Virgines enim ſunt, et ſequuntur Agnum quocumque ierit.* Propter eam cauſam utendum eſt albis in ſolennitatibus ſequentibus, ſcilicet in ſolennitatibus angelorum, de quorum nitore Dominus ait ad Luciferum : *Ubi eras cum me laudarent aſtra matutina?* (Job, xxxviii.) In nativitate Salvatoris et Præcurſoris [326 a] quoniam uterque natus eſt mundus, id eſt carens originali peccato. Aſcendit enim Dominus ſuper nubem levem, id eſt ſumpſit carnem a peccatis immunem, et intravit Ægyptum, id eſt, venit in mundum, juxta quod Angelus ait ad virginem : *Spiritus ſanctus ſuperveniet in te, et virtus Altiſſimi obumbrabit tibi. Ideoque quod naſcetur ex te ſanctum, vocabitur Filius Dei.* Joannes autem, etſi fuit conceptus in peccato, fuit tamen ſanctificatus in utero, ſecundum illud propheticum : *Antequam exires de valva ſanctificavi te* (Hier. i.). Nam et angelus ait ad Zachariam : *Spiritu ſancto replebitur adhuc ex utero matris ſuæ.* In Epiphania, propter ſplendorem ſtellæ, quæ Magos

---

[326] *Byſſus* is here ſpoken of as a colour, *i.e.* white. See note 5 (γ).
[326 a] *The forerunner, i.e.* John the Baptiſt.

adduxit, secundum illud Propheticum : *Et ambulabunt gentes in lumine tuo et reges in splendore ortus tui* (Esa. xl.). In Hypopanti,[307] propter puritatem Mariæ, quæ juxta Canticum Simeonis obtulit lumen ad revelationem gentium, et gloriam plebis suæ Israel. In cœna Domini,[308] propter confectionem Chrismatis, quod ad mundationem animæ consecratur. Nam et evangelica lectio munditiam principaliter in illa sollennitate commendat. *Qui lotus est*, inquit, *non indiget nisi ut pedes lavet, sed est mundus totus* (Joan. xiii.) Et iterum : *Si non lavero te non habebis partem mecum.* In Resurrectione, propter angelum testem et nuncium resurrectionis, qui apparuit stola candida coopertus : de quo dicit Matthæus, quod erat aspectus ejus sicut fulgur, et vestimentum ejus sicut nix. In Ascensione, propter nubem candidam in qua Christus ascendit. Nam et duo viri steterunt juxta illos in vestibus albis, qui et dixerunt, *Viri Galilæi, quid statis aspicientes in cælum, etc.* Illud autem non otiose notandum est, quod licet in consecratione pontificis talibus indumentis sit utendum, consecrantibus scilicet et ministris (nam consecrandus semper albis utitur) qualia secundum proprietatem diei conveniunt, in dedicatione tamen Ecclesiæ semper utendum est albis, quocunque dierum dedicatio celebretur. Quoniam in consecratione pontificis cantatur missa diei, sed in dedicatione Basilicæ dedicationis missa cantatur. Nam et Ecclesia virgineo nomine nuncupatur, secundum illud Apostoli : *Despondi enim vos uni Viro virginem castam exhibere Christo.* De qua sponsus dicit in Canticis : *Tota pulchra es, amica mea, et macula non est in te. Veni de Libano, sponsa mea, veni de Libano, veni.*

Rubeis autem utendum est indumentis in solennitatibus Apostolorum et Martyrum, propter sanguinem passionis, quem pro Christo fuderunt. Nam ipsi sunt qui venerunt ex magna tribulatione, et laverunt stolas suas in sanguine Agni. In Festo Crucis, de qua Christus pro nobis sanguinem suum fudit. Unde Propheta : *Quare rubrum est indumentum tuum sicut calcantium in torculari ?* Vel in Festo Crucis [309] melius est albis utendum, quia non Passionis sed Inventionis vel Exaltationis

---

[307] *Hypopanti* (a corruption of Ὑπαπάντη, or Ὑπάντη, *i.e.* ὑπάντησις, Salutation), one of the names by which the Feast of the Purification is designated. See Durandus, *R. D. O.* lib. vii. cap. 7, and Dufresne *in voc.*

[308] *Cœna Domini, i.e.* Thursday in Holy Week. As to the preparation of the Chrism, or holy oil, on this day, see Beleth. *Div. Off. Expl.* cap. 95.

[309] He alludes to the *Inventio Sanctæ Crucis.* "Cruce Domini inventa ab Helena matre Constantini, per Judam, ut narrat historia, festum ejus primo celebratum est Hierosolymæ. Sed Eusebius, Papa trigesimus a B. Petro, illud postea ubique terrarum celebrari præcepit." *Beleth. Div. Off. Expl.* cap. 125.

eſt Feſtum. In Pentecoſte, propter ſancti Spiritus fervorem, qui ſuper Apoſtolos in linguis igneis apparuit. Nam apparuerunt illis diſpertitæ linguæ tanquam ignis, ſeditque ſuper ſingulos eorum. Unde Propheta: *Miſit de cælo ignem oſſibus meis.* Licet autem in Apoſtolorum Petri et Pauli martyrio rubeis ſit utendum, in Converſione tamen et Cathedra [330] utendum eſt albis. Sicut licet in nativitate ſancti Joannis albis utendum, in Decollatione tamen ipſius utendum eſt rubeis. Cum autem illius Feſtivitas celebratur qui ſimul eſt et Martyr et Virgo, martyrium præfertur virginitati, quia ſignum eſt perfectiſſimæ charitatis, juxta quod Veritas ait: *Majorem charitatem nemo habet quam ut animam ſuam ponat quis pro amicis ſuis.* Quapropter et in commemoratione Omnium Sanctorum quidam rubeis induuntur ornamentis, alii vero, ut Curia Romana, candidis: quum non tam in eadem quam de eadem ſolennitate dicat Eccleſia, quod Sancti, ſecundum Apocalypſim Joannis, ſtabant in conſpectu Agni, amicti ſtolis [50] albis, et palmæ in manibus eorum.

Nigris autem indumentis utendum eſt in die afflictionis et abſtinentiæ, pro peccatis, et pro defunctis. Ab Adventu ſcilicet uſque ad Natalis vigiliam, et a Septuageſima uſque ad ſabbatum Paſchæ.[331] Sponſa quippe dicit in Canticis: *Nigra ſum ſed formoſa, filiæ Jeruſalem, ſicut tabernacula Cedar, ſicut pellis Salomonis. Nolite me conſiderare quod fuſca ſim, quia decoloravit me ſol.* In Innocentum autem die quidam nigris, alii vero rubeis, indumentis utendum eſſe contendunt. Illi propter triſtitiam, quia vox in Rhama audita eſt, ploratus et ululatus multus, Rachel plorans filios ſuos, et noluit conſolari quia non ſunt. Nam propter eandem cauſam Cantica lætitiæ ſubticentur, et non in aurifrigio Mitra [332] defertur. Iſti propter martyrium, quod principaliter commemorans inquit Eccleſia: *Sub throno Dei Sancti clamabant, vindica ſanguinem noſtrum qui effuſus eſt, Deus noſter.* Propter triſtitiam ergo, quam et ſilentium innuit lætitiæ canticorum, Mitra quæ fertur non eſt aurifrigio inſignita, ſed propter martyrium rubeis eſt

---

[330] *Cathedra, i.e.* Cathedra Petri. "De Cathedra S. Petri Eccleſia ſollennizat, quando videlicet apud Antiochiam Cathedrali honore ſublimatus eſſe perhibetur." *Durandus, R. D. O.* lib. viii. cap. 8.

[331] *Sabbatum Paſchæ, i.e.* Eaſter-Eve.

[332] *Non in aurifrigio, &c.* He means that a plain mitre is to be uſed without any golden or embroidered band. The later Roman Liturgiſts diſtinguiſh three kinds of mitres, the Plain Mitre (*ſimplex*) made of linen; the Orfreyed Mitre (*Mitra aurifrigiata,* ſee note 312, p. 152, or *Mitra ſoliennis*); and the Precious Mitre (*Mitra precioſa*), in which the inner Cap (*Mitra,* ſee note 288 [a]) is almoſt entirely concealed by plates made of the precious metals encruſted with jewels.

indumentis utendum. Hodie utimur violaceis : ficut in *Lætare Hieru-falem*,[333] propter lætitiam quam Aurea Rofa fignificat, Romanus Ponti-fex portat Mitram aurifrifio infignitam, fed propter abftinentiam nigris, immo violaceis utitur indumentis.

Reftat ergo quod in diebus ferialibus et communibus viridibus fit indumentis utendum. Quia viridis color medius eft inter albedinem et nigredinem et ruborem. Hic color exprimitur ubi dicitur (Cant. iv.) : *Cypri cum nardo, Nardus et Crocus.*

Ad hos quattuor cæteri referuntur. Ad rubeum colorem coccineus, ad nigrum violaceus, ad viridem croceus. Quamvis nonnulli rofas ad Martyres, crocum ad Confeffores, lilium ad Virgines referunt.[333] a

---

[333] He alludes to the fpecial obfervances (at Rome) of Mid-Lent Sunday, when the Golden Rofe is carried in folemn proceffion by the Pope. "In hac Dominica (4th S. in Lent) Romanus Pontifex celebraturus ad ec-clefiam pergens et rediens ab eadem auream in manu. . . fert rofam. . . (*This Rofe is then given to one whom the Pope defires fpe-cially to honour.*) . . . Demum ille cum multo equitatu et lætitia ingenti civitatem cum rofa circuit, *figuram gaudium illius populi in civitatem Hierufalem reverfi.*" *Durandus, R. D. O.* lib. vi. cap. 53.

[333] a The Veftments of the Roman Church, with the " four Sacred Colours (p. 161) which the Roman Church affigns as proper to various feftivals," are here for the firft time defcribed in their complete development. From the time of this Treatife there have been flight varieties in detail introduced from time to time, in refpect of fhape and ornamentation, but the " *Sacræ Veftes* " of Bifhop, Prieft, and Deacon, proper to the Roman Church, have been accepted, as here defcribed, to this day. [For the " Surplice," which is not mentioned by Innocent III., fee *infra*, p. 166, and Index *in voc.*]

XXXIX.

DVRANDI MIMATENSIS EPISCOPI[331]
RATIONALE[315] DIVINORVM OFFICIORVM.

LIB. III. DE VESTIBUS SACRIS.

CAP. I. CHANGE IN CLERICAL DRESS IN NINTH CENTURY.

. . . Nota quod tempore Ludovici Imperatoris filii Caroli Magni, Epifcopi et Clerici cingula auro texta, exquifitas veftes, et alia fecularia ornamenta depofuerunt.[336]

EPISCOPAL VESTMENTS REGARDED AS SPIRITUAL ARMOUR.

. . . Rurfus Pontifex verfus Aquilonem fufpiciens, quamvis verfus Orientem feu verfus altare, fi fit magis accommodum, refpicere poffit, tanquam advocatus feu pugil cum hofte pugnaturus antiquo, veftibus facris quafi armis induitur, juxta Apoftolum, ut jam dicetur. Primo fandalia pro ocreis habet, ne quid maculæ vel pulveris affectionum inhæreat. Secundo Amictus pro galea [note 178, p. 94] caput contegit. Tertio Alba pro lorica totum corpus cooperit. Quarto cingulum pro arcu, fubcingulum [337] pro pharetra affumit: et eft fubcingulum illud quod dependet a cingulo, quo Stola Pontificis cum ipfo

---

[331] Durandus (Gulielmus), born in France *circ.* 1232 A.D. Bifhop of Mende 1287; died 1296 A.D. The bafis of the text is that of Cellier, Lugduni, MDCLXXII; a very defective one, the punctuation particularly being fuch as often to make nonfenfe of fuch fentences as prefent any difficulties of interpretation. Here, as elfewhere, I have made no alterations, except in punctuation, without notice to the reader.

[315] The third book of this Treatife is entirely occupied with the fubject of veftments. But it confifts in great meafure of large extracts from older writers, many of which have already been before the reader of the prefent work. I have therefore only felected thofe paffages which add to thefe older writers any thing of importance to the fubject of this Treatife.

[336] One effect of the reftoration of an Imperial power in the Weft was that of reftraining the tendency to extravagant fumptuoufnefs and fplendour in the fecular drefs of fome among the Clergy. See, for example, what is faid of Archbifhop Ethelbert by Dr. Hook (*Lives of the Archbifhops of Canterbury*, vol. i. p. 262).

[337] See note 313, p. 153, on the word *fuccinctorium*, which is equivalent to the *fubcingulum* of Durandus.

cingulo colligatur. Quinto, Stola collum circumdans, qua (*Leg.* quasi) haftam contra hoftem vibrans. Sexto, manipulo pro clava utitur. Septimo, Cafula quafi clypeo tegitur. Manus Libro pro gladio armatur. De fingulis etiam aliter dicetur infra. Hæc itaque funt arma quibus Pontifex vel Sacerdos armari debet contra fpirituales nequitias pugnaturus.

Difference in Number between the Vestments of the Law and of the Gospel.

. . . Quindecim ergo funt ornamenta Pontificis . . . Sic ergo nofter Pontifex [336] plura quam octo induit veftimenta quamvis Aaron non nifi octo habuiffe legatur; quibus moderna fuccedunt. Quod ideo eft quoniam oportet juftitiam noftram magis abundare quam Scribarum et Pharifæorum; ut intrare poffimus in regnum cælorum. Poteft etiam dici quod nofter Pontifex octo habet a capite ufque ad pedes, exceptis veftimentis pedum et manuum; fcilicet Amictum, Albam, Cingulum, et Stolam, duas Tunicas, Cafulam et Pallium, Veftimentum enim pedum potius pertinet ad noftros quam ad Aaron: quia noftris dictum eft, *Euntes docete omnes gentes,* etc.

The Surplice.

Denique præter præmiffas veftes facris ordinibus et miniftris deputatas, eft et alia quædam veftis linea, quæ Superpelliceum dicitur, quod quibuslibet fervitiis altaris et facrorum vacantes fuper veftes communes uti debent: prout in fequente titulo dicetur. Superpelliceum autem primo, propter fui candorem, munditiam feu puritatem caftitatis defignat: Juxta illud, *Omni tempore veftimenta,* id eft, opera tua, *fint candida et munda.* Propter nomen vero fuum carnis mortificationem figurat fecundo. Dictum eft enim Superpelliceum eo quod antiquitus fuper tunicas pellicias de pellibus mortuorum animalium factas induebatur; quod adhuc in quibufdam ecclefiis obfervatur, repræfentantes (*fic*) quod Adam poft peccatum talibus veftitus eft pelliciis. Tertio denotat innocentiam; et ideo ante omnes alias veftes facras fæpe induitur, quia divino cultui deputati innocentia vitæ cunctis virtutum actibus fuperpollere debent; juxta illud Pfalmiftæ, *Innocentes*

---

[336] *Pontifex nofter, i.e.* the Pontiff (Bifhop) of us Chriftians in contraft with Aaron the | "*Pontifex in Lege.*" Compare note 194, p. 101.

et recti adhæſerunt mihi. Quarto propter ſui latitudinem congrue charitatem deſignat. Unde ſuper profanas et communes veſtes induitur ad notandum quod Charitas operit multitudinem peccatorum.

Quinto propter ſui formam, quia in modum crucis formatur, Paſſionem Domini figurat, quodque illud gerentes crucifigi debent cum vitiis et cum concupiſcentiis.

Fiunt autem Superpellicea in quibuſdam locis de criſmalibus lineis quæ ponuntur ſuper infantulos baptizatos : exemplo Moiſi qui de purpura et byſſo, et aliis a populo in tabernaculo oblatis, fecit veſtes quibus Aaron et filii ejus induerentur, quando miniſtrabant in Sanctuario.

THE PLUVIAL OR COPE.

Eſt etiam et alia veſtis quæ Pluviale [339] vel Cappa vocatur, quæ creditur a legali tunica mutuata. Unde ſicut illa tintinnabulis, ſic iſta fimbriis infigitur (*Leg.* inſignitur), quæ ſunt labores, hujus mundi ſolicitudines. Habet etiam caputium, quod eſt ſupernum gaudium. Prolixa eſt uſque ad pedes, per quod perſeverantia uſque in finem ſignificatur. In anteriori parte aperta eſt, ad denotandum quod ſancte converſantibus vita patet æterna, ſeu quod eorum vita patere debet aliis in exemplum . . . Rurſus per Cappam glorioſa corporum immortalitas intelligitur. Unde illam non niſi in majoribus feſtivitatibus induimus, aſpicientes in futuram reſurrectionem quando electi, depoſita carne, binas ſtolas accipient, videlicet requiem animarum et gloriam corporum. Quæ Cappa recte interius patula eſt, niſi et [*Leg.* et niſi] ſola neceſſaria fibula inconſuta, quia corpora ſpiritualia facta nullis animam obturabunt anguſtiis. Fimbriis etiam ſubornantur, quia tunc noſtræ nihil deerit imperfectioni ; ſed quod nunc ex parte cognoſcimus tunc cognoſcemus ſicut et cogniti ſumus.

---

[339] The name *pluviale* ("parapluie," as it were), and the Cape or Hood from which was derived the name *Cappa*, and our own "Cope," point to the origin of the veſtment as originally worn out of doors *for protection from the weather*. The form of the later eccleſiaſtical cope may be ſeen in Plate LI., where it is worn by the biſhops officiating at the Coronation of Henry VI. The memory of the original hood is ſtill preſerved in the peculiar ornament on the back of the Cope, upon which the outline of a ſmall cape or round hood is traced in embroidery. See, for example, Bock, *L. G.* vol. ii. pl. xli. [The Cappa is mentioned as one of the monaſtic habits early in the eleventh century. See *Thomaſſinus De Ben.* part i. lib. ii. cap. 48, p. 332.]

XL.

SYMEON
PATRIARCHA THESSALONICENSIS.[340]

Περὶ τῆς ἱερᾶς λειτουργίας.

Κεφ. σι. περὶ τοῦ ἀρχιερατικοῦ Μανδύου[341] τε καὶ τοῦ Ἐγκολπίου[342] καὶ τῆς ποιμαντικῆς ῥάβδου.

Τυθέντος οὖν καὶ θανόντος καὶ ἀναστάντος καὶ ἀνελθόντος Χριστοῦ ὑπὲρ ἡμῶν, τότε τὸ Πνεῦμα κατῆλθε, καὶ τὴν χάριν ἐλάβομεν. Καὶ ἐκ τῆς καρδίας τῶν πιστῶν οἱ ποταμοὶ[343] τῶν δωρεῶν[344] ῥέουσι. Καὶ τοῦτο δηλοῖ ὁ Μανδύας. Καὶ ἡ σφραγὶς δὲ καὶ ὁμολογία τῆς πίστεως ἐν τῷ τοῦ ἀρχιερέως στήθει ἐκκρεμαμένη διὰ σταυρίου ἢ ἐγκολπίου τινος. Καὶ τοῦτο γὰρ ἐν τῷ στήθει διὰ τὴν ἐκ καρδίας ὁμολογίαν.

Ἡ ῥάβδος[345] δὲ, ἣν κατέχει, τὴν ἐξουσίαν δηλοῖ τοῦ Πνεύματος, καὶ τὸ στηρικτικὸν τοῦ λάου, καὶ τὸ ποιμαντικόν, καὶ τὸ ὁδηγεῖν δύνασθαι, καὶ τὸ παιδεύειν τοὺς ἀπειθοῦντας, καὶ τὸ συνάγειν εἰς ἑαυτὸν τοὺς μακράν. Διὸ καὶ λαβὰς ὡς ἀγκύρας ἄνωθεν ἔχει. Καὶ τὸ διώκειν τοὺς θηριώδεῖς τε καὶ λυμαντικούς. Καὶ τελευταῖον τὸν σταυρὸν τοῦ Χριστοῦ δηλοῖ, καὶ τὸ τρισσαῖον, ἐν ᾦ καὶ νικῶμεν, καὶ στηριζόμεθα, καὶ ὁδηγούμεθα, καὶ ποιμανόμεθα, καὶ σφραγι-

---

[340] The writer, here quoted, occupied the See of Theſſalonica from circ. 1410 to 1429 A.D. This Treatiſe was firſt made known in the Weſt by Jacobus Pontanus, a zealous partiſan, who, if Cave ſpeak truly (Hiſt. Lit. ii. p. 113), was anything but a truſtworthy editor.

[341] In this chapter he deſcribes the ordinary dreſs of a Biſhop; his dreſs of miniſtry is ſpoken of in the chapter following. The Mantle, with its three ſtripes, technically called ποταμοὶ, and the Paſtoral Staff may be ſeen in the repreſentation of Patriarch Bekkos among the illuſtrations of this volume. See Plate LIX.

[342] ἐγκόλπιον. See above, note 315, p. 158.

[343] This is uſed in alluſion to Jo. vii. 38, 39. "He that believeth on me . . . . out

of his belly ſhall flow rivers of living water. This ſpake He of the Spirit which they that believe on Him ſhould receive."

[341] δωρεὰ is here correctly uſed of a gift from God to man. Δῶρον, on the other hand, is properly a gift, or offering to homage, from man to God. See Eirenica, vol. i. p. 187 (foot-note.)

[345] In the Greek Church the Staff has not the form of a ſhepherd's crook, as commonly it has in the Weſt, but retains the ſemblance rather of a ſtaff ſuch as men might uſe in walking. The handle is ſet on croſs-wiſe like the horizontal line of the letter T, but the extremities of this handle are generally turned up ſlightly, and terminate in ſome carved ornament. See the Figure referred to in note 341.

ζόμεθα, καὶ παιδαγωγούμεθα, καὶ ἑλκόμεθα εἰς Χριστὸν τὰ πάθη νεκροῦντες,
καὶ τοὺς πολεμίους διώκομεν, καὶ πάντοθεν φυλαττόμεθα.

Κεφ. πά.΄ Περὶ τῶν ἱερῶν τοῦ ἀρχιερέως ἐνδυμάτων.

Ὁ δὲ ἀρχιερεὺς ἐνδύεται μὲν ὡς εἰρήκαμεν τὸ Στιχάριον [346] ὡς ἔνδυμα
ἀφθαρσίας φωτεινὸν καὶ ἁγιωσύνης, τὸ καθαρὸν καὶ φωτιστικὸν [347] Ἰησοῦ, καὶ
τὸ τῶν Ἀγγέλων ἁγνὸν καὶ λαμπρὸν, δηλοῦν. Καὶ τὴν εὐχὴν φησὶν ἀπὸ τοῦ
ψαλμοῦ· Ἀγαλλιάσεται ἡ ψυχή μου ἐπὶ τῷ Κυρίῳ. Εἶτα τὸ Ἐπιτραχήλιον, [348]
τὸ ἄνωθεν ἐκ τοῦ οὐρανίου ἀπὸ κεφαλῆς δοθεῖσαν χάριν σημαῖνον. Καὶ ἡ εὐχὴ
τοῦτο φησίν· Εὐλογητὸς ὁ Θεὸς ὁ ἐκχέων τὴν χάριν αὐτοῦ ἐπὶ τοὺς Ἱερεῖς αὐτοῦ.
Εἶτα τὴν ζώνην, τὴν ἀπὸ Θεοῦ ἰσχὺν ἐπιτοποῦσαν περὶ τὴν ὀσφὺν τιθεμένην. Καὶ
ἡ εὐχὴ μαρτυρεῖ ἐν τῷ περιζωννύεσθαι· φησὶ γὰρ, Εὐλογητὸς ὁ Θεὸς ὁ περι-
ζωννύων με δύναμιν. Ἅμα δὲ καὶ τὸ τῆς διακονίας ἔργον δηλοῖ. Ὁ γὰρ
διακονῶν περιζώννυται. Καὶ ἔτι τὴν σωφροσύνην καὶ ἁγνείαν, ἐπὶ τοὺς νεφροὺς
κειμένη καὶ τὴν ὀσφύν.

Ἔπειτα τὸ Ἐπιγονάτιον [349] τὸ κατὰ τοῦ θανάτου νίκην δηλοῦν, καὶ τὴν
τοῦ Σωτῆρος ἀνάστασιν, ὅπερ καὶ ὡς σχῆμα ῥομφαίας ἔχει. Καὶ ἡ εὐχὴ
τοῦτο φησί· Περίζωσαι τὴν ῥομφαίαν σου ἐπὶ τὸν μηρόν σου, δυνατέ. Ἐκ τούτου
καὶ τὴν δύναμιν καὶ τὴν νίκην, καὶ τὴν ἔγερσιν τοῦ Χριστοῦ, διὰ τῆς καθαρότητος
καὶ ἀναμαρτησίας, δηλῶν (*Leg.* δηλοῖ.) Διὰ τοῦτο γὰρ καὶ αὐτὸ ἐπὶ τῆς ὀσφύος
ἐκκρέμαται. Καὶ τῇ ὡραιότητί σου καὶ τῷ κάλλει σου, φησί, καὶ ἔντεινε καὶ
κατευοδοῦ καὶ βασίλευε, ἕνεκεν ἀληθείας καὶ πραότητος καὶ δικαιοσύνης. . . .

Εἶτα λαμβάνει τὰ ἐπιμανίκια. [350] Ἃ δὴ τὸ παντουργικὸν σημαίνουσι τοῦ
Θεοῦ. Καὶ ἡ εὐχὴ τοῦτο λέγει· Ἡ δεξία σου, Κύριε, δεδόξασται ἐν ἰσχύϊ.

---

[346] Στιχάριον. The derivation of this
word is uncertain. It is the term which in
the Greek Church answers to the *alba* (or
tunica alba) of the West.

[347] The Sticharion as being *white* sets forth
τὸ φωτιστικὸν Ἰησοῦ. With this symbolism
of white garments compare Clemens Alex
Pædag. iii. p. 286. εἰρηνικῶς ἀνθρώποις καὶ
φωτεινῶς κατάλληλον τὸ λευκόν.

[348] ἐπιτραχήλιον *i.e.* what in the Western
Church would be called a stole. See note
144, p. 84.

[349] τὸ ἐπιγονάτιον. This ornament may be
seen in the figures of St. Methodius and St.
Germanus among the illustrations of this
volume, Pl. LVIII. The germ of this orna-

ment may be seen in the somewhat similar
ornaments on the imperial dresses of Justinian
and his courtiers, (known in the language of
the time as *paragaudæ*) in the Mosaic of the
Church of S. Vitalis at Ravenna. See Pl.
XXVIII.

[350] Ἐπιμανίκια. A Byzantine word, half
Greek and half Latin, like many others of
similar character. By derivation it will mean
" what is added to, or set upon, the sleeve ; "
and hence its actual usage as a designation of
the cuffs, worn on either arm, by bishops and
priests in the Greek Church. Their form
may be seen in those of Bishop Nikitas, figured
among the illustrations of this volume. Pl.
LVI.

z

Καὶ τὸ· Αἱ χεῖρες σου ἐποίησάν με καὶ ἔπλασάν με. Ἔτι δὲ καὶ τὸ ταῖς χερσὶν ἱερουργῆσαι τὰ μυστήρια ἑαυτοῦ. Καὶ τὸ τὰς χεῖρας διεῆναι.

Εἶτα τὸ Φαινόλιον,[351] ἢ Σάκκος [352] ὃν ἢ Πολυσταύριον,[353] ἃ δὴ τὴν ἐν τῷ πάθει σημαίνουσι χλαῖναν. Καὶ τὸν Σάκκον μᾶλλον ὁ Σάκκος.[351] Καὶ τὸ Πολυσταύριον δέ. Ἀλλὰ καὶ τὴν προνοητικὴν καὶ φρουρητικὴν ἐν πᾶσι καὶ συνεκτικὴν χάριν τοῦ Θεοῦ, δι' ἣν καὶ καθ' ἡμᾶς ὤφθη, καὶ τὰ πάθη ὑπένεγκε.

Κεφ. πβ΄. Τὸ Ὠμοφόριον.

Καὶ τελευταῖον τὸ Ὠμοφόριον,[355] ὃ ἀπὸ τῶν ὤμων εἱλίττων τὴν τοῦ πλανηθέντος προβάτου τῶν ἀνθρώπων ἡμῶν δηλοῖ σωτηρίαν τε καὶ ἀνάκλησιν. Οὗ δὴ καὶ τὴν μορφὴν ἀνέλαβεν ὁ Σωτὴρ, ἐν ᾗ καὶ παθὼν διὰ Σταυροῦ ἡμᾶς ἔσωσιν. Ὅθεν καὶ ἐξ ἐρίου. Καὶ ἔμπροσθέν τε καὶ ὄπισθεν καὶ ἐπὶ τοῦ στήθους σταυροειδῶς τέσσαρας ἔχει σταυροὺς τὴν σταύρωσιν ἐκτυποῦντας. Καὶ οὕτω μὲν στολισάμενος ἵσταται ὁ ἀρχιερεύς.

Κεφ. πγ΄. Τὰ πέντε ἄμφια τῶν ἱερέων.

[*After describing the ceremonies with which the Liturgy begins, he proceeds as follows:*]

Ἀπέρχεται οὖν οὗτος [*sc.* ὁ ἱερεὺς] καὶ μετὰ τῶν ἄλλων ἱερέων τὰ ἱερατικὰ

---

[351] φαινόλιον. For the *form* of the word as compared with the older φαινόλης, equivalent to *pænula*, see note 153, p. 86. The primitive forms of this vestment may be seen (Pl. XXVII.) in the figure of Eusebius of Cæsarea (from the Syriac MS. at Florence), or in that of St. Sampson, among the illustrations of this volume, Pl. LVI.

[352] Σάκκος. This is a close-fitting vestment worn in place of the φαινόλιον by Metropolitans, as a mark of distinctive dignity. See Goar, *Euchol. Gr.* p. 113. Its form may be seen in the figure of St. Germanus in Pl. LVIII.

[353] Πολυσταύριον, i.e. a Phænolion marked with crosses over its entire surface. It is worn by Bishops generally, or at least was so in the time of St. Symeon here quoted. In his treatise *De Templo* (quoted by Goar, *Euch. Gr.* p. 113) he says, οἱ λοιποὶ τῶν ἀρχιερέων (i.e. those not having metropolitan dignity) τὸ φιλόνιον πλῆρες σταυρῶν ἐνδύονται· ὃ δὴ καὶ πολυσταύριον ὁ λόγος καλεῖν οἶδε.

[354] These words are explained by what the

Patriarch says in another passage (*De Templo,* apud Goar, *Euchol. Græc.* p. 113), ἐξαιρέτως δὲ ἐν ἐνδύσατε ἐμπαιζόμενος ὁ Σωτὴρ ἐξεκονίζει σάκκον· διὸ καὶ σάκκου τύπον ἔχει. Οὐδὲ γὰρ ἔχει τοῦτο ἃ καλοῦσι μανίκια. Ἀριδηλότερος δὲ τοῦτο παρίστησι καὶ ὁ ἱκρφετει τῶν ἀρχιερέων, σάκκος καὶ τοῦτο καλούμενος.

[355] τὸ ὠμοφόριον. This vestment, mentioned first by St. Isidore of Pelusium (see p. 49), and again by St. Germanus (see p. 85), has from the earliest times been worn by all Greek bishops, whether Metropolitans or others. In form, too, it has varied but little, if at all, from the earliest times in which we find it represented, even to the present day. It is worn by all the bishops represented in the picture of the Second Council of Nicæa (Pl. XLI. of the illustrations of this volume), and may be seen also in the figures of St. Methodius and St. Germanus already referred to. An Omophorion of the fourteenth century, that of Archbishop Moses, is figured in Plate LVI.

περιβάλλεται ἄμφια. . . . Ἕκαστον εὐλογεῖ ὡς καὶ ὁ Ἀρχιερεὺς τῶν
ἱερῶν ἐνδυμάτων τι καὶ ἀσπάζεται, καὶ οὕτω δὴ περιβάλλεται, δεικνὺς ὡς
ἡγιασμένα εἰσι, καὶ ἐν τῷ σταυρῷ τοῦ Χριστοῦ ἁγιάζεται, καὶ ἁγιασμοῦ
μεταδοτικά εἰσι πάλιν ἐπενδυόμενα. Περιβάλλεται οὖν πέντε ἐνδύματα, ὡς
τέλειος καὶ αὐτὸς, καὶ τελεσιοποιὸν ἔχων χάριν. Πέντε γὰρ αἱ τέλειαί εἰσιν
αἰσθήσεις τοῦ σώματος, καὶ πέντε αἱ δυνάμεις τῆς ψυχῆς ἃς καὶ ὁ Ἰησοῦς
ἁγιάζει βαπτίζων καὶ ἁγιάζων τὸν ἄνθρωπον. Ἔστι δὲ ἃ ἐνδύεται, Στιχάριον,
Ἐπιτραχήλιον, Ζώνη, Ἐπιμανίκια, καὶ Φαινόλιον. Λευκὰ δὲ ταῦτα, διὰ τὸ
καθαρὸν τῆς χάριτός τε καὶ φωτεινόν.

Πολλάκις δὲ καὶ πορφύρεα κατὰ καιρὸν τῶν νηστειῶν, διά γε τὸ πενθεῖν
ἡμᾶς ἁμαρτήσαντας, καὶ διὰ τὸν σφαγέντα ὑπὲρ ἡμῶν, ἵν᾽ εἰς ὑπόμνησιν ἐλθόντες
τοῦ πάθους αὐτοῦ, αὐτὸν μιμησώμεθα ὃ (fort. ὃν) καὶ μέλλομεν ἑορτάζειν.
Τινὲς δὲ τῶν πρώτων πρεσβυτέρων, ἤτοι οἱ Σταυροφόροι,[356] τῶν Ἀρχιμανδριτῶν τε
τινὲς, καὶ ἐπιγονάτιον ἔχουσι· τοῦτο γὰρ κατὰ δωρεάν ἐστιν ἀρχιερατικὴν ὡς καὶ
ὁ Σταυρός. Οὐδεὶς γὰρ πλὴν τοῦ Ἀρχιερέως τοὺς σταυρούς τε ἐν τῷ φαινολίῳ
καὶ ἐπὶ κεφαλῆς, καὶ τὸ Ἐπιγονάτιον φορεῖν, δύναται. Τούτοις δὲ ὅμως, διὰ
τὸ πρώτους τῶν ἄλλων χειροτονεῖσθαι, τὸ ἐπὶ κεφαλῆς ἔχειν σταυρὸν μόνον, καὶ
ἐπιγονάτιον ἐν τῇ ἱερουργίᾳ φορεῖν, δίδοται.[357]

THE MANDYAS, OR MANTLE, OF THE BISHOP, THE PECTORAL CROSS, AND PASTORAL STAFF.

AFTER that Chrift for us had been facrificed, had died, and rifen again,
and gone up on high, then did the Spirit come down from above, and we
received the grace of God. And now out of the hearts of the faithful
flow the rivers [343] of the divine gifts.[344] And this is fet forth by the

---

[356] οἱ σταυροφόροι. Certain of the clergy at
the principal Church at Conftantinople had
the privilege of wearing a crofs upon their
cowls. See above note 152, p. 86.

[357] From this paffage we find that in the
fifteenth century the recognifed veftments of
the Greek Church were, with few additions
only, identical with thofe defcribed by St.
Germanus feven centuries earlier. St. Germanus mentions Sticharion, Peritrachelion (or
Epitrachelion), and Phelonion, adding mention of the Omophorion as a diftinctive veftment (τοῦ ἀρχιερέως), worn by bifhops. To
thefe we now find added the cuffs (common
to priefts and bifhops), and the " Epigona-
tion," the latter worn by bifhops only. On

the other hand, the ἐγχείριον, or napkin,
mentioned as characteriftic of a deacon by
Germanus, finds no place in this later notice.

Laftly, the σάκκος (note 352) and the πολυσταύριον (note 353) fpoken of in the later
treatife, do not appear to have been known to
the earlier of the two writers. Nor does St.
Germanus make mention of a paftoral ftaff,
or a pectoral crofs, as being in his time diftinctive infignia of a bifhop.

But even with the additions here noticed
the feven facred veftments of the Greek
bifhop ftand contrafted in their greater fim-
plicity and clofe adherence to antiquity, with
the *fifteen* enumerated by Innocent III., and
retained to this day by the Roman Church.

Mantle. The Seal, too, and profeſſion of the Faith, is ſuſpended on
the breaſt of the Biſhop by a Croſs, or Pectoral ornament. For this
alſo is worn upon the Breaſt, becauſe of the profeſſion which from the
heart is made.

Then the Staff,[315] which he holdeth, ſhoweth forth the power of
the Spirit, and what appertaineth to the confirming and paſtoral care of
God's people, and the power to guide, and the chaſtiſing of them that
are diſobedient, and the gathering unto himſelf of them that are afar
off. Wherefore alſo it hath handles [315] on the upper part thereof, like
unto anchors. It ſignifieth alſo the purſuing of them that are fierce
in ſpirit and injurious. And, laſtly, it ſetteth forth the Croſs of Chriſt,
and the memorial of victory, wherein we are both conquerors ourſelves, and are ſtrengthened, and guided, and ſhepherded, and ſealed,
and led by the hand, and drawn unto Chriſt, mortifying our evil
affections, wherewith alſo we purſue our foes, and are protected on
every ſide.

Cap. 81. The Seven Sacred Vestments of a Bishop.

But the (chief prieſt) Biſhop putteth upon him, as we have ſaid,
the Sticharion,[316] as a lightſome garment of immortality and holineſs,
ſetting forth the pure and light-giving nature of Jeſus, and the holineſs
and brightneſs of the angels. And the prayer that he ſaith is from the
Pſalm, " *My ſoul ſhall rejoice in the Lord.*"

Then he putteth on the Epitrachelion,[318] which is a ſign of grace
given from above out of heaven, proceeding from the Head. And this
doth the prayer expreſs, " *Bleſſed be God, who poureth out His grace
upon His prieſts.*"

Then the Girdle, ſetting forth in figure the ſtrength which is from
God, in that this is laid about the loins. And to this doth the prayer
witneſs, which at the girding is uſed, " *Bleſſed be God who girdeth me
about with power.*" By it is likewiſe ſignified the work of miniſtry,
for it appertaineth to one who miniſters that he wear a girdle. And
yet again it is a ſign of ſoberneſs and chaſte purity, reſting as it does
upon the reins and loins.

After this he putteth on the Genual,[319] which ſetteth forth Victory
over Death, and the Reſurrection of the Saviour, which alſo is worn
after the faſhion of a ſword. And this doth the prayer ſay, " *Gird thee
with thy ſword upon thy thigh, thou mighty one.*" And becauſe of this

doth it ſet forth both the power, and the victory, and the riſing of Chriſt from the dead, by the purity and ſinleſſneſs thereof. For this is the cauſe wherefore this veſtment alſo is ſuſpended from the loins. " *In the prime of thy might and in thy beauty,*" ſaith he, " *hold on thy way, and proſper, and reign, becauſe of Truth, and Meekneſs, and Righteouſneſs.*"

Next after this he taketh the Cuffs.[350] By theſe is ſignified the pervading energy of God. And to this do the words of the prayer apply, " *Thy right hand, O Lord, is glorified in ſtrength.*" And again, " *Thy hands made me and faſhioned me.*" By them, too, is figured His conſecrating with His hands the myſteries of Himſelf. And, again, that of His hands being bound.

Next followeth the Phænolion,[351] either Saccos,[352] or Polyſtaurion,[353] by which is ſignified the outer robe which He bare at the time of His paſſion. And by the Saccos that he wears is ſignified rather the like garment of Chriſt.[354] And ſo, too, may we ſay of the Polyſtaurion. Though by this is ſhown alſo the grace of God, provident and protective in all things, and maintenant, by reaſon of which He both appeared among us men, and endured thoſe His ſufferings.

CAP. 82. THE OMOPHORION.

Laſt of all, he taketh the Omophorion,[355] which he rolleth out (unfolds) from his ſhoulders, and ſo ſetteth forth the ſaving and recalling to the fold of the loſt ſheep of our Humanity. Of which ſheep the Saviour did aſſume the form ; wherein alſo He ſuffered, and ſo ſaved us by the croſs. And this is the reaſon that it is made of wool. And both behind and in front, and upon the breaſt, it hath four croſſes, arranged croſſwiſe, figuring forth the Crucifixion.

Such is the faſhion in which the Biſhop doth ſtand arrayed.

CAP. 83. THE FIVE VESTMENTS OF THE PRIEST.

[*After deſcribing the ceremonies with which the Liturgy begins, he proceeds as follows :*]

The Prieſt then goeth thence, and with the other Prieſts putteth upon him the ſacerdotal garments. He bleſſeth each of the ſacred veſtments, and kiſſeth it, even as does the chief-prieſt (Biſhop). And having ſo done he putteth it about him, ſhowing by that he doeth that they have been conſecrated, and are made holy by the croſs of Chriſt, and impart holineſs now that again they are put on. Five garments accordingly he putteth about him, as being himſelf conſummate, and endowed with conſummating grace. For five is the full number of the bodily ſenſes ; and five the powers of the ſoul, which are ſanctified by Jeſus when He baptizeth man and ſanctifieth him. And the veſtments that the Prieſt putteth on are theſe, Sticharion [note 346], Epitrachelion, Girdle, Cuffs, Phænolion. And theſe are white, becauſe of the purity and illumination that belongeth to grace. But oftentimes too they are purple, in times of faſt, becauſe of our mourning in reſpect of ſin, and becauſe of Him who on our behalf was ſlain, in order that being put in remembrance of His paſſion we may follow the example of Him, whoſe feaſt alſo we are about to keep.

But ſome of the principal preſbyters, the Croſs-wearers as they are called, and certain of the Archimandrites, wear a Genual alſo ; for this is a matter of epiſcopal favour, as is alſo the wearing of a croſs. For none ſave the Biſhop hath power to wear both the croſſes (on the Phænolion and the head) and the Genual. Yet, nevertheleſs, thoſe of whom I now ſpeak, becauſe of their being ordained with precedence over others, have given unto them the right to wear a croſs upon the head only, and a Genual, when occupied in the holy office.[357]

APPENDIX.

—◆—

A.

ASSOCIATIONS OF COLOUR IN PRIMITIVE TIMES, AND MORE PARTICULARLY IN THE FIRST FOUR CENTURIES OF CHRISTIAN HISTORY.

PART I. PASSAGES OF PROFANE AUTHORS QUOTED [358] OR ALLUDED TO IN THE INTRODUCTION.

1. Plato, *De Leg.* xii. p. 956. [He is fpeaking of the kind of offerings which may with moſt propriety be offered to the gods: and he fays], ὑφὴν δὲ μὴ πλίον ἔργον [359] γυναικὸς μιᾶς ἔμμηνον· χρώματα δὲ λευκὰ πρέποιτ᾽ ἂν τῆ θεοῖς, καὶ ἄλλοθι καὶ ἐν ὑφῇ· βάμματα δὲ μὴ προσφέριιν ἀλλ᾽ ἢ πρὸς τὰ πολέμου κοσμήματα.

2. *Ibid.* p. 947. He is fpeaking of the honours to be paid to the "Moſt Worthy" citizens in the Commonwealth : that they ſhall have precedence in all Public Aſſemblies ; ſhall repreſent the State in ſolemn religious Embaſſies ; ſhall alone among all be crowned with Bay ; ſhall be Prieſts, all of them, of Apollo and of Helios, and one among them be high-prieſt in each year, and that by his name (as Eponymus) the year ſhall be known. He then adds : —

τελευτήσασι δὲ προθέσεις τε καὶ ἐκφορὰς καὶ θήκας διαφορους εἶναι τῶν ἄλλων πολιτῶν, λευκὴν μὲν τὴν στολὴν εἶναι πᾶσαν κ.τ.λ.

"When they die let them be marked out from all other citizens both by the ſtate in which they are ſet out, and by their carrying out to burial, and by the tombs to which they are committed ; and let their apparel be all of white," etc.

---

[358] Where a tranſlation of any of theſe paſſages has already been given in the Introduction, none is given in this Appendix, nor in cafes where there no difficulty of any kind obſcures the meaning of the author. In other paſſages I have endeavoured to ſupply, either by full Tranſlations or by Notes, what appeared neceſſary for the elucidation of meaning.

[359] μὴ πλίον, κ. τ. λ. He means that the labour expended upon it ſhould not be more than would occupy o e pair of hands for a month. See the tranſlation of what follows, and the explanatory note, Introduction, cap. iii. p. xviii. y.

With this of white apparel wherein to array the dead we may compare the passage that follows : —

3. Plutarch, *Quæst. Rom.* τὸ σῶμα τοῦ τεθνηκότος ἀμφιεννύουσι λευκοῖς, ἐπεὶ μὴ δύναται τὴν ψυχήν· βούλονται δὲ ἐκείνην λαμπρὰν καὶ καθαρὰν προπέμπειν, ὡς προειμένην ἤδη, καὶ διηγωνισμένην μέγαν ἀγῶνα [260] καὶ ποικίλον.

"The body of the dead they array in white, seeing that they cannot so clothe his soul ; and their desire therein is to attend it, all bright and pure, to the grave, as one already released from the body, and that has contended even to the end in the great and chequered battle of life."

4. Horace, *Sat.* ii. 61. White, the colour of social, and in some sort religious, festival, whether of marriage, birthdays, or the like.

> Licebit
> *Ille repotia,*[261] *natales, aliosve dierum*
> *Festos albatus celebret.*

5. Ovid. *Trist.* lib. iii., xii. [He is writing on his Birthday].

> *Scilicet expectes soliti tibi moris honorem*
> *Pendeat* [262] *ex humeris vestis ut alba meis ?*

6. Ovid, lib. v. el. 5. [He writes now of his Wife's Birthday],

> *Annuus adsuetum Dominæ natalis honorem*
> *Exigit . . . .*
> *Quæque semel toto vestis mihi sumitur anno*
> *Sumatur fatis discolor alba meis.*

" Though because of his unhappy condition he should rather be wearing mourning, yet will he, in honour of this day, put on the white robe (*toga*) of festival."

7. Persius, *Sat.* ii.

> Negato
> *Jupiter hoc illi quamvis albata rogarit.*

" Let the gods deny her request, even though (clad in white, *and so*) with all solemnity of outward worship her prayer be uttered."

8. Donatus *on Terence* (apud Wetstenium in Matt. xxvii. 28) *Læto vestitus*

An echo one might almost believe of a thought yet finer and more far reaching still : τὸν ἀγῶνα τὸν καλὸν ἠγώνισμαι· τὸν δρόμον τετέλεκα· λοιπὸν ἀπόκειταί μοι ὁ τῆς δικαιοσύνης στέφανος ὃν ἀποδώσει μοι ὁ Κύριος ἐν ἐκείνῃ τῇ ἡμέρᾳ, κ. τ. λ.

[261] *Repotia.* The return feast given by the bridegroom on the day after a marriage.

Festus apud Scheller : " Repotia postridie nuptias apud novum maritum cænatur. Quia quasi reficitur potatio."

[262] *Pendeat ex humeris.* Note this expression as suggesting that it is of the full and flowing supervesture (and here the Toga) that he speaks, not of the Tunic.

candidus ærumnejo objoletus: purpureus diviti, phœniceus [363] *pauperi datur: militi chlamys purpurea induitur.* [364]

" White vefture is for them that rejoice, and fad clothing for them that are oppreffed with grief. Purple is beftowed upon the rich, dark red [363] upon the poor. A purple chlamys is the mantle of honour [364] for a foldier."

9. Martial, *Epig.* i. lvi. [After defcribing the pleafures of the country, where men can do as they like and drefs as they like, he adds]:

> *Non amet hanc vitam quisquis me non amat opto,*
> *Vivat et urbanis albus in officiis.*

The worft he will wifh for his enemies is that they may be bored as he had often been, when at Rome, by the ceremonious etiquette of the Capital, on occafions in which the wearing of white drefs was a kind of focial neceffity. To the fame effect he expreffes himfelf elfewhere, when defcribing what to him appear the real bleffings of life ; one of which is " *toga rara,*" the times few and far between, when one fhall need to wear the long white robe of burdenfome ceremony. I quote the epigram becaufe of its own worth : —

AD JVLIVM MARTIALEM.

Vitam quæ faciunt beatiorem,
Jucundiffime Martialis, hæc funt :
Res non parta labore, fed relicta :
Non ingratus ager, focus perennis ; [365]
Lis nunquam, toga rara, mens quieta ;
Vires ingenuæ, [366] falubre corpus,
Prudens fimplicitas, [367] pares amici,
Convictus facilis, fine arte menfa :
Mens non ebria, fed foluta curis :

---

[363] *Phœniceus.* There were in Italy common, and not coftly, dyes, of home produce, which furnifhed a colour approaching to purple, but without the luftre and brilliant colour of the more expenfive Tyrian or Laconian dye. This is the " *neftra plebeia purpura ac pæne fufca*" of which Cicero fpeaks (pro Sextio) ; the μελαίνα πορφύρα, which Plutarch attributes to Cato, oppofing it to the ἐρυθρὰ καὶ ἔξιτα (apud Oct. Ferr. p. 707, 2). Some fuch cheap and inferior purple is evidently here meant.

[364] *Militi chlamys purpurea induitur.* He does not mean fimply " the foldier *wears* a purple chlamys," but, that a chlamys of purple would be the *drefs of honour* put about the fhoulders of a foldier, whom an " *Imperator*" defired to honour. For an example, fee the paffage in Commodus' letter to Albinus, quoted in the Introduction, cap. 3, p. xviii.

This ufage of beftowing robes of various kinds as marks of imperial favour was one of the many Eaftern cuftoms imported into the Weft, of which, under the Empire, we find trace, and which in various ways have left their mark upon the ufages even of modern fociety. Witnefs, for example, the *mantle of purple*, with which a Knight of the Garter is folemnly invefted in the prefence of his Sovereign. The hiftory of the Papal " *pallium,*" briefly ftated in the Introduction (fee Index *in voc.*), is a remarkable inftance of the fame kind.

[365] *Focus perennis* (a permanent hearth, *and fo*), a houfe of one's own.

[366] *Vires ingenuæ* (inborn, or natural, ftrength, *and fo*, with the words that follow), " ftrength and health."

[367] *Prudens fimplicitas.* φρόνιμοι ὡς οἱ ὄφεις καὶ ἀκέραιοι ὡς αἱ περιστεραί. (Matt. x. 16.)

A A

Non triftis torus, attamen pudicus :
Somnus, qui faciat breves tenebras :
Quod fis, effe velis, nihilque malis :
Summum nec metuas diem, nec optes.

(Lib. x. Epig. xlvii.)

10. Artemidori [377a] *Oneirocritica*, lib. ii. cap. 3.

Περὶ ἐσθῆτος καὶ κόσμου παντοδάπου ἀνδρίου τε καὶ γυναικείου.

Περὶ ἐσθῆτος καὶ κόσμου παντοδάπου ποιούμενος τὸν λόγον πρῶτον περὶ ἀνδρείας
σκευῆς, ἐγχωρίου τε καὶ ξένης, ἡγοῦμαι δεῖν διαλαβεῖν. Ἐσθὴς ἡ συνήθης πᾶσιν
ἀγαθά· καὶ ἡ κατὰ τὴν ὥραν τοῦ ἔτους. Θέρους μὲν γὰρ ὄντος ὀθονία τε καὶ τριβακὰ
ἱμάτια δοκεῖν φορεῖν ἀγαθὸν ἂν εἴη καὶ ὑγιείας σύμβολον. Χειμῶνος δὲ ἐρέα ἱμάτια,
καὶ ταῦτα καινά. Μόνῳ δὲ τῷ δίκην ἔχοντι καὶ δουλείας ἀπαλλαττόντι πονηρὰ
τὰ καινὰ ἱμάτια. Καὶ χειμῶνος βλέπεται (Leg. βλάπτει) διὰ τὸ πολλὴν ἔχειν
τρίψιν καὶ ἐπιπολὺ ἀντίχειν. Λευκὰ δὲ ἱμάτια τοῖς ἱερεῦσι μόνοις συμφέρει καὶ
δούλοις Ἑλλήνων. Τοῖς δὲ ἄλλοις ταραχὰς σημαίνει, διὰ τὸ τοὺς ἐν ὄχλῳ ἀναστρε-
φομένους λευκὰ ἔχειν ἱμάτια. Χειροτέχναις δὲ ἀργίαν καὶ σχολήν. Καὶ ὅσῳ ἂν
πολυτελεστέρα ᾖ τὰ ἱμάτια τοσούτῳ πλείονα. Οὐ γὰρ πρὸς ἔργῳ ὄντες οἱ ἄνθρωποι,
καὶ μάλιστα οἱ τὰς βαναύσους τέχνας ἐργαζόμενοι, λευκοῖς ἱματίοις χρῶνται. Δοῦλοι
(Leg. δούλοις) δὲ Ῥωμαίων μόνοις τοῖς εὖ πράττουσι· τοῖς δὲ ἄλλοις πονηρόν. Ἐλέγχει γὰρ τοὺς κακῶς πράσσοντας, διὰ τι (Leg. διὰ τι τὸ) τὴν αὐτὴν τοῖς δεσπόταις
ὡς ἐπιπλεῖστον ἐσθῆτα ἐπὶ τούτῳ τῷ ὀντίῳ οὐ γίνονται ἐλεύθεροι ὥσπερ οἱ τῶν
Ἑλλήνων. Ἀνδρὶ δὲ νοσοῦντι λευκὰ ἔχειν ἱμάτια θάνατον προσαγορεύει· διὰ τὸ τοὺς
ἀποθανόντας ἐν λευκοῖς ἐκφέρεσθαι. Τὸ δὲ μέλαν ἱμάτιον σωτηρίαν προσημαίνει· οὐ
γὰρ οἱ ἀποθανόντες ἀλλ' οἱ πενθοῦντες τοὺς ἀποθανόντας τοιούτοις χρῶνται. Οἶδα
δὲ ἐγὼ πολλοὺς καὶ πένητας καὶ δούλους καὶ δεσμώτας νοσοῦντας, οἳ καὶ μέλανα
δοκοῦντες ἔχειν ἱμάτια ἀπέθανον· ἦν γὰρ εἰκὸς τούτους μὴ ἐν λευκοῖς διὰ τὴν ἀπορίαν
ἐκκομισθῆσεσθαι. Ἔστι δὲ ἄλλως ἡ μελαίνα ἐσθὴς πᾶσι πονηρά· πλὴν τῶν τὰ
λαθραῖα ἐργαζομένων. Ποικίλην δὲ ἐσθῆτα ἔχειν ἢ ἁλουργίδα ἱερεῦσι μὲν καὶ
θυμελικαῖς καὶ σκηνικαῖς καὶ τοῖς περὶ τὸν Διόνυσον μόνοις τεχνίταις συμφέρει. Τοῖς
δὲ λοιποῖς ταραχὰς καὶ κινδύνους μόνους ἐπιφέρει, καὶ τὰ κρυπτὰ ἐλέγχει. Τοὺς
δὲ νοσοῦντας ὑπὸ δριμέων χυμῶν καὶ πολλῆς χολῆς ἐνοχληθῆναι σημαίνει. Πορφυρᾶ
δὲ ἐσθὴς δούλοις ἀγαθὴ καὶ πλουσίοις· οἷς μὲν γὰρ διὰ τὸ μὴ μετεῖναι ἐλευθερίαν
σημαίνει· οἷς δὲ διὰ τὸ μὴ ἐπιτάττειν, καὶ τῷ ἀξιώματι κατάλληλον εἶναι, τιμὴν καὶ
εὐδοξίαν προσαγορεύει. Νοσοῦντα δὲ ἀπείρως καὶ πένητα βλάπτει· πολλοὺς δὲ καὶ
δεσμὰ προάγγειλε. Χρὴ γὰρ τὸν ἔχοντα πορφύραν πάντως διάδημα ἢ στέφανον
ἔχειν, καὶ πολλοὺς ἀκολούθους ἢ φύλακας. Τοῖς δὲ περὶ τὸν Διόνυσον τεχνίταις τὰ
αὐτὰ τῇ ἁλουργίδι σημαίνει. Κοκκίνη δὲ [ἐσθὴς] καὶ πᾶσα ἡ τοιαύτη ἐσθὴς ἢ πορφυ-
ροβαφὴς οἷς μὲν τραύματα, οἷς δὲ πυρετὸν ἐπιφέρει. Γυναικεία δὲ ἐσθὴς ἀγάμοις
μόνοις συμφέρει, καὶ τοῖς ἐπὶ θυμέλην ἀναβαίνουσιν· οἱ μὲν γὰρ γαμήσουσιν οὕτω κατα-
θυμίους γυναῖκας ὥστε τοῖς αὐτοῖς χρῆσθαι κόσμοις· οἱ δὲ διὰ τὸ ἐν τῇ ὑποκρίσει
ἰδὸς μεγάλας ἐργασίας καὶ μισθοὺς λήψονται. Τοὺς δὲ λοιποὺς καὶ τῶν γυναικῶν
στερίσκει καὶ κόσμον μεγάλην περιβάλλει, διὰ τὸ μαλθακὸν καὶ ἀσθενὲς τῶν τὰ τοιαῦτα
φορούντων. Ἐν μὲν ταῖς ἑορταῖς καὶ πανηγύρεσιν οὔτε ποικίλα οὔτε γυναικεία βλάπτει

---

377 a See note μ, p. xi., for particulars concerning this Writer.

τινα ἰσθὴς ᴹᴳ Βαρβαρικὴν δὲ ἰσθῆτα ἴχειν ἐπισκευασμένην ὥσπερ οἱ βάρβαροι ἐκεῖ μὲν
ἀπιέναι βουλόμενον ὅπου τοιαύτη ἰσθῆτι χρῶνται οἱ διατρίβοντες, ἀγαθὰς τὰς ἐκεῖ
διατριβὰς σημαίνει. Πολλάκις δὲ καὶ τὸ ἐκεῖ καταβιῶναι προαγγέλλει. Τοῖς δὲ
λοιποῖς νόσον καὶ ἀπραγίαν δηλοῖ. Τὰ δὲ αὐτὰ καὶ ἡ Ῥωμαϊκὴ ἰσθὴς ἣν νῦν
τίβινον ᴷᴮ¹ καλοῦσιν. . . .

Μιλακῇ δὲ ἰσθῆτι καὶ πολυτελῇ χρῆσθαι πλουσίοις μὲν ἀγαθὸν καὶ πένητιν· οἷς
μὲν γὰρ ἡ παροῦσα διαμένει τρυφή, οἷς δὲ φαιδρότερα τὰ πράγματα ἔσται. Δούλοις
δὲ καὶ ἀπόροις νόσον προαγορεύει. Κολοβαὶ δὲ καὶ ἀπερπεῖς ἰσθῆτες ζημίας καὶ
ἀπραξίας σημαίνουσι. Χλανὶς δὲ ἣν ἔνιοι μανδύην, οἱ δὲ ἰφεντρίδα, οἱ δὲ βάρσον,
καλοῦσι, θλίψιν καὶ στενοχωρίαν καὶ τοῖς δικαζομένοις καταδίκην ἐπαπειλεῖται, διὰ
τὸ ἐμπεριέχειν τὸ σῶμα. Τὸ δὲ αὐτὸ καὶ ὁ λεγόμενος φαινόλης· καὶ εἴτε ἄλλο
τούτοις ὅμοιον εἴη ὅθεν ἀπολύειν τὰ ἱμάτια ταῦτα ἢ ἴχειν βέλτιον. Τῶν δὲ ἄλλων
ἱματίων οὐδὲν ἀπολύεσθαι συμφέρει, εἰ μή που τοῖς πένησι καὶ δούλοις καὶ διαμένοις
ἢ καταχρέοις καὶ πᾶσι τοῖς ἐν συνοχῇ οὖσιν. Ἀπολύεσθαι γὰρ ταῦτα τῶν περι-
εχόντων τὸ σῶμα κακῶν ἀπόλλειν σημαίνει. Τοῖς δὲ ἄλλοις οὔτε γυμνοῦσθαι οὔτε
ἱμάτια ἀπολύειν ἀγαθόν· πᾶν γὰρ τὸ πρὸς κόσμον τινὲς ἀπολίσθαι σημαίνει.
Γυναικὶ δὲ ποικίλη καὶ ἀνθηρὰ ἰσθὴς συμφέρει, μάλιστα δὲ ἑταίρᾳ καὶ πλουσίᾳ ᾗ
μὲν γὰρ διὰ τὴν ἐργασίαν, ἡ δὲ διὰ τὴν τρυφήν, ἀνθηραῖς ἰσθήσεσι χρῶνται. Τὰ δὲ
ἰδιόχροα ἱμάτια πᾶσιν ἀγαθὸν σημαίνουσι, καὶ μάλιστα τοῖς εὐλαβουμένοις· ἐλεγχ-
θῆναι γὰρ οὐκ ἐᾷ τὸ τοιοῦτον χρῶμα. Ἀεὶ δὲ ἄμεινον καθαρὰ καὶ λαμπρὰ ἱμάτια
ἔχειν καὶ πεπλυμένα καλῶς ἢ ῥυπαρὰ καὶ ἄπλυτα, πλὴν τῶν τὰς ῥυπώδεις ἐργασίας
ἐργαζομένων.

11. Of the entire paſſage, as given above, I would call more particular
attention to the following, as bearing upon queſtions diſcuſſed in the Introduction to this Treatiſe.

SIGNIFICANCE OF WHITE GARMENTS.

α. "White garments (ſeen in dreams) are a ſign of good only for prieſts,[208]
and for ſlaves in Greece. To all others they are a ſign of troubles, becauſe
it is in the buſy crowd (of great cities) that men wear white garments. But
to artizans they portend idleneſs, and leiſure; and then the more complete in
proportion to their greater coſtlineſs. For men wear not white garments when
at work, eſpecially if engaged in the humble mechanical trades."

THE DEAD CLAD IN WHITE: MOURNERS IN BLACK.

β. "To a ſick man the wearing white garments is an announcement of

---

[208] This ſtatement, that a dreſs like that of
women, and of varied colours, is for harm to
none in time of feaſts or public aſſemblies, has
been already noticed. See Introduction, p.
xi, note μ.

[208]ᵃ Τίβινος or τέβινος, a "toga."

[209] He does not mean that prieſts on days
of ſacrifice wore none but white garments, be-

cauſe, as we ſhall ſee below, this was not the
caſe. But days of ſacrifice, and of public feſ-
tivity accompanied by ſacrifice, were days on
which white dreſs was aſſumed by the people
generally; and ſuch days were days of profit
to the lower order of prieſts, and of public
honour to thoſe higher in ſtation.

death; because it is in white that the dead are carried out to burial. But a black robe is a sign of recovery; for it is not the dead, but they that mourn for the dead, that are so dressed."

Gaudy Coloured Dress.

γ. "The wearing of parti-coloured or of sea-purple dress, bringeth good to priests, to stage-players, and actors, and among artizans to those only who have to do with Dionysus. But to all others they portend trouble and danger only; and serve to the detection of secrets. And for such as are sick they are significant of oppression by acrid humours, and much bile." [To this may be added what follows later in the Chapter.] "To women, parti-coloured garments, coloured like unto flowers, are of good import, especially to harlots, and to the rich. For harlots, because of their occupation, and the rich, out of luxury, wear garments such as these."

Robes of Purple, and Scarlet.

δ. "Robes of purple are of good sign for slaves, and for rich men; to the former because, slaves having no right to such, they are significant of freedom; to the rich, because in respect of wealth alone they have no power to command; and purple, being correlative to official dignity, portendeth to them rank and reputation. But purple is death to a sick man, and harmful to one in poverty. And in many cases they have been found to foretell even bonds. For the wearer of purple must needs have either the band (diadem) that is proper to kings, or a chaplet (στέφανος, note 54) [bound about his brow], and be surrounded with many attendants or guards. But to such as work in matters pertaining to the worship of Dionysus, ordinary purple has the same significance as the sea-purple. Vestments of scarlet and the like, and such as are dyed purple, portend wounds to some, to others fever."

The Chlamys and the Pænula.

ι. "The Chlamys, which some call Mandyas, others Epheatris, others Berion, foretelleth trouble, and difficulty, and to men under trial, condemnation, because of its compassing and confining the body. And like to this is the significance of what is called a 'Pænula,' and of other garments of the same kind."

Vestments of Heathen Priesthood.

12. Tyrian Priests wore a χιτὼν πλατύσημος, *i.e.*, a Tunic with a broad band (*clavus*), probably of purple. Herodianus, lib. v. *apud* Ferrar. He is speaking of the honorary Priests of Elagabalus or Heliogabalus, the Syro-Phœnician

Sun-God. τὰ σπλάγχνα τῶν ἱερουργηθέντων τά τε ἀρώματα ἐν χρυσοῖς σκεύεσιν ὑπὲρ κεφαλῆς οὐκ οἰκέτης δή τινες ἢ εὐτελεῖς ἄνθρωποι ἔφερον, ἀλλ᾽ οἵτ᾽ ἔπαρχοι τῶν στρατοπέδων καὶ οἱ ἐν ταῖς μεγίσταις πράξεσιν, ἀνεζωσμένοι χιτῶνας ποδήρεις καὶ χειριδωτοὺς, νόμῳ Φοινίκων, ἐν μέσῳ φέροντες μίαν πορφύραν.³⁷⁰ Ὑποδήμασι δὲ λίνου πεποιημένοις ἐχρῶντο, ὥσπερ οἱ κατ᾽ ἐκεῖνα τὰ χωρία προφητεύοντες.

13. So in Tyrian colonies, as for example, the Priests of Hercules (Melcarth) at Gades: Silius Italicus, *Punica,* lib. iii.

> Nec discolor ulli
> Ante aras cultus ; velantur corpora lino,
> Ex Pelusiaco præfulget flamine vertex : ³⁷¹
> Discinctis ³⁷² mos thura dare, atque e lege parentum
> Sacrificam lato vestem distinguere clavo.

14. To the same effect is what Tertullian says of the Priests of Saturnus at Carthage. *De Pallio,* cap. 4, p. 213.

" Latioris purpuræ ambitio,³⁷³ et Galatici ³⁷⁴ ruboris superjectio, Saturnum commendat."

In the same place he speaks of the Priests of Ceres as dressed wholly in white, those of Bellona in dark and gloomy garb.

" Cur . . . non spectas . . . illos habitus qui novitati suæ stare religionem mentiuntur, cum ob cultum omnia candidatum, et ob notam vitæ, et privilegium galeri,³⁷⁵ Cereri initiantur ; cum ob diversam affectionem tenebricæ vestis, et tetrici super caput velleris, in Bellonæ mentes (*al.* montes) fugantur."

15. Priests of Dionysus wore purple. See Artemidorus, quoted above, No. 10, and Clement of Alexandria, *Pæd.* lib. ii. cap. 9, quoted later in this Appendix. See No. 39.

16. At Rome the *Pontifices* wore a *Toga prætexta* (*i.e.,* bordered with purple). See Lampridius, quoted in note v, p. xi. And to the same effect is that of Livy (xl. 42), when, in speaking of the *Triumviri Epulones,*³⁷⁶ he says that to them *idem ut Pontifici lege datum togæ prætextæ habendæ jus.*

---

³⁷⁰ μίαν πορφύραν, *i.e.* a single band or stripe (*clavus*) of purple. Compare Silius Italicus in No. 13.

³⁷¹ That is, they wear a cap, or μίτρα, made of fine Egyptian linen.

³⁷² This points to the *long* tunic, not girt up by any *cingulum.*

³⁷³ *Latioris purpuræ ambitio.* This last word (*ambitio*) may possibly be used with reference to its literal meaning, "going round," and so of "the compassing" of the vestment, on its border, by a broad purple stripe. But the more probable meaning (as the previous context shows) is " the ambition of wearing a broad purple stripe " corresponding to the *latus clavus* of Roman use. The words here commented on refer to the *Tunica* ; the *superjectio,* &c. (ἐπένδυμα) to the Super-vestment.

³⁷⁴ *Galaticus rubor, i.e.* scarlet. Plinii *Hist. Nat.* xxii. cap. 11. *Infci vestes scimus admirabili succo. Atque ut filcamus Galatiæ, Africæ, Lusitaniæ cocci granum Imperatoriis paludamentis dicatum, &c. &c.*

³⁷⁵ Note 124, p. 72.

³⁷⁶ *Triumviri Epulones.* Commissioners who regulated the public sacrificial feasts.

17. When facrificing, the Pontiffs commonly covered the head with a portion of this *Prætexta*. To this Virgil alludes, when he reprefents Helenus giving directions to Æneas as to the ceremonial drefs of facrifice : Æn. iii. 404.

> Quin ubi tranfmiffæ fteterint trans æquora claffes,
> Et pofitis aris jam vota in littore folves,
> Purpureo velare comas adopertus amictu,[277]
> Ne qua inter fanctos ignes in honore Deorum
> Hoftilis facies occurrat, et omina turb..t.

18. So alfo Flamens wore purple (Servius on Æneid iv.), and Augurs a *Trabea* of purple and fcarlet, known as διβαφον. Hence the allufion of Cicero when writing to Atticus (*ad Att.* ii. 9), he fays :—

" Proinde ifti licet faciant quos volent Confules, Tribunos plebis ; denique etiam Vatinii ftrumam facerdotii διβάφψ vefliant " (*i.e. let them make Vatinius an Augur.*).

Part II. ASSOCIATIONS OF COLOUR IN HOLY SCRIPTURE.

19. White Robes are fymbolic of joy, Eccl. ix. 8 : of purity and cleanfing from fin, If. i. 18 ; Dan. xii. 10 ; Rev. iii. 4, 5 ; Rev. vii. 13, 14 : of righteoufnefs, Rev. xix. 8.

20. In white angels are clothed, Matt. xxviii. 3 ; Mark, xvi. 5 ; Acts, i. 10. In white, too, our Lord was feen in vifion at the Transfiguration, Matt. xvii. 2 ; Mark, ix. 3. In white "The Ancient of Days" was feen in vifion by Daniel, Dan. vii. 9.

21. White are the robes of Levites at the Dedication of Solomon's Temple, 2 Chron. v. 12. White (becaufe made of *Linen*, note 16) the robes of Priefts. White the robes with which the High-prieft entered the Holy of Holies, on the Day of Atonement. See Philo Judæus, quoted at p. 8, and fee note 17, p. 7.

Red.

22. Red is the colour of wine (*the blood of the grape*), Gen. xlix. 12 ; Pf. lxxv. 8 ; Prov. xxiii. 36 ; If. lxiii. 2.

23. Red is the colour of blood (2 Kings, iii. 22, &c.), and fo affociated with the idea of battle, Nahum, ii. 3 ; Zech. i. 8 ; Rev. vi. 4.

24. Red is alfo a royal colour, and ufed in the decoration of kings' palaces (Efther, i. 6). And as fuch probably ufed in the decoration of the " Houfe of God," King of kings, and Lord of lords.

25. But at other times red is affociated with the idea of fin (" Thy fins,

---

[277] This line is quoted by St. Jerome, on Ezek. xliv. See above, p 30, *in fin.*

though they be red like crimfon"), If. i. 18; or with the imperfonation of Sin defcribed, in Rev. xii. 3, as a great dragon having feven heads and ten horns.

BLUE.

26. Blue is (like red) a royal colour, Either, i. 6, ufed efpecially in "royal apparel," Efther, viii. 15. Compare Ezek. xxiii. 6.

27. It was ufed (compare No. 24) in the decoration of the Tabernacle and Temple (Exod., Numb., 2 Chron., *paffim*) and in the veftments of the High-prieft, Exod. xxviii. 31, &c.

28. We alfo find it mentioned as one of the products of "Tyrus," Ezek. xxvii. 7, 24; and affociated with purple in the clothing of idols, Jer. x. 9.

SCARLET.[370]

29. Scarlet is a royal colour, 2 Sam. i. 24; Lam. iv. 5; Dan. v. 7, 16, 29.

30. As fuch, probably, it was ufed in the decoration of the Tabernacle (compare Nos. 24 and 27) and of the Temple, 2 Chron. ii. 7; and in the veftments of the High-prieft, Exod. xxviii. 6, &c.

31. From its refemblance to the colour of blood it has a fymbolical ufe in "cleanfing from fin" (*"without fhedding of blood there is no remiffion"*). Lev. xiv. 4; Heb. ix. 19.

32. As being a brilliant and very coftly colour it was rarely ufed by unofficial perfons, as an ordinary colour of drefs, fave by the very wealthy, or by immodeft women. (See above, No. 11, γ.) Hence it is fometimes fpoken of in Scripture (as elfewhere) as a meretricious colour, Rev. xvii. 4, 5, or as fymbolical of fin generally, If. i. 18; Rev. xvii. 3.

PURPLE.

33. Purple is a royal colour, Judg. viii. 26; Efther, i. 6; viii. 15; Mark, xv. 17.

34. As fuch (compare Nos. 27, 30) it had its ufe in the Tabernacle, Numb. iv. 13.

---

[370] Scarlet was attainable, from its great coftlinefs, only by the wealthy. This probably explains the phrafe employed in Prov. xxxi. 21, where, in fpeaking of the "virtuous woman," it is faid that "all her houfehold are clothed with fcarlet," *i.e.* by her prudence and wife management there is abundance of clothing, even the moft coftly, for all that need.

35. And for a similar reason, when used by private persons, it is regarded as a proof, sometimes of abundant wealth, Prov. xxxi. 22 (where the clothing of "the virtuous woman" is silk and purple), more often of luxury and self-indulgence, as in Luke, xvi. 19.

Part III. ASSOCIATIONS OF COLOUR IN EARLY CHRISTIAN WRITERS.

36. Clemens Alexandrinus, *Pædag.* lib. ii. p. 233.

"I honour that ancient Lacedæmonian people, who allowed none but harlots to wear garments wrought like unto flowers, and ornaments of gold."

Sellers of Incense and Dyers of Wools should be banished from the Commonwealth of Truth.

37. *Ibid.* p. 208. [He had been speaking with strongest condemnation of the use of unguents, and scents, and incense, and the like (for purposes of luxury), and he adds]:

"With good reason, to my judgment, did they act, who, indignant at seeing pains bestowed on things like these, held scents and unguents in such ill esteem, as emasculating all manliness of character, that they banished the makers of them from well-ordered states, and did treat no otherwise the dyers of various wools. An unrighteous thing it were that garments full of deceit, and unguents, should find their way into the city of truth. . . . And if perchance it should be said, that the Lord, the great High-priest, offereth the incense of sweet savour unto God, let them learn that this is no sacrifice and sweet savour of (actual) incense, but that which the Lord doth offer is the acceptable oblation of holy love, the spiritual sweet savour, upon the altar."

Dyed Garments Signs of an Evil Disposition.

38. *Ibid.* p. 234.

"All dyed colours should be avoided in dress; for these are far away both from man's need, and from truth; and beside this they give proof of evil in the inward disposition."

Garments Dyed like unto Flowers, fit only for Worshippers of Bacchus, for Heathen Priests, and Stage Players.

39. *Ibid.* p. 235. "For men that are pure and unadulterate in heart a white and simple garb is the most fitting for their use. Plainly and purely speaketh Daniel the prophet. *Thrones*, saith he, *were set, and one took his seat thereon as it were the Antient of Days: and His raiment was white like snow.* And the Revelation speaketh of beholding the Lord in the like vesture. "I saw at the foot of the altar the souls of them hat thad testified for Christ, and there was given unto each one white raiment." But if need should be for seeking

any other colour, that natural colour which is of truth, fufficeth. But garments coloured like unto flowers are fit only for Bacchic rites, and for the mummeries of heathen priefts. Purple, too, and filver tiflues, are ' for tragedy players, not for real life,' as the comic poet writes. Whereas the life of us Chriftian folk fhould be anything rather than a vain pomp."

THE SPIRITUAL MEANING OF THAT WHICH IS WRITTEN CONCERNING " THE RAIMENT OF GOLD WROUGHT ABOUT WITH DIVERS COLOURS."

40. *Ibid.* p. 236. He had been fpeaking in ftrong condemnation of women wearing gaudy colours, fuch as thofe above fpoken of. And left any fhould defend this by alleging words of Scripture, which, as he judged, were to be fpiritually underftood, he writes as follows :

" What though the word of God by the mouth of David fpeaketh in Pfalm concerning the Lord, faying, *Kings' daughters were among thine honourable women : on thy right hand ftood the queen in a vefture of gold, and with garments fringed with gold was fhe compaffed about.* [379] In this he would have us to underftand not raiment of luxurious foftnefs, but that which is wrought of faith, he incorruptible adornment of them that have received mercy, the adornment of the Church ; wherein Jefus, the guilelefs one, fhineth out as gold, and the fringes, made of gold, are the elect."

IN WHITE TRUE BEAUTY IS TO BE FOUND.

41. *Ibid.* p. 239. " Why is it then that ye are attracted by that which is rare and coftly, rather than by that which is ready to your hand and of eafy purchafe ? It is becaufe ye know not what is the truly beautiful, and the truly good ; and, in place of realities, beftow your pains upon what is efteemed only among men of no underftanding, to whofe imagination, as with men mad, white and black feem both alike."

TERTULLIAN.[380]

DYED COLOURS DISPLEASING TO GOD.

42. De Habitu Muliebri, cap. 8. " Quis eft veftium honor juftus de adulterio colorum injuftorum ? Non placet Deo quod non ipfe produxit, nifi fi non potuit purpureas et aerias [381] oves nafci jubere. Si potuit, ergo jam noluit : quod Deus noluit, utique non licet fingi."[382]

---

[379] In this prophecy, Amalarius (quoted at p. 99) fees a reference to the dalmatic. The two comments, thofe of Clement and Amalarius, prefent an inftructive contraft.

[380] Born at Carthage, *circ.* A.D. 150. Embraced Chriftianity A.D. 185. Died A.D. 220. His middle life was fpent partly at Rome, and

partly (at a later period) at Carthage.

[381] *Aerias, i.e.* of the colour of the fky.

[382] Whatever may be thought of the logic of this argument, the paffage is good evidence as to the feeling of Tertullian in refpect of the coftly colours of which he is speaking.

DYED COLOURS MERETRICIOUS.

43. *Ibid.* p. 68. " Illa civitas valida quæ fuper montes feptem et plurimas aquas præfidet, cum proftitutæ appellationem a Domino meruiffet, quali habitu appellationis fuæ comparata eft ? Sedet certe in purpura cum coccino et auro et lapide pretiofo."

THE TRUE PURPLE OF THE CHRISTIAN MAN.

44. *De Corona Militis,* cap. 13. [He is addreffing the Chriftian man as at once a foldier of Chrift, and a citizen of the Jerufalem that is above.]

" Coronant et publicos ordines laureis publicæ caufæ, magiftratus vero infuper aureis. . . . . Sed tui ordines et tui magiftratus, et ipfum Curiæ [383] nomen, Ecclefia eft Chrifti. Illic purpuræ tuæ, Sanguis Domini ; et clavus latus, in Cruce ipfius : illic fecuris,[384] ad caudicem arboris pofita : illic virgæ,[385] ex radice Jeffe."

APPENDIX B.

PASSAGES OF EARLY WRITERS INDICATIVE
OF A LEVITICAL ORIGIN FOR CHRISTIAN VESTMENTS.

The monuments, whether of literature or of art, during the firft eight hundred years of Chriftian hiftory, point with an overwhelming weight of concurrent teftimony to the conclufion, that the veftments of Chriftian miniftry were not modelled upon thofe of Levitical priefthood.

In all thofe monuments, as far as we have feen hitherto, there has been no indication of any but white [386] veftments being worn ; no trace anywhere

---

[383] He alludes to the etymological connection between *Curia* and κυριακή.

[384] This points probably to the blood that flowed from the pierced fide.

[385] *Securis,* and again *virga,* in allufion to the axe and rods borne by the lictors of the higher magiftrates.

[386] The only exception to this, of which I am aware, is one of thofe exceptions " that prove the rule." We learn incidentally from a notice in the *Gefta Pontificum Romanorum,* quoted by Walafrid Strabo (p. 106), and by Anaftafius, that attempts were made at Rome, in the pontificate of Sylvefter (314–335), to introduce the ufe of coloured cloth, and of filk, in the veftments of Chriftian miniftry. For

of any intentional imitation of the diftinctive charactcriftics of the dreſs of Levitical prieſthood, viz. the coloured girdle, and the prieſtly cap, of prieſts of the ſecond order ; the gorgeouſly coloured ſuper-veſtments, the jewelled "rational," the cap with its golden plate, worn by the high-prieſt.

But it is deſirable to notice, and to give all due weight to, a few facts that may be alleged as pointing to an oppoſite concluſion. It ſhould not be forgotten, in dealing with queſtions ſuch as thoſe now before us, that between the Aaronic prieſthood and the prieſthood of the Chriſtian Church, there are many points of cloſe analogy, though there are alſo points of important difference. Theſe points of analogy, ſuggeſted as they are by many paſſages of Holy Scripture, were recogniſed from the very earlieſt times by eccleſiaſtical writers. One effect of this was, that titles, properly applicable to the older prieſthood, were, ſparingly at firſt, but with an ever-increaſing freedom as time went on, applied to the ſeveral orders of the Chriſtian miniſtry. And this being the caſe, it would be ſtrange if we did not find here and there ſome recognition, in like manner, of certain features of analogy [386 a] between the veſtments of the Chriſtian biſhop or prieſt, and the Levitical veſtments of the older Church.

Some [387] paſſages, of the kind now ſpoken of, have already been quoted, and their language carefully conſidered. And I take this opportunity of adding thereto ſuch other paſſages of early writers as might be thought to invalidate the general concluſions, as to the origin of Chriſtian veſtments, which have been ſet forth in the Introduction to this treatiſe.

1. The firſt in date occurs in the well-known ſermon, or rather oration, pronounced by Euſebius of Cæſarea, at the opening of the great Church at Tyre, after the public recognition of Chriſtianity by Conſtantine the Great. It is given at full length by its author in the tenth book of his Eccleſiaſtical Hiſtory. Written in a ſtyle of florid rhetoric from firſt to laſt, the leading thought that pervades it is that of a compariſon between the magnificent church, for the conſecration of which they were aſſembled, and the Temple of Solomon. Addreſſing the Biſhop of Tyre, Paulinus, the ſpeaker knows not whether to regard him as a ſecond Bezaleel, or as another Solomon, king of a new and better Jeruſalem, or as the Zorobabel of their own day, crowning

---

Sylveſter found it neceſſary to forbid their uſe. *Hic conſtituit ut ſacrificium altaris non in ſerico neque in panno tincto celebraretur, niſi tantum in linteo ex terreno lino procreato, ſicut corpus Domini Noſtri Jeſu Chriſti in ſindone lintea munda ſepultum eſt, et ſic Miſſa celebraretur.* [Anaſtaſii V. P. R. in S. Sylveſtro, p. 105.] There are abundant proofs (eſpecially in the notices preſerved by Anaſtaſius) of a vaſt acceſſion to the ſplendour of divine ſervice generally, at Rome and elſewhere, from the time of "the converſion of Conſtantine." But it is plain from this paſſage, and from the evidence of ſubſequent centuries, that little if any change

was then permitted in the ſimple but dignified dreſs of Chriſtian miniſtry.

[386 a] As in S. Germanus quoted above, p. 82, note 141. With his expreſſion cloſely agrees, that of Martinus, Biſhop of Braga (*circ.* 572 A.D.), in the collection known as the Capitula Martini Epiſcopi. Labbe, tom. v. p. 912, Canon lxvi. "Non oportet clericos comam nutrire, et ſic miniſtrare, ſed attonſo capite, patentibus auribus; et ſecundum Aaron talarem veſtem induere, ut ſint in habitu ordinato."

[387] See note 59, p. 37; note 62, p. 39; note 65, p. 41.

the temple of God with that glory, better than the former, which belongeth
to thefe laſt times. And it is in accordance with this ſtrain that he addreſſes
the aſſembled clergy as "friends of God, and prieſts (ἰεϱεῖς) clad in the holy
veſture that reacheth to the feet, and with the heavenly crown of glory, and
with the unction of inſpiration, and the prieſtly veſture of the Holy Spirit." [388]

Now I am free to confeſs that I can only underſtand theſe words as highly
figurative throughout. The "ſticharion," white and gliſtening, which was no
doubt worn both by biſhops and prieſts there aſſembled before him, was, in
point of fact, a feature in common between the Jewiſh and the Chriſtian dreſs.
But preciſely for the reaſon (ſo at leaſt it ſeems to me) that in all the other,
and more diſtinctive, features of the Jewiſh ſacerdotal dreſs, *no counterpart was
to be found in the actual dreſs of thoſe before him*, he ſpeaks of "the glory," and
the "unction," and the "Holy Spirit," as ſpiritual robes, which the prieſthood
of the new covenant may rightly claim as their own.

But among modern writers there are ſome who ſee the matter in a very
different light, and find in this paſſage proof that the biſhops of that day wore
mitres (κιδάϱεις) or prieſtly caps, after the model of the Jewiſh prieſts, and had
alſo ſacerdotal robes modelled upon the ſame ſtyle.

I leave it to my readers to decide between the two interpretations.

2. Another paſſage, cloſely reſembling this, is to be found in the fourth
diſcourſe of Gregory Nazianzen. [389] The paſſage referred to is the following.
He is addreſſing his father, then Biſhop of Nazianzum, who had been deſirous
of aſſociating his ſon with himſelf in the duties of the epiſcopal office, for
which at his greatly advanced age he felt himſelf unequal. St. Gregory ſays,
(referring to this), "Thou ſoughteſt that a ſecond Barnabas might be joined,
as helper, to thyſelf a ſecond Paul; that to Silvanus and Timotheus, a Titus
alſo ſhould be added, that ſo the gift of God that is in thee might have free
courſe, by means of them that naturally have care for thee, and that from
Jeruſalem round about unto Illyricum thou mighteſt fulfil the work of an
evangeliſt.' For this cauſe it is that thou bringeſt one forth, and ſetteſt him
in the midſt, and layeſt hold on him, though he would draw back, and ſetteſt
him beſide thyſelf (' This,' you will perhaps ſay, ' is my only wrong'); and
makeſt him partaker both of the cares of thine office, and of its crowns.
Therefore, [390] it is that thou anointeſt the chief prieſt, and putteſt about [him]

---

[388] Ὦ φίλοι Θεοῦ καὶ ἱεϱεῖς, οἱ τὸν ἅγιον
ποδήϱη, καὶ τὸν οὐϱάνιον τῆς δόξης στέφανον,
τό τε χϱίσμα τὸ ἐνθέον, καὶ τὴν ἱεϱατικὴν τοῦ
Ἁγίου Πνεύματος στολὴν, πεϱιβεβλημένοι. By
ἱεϱεῖς here mentioned we ſhould probably
underſtand *biſhops*. See note 61. The paſſage will be found in Euſeb. H. E. lib. x.
cap. 4.

[389] Born A.D. 324, Bp. of Conſtantinople in
378, died in 389. See vol. i. of his collected
works (Morell), p. 136, Oratio v. *in fin.*

[390] The original is as follows. διὰ τοῦτο

τίς μίσον ἅγιις, καὶ ὑπεχωϱοῦντος λαμβάνῃ,
καὶ παϱὰ σεαυτὸν καθίζεις· Τοῦτο τὸ ἐμὶν
ἀδίκημα, φαίης ἄν· καὶ κοινωνὸν ποιῇ τῶν
φϱοντίδων καὶ τῶν στεφάνων. διὰ τοῦτο χϱίεις
τὸν ἀϱχιεϱέα, καὶ πεϱιβάλλεις τὸν ποδήϱη, καὶ
πεϱιτίθης τὸν κίδαϱιν, καὶ πϱοσάγεις τῷ θυσια-
στηϱίῳ τῆς πνευματικῆς ὁλοκαυτώσεως, καὶ
θύεις τὸν μόσχον τῆς τελειώσεως, καὶ τελειοῖς
τὰς χεῖϱας τῷ πνεύματι, καὶ εἰσάγεις εἰς τὰ
ἅγια τῶν ἁγίων ἐπαττενίσαντα, καὶ ποιεῖς
λειτουϱγὸν τῆς σκηνῆς τῆς ἀληθινῆς, ἣν ἔπηξεν
ὁ Κύϱιος οὐκ ἄνθϱωπος.

the (ποδήρη) prieſtly robe, and ſetteſt the prieſt's cap about his head, and bringeſt him unto the altar of the ſpiritual burnt ſacrifice, and ſlayeſt the calf of conſecration, and doſt conſecrate his hands with the ſpirit, and bringeſt him into the holy of holies, as one that ſhall ſee the hidden things of the Lord, and makeſt him a miniſter of the true tabernacle, which the Lord pitched and not man. But whether he [39] be worthy both of you that anoint him, and of Him for whom, and unto whom, is that anointing, this He only knoweth who is the Father of the true 'anointed one' (Χριστός), whom He anointed with the oil of gladneſs above His fellows, beſtowing upon humanity the unction of divinity, ſo as to make of theſe twain one."

Upon this paſſage I need add little to what I have ſaid above upon the ſimilar language of Euſebius. It is evident that many of the expreſſions (ſuch as that of "*ſlaying the calf of conſecration*"), cannot by any poſſibility be regarded as more than figurative phraſes, drawn from the analogies of the rites of conſecration under the Levitical law. And this fact is enough to mark the character of the whole paſſage. On the other hand, it is only right to ſay, that there is a ſtrong probability that in purſuing this compariſon into detail, as he does, the writer would fix upon ſuch points in the older rites as had ſomething analogous to them in Chriſtian conſecration. The "ſticharion," or long white tunic of the Chriſtian miniſtry, offered a point of compariſon with the ποδήρης of Levitical miniſtry. And the mention of the κίδαρις which follows, would lead one to ſuppoſe that among the miniſtering veſtments of St. Gregory's time, there might be ſomething correſponding to the cap or mitre of the Levitical prieſt.

But the more direct evidence of antiquity points, as in the Introduction has been ſhown, to a directly oppoſite concluſion. And if St. Gregory really had preſent to his mind any epiſcopal veſtment (ſo to call it), which he regarded as correſpondent to the Levitical κίδαρις, I ſhould ſuppoſe that it was either a cloſe fitting ſkull-cap, ſuch as that which Euſebius of Cæſarea is repreſented as wearing, in Pl. XXVII., or ſome ſuch diſtinctive head-dreſs as that, with which, at a later time certainly, the *out-door dreſs* of biſhops and patriarchs was diſtinguiſhed.

Dr. Hefele, who has examined this queſtion at ſome length, after referring briefly to the two paſſages above quoted, goes on to ſpeak of the following paſſages, which he thinks point to an early uſe of a diſtinctive head-dreſs by Chriſtian biſhops.

3. Ammianus Marcellinus, lib. xxix. cap. 5. He deſcribes the ſubmiſſion of Firmus to Theodoſius, the general ſent into Mauritania againſt him. He ſays that, *Ne quid ultimæ rationis omitteret, Chriſtiani ritus antiſtites oraturos pacem cum obſidibus miſit.* Theſe being kindly received, two days later, *militaria ſigna et coronam ſacerdotalem cum cæteris quæ interceperat, nihil cunc-*

---

[39] St. Gregory is alluding throughout to himſelf, as the perſon who had been made biſhop againſt his own wiſh. But he avoids | direct mention of himſelf in the firſt perſon.

tatus reſtituit, ut præceptum eſt. The hiſtorian, who writes about this *corona ſacerdotalis* is himſelf a heathen ; and it is in the higheſt degree improbable, even on this ground only, that he ſhould uſe the term *ſacerdotalis* thus abſolutely in ſpeaking of Chriſtian biſhop or prieſt. There can be little, if any, doubt, that this was one of thoſe richer crowns, made of precious metal, which we know [392] to have been worn by the prieſts of ſome among the heathen gods.

4. Dr. Hefele alſo lays great ſtreſs (but I venture to think, without ſtrong ground for ſo doing) on paſſages [393] in which the word *infula* occurs in connection with Chriſtian veſtments. According to *claſſical* uſage *one* meaning of *infula* undoubtedly was that of a long band, made either of linen or of wool, which was faſtened about the head of prieſts, or hung round the neck, or the body, of victims [394] to be offered in ſacrifice. But the word was not confined to this meaning, but was often uſed of the inſignia of imperial or magiſterial rank, and had nearly the meaning (in ſome inſtances) of an " official veſtment," context alone determining what the nature of that veſtment might be. And I am confirmed in the belief that, in the paſſages quoted by Dr. Hefele, *infula* has this wider meaning, by finding moſt certain proof that, even as late as the twelfth century, the word was uſed as a ſynonym for the *caſula* or *planeta.* (See note 268, *in fin.* p. 133.)

5. Another paſſage is quoted from Ennodius, a Chriſtian poet (his Chriſtianity better than his poetry, we may charitably hope, after reading the lines that follow). He wrote about the cloſe of the fifth century. Speaking in praiſe of St. Ambroſe, he expreſſes himſelf as follows [Epig. 77] :

> *Roſcida regifico cui fulſit murice lingua,*
> *Vere ſuo pingens germina quæ voluit.*
> *Serta redimitus geſtabat lucida fronte ;*
> *Diſtinctum gemmis ore parabat opus.*

Dr. Hefele quotes the third line of this paſſage, without its context, as

---

[392] See, *e.g.* the quotation from Tertullian, *De Cor. Mil. ſupra*, p. xiv.

[393] Such are Prudentius Clemens, *Periſtephanon,* iv. 9. He is ſinging the praiſes of the city of Saragoſſa (Cæſar-Auguſta), and of the martyrs of whom it could boaſt. He adds, " *Hinc ſacerdotum domus infulata Valeriorum.*" He writes about the year 400 A.D., and refers in theſe words to Valerius, Bp. of Saragoſſa, and to others of the ſame family.

Again, Pope Gelaſius ſpeaks in one of his letters of a biſhop as being *clericalibus infulis reprobabilis* (unworthy to wear the dreſs of a cleric). Here the uſe of the plural confirms the interpretation given above.

In like manner in a life of St. Willibald,

written in the eighth century, his conſecration as biſhop is ſpoken of as the time when he had beſtowed upon him *ſacerdotalis infulæ honorem.*

And St. Boniface (note 209, p. 106) is repreſented (in a biography dating from the eleventh century) as writing to the Biſhop of Rome concerning Burchard of Wurzburg, to ſay that he was *pontificali infula dignus.*

[394] See, for example, Pl. III., where the bull, being led away for ſlaughter, has ſuch *infulæ* hung about him :

> Stans hoſtia ad aram,
> Lanea dum nivea circumdatur infula vitta.
> Virg.

a proof that bifhops in the days of St. Ambrofe wore a diftinctive head-drefs.[395]   But a moment's reference to the context is fufficient to fhow how entirely ungrounded is fuch an inference.[395a] Throughout thefe lines it is of the eloquence of St. Ambrofe that Ennodius is fpeaking ; and the *" bright garlands which crowned his brow,"* are no more to be taken literally, than is the *"royal purple,"* with which *" his tongue glowed,"* or the *" work bedecked with jewels,"* which he *" fafhioned with his lips."*

Other authorities quoted by Martene in fupport of the antiquity of the epifcopal *"* mitra," are the following :

6. Theodulfus, Bifhop of Orleans, writing *circ.* A.D. 800, is defcribing the *" Ornamenta Pontificis "* (fo Martene writes), and employs the following expreffion (lib. iii. carm. 5) :

<blockquote>Illius ergo caput refplendens mitra tegebat.</blockquote>

In this, Martene fees proof of the early ufe of the mitre by Chriftian bifhops. This, again, is a curious inftance of the miftakes to which even men of great learning are liable, when they quote, without reference to context, fingle lines, or it may be half-fentences, out of ancient authors, in fupport of pre-conceived conclufions.

The quotation is from lib v. carm. 3 (Sirmondi Opera, ii. p. 1106), part of a poem called *Parænefis ad Epifcopos*, written by Theodulph while yet a deacon (*Parva fed in magna cum fim Levitide turba Pars*, is his expreffion in referring to himfelf). In the poem, as it ftands in the edition of Sirmondus, the order of the verfes has evidently become confufed. But there is a long paffage in which a comparifon is made between the outward fplendour of the *pontifex*, or Jewifh high-prieft, and the ornament of diverfe virtues which fhould be confpicuous in the Chriftian "pontifex," or bifhop.

<blockquote>
Illius infignis radiabat lumine veftis,
    Blanditiafque hominum vifibus illa dabat :
At tibi virtutum dent ornamenta decorem,
    Atque oculis cordis, qua potes, ufque fave.
Illi erat in facro pollens reverentia cultu,
    Et decus in habitu pontificalis opis.
Sanĉta eft in fanĉta tibimet reverentia Matre,
    Et vitæ ftudiis, aĉtibus inque piis.
Aurea Pontificis cingebat lamina frontem,
    Qua bis binus apex Nomen Herile dabat.
At tibi frons mentis cingatur fenfibus almis,
    Chriftum Evangelico vox et ab ore fonet.
Sint manifefti aĉtus Fidei, probitatis, et æqui,
    Qui fit virtutum quattuor ordo tibi.
</blockquote>

---

[395] Beiträge, u. 1. w. p. 227. *Aliquando bonus dormitat Homerus.* Dr. Hefele's criti-cifm is generally very accurate, and very un-prejudiced, as far as I have had opportunities of judging. The paffage here commented upon muft not be regarded as a typical fpe-cimen of the author, but quite the reverfe.

[395a] So Hugo Menardus pointed out long ago. See his notes to the Sacramentary of St. Gregory, p. 363.

Then after about hundred lines come in the two following verfes, in a context to which they have no reference whatever :

Illius ergo caput refplendens mitra tegebat :
Contegat et (at ?) mentem jus pictafque tuam.

So far from proving, as Martene thought, the ufe of an epifcopal mitre in France at the clofe of the eighth century, the evidence of this paffage (when examined with its context) points, as will now be feen, to a directly oppofite conclufion. The lines I have quoted are nothing more than a reproduction, in Latin verfes, fuch as were written in thofe times, of the language of Venerable Bede, quoted in p. 78, and commented on in the Introduction. And Theodulphus probably owed the idea, which he has here amplified, to the fame fource as did Bede, viz, to the prayer ufed in the confecration of bifhops, quoted above, Introd. note *t*, p. li.

It is inftructive, on many accounts, to the ftudent of antiquity, to fee in the examples above given, how plaufible a cafe may be made out in favour of any preconceived conclufion, by dint of mutilated quotations fet forth without reference to context. Inftructive, too, to mark (I am obliged to add), how little weight fhould be given, in difputed queftions fuch as thefe, to the reputation, even though deferved, of great and varied learning, on the part of thofe who write concerning them. Erudition, fuch as that of Edmond Martene ; accurate fcholarfhip, thorough impartiality, careful refearch, fuch as are confpicuous in Dr. Hefele ; may all be employed in laborioufly building up arguments, which fall to the ground, as in a moment, when the witneffes, to whom they appeal, are allowed to tell their own tale in full.

I fay this of archæologifts, to whom it applies in fome meafure. But I commend the remark to theologians, to whom, unfortunately, it applies much more.

APPENDIX C.

PASSAGES FROM ANCIENT AUTHORS ILLUSTRATING THE HISTORY OF THE PÆNULA, CASULA, AND PLANETA.

PART I. THE PÆNULA.

1. Plautus (born *circ.* 254 B c.), *Moft.* iv. 11, 74. [Theuropides fays, angrily, to a flave with whom he is difpleafed] :

Jamne abis ? Libertas pænula eft tergo tuo.

" It is only that big cloak of yours that faves your back." Literally, Thy pænula is liberty (*i.e.* the privileges of a free man) to thy back.

2. Lucilius (born B.C. 148), *Sat.* lib. xv. Fr. 6.

> *Pænula, ſi quæris, cantherius, ſervus, ſegeſtre,*
> *Utilior mibi, quam ſapiens.*

3. Cicero (born 106 B.C.), *Pro Milone.* He is ſhowing from the mode in which Milo travelled that he could not have fet out with the intention of attacking Clodius. He ſtates (p. 524, 20) that while Clodius (really bent on violence) had left the city *expeditus, in equo, nulla rheda, nullis impedimentis,* Milo, on the contrary (who had been falſely accuſed of treacherous and intended violence) " *cum uxore veheretur in rheda pænulatus.*" Accordingly, as foon as the followers of Milo attacked him, the firſt thing he did was *rejicere pænulam,* which, by its form and its weight, confined his arms and prevented his de-fending himſelf. *Cum hic (ſc.* Milo) *de rheda, rejeſta pænula, deſiluiſſet, ſeque acri animo defenderet.* And theſe circumſtances, he argues (p. 518, 40), proved of themſelves, " Uter eſſet inſidiator, uter nihil cogitaret mali ; cum alter veheretur in rheda pænulatus, una federet uxor. Quid horum non impeditiſſimum, veſtitus (ſe. pænula) an vehiculum, an comes ? Quid minus promptum ad pugnam, cum pænula irretitus" (entangled in his pænula as in a net), rheda impeditus, uxore pene conſtriſtus eſſet ? "

4. From another paſſage, *pro P. Seſtio,* p. 444 (70), we learn that a rough pænula was commonly worn by mule-drivers, and the like.
" Senſit ruſticulus . . . ſuum ſanguinem quæri . . . mulioniam pænulam arripuit, cum qua primum Romam ad comitia venerat, meſſoria ſe corbe contexit."

5. From its being commonly worn in travelling, *pænulam attingere alicui* ſeems to have been a proverbial phraſe, for what we ſhould call " keeping a man by the button."
Cic. Ad Atticum, lib. vi. p. 288 (113). *Paullo poſt C. Capito cum T. Carri-nate. Horum ego vix attigi pænulam, et tamen remanſerunt.* And to the ſame effeſt juſt before : " De Varrone loquebamur. Lupus in fabula " (" Talk of the devil ! "), " *venit enim ad me, et quidem id temporis ut retinendus eſſet. Sed ego ita egi ut non ſcinderem pænulam.*" In other words, he was not *over preſſing* in his expreſſions of civility, when he inquired whether he would not ſtay. He did not " tear his cloak " rather than let him go.

6. Varro (born B.C. 82), *apud Nonnium,* 14, n. 3.
" Non quærenda eſt homini, qui habet virtutem, pænula in imbri."

7. Horace (born 65 B.C.), 1 Ep. xi. 18.

> *Incolumi Rhodos, aut Mitylene pulchra facit, quod*
> *Pænula ſolſtitio, campeſtre nivalibus auris.*

" If not compelled to live at Rhodes, or at Mitylene, by ill health, a man would no more take up his abode there for good, than he would wear a thick cloak, such as the pænula, at midsummer, or the dress of the exercise ground (scarcely to be called dress) in midwinter."

8. Seneca (born 61 B.C.) *Epist.* lxxxvii. He is describing a little riding tour which he had taken with his friend Maximus, and the manner in which they bivouacked.

Culcita (a mattrass) *in terra jacet, ego in culcita. Ex duabus pænulis altera stragulum, altera opertorium facta est.*

" One pænula served the purpose of a blanket under him ; the other that of a coverlet to throw over him."

9. *Martial* (43 to 104 A.D.) To him, writing at Rome towards the close of the first century of our era, *pænulatus* is an epithet implying a position below that of a gentleman ; while *togatus* (see above, p. 177, No. 9) means a *"needy* gentleman," one not altogether independent of others, and obliged therefore to pay ceremonious court to the rich and influential, to whom he is under obligation. Epig. lib. v. 27.

> *Quod Alpha dixi, Codre, penulatorum*
> *Te nuper, aliqua cum jocarer in charta ;*
> *Si forte bilem movit hic tibi versus,*
> *Dicas licebit Beta me togatorum.*

10. But people of all ranks would wear a *pænula* (as we should carry an umbrella) when on a journey. Hence the allusion in the following lines, where " scortea " means a rough pænula made of sheep-skin or the like. Compare No. 7 :

> *Ingrediare viam cælo licet usque sereno,*
> *Ad subitas nunquam scortea desit aquas.*

11. Another kind of *pænula* known as *gausapina* was of fine and white wool, and so handsome withal, that people who were vain of their dress are represented as wishing for cold weather *that they might have an excuse for wearing them.*

> *Et dolet et queritur sibi non contingere frigus,*
> *Propter sexcentas Baccara gausapinas.*
>
> Epig. lib. vi. 59.
>
> *Pænula gausapina.*
>
> *Is mihi candor inest, villorum gratia tanta est,*
> *Ut me vel media sumere messe velis.*
>
> Epig. lib. xiv. 145.

12. Juvenal (writing circ. 100 A.D.) *Sat.* v.

> *Scilicet hoc fuerat, propter quod sæpe relicta*
> *Conjuge, per montem adversum gelidasque cucurri*
> *Esquilias, fremeret læva cum grandine vernus*
> *Jupiter, et multo stillaret pænula nimbo.*

13. Emperor Adrian (Imp. 117 to 138 A.D.). Lampridius in *Adriano.* " Tribunus plebis factus est, in quo magistratu ad perpetuam tribunitiam po-

teftatem (*i.e.*, to *imperial* power) omen fibi factum afferit, quod pænulas ami-
ferit, quibus uti Tribuni plebis pluviæ tempore folebant, Imperatores autem
nunquam. Unde hodieque Imperatores fine penulis ac togati videntur."

14. Emperor Commodus (Imp. 180 to 192 A.D.) Lampridius in *Commodo.*
[He is fpeaking of a fhow of gladiators (*munus*) exhibited in the circus.]
"Ipfe prodigium non leve fibi fecit. Nam cum in gladiatoris occifi vulnere
manum mififfet, ad caput fibi deterfit; et contra confuetudinem pænulatos
juffit Senatores, non togatos, ad munus convenire, quod in funeribus folebat,
ipfe in pullis veftimentis præfidens."

15. Emperor Alexander Severus (Imp. 222 to 235). Lampridius in
Alexandro. "Pænulis intra urbem frigoris caufa ut Senatores uterentur
permifit." *Ibid.* "Matronas intra urbem pænulis ubi vetuit, in itinere
permifit."

16. Julius Pollux, tom. ii. lib. vii. cap. 13, p. 729. [*Floruit circa*
185 A.D.] ἡ δὲ μανδύη ὁμοιόν τι τῷ καλουμένῳ Φαινόλῃ· Τίνων δί ἐστιν, ὡς μὴ
περιεχόμεθα (*fort.* περιεχόμεθα, Salmas. vel περιεχώμεθα, *i.e.*, ne oberremus
Kuhn), Κρήσσαις ἢ Πέρσαις Αἰσχύλος ἐρεῖ· Λιβυρνικῆς μίμημα μανδύης χιτών·
Καὶ αὐτὸς δὲ ὁ Φαινόλης·[396] ἐστὶν ἐν Ῥίνθωνος Ἰφιγενίᾳ τῇ ἐν Ταύροις· ἐχούσῃ (*leg.*
ἔχουσα) καινὰν Φαινόλην.[397]

From this paffage we learn that the Greek *pænula* in the fecond century
was fomewhat like in fhape to the μανδύη (note 153). This agrees with what
we have already quoted from Artemidorus (*fupra*, Appendix A, No. 11 *i*, p.
180). We learn, too, that the φαινόλη was as old, at leaft, as the time of
Rhinthon (*circ.* 320 B.C.). But there are reafons for thinking that it was very
much older than this.[398]

17. Tertullian (died *circ.* 230 A.D.) *De Oratione*, cap. 12 (tom. iv. p. 14).
[He had been fpeaking of the fuperftitious ufe of various ablutions practifed
by fome in his time, and faying that "*fatis mundæ funt manus, quas cum toto
corpore in Chrifto femel lavimus*" (his thought being of John, xiii. 10). He
follows out his fubject as follows:]

"Sed quoniam unum aliquod attigimus vacuæ obfervationis, non pigebit

---

[396] Compare alfo the expreffion ufed in the
Dialogus de caufis corruptæ eloquentiæ (probably
Quintilian's). *Quantum humilitatis putamus
eloquentiæ attuliffe pænulas iftas, quibus adftricti
ac velut inclufi, cum judicibus fabulamur?*

[397] We have here two forms, φαινόλης and
φαινόλη (here quoted from Rhinthon, a dra-
matic poet, in its Doric form φαινόλα). In
the older Greek, the feminine form φαινόλα
was ufed in fpeaking of the finer and lighter
garment worn by women, the mafculine
φαινόλης of that worn by men. The later

Byzantine Greek, obliterating, as was its wont,
thefe finer diftinctions, merged them both in
the neuter φαινόλιον.

[398] Tertullian ftates (Apolog. adv. Gentes)
that the pænula was "invented" by the Lace-
dæmonians, to enable them, as fpectators, to
enjoy, even in cold weather, the fpectacles of
the ftadium. *Ne voluptas impudica frigeret,
Lacedæmonii pænulam ludis excogitarunt.* But
an unfupported ftatement of this kind does
not carry much weight.

cetera quoque denotare, quibus merito vanitas exprobranda eſt, ſiquidem ſinc ullius aut Dominici aut Apoſtolici præcepti auctoritate fiunt. Hujuſmodi enim non religioni ſed ſuperſtitioni deputantur, affectata et coacta, et curioſi potius quam rationalis officii, certe vel eo coercenda, quod gentilibus adæquent. Ut eſt quorundam poſitis pænulis orationem facere: ſic enim adeunt ad idola nationes. Quod utique ſi fieri oporteret, Apoſtoli, qui de habitu orandi docent, comprehendiſſent; niſi ſi qui putant [399] Paulum pænulam ſuam in. oratione penes Carpum reliquiſſe. Deus ſcilicet non audiat pænulatos; qui tres ſanctos in fornace Babylonii regis orantes cum Sarabaris et Tiaris ſuis exaudivit."

[This is a very inſtructive paſſage concerning the Pænula. From it we learn that heathen worſhippers, in Tertullian's time, thought it indecorous to wear a Pænula when engaged in public prayer, that on ſuch occaſions therefore they put them off. We learn, too, that many Chriſtians had adopted the ſame cuſtom, and that ſuch ſcruples were regarded by Tertullian as favouring of ſuperſtition rather than of religion. He then puts it as an abſurd (note 399) ſuppoſition, which ſome might poſſibly adopt, that St. Paul loſt his Pænula in conſequence of his taking it off when about to engage in prayer at the houſe of Carpus. As to St. Paul's Pænula being itſelf a "ſacrificial veſtment," it is evident that ſuch an idea had never entered Tertullian's head. No one having any real acquaintance with antiquity could ſuppoſe ſo now. The "ſuperſtition," in Tertullian's time, was that of ſuppoſing that it was ſuch a garment as none could fitly appear in church at all.

18. From another paſſage of Tertullian (*De Cor. Mil.* p. 346) we find that, in his time, the Pænula was worn by ſoldiers, not of courſe when actively engaged (compare No. 3), but much as our own ſoldiers wear "great-coats" for protection againſt the weather. He is ſpeaking of a Chriſtian ſoldier, who had refuſed to wear the *corona* of heathen ſacrificial rites. *Reus ad præfectos. Ibidem graviſſimas pænulas poſuit, relevari auſpicatus.* A ſimilar uſe of the Pænula by ſoldiers appears in a paſſage of Suetonius (in Galba). Speaking of Ser. Sulpicius Galba (afterwards emperor) in the year 45 A.D., he ſays, "A Caio Cæſare Gætulico ſubſtitutus, poſtridie quam ad legiones venit, ſollenni forte ſpectaculo plaudentes inhibuit, data teſſera ut manus pænulis continerent."

19. St. Jerome, ad *Damaſum*, Epiſt. cxxv. 9, 2. "Volumen [400] Hebræum replico, quod Paulus Φαιλόνην juxta quoſdam vocat." [Compare No. 21, below.]

20. *Ibid.* in 2, Epiſt. ad Timoth. iv. 13.[401] "*Pænulam quam reliqui, &c.* Non dixit pænulam meam: potuit enim converſus aliquis, ad pedes ejus, inter cætera, impoſuiſſe vendendum." [Ed. Benedict. vol. v. p. 1100.] *He ſuppoſes*

---

[399] *Niſi ſi qui putant.* This is a formula with which Tertullian introduces a hypotheſis, the abſurdity of which he deems to be ſelf-evident. Compare the paſſage quoted above, Appendix A, No. 42, *niſi ſi non potuit Deus* etc.

[400] He uſes the words *volumen* and *replico* in their technical ſenſe. See note 79, p. 50.

See, too, the words of Theodoret (on 2 Tim. iv. 13) quoted under No. 21, note 403.

[401] This commentary on 2 Ep. Tim. is regarded as ſpurious by the Benedictine editors. But the authorſhip is not, to the preſent queſtion, a matter of primary importance.

that this Pænula may have been brought by some convert, as a superfluity of which to make an offering to God, "laying it at the apostles' feet " (Acts, iv. 35), that it might afterwards be sold, and the proceeds made use of as St. Paul should think fit.

21. St. John Chrysostom (born *circ.* 347, died 407 A.D.) Tom. xi. p. 780 A, in 2 Tim. iv. 13. Τὸν Φιλόνην ὃν ἀπέλιπον ἐν Τρωάδι παρὰ Κάρπω, ἐρχόμενος φέρε, καὶ τὰ βιβλία, μάλιστα τὰς μεμβράνας. Φιλόνην ἐνταῦθα τὸ ἱμάτιον λέγει. Τινὲς δὲ φασὶ τὸ γλωσσόκομον,[402] ἔνθα τὰ βιβλία ἔκειτο. Τί δὲ αὐτῷ τῶν βιβλίων ἔδει μέλλοντι ἀποδημεῖν πρὸς τὸν Θεόν; Καὶ μάλιστα ἔδει, ὥστε αὐτὰ τοῖς πιστοῖς παραδίσθαι, καὶ ἀντὶ τῆς αὐτοῦ διδασκαλίας ἔχειν αὐτά . . . . Τὸν δὲ Φιλόνην ζητεῖ ὥστε μὴ δεηθῆναι παρ' ἑτέρου λαβεῖν.

"By the word φιλόνης, here used, is meant the outer garment so called. But some think that it was the case (*capsa*) in which lay the Books.[403] But for what could he need these Books, when he was about to depart hence unto God ? Nay, he had in truth the greatest need of them, that so he might commit them into the hands of the faithful, to be to them in place of his own teaching. . . . And his inquiring for this cloak was for this cause, that he might not need to receive one (as a gift) from some other. For thou seest that this is a matter about which he is specially careful, saying, as he does, in another place, when discoursing to them of Ephesus, *Ye know that these my hands did minister to my necessities, and to them that were with me.* And again, *It is blessed to give rather than to receive.*"

It is evident from the above that St. Chrysostom regarded the φιλόνης of St. Paul as an ordinary ἱμάτιον; and that the *membranæ*, or parchments, were in his judgment MSS. containing St. Paul's own teaching.

22 The Theodosian Code, published in 438 A.D., and that simultaneously for the Eastern and the Western empire, furnishes us with an important indication of the changed use of the Pænula established by that time. In lib. i. *De Habitu*, we read as follows :

"Nullus senatorum habitum sibi vindicet militarem, sed chlamydis terrore deposito, quieta colobiorum ac pænularum induat vestimenta. . . . officiales quoque per quos statuta complentur ac necessaria peraguntur, uti quidem pænulis jubemus, verum interiorem vestem admodum cingulis observare."

The chlamys being (note 142) a military garb, is unsuited for senators when at Rome. In earlier times their proper garb would have been the *tunica laticlavia* and the *toga.* The corresponding vestments are now (fifth century) the *colobium* and *pænula.*

---

[402] That is a case for books, such, perhaps, as is represented in Pl. XII., XIV.

[403] For this interpretation of τὰς μεμβράνας, compare Theodoret on this passage. He follows St. Chrysostom closely as was his wont. Μιμβράνας τὰ εἴλητα κίκληκε ' (εἴλητον i.e.

volumen) οὕτω γὰρ Ῥωμαῖοι καλοῦσι τὰ δέρματα. Ἐν εἰλητοῖς δὲ εἶχον πάλαι τὰς ἰδίας γραφάς. Οὕτω δὲ καὶ μέχρι τοῦ παρόντος ἔχουσιν οἱ Ἰουδαῖοι. [This may be said with truth of the Jews even to the present day.]

23. St. Isidore of Seville, *circ.* 600 A.D. See the quotation at p. 72 and note 130 *in loc.* This passage, however, does not prove any *contemporary* usage of the word Pænula, either in Spain or in other parts of the West. For the gloss in question is simply transferred (as was St. Isidore's wont) *totidem verbis* from a *vetus interpres* on Persius.

24. St. Germanus, Patriarch of Constantinople, *circ.* 715 A.D. See his words quoted at p. 84, l. 4. From another mention of the Phænolion at p. 86, l. 1, we learn that in the eighth century, at Constantinople, if not elsewhere, this vestment was either of a purple or a scarlet colour, or at least of a colour which served to recall the "scarlet (or purple) robe" put in mockery upon our Lord.

25. Patriarch Nicephorus of Constantinople writes (in the year 811) to Leo III., *inter alia :*

"In signum mediatricis inter nos in Domino dilectionis, misimus vestræ fraternæ beatitudini encolpion [315] aureum, cujus una facies cristallum inclusum, altera picta nigello [401] est, et intus habet alterum encolpion, in quo sunt partes honorandi ligni in figura Crucis positi : tunicam candidam, et pænulam castaneam inconsutilem (*leg.* inconsutiles) ; stolam et semicinctium,[405] auro variata."

The word *pænula*, here used, represents the φαινόλης (or more probably φαινόλιον) of the original text. The description of this φαινόλιον as ἄῤῥαφον (*inconsutilis*) may be regarded as probably pointing to those words of St. John, ἦν δὲ ὁ χιτὼν ἄραφος (*al.* ἄῤῥαφος) ἐκ τῶν ἄνωθεν ὑφαντὸς δι᾽ ὅλου.

Part II. The Casula.

26. The earliest notices of the Casula are two following from St. Augustine (born 354, died 430).

The Casula as an Out-door Dress for Working Men, *circ.* 350 A.D.

α. *De Civit. Dei,* lib. xxii. cap. 8, § 9. "Erat quidam senex Florentius, Hipponensis noster, homo religiosus et pauper ; sartoris se arte pascebat. Casulam perdiderat, et unde sibi emeret non habebat. Ad [406] Viginti Martyres, quorum

---

[401] δι᾽ ἐγκαύσεως. Enamelling. Baronius edits the letter from the Latin of Anastasius Bibliothecarius. The original Greek text will be found in Harduin's Concilia, vol. iv. p. 1000.

[405] ἐγχείριον. A handkerchief. Here, probably, something resembling the *sudarium* or *mappula* of the Latin Church. *Stola* is here used as the Latin rendering of ἐπιτραχήλιον, which corresponded (see note 144 p. 84) to the Orarium or Stola of the West.

[406] *Ad viginti, &c.* "At the chapel of the twenty Martyrs." The word "memoria," which follows is here used in its technical sense of a "memorial chapel," or church. St. Augustine's Sermon CCCXXV. is on the "birthday" (day of martyrdom) of these "twenty martyrs," whose number "cœpit ab Episcopo Fidentio, clausit ad fidelem feminam sanctam Victoriam. Initium a fide. Finis ad victoriam."

memoria apud nos eſt celeberrima, clara voce, ut veſtiretur, oravit. Audierunt eum adoleſcentes, qui forte aderant, irriſores ; eumque diſcedentem exagitantes proſequebantur, quaſi a Martyribus quinquagenos folles, unde veſtimentum emeret, petiviſſet. At ille tacitus ambulans ejectum grandem piſcem palpitantem vidit in littore, eumque illis faventibus atque adjuvantibus apprehendit, et cuidam coquo, Catoſo nomine, bene Chriſtiano, ad coquinam conditariam, indicans quid geſtum ſit, trecenis follibus vendidit ; lanam comparare inde diſponens, ut uxor ejus, quomodo poſſet, ei, quo indueretur, efficeret. Sed coquus, concidens piſcem, annulum aureum in ventriculo ejus invenit ; moxque miſeratione flexus, et relligione perterritus, homini eum reddidit, dicens, Ecce quomodo Viginti Martyres te veſtierunt."

THE CASULA AN ORDINARY OUT-DOOR GARB, *circ.* 400 A.D.

27. β. *Ibid.* Sermo CVII. cap. 5 (tom. v. p. 530). "Quid eſt iniquius homine qui multa bona habere vult, et bonus ipſe eſſe non vult? Indignus es qui habeas, qui non vis eſſe quod vis habere. Numquid enim vis habere villam malam? Non utique, ſed bonam. Numquid uxorem malam? Non, ſed bonam. Numquid denique caſulam malam? Numquid vel caligam malam? Quare animam ſolum malam?"

THE CASULA WORN BY MONKS (AND BY BISHOPS IN MONASTIC LIFE),
circ. 500 A.D.

28. Of Fulgentius, Biſhop of Ruſpa (*circ.* 507), his diſciple and biographer Ferrandus writes as follows, l. 18 (*apud Thomaſſinum, Vet. et Nov. Ecc. Diſc.* lib. ii. cap. 47) :

"Nunquam pretioſa veſtimenta quæſivit : una tantum viliſſima tunica, ſive per æſtatem, ſive per hiemem, eſt patienter indutus. *Orario quidem ſicut omnes epiſcopi nullatenus utebatur. Pellicio cingulo* (note 74) *tanquam monachus utebatur . . . . Caſulam pretioſam vel ſuperbi coloris nec ipſe habuit, nec ſuos monachos habere permiſit.*[407] . . . . In qua tunica dormiebat in ipſa ſacrificabat ; et in tempore ſacrificii mutanda eſſe corda potius quam veſtimenta dicebat."

A CASULA WORN (AS A CLOAK) BY AN ARCHBISHOP.

29. Extracts from the laſt will and teſtament of S. Cæſarius, Archbiſhop

---

[407] Compare what is ſaid, by Ven. Bede, of S. Cuthbert and the monks of Lindisfarne (Vita S. Cuthberti, cap. 16, Bedæ Opera, tom. iv. p. 262). "Veſtimentis utebatur communibus, ita temperanter agens, ut horum neque munditiis neque ſordibus eſſet notabilis. Unde uſque hodie in eodem monaſterio exemplo ejus obſervatur, ne quis varii aut pretioſi coloris habeat indumentum, ſed ea maxime veſtium ſpecie ſint contenti, quam naturalis ovium lana (note δ, p. xviii) miniſtrat."

of Arles, † 540. [A copy of this will was obtained for Baronius, from the
archives preferved at Arles.   See the *Annal.* tom. vi. p. 602, *ſqq.*] " Sanͨto
et domino meo archiepiſcopo, qui mihi indigno digne ſuſceſſerit, licet omnia in
fua poteſtate ſint, tamen, fi lubet, et dignum ducit, indumenta paſchalia [408]
quæ mihi data funt, omnia illi ſerviant, ſimul cum caſula villoſa [409] et tunica
vel galnape quod melius dimiſero.   Reliqua vero veſtimenta mea, excepto
birro amiculari, mei tam clerici quam laici, cum gratia vel ordinatione domini
archiepiſcopi, fibi ipſo jubente, immo donante, dividant."

30. [In the life of the ſame Archbiſhop Cæſarius, we find mention of
his wearing a Caſula both in his ordinary walks about the city, and in pro-
ceſſions.]   " Ambulans per plateam civitatis, vidit contra in foro hominem qui
a dæmonio agebatur.   In quem cum attendiſſet, *habens manum ſub caſula, ut
a ſuis non videretur, crucem contra eum fecit.*"   And again:

31. Lib. ii. cap. 19. [A poor man begs of him, and the biſhop having no
money to give him] "*caſulam qua in proceſſionibus utebatur,* et albam paſchalem [108]
profert, datque egeno, jubetque ut vendat uni ex clero."

THE CASULA A DRESS FOR PEASANTS, *circ.* 530 A.D.

32. Procopius (Fl. *circa* 530 A.D.) *De Bello Vandalico,* lib. ii. cap. 26.
He is deſcribing the abject ſubmiſſion of Areobindus when defeated by Gon-
tharis.   He ſpeaks of him as ἱμάτιον ἀμπιχόμενος οὔτε στρατηγῷ οὔτε ἄλλῳ
στρατευομένῳ ἀνδρὶ ἐπιτηδείως ἴχον, ἀλλὰ δούλῳ καὶ ἰδιώτῃ παντάπασι πρέπον,
Κασοῦλαν αὐτὸ τῇ Λατίνων φωνῇ καλοῦσι 'Ρωμαῖοι.[410]

CASULA AS AN OUT-DOOR DRESS AT ROME, *circ.* 600 A.D.

33. S. *Gregorii Vita* a Joanne Diacono conſcripta, lib. iv. cap. 63.   The
biographer quotes a ſtory of St. Gregory told by Abbot John, a Perſian.
" Olim ivi Romam ad adorandum loculos ſanͨtorum apoſtolorum Petri et
Pauli: et una dierum cum ſtarem in medio civitatis, video Papam Gregorium
per (prope ?) me tranſiturum : et cogitavi me mittere ante eum.   Cum ergo
appropinquaſſet mihi Papa, videns quia pergerem ut mitterem me ante eum, [411]
ſicut coram Deo dico, fratres, primus miſit ſe ante me ſuper terram : et non

---

[408] By the *alba paſchalis,* here mentioned,
we are probably to underſtand an alb of ſome
more than uſually rich material to be uſed at
the Eaſter feſtival.   Dr. Hefele, however, in-
terprets the parallel expreſſion *indumenta paſchalia,* (*ſupra,* No. 29) as " Sonntagsgewünder."
I can hardly ſuppoſe this to be correct.

[409] Dr. Hefele obſerves (D. L. G. p. 196) that
this *caſula villoſa,* or long-napped cloak, is
here diſtinguiſhed from the *indumenta paſchalia*

(note 409), and is a garment for out-door
wear, not an eccleſiaſtical "veſtment," properly
ſo called.

[410] Procopius evidently conſiders the *caſula*
to be a garb fit only for peaſants.   It is aſſumed on this occaſion as a *veſtis ſordida,* in
token of abject humility and ſubjection.

[411] *Me mittere ad eum,* i.e., " bowing himſelf to the ground before him," as is the
wont of Eaſtern people.

ante furrexit, quam ego prior furgerem ; et amplexatus me cum multa humilitate, *tribuit mihi per manum numifmata tria: et juffit mihi dari cafulam
et neceffitates meas omnes.*"

A Casula sent as a Present to a King.

34. Bonifacii III. PP. Epift. iii. (*apud O. Ferrarium, D. R. V.* p. 685,)
a.d. 606. "Litteras et munufcula parva tranfmitto vobis, id eft, Cafulam non
holofericam, fed caprina lanugine miftam, et villofam, ad tergendos pedes [414]
dilectionis veftræ."

35. St. Ifidore, *Hifp. De Originibus*, lib. xix. (quoted above, at p. 74),
circ. a.d. 620. He does not mention the Cafula as in any way a *facred*
veftment, but merely defcribes it as a *veftis eucullata.*

A Casula the Out-Door Dress of the Clergy.

36. Concilium Germanicum I. Celebratum xi. Kal. Mai, a.d. 742. Sub
Carlemanno Majore Domus Regiæ, auctoritate S. Bonifacii, Can. vii. "De-
crevimus [415] quoque ut prefbyteri vel diaconi non fagis laicorum more, fed
cafulis utantur, ritu fervorum [416] Dei." [Labbe, Concil. tom. vi. p. 1533,
fqq.]

37. To the paffages above given may be added a reference to a fingular
fragment, illuftrating the old Gallican ufe, and which may poffibly date from
the eighth [417] century, though it would feem to belong rather to the ninth.
See Appendix E. The fecond paragraph, there quoted, contains not only a

---

[414] This letter is addreffed to king Pepin.
It is difficult to underftand how a cafula
fhould be ufed *ad tergendos pedes.* Either
therefore *villefa* muft here be taken as a
virtual fubftantive (compare *linea, alba, gau-
fapina, fcortea*), or we muft fuppofe fome word
fuch as *mappam* to have been dropped.

[415] It is worth noting as a characteriftic
feature of thefe times, that the decrees of this
Council iffue in the name of "*Ego Carleman-
nus Dux et Princeps Francorum,*" acting "*cum
confilio fervorum Dei et optimatum meorum ;*"
and in purfuance of fuch counfel, decreeing
(*ftatuimus*) that fynods fhould be held, yearly,
"*ita ut nobis præfentibus canonum decreta et ecclefiæ jura reftaurentur, et religio Chriftiana
emendetur.*"

[416] In fpeaking of the Cafula as befitting
thofe who are "*fervi*" of God, St. Boniface
may not improbably have had in view the
lowly origin of this garb, as worn by peafants
and by monks. The *fagum*, which prefbyters
and deacons in Germany are forbidden to

wear, is the fhort military cloak which in
the eighth century had come into general
fecular ufe. Some (as Dr. Hefele) underftand
the words *ritu fervorum Dei* to mean "as do
monks." But in the Preface, quoted in note
415, the words evidently are ufed of "the
clergy."

[417] There is mention made of the *cafula*
as the veftment of a prefbyter in the Sacramentary of St. Gregory, and from this fome
writers have careleffly inferred that the cafula
muft *in his time*, i.e., *circ.* 600 a.d., have been
recognifed as a veftment of Chriftian miniftry.
But, as Profeffor Hefele remarks, the Sacramentary proves nothing of the kind, feeing
that it dates, *in its prefent form*, from a period
confiderably later than St. Gregory, probably
not earlier than the ninth century. The
words occur in the *Ordinatio Prefbyteri*, p.
238, when, juft before the bleffing is conferred, the direction following is given : *Hic
veftis et cafulam*, i.e. At this point thou art to
inveft him with the chafuble.

reference to the Chasuble as a vestment of holy ministration, but a description of its form. *Casula . . . sine manicis, unita prinsecus, non scissa non aperta.* See p. 204, below.

PLANETA TOO COSTLY TO BE WORN BY MONKS.

38. Cassianus (*circ.* 418 A.D.) *De Habitu Monachorum*, lib. i. cap. 7. "Post hæc angusto palliolo tam amictus humilitatem, quam vilitatem pretii compendiumqne sectantes, colla pariter atque humeros tegunt quæ masortes tam nostro quam ipsorum nuncupantur eloquio, et ita Planeticarum simul atque birrorum (note *ω*, p. lvi) pretia simul et ambitionem declinant."

THE PLANETA WORN BY LAYMEN OF RANK.

39. Vita S. Fulgentii († 533) *Acta Sanctorum*, tom. i. Januar. p. 43. [The writer, Nolanus, a contemporary of Fulgentius, is describing the return of Fulgentius to Carthage after his exile.] "Tantum fides Nobilium crevit, ut Planctis suis super B. Fulgentium gratanter expansis, repellerent imbres, et novum tabernaculi genus artificiosa caritate componerent."

PLANETA WORN BY THE ATTENDANTS OF A BISHOP OF ROME.

40. Joan. Diac. Vita D. Gregorii, lib. ii. cap. 43. [The writer is speaking of a plot laid by certain sorcerers (*magi*) to throw St. Gregory off his horse as he rode through the city.] "Cumque magi ex planetatorum [42] mappulatorumque processionibus magnum pontificem cognovissent," &c., &c.

PLANETA WORN BY A ROMAN SENATOR, AND A ROMAN BISHOP.

41. Joan. Diac. Vita D. Gregorii, lib. iv. cap. 83. [Describing the dress of Gordianus, a senator, father of St. Gregory, he says,] "Gordiani habitus castanei coloris planeta est, sub planeta dalmatica, in pedibus caligas habens."

And in cap. 84, speaking of St. Gregory himself, "Planeta super dalmaticam castanea."

THE PLANETA NOT TO BE WORN BY MONKS.

42. St. Isidore (*circ.* 620), *in Regula*, cap. 13 (*apud Ducange*). "Linteo non licet Monachum indui. Orarium, birros, planetas, non est fas uti, neque illa indumenta vel calceamenta quæ generaliter cætera monasteria abutuntur" ("do not use").

---

[42] The people dressed in *planeta* are probably presbyters, and high officials; the mappulati, deacons, and sub-deacons.

THE PLANETA WORN AS A DISTINCTIVE VESTMENT BY BISHOPS AND PRESBYTERS.

43. *Concil. Tolet.* iv. *ann.* 634. See p. 75, *sqq.*

A PLANETA ONE OF THE VESTMENTS OF A POPE.

44. *Ordo Romanus* i. (eleventh century), *apud Mabillon, Museum Italicum,* and Martene *De Antiq. Eccl. Rit.* tom. ii. lib. iii. cap. 11.

In § 6 the vestments of the Pontifex Romanus are enumerated :

"Subdiaconi regionarii fecundum ordinem fuum accipiunt ad induendum Pontificem ipfa veftimenta: alius lineam, alius cingulum, alius anagolaium, id eft amictum, alius lineam dalmaticam, et alius majorem dalmaticam, *et alius planetam;* et fic per ordinem induunt Pontificem. . . . Noviffime autem, quem voluerit Dominus pontifex de diaconibus, vel fubdiaconibus, cui ipfe jufferit, fumit de manu fubdiaconi fequentis pallium, et induit fuper Pontificem, et configit eum cum acubus in planeta retro et ante, et in humero finiftro et falutat Domnum et dicit," &c.

PLANETA WORN BY DEACONS, SUB-DEACONS, ACOLYTES.[119]

45. *Ibid.* §§ 7 to 11. From a variety of notices in this portion of the *Ordo Romanus I.,* it is clear that at Rome, in the eleventh century (and probably at a fomewhat earlier time alfo), deacons, fub-deacons, and other of the inferior orders, wore a planeta when in attendance on a pope at a folemn function.[120]

---

[119] Compare Ordo Rom. viii., where an acolyte, at his ordination, is defcribed as invefted with *orarium* and *planeta.* Dr. Hefele, referring to this, conjectures (p. 201), that the *planeta* of the minor orders was a fcantier and fhorter veftment than that worn by bifhops and prefbyters, refembling the little phænolion fo called, worn by ἀναγνῶσται in the Greek Church. But he has apparently overlooked the paffage in the Ordo I., which is inconfiftent with his explanation. For the fub-deacon is there defcribed (§ 7) as carrying the mappula of the pontiff on his own left arm, *fuper planetam revolutam.* A veftment fuch as Hefele defcribes could not be rolled (folded) back upon the arm, and then have a mappula refting upon it. But thefe are minor matters, of antiquarian intereft only.

[120] From the clofe of the eighth century the terms *Planeta* and *Cafula* ceafed to be diftinguifhed the one from the other. See Rabanus Maurus (quoted p. 91, "Cafula . . . hanc Græci planetam vocant") ; Honorius of Autun (quoted p. 137, "Cafula . . . hæc veftis et Planeta . . . vocatur") ; Innocent III. (quoted p. 155, "Cafulam vel Planetam.") To thefe paffages may be added the following from the life of Abbot Anfegifus (written in the ninth century), edited by Mabillon in the *Acta Sanctorum Ord. Benedict.* Sæc. iv. p. 945. Mention is made of various gifts to the church made by St. Anfegifus, and amongft them of *Planetas cafulas quattuor . . . mappulas duas . . . ftolas duas.* And fo Luitprand (Hift. vi. cap. xi). Cui (fc. Benedicto Pfeudo-Papæ) "Cafulam quam Planetam vocant, cum ftola pariter abftulit."

APPENDIX D.

VESTMENTS WORN IN THE GALLICAN CHURCH.

From a ms. of Uncertain Date Edited by Martene.[421]

Epist. Secunda De Communi Officio. . . . . "Pallium in pascha cum tintinnabulis Eucharistia velatur, instar veteris testamenti ubi tonica [h. e. tunica] sacerdotis plena tintinnabulis, signans verba prædicationis, ostenditur. Præcinctio autem vestimenti candidi, quod sacerdos baptizaturus præcingitur, in signa sancti Joannis agitur, qui præcinctus baptizavit Dominum. Albis autem vestibus in pascha induetur, secundum quod angelus ad monumentum albis vestibus cerneretur. Albæ etinim vestis exaltationem significant.

" Casula, quam amphibalum vocant, quod sacerdos induetur, tota unita, per Moysem legiserum instituta primitus demonstratur. Jussit ergo Dominus fieri dissimilatum vestimentum, ut talem sacerdos induerit quali indui populus non auderetur. Ideo sine manicas, quia sacerdos potius benedicit quam ministrat.[422] Ideo unita prinsecus, non scissa, non aperta : quia multæ sunt Scripturæ sacræ secreta mysteria, quæ quasi sub sigillo sacerdoti doctus debet abscondere, et unitatem custodire, non in hæresi vel schismata declinare.[423]

" Pallium [424] vero quod circa collo usque ad pectus venit, rationale vocabatur in vetere testamento, scilicet signum sanctitatis super memoriam pectoris, dicente propheta ex persona Domini, ' Spiritus Domini super me.' Et post pauca, ' ut ponerem gloriam lugentibus Sion, et darem eis coronam pro cinere, oleum gaudii pro luctu' (Is. lxi. 3). Pallium laudis pro spiritu mœroris. Quod autem collo cingit, antiquæ consuetudinis est, quia reges et sacerdotes circumdati

---

[421] These extracts are from a MS. edited by Martene (*Thesaurus Anecdotorum*, tom. v). He describes it as follows ; *Sancti Germani Parisiensis episcopi expositio brevis antiquæ Liturgiæ Gallicanæ* ; and gives it as his opinion that *this work was written* (hoc opus scriptum) about the middle of the sixth century. This, he says, because St. Germanus was Bishop of Paris from 556 to 576 A.D. The only link of connection, however, between this anonymous MS. (found in the Monastery of St. Martin at Autun) and St. Germanus, is the fact that the writer begins by referring to (and quoting) what *Germanus episcopus Parisius scripsit de Missa*. Internal evidence points to the ninth or tenth century as the earliest at which the MS. could have been actually

written. [The spelling of the original is preserved throughout.]

[422] He refers to the fact that the form of the Casula was inconsistent with the use of the arms for anything like *active ministration*.

[423] This furnishes, as will be seen, a new mystical meaning for the *Casula*.

[424] The word Pallium is probably not used here in the technical sense of an archbishop's Pallium. In early representations (ninth century) of Gallican Bishops, the older form of the Pallium is seen, resembling that of Pl. XXX., XXXI., but meeting it at a point at the breast. And so the words here commented on may point to the *Pallium Gallicanum* (so called), of which more in Appendix E.

erant pallia vefte fulgente, quod gratia præfignabat. Quod autem fimbriis veftimenta facerdotalia adnectuntur, Dominus Moyfi præcepit in Numeris, ut per quattuor angulos palliorum filii Ifrael fimbrias facerent, ut populus Domini non folum opere, fed etiam et veftitu, mandatorum Dei fignum portaret.

" Manualia vero, id eft manicas,[425] inducere facerdotibus mos eft, inftar armillarum quas regum vel facerdotum brachia conftringebantur. Ideo autem ex quolibet pretiofo vellere, non metalli duritia, extant, vel ut omnes communiter facerdotes etiam minoris dignitatis in fæculo facilius inveniant.

" Veftimentum parvolum [425a] quod non fit in alio ufo nifi ad frequentandum facrificium, vel fignificat quod non graventur manus noftræ honoribus feculi, fed circumdentur fubtilia exercitia mandatorum Dei. Prohibet autem manica, tonica ne appareat vile veftimentum, aut quocunque indignum tactum fordium fuper divina facrificia, quo manus immolantis difcurrunt.

" Albas vero quas levitæ utuntur ideo ftatuerunt Patres, quia in veftimento tincto non fic apparet cito macula quomodo in albo: et minifter altaris ideo utitur, ut obfervet et caveat omnem maculam et nullatenus veftimenta miniftrantium vel leviore tactu appareant fordida ; fed candida fint, exterius vefte, interius mente. Sirico aut vellere fictur, quia Dominus facerdotibus ideo exinde habere indumenta mandavit, ut eorum veftis fpem refurrectionis oftenderet. Sirico enim de ligno per verme fictur. Vermis poft mortem procedit in alate, et poft occafum et volatum figurans Chriftum, qui ex ligno crucis quiefcens in fepulchro, tanquam vermis claufus in facculo angufto, furrexit de tumulo, et ad cælos fumfit volatum. Alterius vero velleris albi innocentiam tantum vitæ demonftrant. Alba autem non conftringitur cingulo, fed fufpenfa tegit levitæ corpufculum, quia omnis converfatio Levitica in defiderio cæleftis patriæ a terrenis operibus debet effe fufpenfa, nec cingulo peccatorum conftricta.

" Stola autem, quam fuper alba diaconus induit, fignificat fubtilitatis intelligentiam in divina myfteria, licet veteri (h. e. veteres) ftola induentes gaudium follennitatis fe habere monftrabant. Et pro hac caufa in quadragefima pro humiliatione non utitur, ficut nec alleluia in noftra ecclefia, fanctus, vel prophetia, hymnum trium puerorum, vel canticum rubri maris, illis diebus decantantur. Stola alba namque angelus præcinctus apparuit, quando fedens in monumento Domini follennitatem refurrectionis illius nunciavit. Ideo in quadragefima prohibendum hæc cantica, quia cæleftia et angelica funt."

---

[425] The *manicæ*, here mentioned, " *inftar armillarum*," feems to point to a veftment refembling the Greek ἐπιμανίκια (note 350, p. 169).

[425]a This " fmall veftment " is evidently the maniple.

APPENDIX E.

PASSAGES FROM EARLY WRITERS ILLUSTRATING THE HISTORY OF THE ORARIUM ("STOLE,") AND THE PAPAL PALLIUM.

The Orarium of Secular Use.

1. The following passages will indicate the form, and usage, of the Orarium in ordinary life. α. St. Jerome, *ad Nepotianum*, 529. *Plenum dedecoris est, referto marsupio, quod sudarium orariumque non habeas gloriari.* β. St. Ambrose, *De Resurrect. Et facies ejus (sc. Lazari) orario colligata erat.* γ. St. Augustine, *De Civit. Dei*, lib. xxii. cap. 8, § 7. [An Orarium used as a bandage to tie up a wounded eye.] *Tunc, sicut potuit, oculum lapsum atque pendentem loco suo revocatum ligavit orario.* δ. Prudentius (fifth century), *Peristeph.* 1, 86. [Speaking of two martyrs, Hemeterius and Celedonius, he says that the ring worn by one, and the handkerchief of the other, were miraculously carried up to heaven.] *Illa laus occulta non est, nec senescit tempore, missa quod sursum per auras evolarunt munera.* . . . *Illius fidem figurans nube fertur annulus; Hic sui dat pignus oris, ut ferunt, orarium.* ε. With this last compare St. Gregory of Tours, *De Glor. Martyr.* cap. 93, where he relates the same tale. In another passage of the same author we read of the son of Sigismund being strangled by means of an *Orarium. Hist. Franc.* lib. iii. cap. 5. *Sopitum vino dormire post meridiem filium jubet: cui dormienti orarium sub collo positum ac sub mento ligatum, trahentibus ad se invicem duobus pueris, suggillatus est.* [This was in the year 522 A.D.] η. St. Gregory the Great (close of the sixth century), writing to a friend at Constantinople, a *vir religiosus*, but not a priest, sends him as a present *duas camisias et quattuor oraria*, much as the Emperor Gallienus had done when writing to Claudius, three centuries earlier. [Epist. lib. vii. xxx. Indict. xv.]

Oraria as Imperial Presents.

1 *b.* Trebellius Pollio in *Claudio (prope finem).* He is quoting a letter of the Emperor Gallienus in which he enumerates the presents (chiefly plate and rich garments) which he had sent to Claudius (afterwards emperor from 268 to 270). "Albam subsericam, paragaudem tunicam unam. Zanchas[407] de nostris Parthicis paria tria, . . . Penulam Illyricianam unam . . . *Oraria Sarabdena quatuor.*"

Flavius Vopifcus in *Aureliano* (*Imp.* 270-275), *prope fin.* (p. 428). "Sciendun . . . illum . . . donaffe populo Romano tunicas albas manicatas ex diverfis provinciis, et lineas Afras atque Ægyptias puras; *ipfumque primum donaffe oraria populo Romano quibus uteretur populus ad favorem.*" [On this ufe of *oraria*, "ad favorem," fee F. B. Ferrarius, *De Veterum Acclamationibus*, lib. ii. cap. 7, p. 63.]

THE ORARIUM, AS A SACRED VESTMENT, NOT TO BE WORN BY ANY BELOW THE RANK OF A DEACON.

2. Council of Laodicea, A.D. 327. [Harduin *Concil.* tom. i. p. 786.] Can. xxiii. οὐ δεῖ ὑπηρέτην ὠράριον φορεῖν, οὐδὲ τὰς θύρας ἐγκαταλιμπάνειν· *Ibid.* Can xxiv. ὅτι οὐ δεῖ ἀναγνώστας ἢ ψάλτας ὠράριον φορεῖν, καὶ οὕτως ἀναγιγνώσκειν ἢ ψάλλειν.

ORARIUM WORN BY DEACONS, *circ.* 467.

3. St. Chryfoftom († 407). In *Parab. de Filio Prodigo. Inter opera fpuria.* [Though probably not St. Chryfoftom's, it is of a date not much later than his]. Tom. viii. p. 655. Μεμνημένοι τῶν φρικτῶν μυστηρίων τῶν λειτουργῶν τῆς θείας λειτουργίας, τῶν μιμουμένων τὰς τῶν ἀγγέλων πτέρυγας ταῖς λεπταῖς ὀθόναις ταῖς ἐπὶ τῶν ἀριστέρων ὤμων κειμέναις, καὶ ἐν τῇ ἐκκλησίᾳ περιτρεχόντων.

THE SAME, *circ.* 412.

4. St. Ifidore of Pelufium, *circ.* 412 A.D. He fpeaks (fee above, p. 49) of ἡ ὀθόνη μεθ' ἧς λειτουργοῦσιν οἱ διάκονοι ἐν τοῖς ἁγίοις; and he adds that this ὀθόνη, or piece of fine linen, recalls the humility of our Lord in that of His wafhing, and wiping dry, the feet of His difciples.

ORARIUM FORBIDDEN TO MONKS, A.D. 511.

5. Concil. Aurelian. (anno 511) Canon xx. "Monacho uti orario [426] in Monafterio, vel tzangas [427] habere non liceat." [Labbe, Concil. tom. iv. p. 1407.]

---

[426] All commentators on this paffage confider the word Orarium to be here ufed with its older meaning of a "pocket hankerchief."

[427] *Tzangas.* A kind of boot. τζάγγα or τζαγγία in Byzantine Greek. As being of barbarous origin they were not allowed to be worn at Conftantinople, *intra urbem*, even by laymen. [Codex Theod. *De Habitu*, &c. 14, 10. *Ufum Tzangarum atque braccarum*

intra urbem venerabilem nemini liceat ufurpare.] Nearly four centuries later Charlemagne interdicted their ufe by the Clergy. *Capitul.* lib. vii. cap. 314. *Ut clerici pampis* [al. pompis] *aut tzangis vel armis non utuntur.* The paffage in the letter of Emperor Gallienus quoted in p. 206 (overlooked by Ducange), determines their origin. *Zanchas de noftris Parthicis paria tria.*

DEACONS ARE NOT TO HIDE THEIR ORARIA.

6. Concil. Bracar. II. A.D. 563, capitulum ix. " Item placuit ut quia in aliquantis hujus provinciæ ecclesiis diaconi absconsis infra tunicam utuntur orariis, ita ut nihil differre a subdiacono videantur, de cetero superposito scapulæ utantur orario." For Concil. Bracar. III. A.D. 572, see Innocent III., *sup.* p. 154.

7. Concil. Tolet. IV. A.D. 633. [See above, p. 76.] Bishops and presbyters alike wear *Oraria*, but not more than *one*. Deacons also are to wear but one, and that upon the left shoulder only. They are to wear it plain (*purum*), not decked out with colours nor with gold.

8. Concil. Bracar. IV. A.D. 685 [Labbe, tom. vii. p. 581] Can iv. " Cum antiqua ecclesiastica noverimus institutione præfixum ut omnis sacerdos, cum ordinatur, orario utroque humero ambiatur, scilicet ut qui imperturbatus præcipitur consistere inter prospera et adversa, virtutum semper ornamento utrobique circumseptus appareat; qua ratione tempore sacrificii non assumat quod se in sacramento accepisse non dubitatur? Proinde modis omnibus convenit ut quod quisque percepit in consecratione, hoc et retentet in oblatione, vel perceptione suæ salutis; scilicet ut cum sacerdos ad solemnia missarum accedit, aut pro se Deo sacrificium oblaturus, aut sacramentum Corporis et Sanguinis Domini nostri Jesu Christi sumpturus, non aliter accedat quam orario utroque humero circumseptus, sicut et tempore ordinationis suæ dignoscitur consecratus: ita ut de uno eodemque orario cervicem pariter et utrumque humerum premens signum in suo pectore præferat crucis. Si quis autem aliter egerit, excommunicationi debitæ subjacebit."

9. St. Germanus of Constantinople, *circ.* 715 A.D. [See the passage quoted, *supra*, p. 84.] He speaks of the deacons as distinguished by the light wings of their light oraria.

10. Concil. Moguntiacum (Mayence), A.D. 813, Can. xxviii. [Labbe, vol. xi. p. 336, Venet.] " Presbyteri sine intermissione utantur orariis propter differentiam sacerdotii dignitatis."

ORARIUM AND OTHER VESTMENTS, NINTH CENTURY.

11. Riculfus, Bishop of Soissons [† 902] Statutum vii. " Studere etiam debetis ut digne atque honeste vestra ecclesiastica vestimenta præparata habeatis; Albam videlicet ad divinum mysterium unam vel duas nitidas, cum orariis, id est, stolis duabus nitidis, et amictus duobus nitidis, corporalibus quoque totidem nitidis, item zonis duabus, id est cinctoriis, ac manipulis totidem nitidis; ac linteamina altaris habeatis nitida, et casulam sericam, cum qua missa celebretur. Hoc autem omnimodis prohibemus, ut nemo illa alba utatur in sacris mysteriis, qua in quotidiano vel exteriori usu induitur."

ORARIUM TO BE WORN WHEN TRAVELLING.

12. From the *Capitula* of Hincmar, Archbishop of Rheims († 882), and from the *Difciplina Ecclefiaftica* (lib. i. 62) of Regino, Abbot of Prume, in the following century, we find that a priest, when on a journey, was bound to wear his *ftola* or *orarium*, that his facred character might be known. If he were robbed, or murdered, *non ftola veftitus*, the crime was to be atoned *fimplici emendatione*, but if *cum ftola*, then *emendatione triplici*. This laft provifion was made by a council held at Tribur, near Mayence, in 895.

THE PALLIUM (PAPAL OR ARCHIEPISCOPAL).

13. The political hiftory (fo to call it) of the "Pallium Pontificium" in the Weft, may be briefly fummed up as follows :

It was at firft [428] conferred on archbifhops [429] and metropolitans, not as a neceffary qualification for that dignity, but as a fymbol of acceffion of honour and of authority through *vicarial powers* (vices Apoftolicæ Sedis), beftowed by the Roman See. Arles,[430] for example, had been an archiepifcopal See long before Symmachus beftowed the Pallium on Cæfarius. See note ‡, p. lviii. And when, nearly a century later, another Archbifhop of Arles, Virgilius, applied (by letter) to St. Gregory the Great, for a fimilar privilege, he had been already for four years in poffeffion of his See, and in the full exercife of his office.

This being fo, a queftion of fome difficulty arifes out of the language of the firft Council of Macon, A.D. 581, which in its fixth canon directs that no archbifhop fhall celebrate mafs *fine Pallio*. Interpreted by the later difcipline of the Weftern Church, when the power of the Papacy had been firmly eftablifhed,

---

[428] Anaftafius, in the *Gefta* of Marcus, Bp. of Rome, A.D. 336, writes as follows: "*Hic conftituit ut epifcopus Oftienfis, qui confecrat epifcopos Urbis,*[113] *tunc pallio uteretur, et ab eodem Urbis*[113] *epifcopus confecraretur. Hic fecit conftitutum de omni ecclefiaftico ordine.* If the "Pallium" here fpoken of is the Papal pallium, which is open to doubt, we have here the firft inftance of its being conferred by favour of the Roman See, but only for this fpecial occafion of the confecration of the *Urbis epifcopus.*

[429] Millin, Voyage en Italie, tom. i. p. 108, fpeaks of a farcophagus of S. Celfus, Archbifhop of Milan, on which the Archbifhop is reprefented wearing a Pallium marked with a fingle crofs. [Martigny, D. J. A. C., *in voc.* Pallium.]

[430] "Primate and Metropolitan had been

fynonymous terms applied to the firft Bifhop of a Province" [*Primæ fedis epifcopus* is the only term allowed by Concil. Carth. iii. A.D. 397], "and fo they continued to be for fome time : fubfequently the heads of the nations, or exarchs of a diocefe, monopolifed the title. Conc. Chalced. can. 9 et 17. Thus there were three Gallican primates over Celtica, Belgica, and Aquitania, refpectively, whofe Sees were Lyons, Treves, and Bourges. Again, the Bifhop of Arles was ftyled Primate after that city had been made the refidence of the prætorian Prefect; and hence the frequent contentions between him and the Bifhop of Vienne about the primacy, in which the Roman bifhops interfered, conftituting themfelves, as it were, primates over primates." Foulkes' *Manual of Ecc. Hift.* Oxford, 1851.

E E

this might be fuppofed to mean *till he had been to Rome and there received the Pallium*. But fuch an interpretation in regard of the churches of Gaul in the fixth century would be altogether an anachronifm, as well as a forcing of the language of the canon itfelf. Hence fome ritualifts [431] have fuppofed that in the fixth century a Pallium (but not neceffarily the Roman Pallium) was worn by all archbifhops as the fymbol of their office, in the Gallican churches, as in the Eaft, whofe cuftoms in many particulars they followed. It is believed, accordingly, that there was a *Pallium Gallicanum*, fuch as Gallican archbifhops wore, exifting fide by fide with the *Pallium Romanum*, worn by fuch bifhops only as had the *vices Apoftolicæ Sedis*. Hence the language of the canon will imply that an archbifhop muft wear a *Pallium*, when celebrating mafs, juft as a prieft was bound at fuch time to wear an "orarium" (fee Appendix E, No. 8). Compare note 424.

A further point of great intereft in the hiftory of the Papal Pallium is that of the joint action in regard to it of the chief powers in church and ftate. With regard to this there are fome points which are abfolutely beyond queftion, — others upon which Roman and Gallican (or German) authorities are at iffue. It is admitted that at the clofe of the fixth century St. Gregory the Great fpeaks of himfelf as fending the Pallium with vicarial authority, to an archbifhop of Arles, *with the affent of the Emperor* [430] (*i.e.* of the Byzantine Emperor, Maurice), and in compliance with the requeft (*petitio*) of the King. It is admitted, too, that at a fomewhat earlier date (A.D. 545), Pope Vigilius, when conferring fimilar privileges on Auxanius, Bifhop (really Archbifhop) of Arles, did fo *pro gloriofiffimi filii noftri Regis Childeberti Chriftiana devotione mandatis*, " as our moft glorious fon, King Childebert, with Chriftian devotion, has commiffioned us to do." But when, going back yet a hundred years earlier, a refcript of the Emperor Valentinian is produced, which purports to confer, by exclufively imperial authority, archiepifcopal powers, and the right of wearing the Pallium, upon one Joannes, Bifhop (thenceforth archbifhop) of Ravenna, and attaching thefe privileges to that fee in perpetuity, we reach ground which is, naturally, intolerable to fome. Hieronymus Rubeus, who was the firft to publifh the document, fought to evade the difficulty by fuppofing, that the Pallium fpoken of by Valentinian was an imperial (or fecular) Pallium, not the Pallium of an archbifhop. Cardinal Baronius fhows conclufively that the whole context is fuch as to exclude fuch a meaning. And he intimates, what is evidently true, that even were it otherwife, the really important queftion would be left untouched, that of the power of an emperor to conftitute, by his own act and authority, a metropolitan province,

---

[431] See Hefele, L. G. p. 217 ; Ruinart. Dif-fertatio de Palliis Archiepifcop., printed among the Opera Pofthuma of Mabillon.

[430] But on other occafions, in dealing with Churches, which were created by the miffion-ary zeal of the Roman See, St. Gregory acts upon the principle alluded to in Note 116. And fo (knowing nothing of the older *Britifh* Church in the *Anglia* of his day) he created in England the two Archiepifcopal Sees of Canterbury and York, and fent over two Pallia for their ufe.

and affign archiepifcopal powers. He maintains therefore (followed in this by Cardinal Bona) that the entire document is a forgery. Dr. Hefele, a Roman Catholic, but not an Ultramontane, points out a fatal flaw in *one* of Baronius' arguments, viz. his affuming (what is notoriously [433] contrary to fact) that the conferring of fuch powers was *in thofe days* a matter of *exclufively* ecclefiaftical jurisdiction, pertaining to the See of Rome. But I cannot help obferving that he has not dealt with a far ftronger argument, with which the Cardinal backs up his firft. If fuch a refcript as this had been in exiftence among the archives of Ravenna (or even kept in memory by tradition), in the time of another John of Ravenna (fee above, p. 66), contemporary of St. Gregory the Great, how came it that when there was a warm difpute, as in his time there was, concerning the nature and extent of the privileges of the Pallium attaching to the See of Ravenna, *no reference was made to this refcript* either by John himfelf (as far at leaft as we can judge from the correfpondence), or by St. Gregory?

On the whole, I incline to think the Cardinal's theory probable, viz. that at fome fubfequent time of divifion between the Bifhops of Ravenna and of Rome, this document was forged, in order to fupport the claims to independence put forward by the Northern See. Well would it be if Chriftian hiftorians could fay with truth, that fuch politic forgeries were without precedent elfewhere in Mediæval times.

Such is the earlier hiftory of the Roman Pallium. If we turn to later hiftory, we fhall find another phafe of thought concerning the Pallium, fymbolifed by the interefting hiftorical monument reproduced in Plates XXXII. and XXXIII., and with more exactnefs of reprefentation at p. lii. And fome fifty years after the date of Leo III., and of Charlemagne (the embodied " Church and State" of thofe Mofaics), we find Pope Nicholas I., in his *Refponfa ad Bulgaros,* laying down (for the firft time) the rule which, whenever poffible, has been adhered to ever fince by the Roman Curia, viz. that no archbifhop fhall venture to exercife any of his functions, even after confecration, till he has received the Pallium from the tomb of the chief of the apoftles. Labbe, Conc. tom. viii. p. 541; Innocent III., quoted at p. 160.

Thofe who would purfue this fubject further will find the materials for doing fo in the treatifes named in note 110, p. 63; and in the paffages of ancient authors quoted or referred to in the later editions of *Du Cange* (G. M. et I. L. *in voc.* Pallium), and of *Meurfius, in voc.* 'Ωμοφόριον.

---

[433] In the Codex Theodofianus, for example, we find an imperial refcript (lib. xvi. tit. ii. No. 45) addreffed to the Prefect of Illyricum, which places all ecclefiaftical affairs in the Illyrian Provinces under the jurifdiction of the " *vir religiffimus, facrofanctæ Legis Antiftes,*" the Bifhop of Conftantinople. With this compare the refcript of Gratian, giving jurifdiction over other metropolitans to Damafus Bifhop of Rome. [Giefeler, E. H. p. 434.]

APPENDIX F.

THE SACRED VESTMENTS OF THE ROMAN CHURCH.

1. The Amictus, or Amice.[434]

The Amice is described in note 178, p. 96. It is nowhere mentioned as a vestment till the ninth century. Walafrid Strabo, even in that century, is silent with regard to it. Note 217, p. 108. There is no corresponding vestment in the Greek Church.[435]

But though not named in the first eight centuries as a sacred vestment, we can trace its origin in some expressions of St. Jerome, which suggest also the reason of its late appearance among church vestments. In a letter to his friend Nepotianus (a priest), he is warning him not to think that there is any merit in being dirty, and bids him not to take pride, *quia linteolum*[436] *in collo non habeas ad detergendos sudores,* i.e. because, following monastic rule, you wear no linen between the neck and the outer woollen garments. As long as church vestments were themselves *of linen,* such a *linteolum* was not needed *in Church.* But when silk and rich ornaments (especially about the *upper border* of the planeta) came to be worn, it was necessary to prevent their actual contact with the skin, and hence the introduction of the " Amice."

The mystical meanings attached to it may be seen detailed at p. 88 (Ephod Bad), 96, 111,[*] 115,[*] 122, 126, 128, 132, 135.

Dr. Bock gives a plate (vol. ii. Pl. II.) showing the mode of wearing the Amice, both on the shoulders, and (in passing) as a *galea* (note 178, and Durandus, quoted at p. 167) on the head. The same writer furnishes details as to the *paruræ,* or ornamental borders, sometimes attached to the Amice, from the tenth century onward (as he thinks). Weiss (*Kostümkunde,* p. 667) dates these a full century later. [The former is right. See note 441, below.]

2. The Alb.[437]

The history of the Alb during the first eight centuries has been already given. See Introduction, Chap. vii. p. liv.

---

[434] Other names are *Humerale,* i.e. shoulder-piece, *Superhumerale* or *Ephod* (so, perhaps, Rabanus, p. 88); *Anabolagium* (i.e. ἀναβολάδιον or ἀναβολαῖον) or *Anagelaium.*

[435] M. Victor Gay admits that the Amice cannot be traced back farther than the 8th century; A. A. vol. vi. p. 158. He adds (p. 161), "Les Orientaux plus stricts observateurs des traditions du costume primitif ne l'ont jamais adopté."

[436] When in the same letter (Ep. 52) St. Jerome speaks of one who *absque amictu lineo incedit,* the word *amictus* is probably used in its older classical sense. *Non absque amictu lineo incedere, sed pretium vestium linearum non habere, laudabile est. Alioquin ridiculum est et plenum dedecoris, referto marsupio, quod sudarium orarium-que non habeas gloriari.*

[437] *Tunica linea,* or *tunica talaris, linea, ca-*

Like other veftments which in primitive times, and even till the clofe (or nearly fo) of the eighth century, were of white linen only, the Alb became enriched in the later centuries,[438] both in refpect of material and of ornament. See Bock, L. G. vol. ii. p. 33, *fqq.*, and Hefele, p. 171, *fqq.* Their ornamentation was effected by adding *paruræ*, the pofition of which may be feen in Pl. LXI., on the Alb worn by the priefts. Such Albs were known in France as *Albæ Romanæ* (V. Gay in Didron, A. A.).

The myftical meanings attached to this veftment may be feen on reference to pp. 69, 89, 95, 96, 110, 116, 135, 165.

The full and flowing fhape of the Chriftian *Alba* was contrafted in the ninth century (fee Amalarius, p. 96) with the clofely fitting (note 6, p. 2) tunic of Levitical priefthood. But as fuper-veftments were multiplied in the tenth and eleventh centuries, the Alb was neceffarily more and more confined, and the modern Alb is almoft as clofely fitting as was that of the Levitical prieft. Compare Pl. IX. and LXI. Even in St. Hugo's time (fee p. 132, l. 4) the *linea interior*, correfponding to the original Alb, was altogether hidden (*latet*) by the additional veftments worn.

3. THE GIRDLE.

Cingulum, Zona, Balteus.

The Girdle was almoft univerfally worn in ancient times as a matter of convenience, to faften up the tunic, and in that cafe, generally, fo worn as not to be vifible. Exceptionally, too, by kings (note 81, p. 51) and other great perfonages in the Eaft, it was worn as a diftinctive ornament, and in fuch cafes was richly ornamented. Such was the Girdle (fee Pl. VIII. and IX.) of the Levitical priefthood.

Hence a double fignificance of the Girdle, α. as a fymbol of *activity* (fo, generally in Scripture, and in claffical authors); β. as a fymbol of royal or prieftly dignity.

A third fymbolifm, that of chaftity, which in ecclefiaftical writers has almoft exclufive place, is to be referred to affociations of idea in regard to the Girdle fufficiently familiar to fcholars, and upon which it is not neceffary to dwell.

Thefe confiderations will explain the myftical fignificance attached to the Girdle from the ninth century onwards. Thefe may be feen in pp. 89, 113, 116, 122, 132, 136.

Till, in the eighth or ninth century, the idea of an intended refemblance

---

mifia, fupparus, linea interior, are various names ufed in fpeaking of this veftment.

[438] "After the 10th century," fays Weifs (K. p. 667). The two kinds of albs were diftinguifhed as "*Alba pura*" (the "white alb *plain*" of Edward's firft Prayer-book), and the *Alba parata*.

in detail between the Christian and the Levitical vestments was first broached, the Girdle, naturally, was either not [439] worn at all (with the *tunica talaris* it was not necessary), or, when worn, was not visible, and was thought of only as a matter of convenience. In none of the early monuments of the West before A.D. 800, is any trace of it to be seen. But in the East we have mention of a Girdle as worn by deacons, early in the eighth century. (See p. 86, *in fin.*)

The mode in which the Girdle was worn in the ninth century is well illustrated in Pl. XXIII., where the priest is in an alb, with close-fitting sleeves (for obvious reasons of convenience in the administration of baptism by immersion) without chasuble.[440] And the alb is evidently girt in at the waist, though no pendent ends are visible. The mode in which these ends appear in the later Roman costume may be seen in Pl. LXI., where they hang down beside the stole. These pendents probably correspond to the *subcingulum,* or *succinctorium* of Honorius, p. 136, note 275 *α*; Innocent III., p. 144, note 301 ; and Durandus, p. 165, note 337.

It will readily be understood that a richly ornamented girdle, like that of Levitical priesthood (see Pl. VIII. and IX.) would be out of place (because wholly unseen) in the primitive dress of Christian ministry. Hence the *cingula auro texta* worn by bishops and others of the clergy in the ninth century were, as Durandus says (p. 165, note 336), *sæcularia ornamenta,* worn as part of the splendid secular dress then in fashion.

A variety of documents dating from the ninth century lead to the conclusion, that the Zona, *as a sacred vestment,* was not then in *general* use, but that costly Girdles (Zonæ Romanæ, p. 111) were in some cases used by bishops, as, for example, by Riculfus [441] of Soissons († 915 A.D.). These could

---

[439] Note, as bearing upon this, the reproof given by St. Celestine (*sup.* p. 45), to certain Bishops in Gaul, who fought " by wearing a girdle (Note 74) round their loins to fulfil the truth of Scripture, not in the spirit, but in the letter."

[440] Curiously parallel to this are the words, quoted at p. 204, where the priest is described as dressed *in albis,* and wearing a girdle *when about to baptize.*

[441] The Will of Bishop Riculfus is a complete inventory of Church vestments such as were used in the wealthier Churches of the 10th century. I subjoin those portions of it which refer to this subject, from the text of Migne (P. C. C. tom. cxxxii. p. 468). For the credit of the Bishop's Latin I will add that such expressions as *capas duas, una purpura,* &c., may arise simply from copyists not recognising the abbreviation commonly employed for the accusative case in MS.

Among the various things *quæ in cultu*

Dei pertinent, which he leaves for the use of his Church, and of his successors in the See, he names—

"Caligas et sandalias paria duo, amictos cum auro quattuor; albas quinque, tres claras et planas duas; roquos quattuor, unum purpureum cum auro, et alium palleum Græco, et alios duos in Græcia factos; zonas quinque, una cum auro, et gemmis pretiosis, et alias quattuor cum auro; stolas quattuor cum auro, una ex illis cum tintinnabulis; et manipulos sex cum auro, unum sex [*leg.* ex] iis cum tintinnabulis; casulas episcopales optimas tres, unam dioprasiam, et alias duas de orodonas; annulum aureum unum cum gemmis pretiosis, et uvantos paria unum; camisas ad textum et missalem quattuor, unum cum auro purpureum, et alios palleos corporales quattuor; palleos quattuor, e brosdo unum ; dalmaticas tres; capas duas, una purpura et alia bition " (*blatea ?*). [For *de orodonas* above, Dr. Hefele reads *diarodinas, i.e.,* διαρόδινας, " rose-coloured."]

be worn *fo as to be feen* with a *capa* or cope (two of which are mentioned among the bifhop's veftments), though not with a *cafula*.

Full details as to the later forms of the Girdle, and the changes in it at various times, will be found in Bock, L. G. tom. ii. p. 50, *fqq.* Compare Hefele, L. G. p. 78.

4. THE STOLE [ORARIUM OR STOLA].

For the earlier hiftory fee Introduction, p. lxii., *fqq.* and Appendix D. And for the two names fee note 144, p. 84.

No fatisfactory [442] account has yet been given of the introduction of this later term *Stola.* I venture to think that it is to be accounted for by the fact that the word, *as employed in the Vulgate*, is fuggeftive of a veftment of folemn ftate or dignity, particularly of "a prieftly robe." And as in the eighth century the *Orarium* was regarded as *the fpecial veftment of Chriftian prieft-hood*, to be worn *hora facrificii* under pain of excommunication, it feems not improbable that the *Orarium* may then have been called, *by certain perfons*, as Raban fays, "the Stole," or, as we might now fay, "the veftment" of the prieft. The technical terminology of the Mediæval Church in the Weft was formed not upon claffical Latin, ftill lefs upon claffical Greek, or, indeed, any Greek at all, but upon the Latin of the Vulgate, [443] and of the Latin fathers. We find, accordingly, fome indications that the word *ftola* was occafionally ufed in early writers, as it is occafionally in Scripture, of a long white garment, "a prieftly robe," as the *tunica talaris.* Such probably is the meaning of the word in the only paffage in which *ftola* is exprefsly diftinguifhed from the *Orarium* by any of the mediæval writers. [Acta Sanctorum, Maius xxvi. p. 393, " *Addit Stolam et Orarium.*"]

This veftment was originally of white linen. But fo early as the beginning of the feventh century we find that fome of the younger clergy of Spain had taken to "coloured oraria," decked out with gold ; and were not even content with *one* only. Hence the Canon of the Fourth Council of Toledo, quoted at p. 75.

---

[442] The fuppofition that it was the *border* of a long and full garment called " ftola " (fuch as the older *ftola matronalis*), is defervedly rejected by moft writers on this fubject. The fuggeftion made by Honorius (fee p. 136), points rather to fuch an explanation as that made in the text, in this, at leaft, that he traces back the ecclefiaftical ufe of " ftola " to the fcriptural (Vulgate) ufe of the fame word. See next note.

[443] Thus Honorius (*fupra*, p. 139, l. 17)

fpeaks of the *prima ftola* " the beft robe," with which the prodigal on his return was clad. And Innocent III., in like manner, quotes the words of the Apocalypfe, "*ftabant . . . . amicti ftolis albis* " (p. 163, l. 15), without any thought whatever of the "*Stole*" technically fo called. Compare the paffage of Ezekiel, xliv., quoted at p. 29, where fee note 50. And that of Honorius (p. 156) referred to in laft note.

By the ninth century we find such coloured stoles, bedecked with gold, reprefented both in Italy and in Gaul.[411] In the Pontifical of Bishop Landulfus, fome of the prefbyters wear *two* Stoles, differing in pattern one from the other, one being white, with black croffes, the other gold colour.

For notices of the Stole (other than thofe in Appendix E), fee pp. 126, 129, 132, 136, 142, 147, 154, 165, 166, 207.

For reprefentations of it, Pl. XXIII., XXXV., XXXVI., XLIV., XLV., LXI. In the three laft, only the lower [415] extremity of the Stole is vifible under the dalmatic.

5. The Maniple.

[*Pallium Linoftimum, Mappa, Mappula, Manipulus, Sudarium, Phanon* [161] *or Fanon,*[233] *Mantile, Manutergium.*]

The earlier hiftory of the Mappula has been already touched upon. Introduction, p. lxx.

Till the clofe of the eighth century, we hear of it only as a proceffional veftment, diftinctive of the Roman clergy. But from the beginning of the ninth it has been recognifed as one of the *facræ veftes.* See pp. 65, 90, 101 (*fudarium in manu*), 103, 113 (note 233), 117, 127, 137, 149, 156, 161, (*manipulo pro clava utitur*).

The ἐγχείριον, or ὀθόνη, which in the eighth century was carried fufpended from the Girdle by *deacons* in the Eaft, conftituted, in all probability, a real parallel to this veftment. But the epifcopal ἐπιμανίκια (fee note 350, and Pl. LVI.), differ from it in origin, in fhape, in fymbolifm, as they do in name.

For reprefentations of the Maniple, fee Plates XLIII., XLVIII., LXI.[146]

---

[411] In the Pontifical of Landulfus, and in the illuminations, dating from the ninth century, publifhed by Louandre et Maugé, L. A. S. vol. ii. " Le Prince Franc." In this picture the ends of the Stole (which alone are vifible) in two figures of bifhops, are decked with gold.

[415] In this we fee the reafon for the concentration of ornament in the *ends* of the Stole, in mediæval times, and for their gradual enlargement confequent upon this.

[146] In a French MS. of the ninth century (fubfequent to the adoption of the Roman ritual), bifhops and priefts are reprefented *holding* a Maniple, generally in the right hand (not wearing it pendent from the left wrift as in later ufe). See Louandre et Maugé

Les A. S. vol. ii. Les Chanoines de St. Martin. So Amalarius (*fup.* p. 112, 113) *writing in Gaul*, " fudarium quod . . . . in manu geftari mos eft."

But in the Pontifical of Landulfus, affigned by all Roman antiquaries to the ninth century (fee Pl. XXX. to XXXIII. of this work) none of the priefts have Maniples. In No. 3, 5, 9, the bifhop has on his right hand what might be miftaken for a Maniple, but which on clofe examination of the facfimiles (drawn and coloured from the originals) now before me, appear rather to be the extremity of a kind of pallium, worn by the bifhop over his chafuble; and which appears to be a detached veftment, not a mere " orfrey " (note 312) of the chafuble itfelf.

6. The Chasuble.

[*Planeta, Cafula, Infula, Amphibalum.*]

For earlier hiftory, fee Introduction, p. lxiii, *fqq.*, and Appendix C.

For fubfequent notices fee Rabanus, p. 91; Amalarius, p. 97; Walafrid, p. 108; Alcuinus, p. 117; St. Ivo, p. 127, (note 217); St. Hugo, p. 132, 133 (note 268); Honorius, p. 136; Innocent III., pp. 148 and 156; Durandus, p. 166, l. 3 (cafula quafi clypeo tegitur).

For reprefentations, fee Pl. XXVIII., XXX., XXXI. (all thefe, however, *Planetæ* rather than *Cafulæ*), XXXIII. (but ?), XXXIV., XXXV., XXXVI., XXXVII., XXXIX., XL., XLII., XLIV., XLV., XLVI., XLVIII., LXI.

With thefe compare the Greek φαινόλια, both fecular, as in Pl. XVIII., XIX., XX., XXI., XXVII., and liturgical, as in Pl. XLI. and LVIII.

For details of ornamentation at various times, fee Bock, L. G. p. 101 to 128; Hefele, L. G. p. 199, 200; and Pugin G. G. A. *in voc.*

This veftment is utterly unlike any of thofe of Levitical priefthood. And as long as the humble origin of the veftment (fee Appendix C, No. 32) was remembered in the church, and it was regarded as common to all clerics, and to monks alfo (Appendix C, No. 33, 34, 35), as a fecular drefs, there was of courfe no fpecial affociation of ideas of "facrifice" with this veftment. Accordingly we find the earlier writers fpeaking of it as typical either of "charity," the fymbolifm [447] which it has retained through all the later liturgical writers, or of thofe good works and duties which are "*common to all of the clerical order,*" hungering, thirfting, watching, nakednefs; reading, finging of pfalms, prayer; activity in good works, teaching, filent meditation, and the like (Amalarius, p. 98). But as time went on, and the fecular [447 a] drefs of the clergy no longer refembled the *cafula* in form or in name, the chafuble came to be regarded as *the* diftinctive veftment of Chriftian priefthood, and *therefore* (according to the prevailing idea of mediæval times) became fpecially affociated with the idea of facrifice. See Appendix G, No. 2, and note 458.

NINE ADDITIONAL VESTMENTS PROPER TO BISHOPS ONLY.

7. The Caligæ, Leggings or Stockings.

First mentioned among the facred veftments by St. Ivo, p. 128, l. 6. He defcribes them as made of linen, and *reaching* (from the foot) *to the knee,*

---

[447] See Rabanus, p. 91. The paffage there quoted will fhow the fanciful ground on which this fymbolifm was originally bafed.

Compare St. Ivo (p. 127). *Cafula . . quæ quia communis eft veftis charitatem fignificat.*

[447 a] On the fecular drefs of the clergy, both in Eaft and Weft, from the ninth century downwards, fee Thomaffinus, *De Bea.* part i. lib. ii cap. 48, 50, 51. *Cappa* was, as we fhall fee, the prevailing name for the out-door drefs both of clergy and monks.

where they are closely fastened. Hence the symbolism which he gives them. Compare Innocent III., p. 150. In later times the *tibialia* [448] of a bishop were always made of silk. Of this regulation we retain, by custom, some traces among ourselves.

8. The Shoes.

Sandalia, Soleæ, Campagæ or Campobi.

First noticed *as a sacred vestment* by Rabanus (*supra*, p. 92). Compare Amalarius, p. 97, l. 15, and p. 104 (where every minute part of the Shoe has its special symbolism assigned); Alcuinus, p. 112 (*in fin.*), 115, 118, and note 243; St. Ivo, p. 127; Innocent III., pp. 150 and 157.

Even at an earlier time we find that the kind of Shoes to be worn by ecclesiastics was matter of strict regulation in churches subject to the Roman See. Note 184, p. 97. Such matters had not been thought unworthy of imperial legislation, in reference to the etiquette of dress at Rome and at Constantinople. See note 427, p. 207, and Plates XXII., XXIV., XXV., XXVIII., XLIII.

9. The Under-Girdle.

Subcingulum, Succinctorium.

This vestment has been already noticed, in connection with the Girdle, and in note 313.

But since that note was written I have discovered what appears to be the real explanation of what is written about the Under-Girdle, by Honorius (p. 136); Innocent III. (pp. 143, 144); and Durandus (quoted in note 313). They all speak, directly or by implication, of *two* Girdles. And though the language of Durandus and of Innocent III. in p. 153, might admit of the explanation given in note 313, that of Honorius seems inconsistent with it. But the Ordo Romanus V., when describing the vestments of the *Pontifex* (*i.e.* the Pope), [449] shows that there really were two

---

[448] *Tibialia* is another name for the caligæ. The *caligæ* of a bishop, wearing ecclesiastical dress, are, of course, not visible. Similar *caligæ* worn by Charlemagne are seen in the woodcut at p. lii.

[449] Though in the language of the Western Church *generally*, Pontifex has the meaning "bishop," as pointed out in note 45, yet *at Rome itself* (to which, as shown in that note, the word *Pontifex* has a special relation), this title was distinctively used of the Pope, while to other bishops was given the ordinary title of *episcopus.* Both these usages of Pontifex are

illustrated by John the Deacon (*circ.* 875). He sometimes uses it of ordinary bishops, as in lib. iii. cap. 15, 33, 33, or of archbishops, as of John of Ravenna. But in lib. iv. cap. 91, he speaks of Bishop (*episcopus*) Lucidus, *then resident at Rome*, going up to dine in full dress (*sacerdotalibus infulis redimitus*) at the patriarchium, with the *Pontifex*, St. Gregory. In accordance with this, the Ordo Romanus V. distinguishes between the *Vestimenta Pontificalia*, and the *Vestimentum alii* (*i.e.* alius) *Romani Episcopi.* [See Mabillon's Preface, p. 63.]

diftinct Girdles, as indicated by Honorius. The veftments are enumerated as follows: *De Veſtimentis Pontificalibus. In primis cam* (i.e. camiſia) *et cingitur ſupra. Dein linea cum cottis, ſerica, et cingulum. Poſt hæc mittitur anagolai* (i.e. amictus); *exinde dalmatica minore, poſtea majore dalmatica, et ſupra orarium. Poſt hæc planeta, et ſupra mittitur pallium.* The inner Girdle over the *camiſia*, or ſhirt, reprefents the older Girdle of primitive ufage, without ornament, and altogether out of fight. The *cingulum*, afterwards ſpoken of, is an ornamented girdle, introduced among the " veſtments " at a much later period, in imitation of the ornamented Girdle of Levitical prieſthood.

10. The Episcopal Tunic.

Tunica Pontificalis, T. poderis, T. interior vel hyacinthina.

Innocent III., in his enumeration of the pontifical (*i.e.* epifcopal) veſtments, diftinguiſhes between the Alb, p. 145, *ſqq.*, the Tunic, and the Dalmatic. All thefe are really Tunics, the two latter having been fuperadded one after the other for richer ornament. The procefs was probably this. The *tunica alba*, made of linen, of the more primitive drefs, was replaced by one of filk, often of *blue* filk, in imitation of the *tunica hyacinthina* of the Levitical high-prieſt. A rich veſtment of this kind required *an under tunic*, for obvious reafons. And, accordingly, that under Tunica was now called *alba* fimply, the fecond Tunic (which was *talaris*, but not quite fo long as the alb) followed ; and the Dalmatic, ſhorn now of its ancient length, *in order to leave the fecond tunic viſible*, followed third in order. All this will readily be underſtood by reference to the figure of the biſhop in Pl. LXI. The gradual addition of one Tunic after another may be traced from the ninth century downwards in Pl. XXXVII. (one only); XXXIX. and XLIV. (two); XLVIII. and LXI., (three). The Ordo Romanus V. (*ſup.* § 9) enumerates three Tunics in all, befides the *camiſia*.

The language of St. Ivo (fee p. 122), and previoufly of Amalarius (p. 100, 101), fully confirms this fuppofition. St. Ivo fays, that both in the old and the new covenant, only *Pontifices* (high-priefts in the one cafe, biſhops in the other), wear two Tunics, the fecond Tunic, the *tunica hyacinthina*, being that which was exclufively theirs. This Tunica he calls *interior*, as does Amalarius (p. 101), not of courfe in reference to the *alba* [450] (or to the *tunica talaris* of the high-prieſt), but in reference to the dalmatic. Alcuinus, on the other hand, ſpeaks of the Levitical Tunic of blue (p. 110) as *tunica exterior*, an *outer* Tunic, in refpect of the white Tunic of linen beneath it. St. Hugo varies yet again from thefe. The *two Tunics* are to him the *linea interior*

---

[450] Hence Amalarius fpeaks of the alba as *camiſia*, and of the two others as *duæ tunicæ.* See p. 101, and note 194. And what Amalarius calls *duæ tunicæ*, appear in the fifth of the *Ordines Romani* as *dalmatica major* and *minor*.

(anfwering to our fhirt), which (*latet*) is unfeen, and the *linea exterior* or alb, which was vifible. See pp. 131, 132.

11. THE DALMATIC (OF THE BISHOP).

The general hiftory of the Dalmatic has already been fully inveftigated See Introduction, p. lv, *fqq.*

But the Dalmatic now in queftion is not the full and flowing white linen veftment of primitive times (with fimple ftripes for ornament, fee Pl. XVII., XXXIII.), but the highly ornamented veftment worn by bifhops and other high officials of the Church, immediately under the *cafula* or *planeta*. In fome inftances (Ordo Rom. V. quoted in § 9) two fuch Dalmatics are fpoken of. Reprefentations of this veftment may be feen (immediately under the chafuble) in Pl. XXXIX., XLII., XLIV., XLV., XLVI., LXI., in which laft is feen the deacon's Dalmatic alfo.

12. THE MITRA.[451]

Firft mentioned among the *Sacræ Veftes* by Honorius of Autun, about the middle of the twelfth century. See p. 138. But it had been in ufe, in fome parts at leaft of the Weft, fome time previoufly. The figure of St. Dunftan (Pl. XL.) in a MS. of the eleventh century, fhows him wearing a cap *ex byffo confecta*, much fuch as that to which the language of Honorius points, and this is the earlieft example of the kind which I have feen. I fhould except, perhaps, one of the bifhops reprefented in the Benedictional of St. Ethelwald, belonging to the Duke of Devonfhire. This is of the tenth century. The figure is reprefented with a kind of diadem, a narrow circlet of gold, with jewels round the head. This, however, is not really of the nature of a "Mitra," and may not improbably be fuggeftive of royal rank, to which church dignitaries could then not unfrequently lay claim. Some ritualifts have fought to affign a much earlier date to the "Mitra." The paffages they allege have been already confidered (Appendix B, No. 1 to 6). If we omit thefe (for the reafons given in that Appendix) we fhall find that the earlieft mention of the Mitra, which Dr. Hefele can adduce as genuine,

---

[451] The word μίτρα (quafi μίτρια from μίτος thread), was probably by origin an adjective. Hence its double ufe in claffical Greek, meaning a woman's cap (στεφάνη being underftood), or a girdle, when ζώνη is the word to be fupplied. In the LXX it is ufed as the rendering of Miznepheth, the prieft's cap (Exod. xxviii. 33; xxix. 6; xxxix. 31), for which elfewhere (Exod. xxviii. 4, 35, and 36; xxix. 9; xxxix. 27) κίδαρις is employed. The Vulgate has in correfponding paffages either *cidaris* (Exod.

xxviii. 4) or *tiara* (fee note 84, p. 52), as in Exod. xxviii. 37, 40; xxix. 6; or *mitra*, as in xxix. 9; xxxix. 26 and 20. In St. Ifidore, *mitra* (as in claffical Latin) means a cap worn by women. *Orig.* xix. 31, and *De Off. Ecc.* lib. ii. cap. 17. So in Tertullian, *De Virg. Vel.* (vol. iii. p. 32).

Other names for the Mitra are Tiara (note 84, p. 52), Pileus, Cidaris, Infula (note 296[a], and Appendix B, No. 4) Phrygium (Menardus in *Lib. Sacram. S. Gregor.* p. 212).

is of the eleventh century, where in 1049 A.D. mention [452] is made, on more than one occasion, of a *Mitra Romana*, a kind of Mitra specially characteristic of the Roman Church. And to the same effect, Peter Damian, writing *circ.* 1073, to Cadalous, then " antipope," says, " *Habes nunc forsitan mitram, habes juxta morem Romani pontificis rubram cappam* (opp. tom. i. p. 121, Epist. lib. i. 20); " It may be that you now are wearing the vestments which properly belong to the pope, the mitre and red cope." Menardus states that in all the ritual books before 1000 A D. which he had examined, there was no mention of the *Mitra*, and that he believes *vix ante annum post Christum natum millesimum mitræ usum in ecclesia fuisse*. The documents quoted in this work all point to the same conclusion. See the language of Alcuinus, quoted at p. 112. *Tiara* (that of the Lævitical priest) *erat vestis, pileolum videlicet rotundum.* . . . . . . *habens vittas.* . . . . *Summus Pontifex* (the high-priest) *præter pileum habebat coronam auream triplicemque.*[453] . . . *Hujuscemodi vestis non habent* (*leg.* habetur) *in Romana ecclesia vel in nostris regionibus,* and then again, after speaking of the *lamina aurea,* he adds, *Neque hanc ornamenti speciem Christi accepit ab illis ecclesia.* This treatise dates (note 218) from late in the tenth century. Compare note 217, *in fin.*

Various forms of the Mitra will be seen in Plates XLIV., XLVI., XLVII., XLVIII., L., LI., LII. to LV., LXI. And see description of Pl. XXXIX.

For details as to the ornamentation of the Mitra, and its varieties of form at different periods, see Bock, L. G. tom. ii. p. 153, *sqq.*

---

[452] In a charter of Leo IX., conferring privileges on Eberhard, Archbishop of Treves: *Quapropter omnibus ipsis laudantibus et respuentibus* [respondentibus?] *pro investitura ipsius Primatus, Romana mitra caput vestrum insignimus, qua et vos et successores vestri in Ecclesiasticis officiis Romano more semper utamini, semperque vos esse Romanæ sedis discipulos reminiscamini.* [*Apud* Dufresne *in voc.*]

[453] Among the expressions in ancient writers alleged as bearing upon this point, are some few, from which it appears that *corona vestra* (literally " *your chaplet* ") was a term of formal courtesy in addressing bishops and others of the clergy as early as the fourth century. The only *corona* of Christian ministry known to antiquity, even as late as St. Isidore's time (see p. 68, above), was the chaplet or circle of hair beneath the tonsure. Tertullian, as is well known, regards *coronæ* as essentially symbols of heathenism, and asks (after his rhetorical manner), *Quis Patriarcha, quis Propheta*

. . . . *vel postea Apostolus* . . . *aut Episcopus invenitur coronatus?* *De Cor. Mil.* 350. I can only suggest that " *corona vestra* " may have been, in the conventional language of Rome in the fourth century, an expression of courtesy answering to " Your Reverence," " Your Grace," and the like in modern times; and *imported into Christian usage from an idiom, which originally had reference to the coronæ of heathen priesthood.* The passages, of which I speak, are, α. Hieronymus ad Augustinum, No. 26. " *Fratres tuos, dominum meum Alypium et dominum meum Evodium, ut meo nomine salutes, precor coronam vestram;* and β. St. Augustine, ep. 147, ad Proculianum. *Per coronam nostram nos adjurant vestri* (h. e. the Donatists); *per coronam vestram vos adjurant nostri.* Many passages to the same effect are quoted by Dufresne, *in voc.*, and he adds that the phrase ὁ ὑμέτερος στέφανος is used in the same sense by some of the Greek Fathers.

13. The Gloves.

Chirothecæ, Guanti,[451] *Uvanti.*

Like many other parts of the full episcopal costume as developed in the twelfth century, the Gloves (*chirothecæ*) had long been in use, for practical purposes, before they were exalted to the rank of "sacred vestments," and invested with a symbolism of their own. The first writer who so mentions them is Honorius (note 296 ª), early in the twelfth century.

Full details concerning these will be found in Bock, L. G. ii. 131, *sqq.*

14. The Episcopal Ring.

In Roman usage, of the classical times, Rings were used as insignia of rank, and a Ring of a particular kind was exclusively appropriated to those of the equestrian order.

Early in the seventh century we find mention (see p. 75) of a Ring as one of the distinctive insignia of a bishop. When the coffin of Bishop Agilbert of Paris (seventh century) was opened, De Sauffay, who was present, saw on his finger a gold ring, with a jewel on which was a likeness of our Lord and St. Jerome. Other similar instances are referred to by Bock, L. G. ii. p. 207, *sqq.*

That no mention of the Ring, as one of the insignia of a bishop, should be made by any of the writers of the ninth, or even tenth century, quoted in this volume, may be accounted for by the fact, that they occupy themselves more particularly with those vestments which resembled (or were thought to resemble) those of Levitical priesthood. Of the later writers, Honorius is the first to speak of it (see p. 139); and he is followed by Innocent III., p. 149 and 157; as afterwards by Durandus, and all the later ritualists.[455]

15. The Staff, and the Crozier.

Baculus, Pedum, Virga, Cambuca, Ferula.

The Staff, as a distinctive mark of a bishop, is mentioned in the Acts of the Fourth Council of Toledo. The allusion to the Baculus in the letter of Celestine, Bishop of Rome (quoted at p. 45), is such as so indicate that the carrying of a *Baculus*, by bishops, as matter of ceremonial, was an innovation peculiar to certain parts of Gaul at that time (*circ.* 430 A.D.). The earliest

---

[451] These forms, which with *Wantus, Quanto, Gantus* (whence the French " gant "), are all of German origin, and indicate the source from which the use of gloves was introduced into Europe.

[455] For this see Innocent III., quoted at p. 147, and p. 155; and Honorius, p. 139.

reprefentation of a Staff in art-monuments, that I have feen, are thofe in Pl. XLII. and XLIII. But a "crofs," fomewhat refembling the later Crozier of an archbifhop (fee Pl. XLVIII.), is attributed both to St. Peter and to St. Laurentius, in the mofaic dating from the time of Pelagius II. (*fed.* 578 to 590), reproduced from a drawing in the collection at Windfor in Pl. XXIX. The fame plate reprefents a *Virga* in the hand of our Lord, the fymbolifm of which, as the "rod" or "fceptre" of *divine power*, has already been noticed. (Introduction, p. xl.) For the later forms of the Staff and Crozier, appropriated to bifhops and archbifhops refpectively, fee Plates XLII., XLVII., XLVIII., LI., LXI; and for the abbot's Staff, Pl. XLVII. and XLIX. For the Pallium, fee Introduction, p. lxxi, *fqq.*, and Appendix E, No. 13, to end. For the Orale (or *Fanon*) of the Pope, note 314, p. 153; and for the Pectoral Crofs, note 315. To this laft ornament anfwers the ἐγκόλπιον (note 342), worn by bifhops in the Eaft.

APPENDIX G.

THE VESTMENTS PRESCRIBED IN THE FIRST PRAYER-BOOK OF EDWARD VI., AND IN THE LATER BOOKS.

The veftments ordered in the Prayer-book of 1549, are at the holy Communion, *a.* "for the prieft that fhall execute the holy miniftry, the vefture appointed for that miniftration, that is to fay, *a white alb plain, with a veftment or cope;*" *β.* where there are priefts or deacons, ready to help, thefe are to wear "albs with tunacles."

1. The firft-named is the "*white Alb plain.*" By the Alb, when diftinguifhed, as here it is, from the furplice, is meant a white tunic, of much fcantier [456] dimenfions than the furplice, and, as fuch, fuited for wearing under a fuper-veftment, fuch as the "veftment or cope." By plain (*pura*) is meant without the "apparels" (note 438, p. 213), which, in mediæval times, had been adopted as ornaments to the Alb.

For the earlier hiftory of the Alb, fee Introduction, p. liv, *fqq.* and Appendix F. No. 2.

2. The "*veftment.*" In ftrictnefs of grammar, one who fpeaks of wearing

---

[456] See p. 213, l. 10, *fqq.*

"*a veftment or cope*," would be underftood to mean but *one* veftment, of which
"cope" was an alternative name. But it appears clear that in the fifteenth
and fixteenth centuries, the word "*veftimentum*" was often [457] ufed, with a
limited meaning, of that which was *then* regarded as *the* fpecial veftment
of Chriftian miniftry, viz. the chafuble.

It is clear that the laft-named veftment was in the later pre-Reformation
times regarded as fpecially appropriate to "the facrifice of the altar." This
will appear firft from the language of the older Inventories, quoted and examined below (p. 226). And the inference thence made is curioufly confirmed
by another rubric of the fame firft Prayer-book. Though an option is given
(in the rubric already quoted) between "veftment or cope," for the prieft
at holy communion, yet in the rubric providing for fervices on Wednefdays and
Fridays, when there is no communion, a "cope" is prefcribed without any
alternative. [458]

3. The veftment next named is the Cope (Cappa or Capa). A reprefentation of the Cope, dating from the time of Henry VII., will be feen in
Pl. LI. An earlier example at Pl. XLVII., and XLVIII.

The word *capa* is firft met with in the *Origines* of St. Ifidore. And the
two definitions which he gives to the word (anfwering, refpectively, to our
"cape," or hood," [459] and "cope"), ferve to cover the whole range of
meanings attached to the word even to the prefent time. "*Capa*," he fays,
in one place, "*dicta, quod capitis eft ornamentum ;*" and then again, "*capa
. . . quia quafi totum capiat hominem.*"

It is with the fecond of thefe two meanings that we are now concerned.
The Cope was originally a garb for out-door ufe, and was therefore furnifhed,
as were almoft all fuch garments in primitive times, with a "hood," for
protection of the head againft cold or rain. [460]

---

[457] It was alfo ufed as an inclufive term, for
a complete fet of veftments for "Celebrant,
Epiftoler, and Gofpeller," with altar-hangings
to match (*ejufdem fecta*). See paffages to this
effect quoted below in note 463.

[458] I have to thank Mr. Droop for calling
my attention to this. He adds, as further,
and very conclufive proof of the diftinctive
pofition then affigned to the chafuble, a reference to a kind of "*directorium*," in the
Lutheran Church in Brandenburg, publifhed
in MDXL. Provifion is there made for part
of the communion office being performed
when there are no communicants, but with the
direction appended, that the priefts are in that
cafe *not to wear a chafuble*, but a cope (kor-
kappe) only, or in village churches where
there are no copes, a common furplice (ein
fchlechten Corrock), *left fimple folk fhould
fuppofe that it was intended to celebrate mafs,*

after the former fafhion, without communicants.
[Kirchen Ordnung in Churfürftenthum der
Mareken zu Brandenburg u. s. w. Berlin,
MDXL. In the Britifh Mufeum under
"Liturgies." Brandenburg, c. 47, d.]

[459] For this we have direct authority at a
later time. Theodemarus, writing *from Italy*
to Charlemagne, and fpeaking of the drefs of
the monks of Monte Caffino (Dufrefne, *in
voc. Capa*). Illud indumentum quod a Gallis
monachis cuculla dicitur, nos Capam vocamus.
We may trace the fame meaning of *Capa* as
equivalent to "hood" in the eleventh century (Concil. Metenfe, A.D. 888). when the
ufe of *Citti* and *Mantelli*, with *Capæ*, was forbidden to laymen, and prefcribed to monks.

[460] Hence the name *Pluviale*, by which the
cope is often known. See p. 167, and note
339, *in voc.*

Such a garment, it is obvious, admits of every poffible variety in material, and colour, and ornamentation. And we find, accordingly, that the *Cappa* was ufed by laymen, by monks, by the clergy of all orders.[460a] But even the richeft Copes were for the moft part confidered as veftments of ftately dignity to be worn *in proceffions*, and on ceremonial occafions, not as having any efpecial relation to the *miniferium Altaris*.

One very common ufage of the fimpler *Cappa* was that of a choir-veftment for the *Cantores*. See note 295, p. 141. Being made of a thick woollen material, and furniflied with a hood, it was well fuited for fuch a purpofe as a protection from cold.[461]

4. The *Tunacle*.[462] The rubrics of 1547 were written fo as to be under-ftood by perfons who, with very few exceptions, were neither fcholars nor antiquaries, but who were acquainted with the conventional meaning of terms in common ufe in this country at the time. That common ufe we may now trace in the barbarous Latin, or the Latinifed Englifh, of church Inventories. And in thefe we find that *Tunicæ* are diftinguifhed, as in this rubric, from *Albæ*. And it is clear that the direction given in this rubric of the firft Prayer-book of 1549, is bafed throughout upon the old arrangement. Such lifts as thofe given below,[463] when carefully examined with fpecial reference to the *numbers* of each feparate veftment named, will at once illuftrate, and be illuftrated by, the rubric we are now confidering. In each cafe the " *veftimentum*," fpoken of (the word here meaning a *complete fet of veftments* for *three* perfons, the Celebrant, Epiftoler, and Gofpeller), contains *three* of all fuch veftments as in pre-Reformation ufe *would be worn by all three*, but has *one* Cafula only, and *two* Tunicæ. In mediæval times, thefe *Tunicæ*,

---

[460a] A *cappa rubra* is fpoken of as one of the diftinctive marks of a pope in a letter of Peter Damianus, quoted at p. 221. A *cappa pavonacea* (violet colour) is worn by Roman cardinals.

[461] For detailed information as to the fhape, fize, and ornamentation of the Cope, fee Bock, *L. G.* ii. 287 *sqq.* or Pugin's *Gloffary, in voc.*

[462] The very form of the word Tunacles (inftead of the more correct Tunicles) indicates the debafed period from which the word dates. Properly fpeaking, the diminutive *Tunicula* anfwers to the χιτωνισκος of the Greek Church, and is correctly ufed of any of thofe *fhorter* forms of the Tunic, which from early times, and from affociations of idea which were all but univerfal, ferved to mark *inferiority of dignity* on the part of thofe who wore them. They were alfo fuggeftive of the *more active miniftration* required of the inferior

orders of the clerical body.

[463] *Inventory of St. George's Chapel, Windfor.* " Item de dono Regis Henrici quarti unum veftimentum blodii coloris intextum cum albis canibus, viz., duabus frontellis, duabus ridellis [Fr. *rideaux*] una cafula, duabus tunicis, tribus amictibus, cum ftola et fanone [230] ejufdem fectæ. Item unum veftimentum album bonum de panno adaurato pro principalibus feftis beatæ Mariæ, cum cafula, duabus tunicis, tribus albis, tribus amictibus, cum ftola et fanonibus, quattuor capis ejufdem fectæ, cum diverfis orfreis,[312] et quatuor aliis capis diverfæ fectæ de panno adaurato, cum duabus ridellis et toto apparatu Altaris five frontello." [In another " veftimentum," three Cafulæ are mentioned without any mention in detail of other veft-ments.] Quoted by Pugin, *G. G. A. in voc.* " veftment."

which in Englifh [461] Inventories appear as "Tunacles" (note 462), were in many cafes of coftly material, and richly embroidered. Their fhape re-fembled that of the later Dalmatics, and may be feen in the reprefentation of the deacon in Pl. LXI.

2. Ministering Vestments of a Bishop, a.d. 1548.

In the laft page of the Liturgy authorifed by the Act of 1548, occurs the following rubric :

"In the faying or finging of Mattins and Evenfong, baptizing and burying, the minifter in parifh churches, and chapels annexed to the fame, fhall ufe a furplice. And in all cathedral churches and colleges the archdeacons, deans, provofts, mafters, prebendaries, and fellows, being graduates, may ufe in the quire, befide their furplices, fuch hood as appertaineth to their feveral degrees. And whenfoever the bifhop fhall celebrate the holy communion in the church, or execute any other public miniftration, he fhall have upon him, befide his rochette, a furplice or albe, and a cope or veftment, and alfo his paftoral ftaff in his hand, or elfe borne or holden by his chaplain."

Taking thefe in their order, we have,—

1. The Rochette [465] [*Rochetum*, or *Roquetum*, It. *Rochetto*, Fr. *Rochet*.]

This is by origin a German word, of which *Rock* (a coat) is the modern form, appearing, in refpect of Church ufage, in the form *roquus*, as early as the tenth century, in the will of Bifhop Riculfus above quoted (p. 214, note 441); and in modern German in the word "*chorrock*," *i.e.* quire drefs, or furplice. The Rochet anfwers to the *colobium* of primitive ufe, being a *tunica talaris* without fleeves.[466] It came to be affigned more efpecially to epifcopal ufe, becaufe it was fuited, as the full furplice is not, to be worn under a fuper-veftment, fuch as the cope.[467]

2. A Surplice or Alb. Thefe two veftments are (as their juxtapofition in this rubric intimates) flight variations of what was by origin one veftment.

---

[461] "Item, a Chafuble of green bauiekin, with tunacles of one fuit, ... with three albes of divers forts with their apparel." "A Chafuble of purple velvet . . . with two tunacles and three albes of the fame fuit." From Dugdale's Inventory of veftments belonging to Lincoln Cathedral, quoted by Pu-gin *in voce.* "Chafuble."

[465] In Anglo-Saxon, *Roc.* Leofric, Bifhop of Exeter, in the eleventh century, bequeathed to the ufe of the cathedral church, *inter alia*, (ii *dalmatica*, and iii *piftel roccas*, *i.e.* Epiftoler's rochets). [Dr. Rock, *C. O. F.* vol. i. p. 385.]

[466] Lindwodus (*apud* Dufrefne) ad Provincial. Eccl. Cantuar. lib. iii. tit. 27. "Rochetum differt a fuperpelliceo quia fuperpelliceum habet manicas pendulas, fed Rochetum eft fine manicis, et ordinatur pro clerico miniftraturo facerdoti, vel forfan ad opus ipfius facerdotis in baptizando pueros ne per manicas ipfius brachia impediantur."

[467] The Chimere [It. Zimarra, Sp. Chamarra, Fr. Chamarre, or Cimarre] is itfelf probably a modification of a Cope. See mention of the Chimere in the *Ordo*, &c., of Archbifhop Parker's confecration, quoted at p. 229, No. 3.

One of the earlieſt notices of the *Superpelliceum*,[468] [O. Fr. Sourpelis] has been already quoted (p. 166). The firſt in date to ſpeak of the *Superpelliceum* is Stephanus [469] Tornacenſis, towards the cloſe of the twelfth century (born 1135 A.D., Biſhop of Tournay 1192). The alluſions he makes to it imply that the veſtment was one which had long been in uſe. It was of linen, and *talare* of full length, while the *cappæ* mentioned by the ſame author are of wool.

It is impoſſible to ſay how long this name may been in popular uſe before it appeared in eccleſiaſtical literature. But in ſhape and general arrangement it is a combination into one veſtment of the *tunica* and ſuper-veſtment of the primitive Chriſtian dreſs, as ſhown in the earlieſt monuments of the Weſt. [Plates XIV., XV., XVII.] And it ſtill more cloſely reſembles the dreſs which by the traditions of the Eaſtern Church was aſſigned as a ſacred veſtment to the Apoſtles. See the figure of St. James in Pl. LXIII.

The ſurplice is, in point of faƈt, a *tunica talaris*, made full and flowing, as was the primitive *tunica alba* of Chriſtian miniſtry, and with ſleeves which correſpond to the early *Greek* type juſt ſpoken of, rather than to the comparatively ſmall ſleeve of the Roman dalmatic.

The difference between the Roman and Engliſh Surplice may be ſeen in Pl. LXIII. And the all but exaƈt correſpondence in appearance between our preſent Engliſh Surplice and Stole, of ordinary uſage, and the primitive dreſs attributed to apoſtles, may be ſeen on reference to the central figure of the right-hand group (*ſpeƈtator's* right) in Pl. XV.

3. The Alb has been already noticed. *Sup.* p. 223, No. 1.

4. The Veſtment or Cope. *Sup.* pp. 223, 224, No. 2 and 3.

5. The "Paſtoral Staff." See above, p. 222, No. 15. In the *Ordo*, &c., quoted at p. 229, it is made matter of ſpecial remark that there was no ceremonial *traditio* of a paſtoral ſtaff to the archbiſhop. In mediæval times this [470] conſtituted a ſpecial ceremony of which a full account is given by Gervaſe of Canterbury [Rock, *C. O. F.* p. 226] at the cloſe of the twelfth century.

6. The *Hood*. Both the *Caſula* and the *Cappa* were originally furniſhed with a hood (*cuculus, capitium, cappa*) for the proteƈtion of the head. So were the Pænula and Caracalla,[25] of ſtill earlier uſe.

Our own word *Hood* is derived from the Anglo-Saxon *Hod*, virtually identical with the German *Hut*, and our own more modern " hat."

---

[468] So called as being worn *over* the *pelliceum*, the woollen or furred coat.

[469] In his 106th letter (Migne, *P. C. C.* tom. ccxii. col. 394), which he ſends with a preſent of a new ſurplice to Cardinal Albinus, and with it a ſermon which he had preached ſhortly before " *de myſtica ſuperpellicei conſec-* *tione*." In another form (*linea ſuperpellicealis*) the word occurs in reference to the veſtment of John, Archbiſhop of Rouen († 1076). Dufreſne *in voc.*

[470] Or rather the delivery of the *Croz'er*. See p. 222, No. 15.

The Hood which in primitive times formed part of the super-vestment, was afterwards separated from it. Thus separated, it was lined with fur for the greater comfort (and with *costly* fur for the greater dignity) of them who wore it. The material of which it was to be made, the lining with which it was to be furnished, became matters of minute regulation. Hence the various Doctor's, Master's, Bachelor's hoods, of our present Universities.[471]

2. The Prayer-book of 1552.

In the first Prayer-book, authorised by the Act of 1548, the more important of the older vestments were retained, no mention, however, being made of Amice, Girdle, or Under-Girdle, Stole, Maniple, Caligæ, and Sandalia, Mitre, Gloves, or Ring.

In the second Prayer-book a further change [472] was made. The second rubric before Morning Prayer runs as follows:

"The minister at the time of the Communion, and at all other times in his ministration, shall use neither alb, vestment, nor cope, but, being archbishop or bishop, he shall have and wear a rochette, and being a priest or deacon, he shall have and wear a surplice only."

3. Injunctions of Queen Elizabeth, A.D. 1559.

In the injunctions issued in the first year of Queen Elizabeth no mention is made of vestments. But in the interpretations appended to them by the archbishop and bishops (Cardwell, *Doc. Ann.* p. 203, *sqq.*), there occurs the following direction:

"That there be used only but one apparel; as the cope in the ministration of the Lord's Supper, and the Surplice in all other ministrations."

4. Prayer-book of 1559.

This book, the use of which was enjoined by the Parliament of 1558–1559, has the following rubric on vestments:

"And here is to be noted, that the minister at the time of the communion, and at all other times of his ministration, shall use such ornaments in the church, as were in use by authority of Parliament in the second year of the

---

[471] Of similar origin is the Amess (often confused with the Amice). The word Amess appears in its earliest form in the Provencal *Almusse*, in which the Arabic article is combined (as in many words dating from after the Saracen conquests in Europe) with a European word, the German *Mutze* (a cap) Sp. *Mozzo*. In mediæval Latin it is *Almutium*, in O. Fr. *Aumuce*, now *Aumusse*. In Spanish and Italian we find two sets of derivates, some from the compound form, as Sp. *Almucio*, It. *Almucia*; others from the simple word, as Sp. *Muceta*, It. *Mozzetta*.

[472] The question of the vestments had in the interval been brought prominently into discussion in consequence of Bishop Hooper refusing to be consecrated unless the use of the Pontifical vestments were dispensed with.

reign of King Edward VI. according to the act [473] of parliament set in the beginning of this book."

5. Vestments [474] worn by the Bishops at the Consecration of Archbishop Parker, Dec. 16, 1559.

1. At Morning Prayer (*mane, circiter quintam aut sextam*) and Sermon, the archbishop elect wore his doctor's gown and hood (*toga talari coccinea caputicque indutus*).

2. Sermon ended, the archbishop, and the four bishops, *sacellum egrediuntur . . . . se ad sacram communionem paraturi.* They return vested as follows :

α. The archbishop (elect) *linteo superpelliceo (quod vocant) induebatur.*

β. The Bishop of Chichester in a Cope : *capa serica ad sacra peragenda paratus utebatur.*

γ. Two chaplains of the archbishop who assisted at holy communion wore silk copes also.

δ. The Bishop of Hereford (elect) [475] and the suffragan Bishop of Bedford *linteis superpelliceis induebantur.*

ε. Milo vero Coverdallus non nisi toga lanea talari utebatur.

3. After the Consecration Service, and the Communion, the archbishop went out, accompanied by the four bishops, and speedily returned, "*alba episcopali, superpelliceo, chimeraque* [467] (*ut vocant) ex nigro serico indutus, circa collum vero collare quoddam ex preciosis pellibus sabellinis (vulgo ' sables ' vocant) consutum gestabat. Pari quoque modo Cicestrensis et Herefordensis suis episcopalibus amictibus, superpelliceo se. et chimera* [467] *uterque induebatur. D. Coverdallus vero, et Bedfordiæ suffraganeus, togis solummodo talaribus utebatur.* The archbishop then formally delivered the white wands of office to the principal persons of his household, and then left the chapel attended by them, and accompanied by the bishops.

6. The Advertisements [476] of 1564.

"Item. In the ministration of the holy communion in cathedrall and

---

[473] This refers to the Act for the Uniformity of Common Prayer (1 Eliz.), re-enacting the second Prayer-book of Edward VI., but with certain specified alterations, whereof this of the vestment is one. The direction, however, is thus modified, "until other order shall be therein taken by the authority of the Queen's Majestie, with the advice of her commissioners appointed and auctorised under the great Seale of England, for causes ecclesiastical, or of the metropolitan of this realme."

[474] Rituum et ceremoniarium Ordo in consecratione, &c. Cardwell, *Doc. Ann.* i. p. 243.

[475] John Scory, late Bishop of Chichester, but now of Hereford elect.

[476] Put forth, at the Queen's injunction, by the Archbishop of Canterbury, Metropo-

collegiate churches, the principall minister shall use a cope, with gospeller and epistoler agreably; and at all other prayers to be sayde at the communion table, to use no copes, but surplesses.

"Item. That the deane and prebendaries weare a surplesse with a silk hood in the quyer; and when they preach in the cathedrall or collegiate churches to weare their hood.

"Item. That every minister saying any publique prayers, or ministringe the sacraments, or other rites of the churche, shall wear a comely surples with sleeves. . . . ."

7. CANONS OF 1603.

XVII. "All masters and fellows of colleges or halls, and all the scholars and students in either of the universities, shall in their churches and chapels, upon all Sundays, holy days, and their eves, at the time of Divine Service, wear surplices according to the order of the Church of England; and such as are graduates shall agreeably wear with their surplices such hoods as do severally appertain unto their degrees."

XXIV. and XXV. By the terms of these canons, the "principal minister" at the holy communion, in cathedral and collegiate churches, is to wear a decent cope. But "when there is no communion, it shall be sufficient to wear surplices. Saving that all deans, masters, and heads of collegiate churches, canons, and prebendaries, being graduates, shall daily at the times both of prayer and preaching, wear with their surplices such hoods as are agreeable to their degrees."

PRAYER-BOOK OF 1604.

In this Book the ornaments of the first Prayer-book of Edward VI. are re-enacted as follows:

"And here is to be noted, that the minister at the time of the communion, and at all other times in his ministration, shall use such ornaments in the Church, as were in use by authoritie of Parliament in the second yeere of the reigne of Edward the Sixt, according to the Acte of Parliament [177] set in the beginning of this booke."

8. PRAYER-BOOK OF 1662.

To this are prefixed, *a.* The Act I. Eliz. (see note 473); *β.* The Act of

---

litan, the Bishops of London, Ely, Rochester, Winton, and Lincoln, "Commissioners in causes ecclesiastical with others." See Note 473 above. As to their authority, see Cardwell, *Doc. Ann.* vol. i, p. 287.

The same advertisements contain some-

what minute directions for the "outwarde apparell of persons ecclesiasticall," *i.e.* for their secular dress.

[177] This Act being 1 Eliz. For the uniformitie, &c., containing the modifying clause, "*until other order shall be taken*," &c.

Uniformity, XIV. Carol. II. "Whereas in the firft year of the late Queen Elizabeth," &c.

The rubric as to veftments is as follows :

" Here is to be noted, that fuch ornaments of the church and of. the minifters thereof, at all times of their miniftration, fhall be retained and be in ufe, as were in this Church of England, by the authority of Parliament, in the fecond [478] year of the reign of King Edward the Sixth."

---

[478] The Parliament which authorifed the firft Prayer-book of Edward VI., met Oct. 15, 1548; was prorogued till Nov. 24 by reafon of the Plague. The Bill for confirming " the order of divine worfhip," which had been drawn out " by the Archbifhop of Canterbury, with other learned and difcreet bifhops and divines," was brought in Dec. 9 to the Commons, Dec. 10 to the Lords, and was agreed to Jan. 15, 1549. The Parliament was not prorogued till March 14. And as Edward's acceffion dates from Jan. 28, 1547, the feffion is technically defcribed as 2 and 3 Edward VI., and yet the "authority of Parliament" is faid to be given to this book *"in the fecond year of King Edward VI."*

PART III.

PLATES AND DESCRIPTIONS.

Frontispiece. DIPTYCH OF S. PAUL.[479] Photographed from a facsimile in fictile ivory in the British Museum. Imperfectly represented, and wrongly described, as a *Consular* diptych, by Duval.

In the centre compartment is the scene described in Acts, xxviii. 1 to 6. The viper is falling from St. Paul's hand; the "fire of dried wood" is at his feet; the πρῶτος τῆς νήσου, the chief officer of the island, is looking on in astonishment; a soldier (the dress marks him as a "barbarian") is in attendance upon him.

In the lower compartment are some of those "which had infirmities in the island," whom the soldier, mentioned above, is directing to St. Paul for healing.

In the upper compartment St. Paul[480] is seated on an apostolic throne, and giving his blessing to a bishop.[481] In this we may probably see a trace of an early Roman tradition, coinciding with the conclusions to be drawn from Scripture, and from the epistle of St. Clement of Rome. From these it appears clear that St. Paul, and not St. Peter,[482] was the first "apostle and bishop" of Rome; though St. Peter no less than St. Paul witnessed there, by his death, for Christ. Compare p. xlii. l. 1, *sqq.*

PLATES I. TO VII., ILLUSTRATIONS OF CLASSICAL COSTUME.

Pl. I. *The Monument of Caius Sestius.* The father (dressed in *tunica talaris* and *toga*) bids "Farewell, for ever," to his daughter.

---

[479] The original was at one time in the possession of Baron Denon, and belongs now to M. Carrand of Lyons.

[480] This is plain from a comparison of this figure with that of St. Paul in the central compartment. Contrast the figures of consuls in Plates XXII., XXIII.

[481] So I infer from the book of the Gospels held in the left hand, this having been in early times the distinguishing *insigne* of a bishop. See p. xlii, and compare Plates XXX., XXXI., XLIV., XLV., XLVI., and, for the East, the figure of St. James in Pl. LXIII.

[482] This will account for the fact that in very many of the early monuments at Rome precedence is given to St. Paul over St. Peter; the former being often placed on the *right* hand of our Saviour, St. Peter on the left.

Pl. II. *From the Arch of Titus.* The Emperor, in the long garb of peaceful (p. ix, *4*) rule, gives audience [483] to his people. The figures standin n around and below him illuftrate the various types of drefs defcribed in Introduction, Chap. ii. p. vii, *fqq.*

Pl. III. *From the Column of Trajan.* [484] The Emperor, before the Prætorian tent, offers the facrifice known as the *Suovetaurilia.* He is clad in a *toga* (fee p. xiv), and has the head covered (p. 182, No. 17); in his hand a patera. The actual facrificers are *nudi* (note *π*, p. xxi), naked to the waift. ·

Pl. IV. *From the Arch of Conftantine.* The Emperor, in the garb of war [485] (p. xl, *1*), addreffes the people of Rome.

Pl. V. *The Ornamented Planeta* [486] *and the Dalmatic.* [487] The firft of thefe figures is by moft antiquaries defcribed as dreffed in a Pænula. [488] There is little doubt that in *form* it refembles the Pænula, and it may be fuch a Pænula as in the fifth century (p. 197, No. 22) was worn even *intra Urbem* by fenators. The ornamental *clavi* worn, as here, *upon a fuper-veftment*, are of very rare occurrence.

The other figure is clad in a Dalmatic.

Both figures are *"orantes,"* in what was in early times the attitude of prayer.

Pl. V. *bis. Roman Drefs* [489] *of the Imperial times.*

1. A Roman marriage, as generally defcribed, but rather perhaps a betrothal (*fponfalia*). For the drefs of the man, fee pp. x, xi. The head-drefs of the bride may either be the (*Flammeum*) bridal veil, or a *Mafortis*, if the ceremony be not a marriage.

2. A mode of wearing the *Pallium*, [490] common in works of late Greek or Roman art, and reproduced in many of the early frefcoes and mofaics in reprefentations of Apoftles. Plates XXIX., XXXVIII., XLV.

---

[483] This fculpture is intended to reprefent the bleffings of peace and plenty reftored by the emperor to Italy. FEMINARVM FOE-CVNDITATI GENITORVMQ SPEI CON-SVLVIT PVBLICVS PARENS PER VNI-VERSAM ITALIAM PVERIS PVELLISQ VLPIIS (?) ALIMENTARIIS INSTITVTIS. See Bellori (*Vet. Arc. Aug*), by whom the relievi of this arch are fully defcribed and figured. Compare Pliny, *Paneg.* cap. 26. *Adventante congiarii die . . . labor parentibus erat oftentare parvulos, impofitofque cervicibus adulantia verba blandafque voces edocere.*

[484] For a full defcription, fee Bellori, *Colonna Traiana.*

[485] Becaufe he is here reprefented at the moment of his entering Rome, *immediately after his victory* over Maxentius, Oct. 28, A.D. 312. See Bellori, *Vet. Arc. Aug.*

[486] For the Planeta, fee Appendix C, No. 38, *fqq.*

[487] See Introduction, p. lv, *fqq.*

[488] See Appendix C, Nos. 1 to 25; Introduction, p. lx, *fqq.*

[489] Thefe outlines are from Weifs, K. Abt. ii. fig. 376, 423; K. i. M. fig. 3, 8.

[490] This term is here ufed, as by the Romans under the empire, as the equivalent for the Greek *ἱμάτιον*, a general term for a fuperveftment, as diftinct from the *χιτών.*

H H

3. The Toga, with a sketch showing its supposed form and proportion when opened out.

4. The Pænula, with its hood attached. An outline appended, showing its *cucullus* (or " hood ") as worn upon the head.

5. The *tunica talaris* (p. viii, and note λ, p. ix) *manicata*.

Pl. VI. *Greek Dress.* From Montfaucon, A. E. tom. iii. Pl. I. The smaller groups are from the Parthenon, and of the time of Pericles. The larger figures (wearing ἱμάτιον and χιτών) are of the Roman Period. See Boissard, Pl. 51, 123.

Pl. VI. *bis* and VII. *Roman and Greek Sacerdotal Costume.* The figures here given (from Montfaucon and Boissard) will serve to show the conventional modes of designating official priesthood in classical art. See p. xxxix, *sqq.*

Pl. VIII. and IX. *Dress of Jewish Priesthood.* These Plates, which are reproductions of those given by Dr. Bock [491] (*L. G.* vol. i. Pl. III., IV.), are probably near approaches to those of actual Levitical priesthood. Compare the accounts of Josephus (p. 2 to 7), and of St. Jerome (p. 10 to 19). But the mitre of the Levitical priest was probably very different from that here represented. Braunius himself, whom Dr. Bock here follows, speaks with great diffidence upon this point, and expresses his opinion that if we could determine what was the *pileolum* assigned to Ulysses [492] in works of ancient art, this would determine the real form of the Levitical cap. Such a cap is in point of fact seen in several works of art still existing, [493] and is what we should call a " skull-cap," of the shape of the head, and " *like a sphere divided in twain,*" as St. Jerome described it. Such a cap as that attributed to the high-priest in Pl. IX., was probably common to both orders, the difference consisting only in the insignia (pp. 6 and 19), proper to the high-priest, the additional overing, *coloris hyacinthini,* and the *lamina aurea.*

Pl. X. *The Holy Family.* From the chromolithograph of De Rossi [I. S. D. V.] This fresco, in its original place in the cemetery of S. Priscilla, occupies, strange to say, a wholly subordinate position amongst a number of unimportant figures. It is probably the oldest picture of the subject now extant. [For a very early *Eastern* representation, see Texier and Pullan, B. A. Pl. V.] The Star of Bethlehem is seen above. And De Rossi very ingeniously (but somewhat fancifully) suggests, that the standing figure is not that of St. Joseph, but the embodiment of the Jewish prophet of the older

---

[491] Dr. Bock's authority is Braunius *De Hab. Sac. Hebræorum,* a very learned writer, but one who has followed Maimonides, and other late Jewish authorities, upon some points in which they differ from Josephus and St. Jerome.

[492] *Pileolum quale pictum in Ulysse* (al. Ulysseo) *conspicimus, quasi sphæra media sit divisa.* St. Jerome, *ad Fabiol.* quoted at p. 14.

[493] See, for example, Gell's *Pompeii,* Pl. XV., vol. ii.

covenant, pointing to that Star as the symbol of the fulfilment, in the Nativity, of the great subject of Old Testament prophecy. A comparison of this with Plates XXXVIII., XL., XLV., and XLVI., will show at a glance the difference of belief at Rome in the third or fourth century (from which, if not from an earlier time, this first representation dates), and in the ninth, and eleventh, and twelfth, to which those later pictures belong.

Pl. XI. *Our Lord blessing a young child.* From the Cemetery of SS. Marcellinus and Peter. Aringhi, R. S. tom. ii. p. 71. For the *virga* in the hand of our Lord, see p. xl.

Pl. XII. *Our Lord as the giver of the Divine Word.* Cemetery of St. Agnes. Aringhi, R. S. tom. ii. p. 213. On either side are two Apostles, who, as well as our Lord, have the nimbus, indicating a somewhat late date for this picture. The two *capsæ*, on either side, filled with *volumina*, are intended (almost without doubt) as representations of the Old and New Testament respectively. The open *codex* in the hand of our Lord shows the later form of Book.[494]

Pl. XIII. *Our Lord as the Good Shepherd.* [Aringhi, R. S. tom. ii. p. 111.] From a drawing made for me by a valued friend, and most accomplished artist, the late Mrs. C. Newton.

For the type of dress represented, see pp. viii and ix.

Pl. XIV. *Our Lord with Six Apostles.* From the Cemetery of St. Agnes at Rome. Aringhi, R. S. tom. ii. p. 195. On the dress here attributed to our Lord and to the Apostles, and with very slight variations perpetuated in much later monuments, see Introduction, Chaps. IV. and V.

Pl. XV. *Our Lord with the Twelve Apostles.* From the Cemetery of S. Callixtus at Rome. Aringhi, R. S. tom. i. p. 529.

Pl. XVI. *A Passover Celebration.* The *lamb* (as I suppose it to be) dressed whole, which is upon the table, the cup, and the youth, dressed, not as a slave, but as a son of the house (compare Exod. xii. 26), all indicate such an interpretation as is implied by the title I have given to this picture. Aringhus (R. S. ii. p. 119) regards it as an *Agape Funeralis.*

Pl. XVII. *The Ordination of a Deacon.* From the Cemetery of St. Hermes. Aringhi, R. S. ii. p. 329. Anastasius states (D. V. P. in Pelagio II.) that Pope Pelagius II. "made" (*fecit*) this cemetery, and held ordinations there. The style of a mosaic (Pl. XXIX.), which Pelagius constructed elsewhere, confirms the probability of the conjecture, that the fresco reproduced in this plate dates from his time. It may probably be regarded as an ideal

---

[494] In accordance with this somewhat late date, probably the fifth century, is the curious fact that in this picture our Lord is distin- | guished from the two Apostles by an *Orarium*, corresponding in arrangement to those shown in Pl. IV.

reprefentation of ordination, as proceeding ultimately from our Lord. If fo, the two figures on either fide will reprefent St. Peter and St. Paul, as the joint founders, under Chrift, of the Church at Rome.

Pl. XVIII. **PWMANOY ΠPECBEYTOY** (probably the Prefbyter Romanus, martyred Nov. 17, A.D. 303) and **EYKAPΠIWNOC CTPA-TIWTOY** St. Eucarpion, foldier and martyr in the Reign of Diocletian. This and the three plates which follow are from chromolithographs publifhed by Texier and Pullan ("from careful drawings coloured on the fpot") in their "Byzantine Architecture." The mofaics reprefented decorate the vault of the Church of St. George at Theffalonica, and are among the very few early Greek mofaics which efcaped deftruction either from the Iconoclafts, or at the hands of the Turks. The learned authors of the work above mentioned give reafons for their belief, that this church was built by Conftantine himfelf during his firft fojourn at Theffalonica. The drefs feen in all thefe plates is not the drefs of holy miniftration (which would have been white), but the drefs of folemn ceremonial, fuch as could appropriately be attributed, as here it is, to laymen, as well as to bifhops and priefts.[495] For details concerning this, fee Introduction, Chapters II., III., IV., and for the queftion of colour, Appendix A.

Pl. XIX. **KOCMOY IATPOY** and **ΔAMIANOY IATPOY** SS. Cofmas and Damianus, natives of Arabia. They practifed Medicine at Ægæ in Cilicia, A.D. 283.

"They traverfed the country curing difeafes, and demanded no other re-compenfe from thofe whom they cured than that they fhould embrace the Chriftian faith. But the partifans of idolatry, believing that they worked by magic, denounced them to the Emperor (Carinus). When arrefted they were ordered to deny Chrift; upon their refufal they were about to be conducted to execution, when, through divine infpiration, the emperor was convinced of his error by means of a cure effected by thefe two Chriftians. The emperor and all his fervants thenceforth believed in Chrift; but the honours rendered to the two phyficians excited the jealoufy of the courtiers, and one day, when Damian and Cofmas were gathering plants upon a mountain, they were fur-prifed and put to death." *Byz. Archit.* p. 141.

Pl. XX. **ΦIΛIΠΠOY EΠICK** and **ΘEPINOY CTPAT** *i.e.* Philip, Bifhop of Heraclea; Therinus, foldier and martyr.

"Philip was Bifhop of the town of Heraclea, in the fourth century. . . . . Baffus, being Governor of Thrace, fent the procurator Ariftoma-chus, to clofe the church and feize the treafure. Philip ftill perfifted in performing fervices under the portico, and in exhorting Chriftians to remain fteadfaft in the faith: for this he was fent to the ftake. . . ." *Ibid.*

---

[495] Slight variations may, however, be noticed as between the drefs attributed to a bifhop (Pl. XX.) and a prefbyter (Pl. XVIII.), compared with that of the laymen.

Of Therinus nothing is known with certainty, save what the title of "soldier," here given him, indicates. His position relatively to St. Philip makes it probable that he was of the same province (Macedonia) and probably an officer, or soldier, of the Macedonian Legion.

Pl. XXI. ΟΝΗCΙΦΟΡΟΥ CΤΡΑΤC and ΠΟΡΦΟΙΡΙΟΥ.

"Onesiphorus and Porphyrius . . . . suffered martyrdom on the same day. Onesiphorus was a native of Iconium, and a relative of the Empress Tryphæne. He lived at Iconium, and having received there the Apostle Paul, he was instructed by him, and baptized with his whole houschold. Having become a Christian he quitted Iconium and went to dwell at Paros, where he preached the Christian doctrine; but having been seized by the order of the Archon, at the same time as his servant Porphyrius, he was tortured and afterwards put to death by being tied to the tail of a spirited horse, and dragged over a stony road. Porphyrius suffered the same torture, and died with his master." Texier and Pullan, B. A. p. 140.

Pl. XXII. *Diptych of Boethius, Consul of the West,* A.D. 510. For the history of the diptych, and a statement of the various questions suggested by it, see Gori. Thes. Diptych, tom. i. p. 137, *sqq.* A comparison of this with Pl. XXIII. will show the identity (with very slight modifications only) of official costume in New and Old Rome, in the sixth century, and will indicate the probable source of the Omophorion, worn (as matter of privilege) by Patriarchs and Metropolitans in the East, and, out of usage rather than of theoretical right, by almost all bishops.

Pl. XXIII. *Diptych of Clementinus, Consul of the East,* A.D. 513. For a description of this diptych, see M. D. Wyatt, *Notices of Sculpture in Ivory,* p. 6; Gori, *Thes. Dipt.* i. p. 229, *sqq.* This, and the following Plate, are photographed, by permission, from the facsimile, in fictile ivory, published by the Arundel Society.

Pl. XXIV. *Diptych of St. Gregory the Great, in the Costume, and with the Insignia,*[496] *of a Consul.* This singular monument, assigned by antiquaries to the year 700, or thereabouts, now forms the cover of an antiphonary, presented by St. Gregory to Theodolinda, Queen of the Lombards. It is preserved in the Treasury of the Cathedral at Monza.[497] The received opinion among the older antiquaries was, that this was originally a consular diptych, *converted* into a representation of St. Gregory. Fuller information, however, has led the most eminent modern antiquaries to regard this as an original work. The inscription above the bishop's head is thus worded: GREGO-RIUS PRÆZVL MERITIS ET NOMINE DIGNV VNDE GENVS DVCIT MERITVM CONSCENDIT HONOREM.

---

[496] The *Mappa* in the r. h. of a consul (thrown into the arena as a signal for the games to commence), as in Plates XXII., and XXIII., may here perhaps be interpreted as a *Mappula,* or Maniple.

[497] Photographed, by permission, for this work, from the facsimile of the Arundel Society.

Pl. XXV. *Picture of St. Gregory the Great, of his Father Gordianus, and his Mother Sylvia.* This picture corresponds with the description [498] given of the original by Joannes Diaconus, in the tenth century. Roman antiquaries constantly refer to it as authentic; and Cardinal Baronius, who had opportunities of knowing its history, and Papebrochius (AA. SS. Maius Propyl. p. 177) publish it as such. Reference is made to a *tabula æri incisa* used by Baronius, but the actual drawings (if any), of older date, from which this derived, are not specified.

Pl. XXVI. *The Ascension.* Facsimile of an illustration in a Syriac MS. of the Gospels, written A.D. 586, at Zagba, in Mesopotamia, and acquired for the Library of the Medici, at Florence, A.D. 1497. The picture represents the Ascension. The dresses of the Apostles correspond exactly with those assigned to them in early Roman frescoes and mosaic pictures. It is noticeable that in this picture we have already traces, slight in themselves, of a tendency to exalt the blessed Virgin to a position beyond that assigned to her in Holy Scripture, or in the earlier monuments of Christian antiquity. She here occupies the central place amid the Apostles, as present at the Ascension, an event with which, in the narrative of Scripture, she is not in any way connected. And to her, as to our Lord and to the angels, the nimbus is assigned, though the Twelve have it not. In these respects this picture forms a connecting link, in the thought implied, as in the time from which it dates, between Pl. X., and XXXVIII. [From Seroux d'Agincourt, Histoire, &c., vol. v. Pl. XXVII.]

Pl. XXVII. *Eusebius, Bishop of Cæsarea, and Ammonius of Alexandria.* [From the same MS. as No. XXVI.] After Asseman. Bib. Med. Pl. III.

Pl. XXVIII. *The Emperor Justinian, and Archbishop Maximianus, at the Consecration of the Church of S. Vitalis, at Ravenna.* From a mosaic dating, probably, from the close of the sixth century. The Archbishop wears a Dalmatic under a Planeta.[499] Over the Planeta is a Pallium of the older [400] form and arrangement, and in his hand a jewelled cross. The two personages

---

[498] Joan. Diac. D. G. P. lib. iv. cap. 83. 84. In this description, note particularly the following concerning St. Gregory's dress: "Planeta super Dalmaticam castanea: evangelium in sinistra, modus crucis in dextra: pallio meniotici, a dextro videlicet humero sub pectore super stomachum circulatim deducto: deinde sursum per sinistrum humerum veniens propria rectitudine non per medium corporis sed ex latere pendet: circa verticem vero tabulæ" (the "*square nimbus*," so called) "similitudinem, quod viventis insigne est, præferens, non coronam" (the "*nimbus*"). The *Pallium* described is evidently such as that ascribed to Leo III. in the drawing at p. lii. The language of John the deacon implies that

in his own time (tenth century) the form and arrangement of the pallium had undergone a change. Compare cap. 80 of the same book, whence it appears that the pallium was in St. Gregory's time of *linen* and *nullis accubiis* (i.e. *acubus* [322]) perforatum.

[499] As to the colour of this Planeta it is difficult to speak with authority. Ciampini speaks of it as *aurea*. Hefner-Alteneck (Pl. XCI) in his coloured drawing represents it as a very dull green, the Dalmatic white, with black stripes; and Gally Knight (E. A. Pl. X.) both figures and describes the whole dress as white. All the coloured drawings that I have seen represent the *lora* (or *clavi*) as black.

on his left (probably archdeacon and deacon) wear Dalmatics of the older form, with black *clavi* (not clearly fhown in this Plate), and correfponding ftripes at the edge of the fleeve. [After Gally Knight, E. A. Pl. X]

Pl. XXIX. *A mofaic, dating from the clofe of the Sixth Century, from the Church of S. Laurentius, at Rome.* The figures reprefented are our Lord, S. PETRVS and S. PAVLVS, S. LAVRENTIVS and S. STEPHANVS, S. YPPOLIT (St. Hippolytus) and PELAGIVS EPISC. (Bifhop of Rome from 578 to 590). Pelagius is without the nimbus affigned to the other fix perfonages, and wears the drefs traditionally attributed to our Lord and the Apoftles. [From a drawing in Her Majefty's Collection.] The figure of Pelagius has been in great part deftroyed by accident, and is here reprefented as reftored by Roman antiquaries. In one particular,[500] not of importance to this inquiry, the arrangement of the two figures on the fpectator's left is probably incorrect.

Pl. XXX. SCS CORNELIVS PP. (Bifhop of Rome A.D. 251–252), and SCS CIPRIANVS (Bifhop of Carthage A.D. 248–258). [From a frefco lately difcovered by Chevalier De Rofli, and dating[501] (probably) from the clofe of the eighth century.]

Pl. XXXI. Frefco of the fame date[501] as the above, in which are reprefented S. XVSTVS [Bifhop of Rome from A.D. 257 to A.D. 259], and a contemporary Bifhop [SCS. O. perhaps St. Optatus] of fome unknown fee.

Pl. XXXII. *The TRICLINIVM LATERANVM.*[500] A portion of the Banquet-room of the Lateran Palace, built and decorated with mofaics by Leo III., at the beginning of the ninth century.

Pl. XXXIII. *Two groups from the Mofaics of the TRICLINIUM LATERANUM.*[502] In the one our Lord beftows a Pallium (fymbol of eccle-fiaftical authority), upon St. Sylvefter, and a *Vexillum* (fymbol of imperial rule) upon CONSTANTINVS REX. In the other, St. Peter gives a Pallium to D. N. SCTISSIMVS LEO PP. (Dominus nofter Sanctiflimus Leo Papa); and a *Vexillum* to CAROLVS REX (Charlemagne). By thefe two groups is fymbolifed the Divine origin of both fpiritual and temporal power ; and the alliance, and partition of the two, in the perfon of the Pope and the Emperor. A more exact reprefentation of this Plate, photographed

---

[500] According to one reftoration the model of the church is held in the hands of Pope Pelagius, fo as to defignate him as the reftorer of the church.

[501] As to the date of thefe monuments fee De Rofli, R. S. p. 298 to 304. He pronounces them as "certainly not older" than the feventh century, and mentions various reafons for attributing them to the ponti-

ficate of Leo III.

[502] For full details concerning this monument fee Alemannus, *De Parietinis Lateranis,* from which the above drawings are taken. The firft is altogether, and the fecond in great part, a reftoration, authority for which was found in drawings preferved in the Vatican, after the original itfelf (even as reftored by Leo IV.) had been in great part deftroyed.

from a drawing in Her Majesty's collection, will be found at p. lii. See description of woodcuts below.

Pl. XXXIV. to XXXVI.[503] A series of illustrations from the Liber Pontificalis of Landolfus, a MS. of the ninth century, in the Library of S. Minerva, at Rome. These represent the Costume and Insignia, and the modes of Ordination, regarded as proper to priests, deacons, sub-deacons, exorcists, and the other minor orders, at the period in question.

Pl. XXXIV. *Ordination of Ostiarii* (doorkeepers) *and of Lectores* (readers).

1. The Bishop delivers to the Doorkeepers the keys of the Church. *Tradendo eis claves ecclesiæ Dei.*

2. The *Ostiarii* prostrate themselves before the Bishop to receive his blessing. *Prosternuntur ante pontificem.*

3. Ordination of Readers. *Tradidit eis episcopus codicem.*

4. The Bishop gives his blessing to the Readers. *Deinde prostratis in terram (benedicit).*

Pl. XXXV. *Ordination of Exorcists, Acolytes, Sub-deacons, and Deacons.*

5. The Bishop gives a book to the Exorcists. *Exorcistis tradit episcopus libellum.*

6. The Bishop hands a candlestick to the Acolyte. *Acolitis tradit episcopus cerostatam.*

7. The Sub-deacons receive the Paten and the Chalice. *Subdiaconi patenam et calicem.*

8. The Bishop lays the *Orarium* (Stole) on the left shoulder of the Deacon. *Ponens oraria super humeros.*

Pl. XXXVI. *Ordination of Deacons and Priests.*

9. The Bishop bestows Benediction on the Deacons. *Dum in terram prostrati fuerint.*

10. Ordination of Priests. The Bishop places the *Orarium* (Stole) about their necks. *Oraria super colla eorum.*

11. They bow the head to receive imposition of hands, and episcopal Benediction. *Super quos inclinatis capitibus* (benedicit).

12. The Bishop anoints their right hands, tracing thereon the sign of the Cross. *Cum pollice dexteræ faciens crucem.*

---

[503] From the outlines published by Seroux d'Agincourt. Facsimiles of the original drawings are in the author's possession.

Pl. XXXVII. *A Bishop giving the Chrism to a newly baptized Infant.* From a Latin MS. of the ninth century, in the Library of the S. Minerva, at Rome.[504]

Pl. XXXVIII. *The Virgin Mother and Holy Child.* The former wears a royal diadem, and a dress of purple and gold, with scarlet shoes (insignia of royalty). On either side are, *r.* S. IACOBVS and S. IOANNES; *l.* S. PETRVS and S. ANDREAS. This mosaic dates from *circ.* 848 A.D. [Photographed from a drawing in Her Majesty's Collection.]

See above on Plates X. and XXVI.

Pl. XXXIX. *Pope Nicholas I.* [*sed.* A.D. 858–867] *and the Emperor Lewis II.* [*regn.* A.D. 843–876.] From the *Chartularium Prumiense*, a MS.[505] partly of the ninth century, partly of later date, in the Stadtbibliotek, at Treves. The Cap here worn by the Pope is not a *Mitra*, but a *Camelaucium*, so called. Compare Florovantes, *Ant. Pontif. Rom. Den.* p. 37. He is speaking of a coin of Hadrianus I. *Figura in medio Pontificali habitu et bireto, quod Camelaucium ab Anastasio in Constantino, hodie vero Camaurum dicitur.* The first change of head-dress on the coins is early in the tenth century. Describing a coin of Sergius III. (*sed.* 904–911), Flor. says, p. 63, *Sergium III. pontificia veste indutum, et mitra ornatum, hic exhibet nummus;* at in superioribus nummis Pontificum capita camelaucio tantum tecta visuntur: *quæ res mire favet eorum sententiæ qui Pontifices serius mitram gestasse arbitrantur.* These facts bear out the opinion already expressed (note 265, p. 129), that the Mitra had been introduced at Rome before the time (close of eleventh century) of St. Ivo's writing. Compare Appendix F, No. 12. But they throw back the *Mitra* at Rome itself to a somewhat earlier date than most modern antiquaries have assigned to it. [The book above quoted is of great rarity. But these coins are figured in another work, the *Memoria di Domenico Promis. Monete dei Rom. Pontef.* Torino, 1858.] See further on Pl. XLVII.

Pl. XL. A fresco from the hypogene Church of S. Clemente, at Rome (lately discovered). It presents a picture of the Assumption, and contains a representation of Leo IV., and S. Vitus. This picture, when first discovered, was supposed, by such of the Roman clergy as were not antiquaries, to prove the recognition of the doctrine of the Assumption as early as the second or third centuries. They forgot that, though the walls on which these frescoes are painted are undoubtedly very ancient, it by no means follows that the paintings upon them are of the same date. The square nimbus (*quod viventis insigne est,* Joan. Diac. note 498) on the head of Leo IV., *and the position assigned him in the picture,* indicate that he was the giver of this fresco. SANCTISSIMVS DOM. LEO QRT. PP. ROM. may be seen inscribed about his head. The signature QVOD HÆC PRÆ CVNCTIS FVLGET PICTVRA COLORE COMPONERE HANC STVDVIT PRESBYTER ECCE LEO shows that he gave the picture before he became Pope, and that the smaller inscrip-

---

[504] Photographed from a drawing in Her Majesty's collection.

[505] This Plate is from Ramboux (Beitrage zur Kunstgeschichte, u. s. w).

I I

tion was added fomewhat later, probably foon after his death.   A.D. 855.
[On the title *Papa Romanus*, derived from the earlier times of the Church,
when there were other "Papæ" even in the Weſt, befide the Biſhop of
Rome, fee De Roſſi, R. S. p. 303, and Dufreſne, *in voc.*]

Pl. XLI.   The Emperor Conſtantine VI. prefiding at the Seventh General
Council (fo called), held at Nicæa, A.D. 787.   From a Greek MS. of the tenth
century, the *Menologium Græcorum, &c.*, in the Vatican Library.   This Plate
is from the outline publiſhed by Seroux d'Agincourt.   An accurate copy of the
original is in the author's poſſeſſion.   The Sticharia of the biſhops, as well
as their Phænolia, are coloured.   The Phænolion of the biſhop on the emperor's left (Taraſius, Patriarch of Conſtantinople), is lavender purple ; the
others (apparently) black and gold.   Two of the patriarchs here repreſented,
though *fuppofed to be prefent* (by their deputies), had not even heard of the
Council, the occupation of the country by the Saracens preventing communi-
cation.   The proſtrate figure repreſents the "defeated party," in this cafe the
Iconoclaſts.   The determinations of this Council were fully fanctioned by the
Pope (Hadrian I.), as before by his legates.   But Charlemagne fummoned
another Council of three hundred biſhops, at Frankfort, A.D. 794, at which the
authority of this Nicene Council (claiming to be the Seventh General Council)
was rejected, and its decrees reverfed.   [An entirely different account is given
by moſt of the Roman authorities.   For the above, and the evidence on which
it reſts, fee Cave, *Hiſt. Lit.* i. 652.]

Pl. XLII.   Egbertus, Archbiſhop of Treves (*fed.* 975 to 993), receives
a book offered to him by Keraldus Augienſis and another Benedictine Monk.
This picture forms the title-page of an Evangeliarium, written at the clofe of
the tenth century.   [From the drawing of Ramboux.]

Pl. XLIII.   *St. Clement at the Altar.*   The miraculous blinding of Sifin-
nius.   [The fame fubject in one of the frefcoes of the Church of St. Mark,
at Venice.   Kreutz, *Mof. Sec. &c.*, tav. xxiii.]   The donors of this frefco,
Beno de Rapiza, and Maria his wife, are repreſented *de more* at the left of the
picture ; and *of fmall fize* (compare Pl. XLI.) in token of humility.   There
is ſtrong internal evidence, to an antiquarian eye, of the late date of this
picture.   And I hear that diplomatic evidence, lately difcovered at Rome,
ſhows that Beno de Rapiza and his wife lived in the eleventh century.

Pl. XLIV.   *St. Gregory the Great and St. Dunftan.*   From a MS. of the
eleventh century, in the Britiſh Mufeum.   St. Gregory wears a Mitre of the
earlieſt form, the *tæniæ* or *fafciæ* of which hang down on either fide, fo as to
appear like large earrings.   The archbiſhop (who alfo wears a Mitre) is kneeling,
with two monks, at St. Gregory's feet, and embracing them.   The dove
whiſpering, as it were, into the ear, is an emblem of divine infpiration.   For
further details, fee the great work of Profeſſor Weſtwood (*Miniatures and Ornaments, &c.*, p. 126) to which I owe this more correct defcription of the picture.

Pl. XLV.   The Bleſſed Virgin, as the Queen of Heaven, feated on the
fame throne with our Lord.   In her hand a fcroll (painted black in the

drawing at Windſor, from which this is photographed) on which in the original are inſcribed the words *Læva ejus ſub capite meo* (Cant. ii. 6; viii. 3). The figures on either ſide are (on the ſpectator's left) INNOCENTIVS PP., (Innocent II. *ſed.* A.D. 1130-1143, the donor of this moſaic), LAVRENTIVS (St. Laurence carrying a croſs, as in Pl. XXIX.) CORNELIVS PP. On the *r.* PETRVS, CALIXTVS PP. IVLIVS PP. and CALEPODIVS PRESBYTER. [From a drawing in Her Majeſty's collection, as is Pl. XLVI. which follows.]

Pl. XLVI. PRÆSIDET ÆTHEREIS PIA VIRGO MARIA CHO-REIS. [A moſaic[506] in the apſe of the Oratory of St. Nicolaus, at Rome, commenced by Calixtus II., and completed[507] by Anaſtaſius II.] The in-ſcription on this moſaic is too characteriſtic of the times to be omitted :

> SVSTVLIT HOC PRIMO TEMPLVM CALLIXTVS AB IMO
> VIR CLARVS LATE GALLORVM NOBILITATE.
> VERVM ANASTASIVS PAPATVS CVLMINE QVARTVS
> HOC OPVS ORNAVIT VARIISQVE MODIS DECORAVIT.

Pl. XLVII. Pope Innocent II. giving Benediction to Abbot Adalbero. From an *interpolated* copy of the *Chartularium Prumienſe*, now in the Stadt-Bibliothetek, at Treves. For the Hiſtory of the MS., ſee Ramboux. The greater part of it dates from 1222 A.D. But there have been additions to it, of which this picture muſt be one. For the *triple* crown, here ſhown, points to the fourteenth century. According to Roman antiquaries of the higheſt repute, the *double* crown (ſignificant of ſpiritual and temporal power combined) was introduced by Boniface VIII. A.D. 1299-1303, (Alemannus, *De P. L.* cap. 13, p. 129; and Florovantes, *Ant. Pont. Rom. Den.* p. 57); and the *triple* crown by Urbanus V. (A.D. 1362-1370). Compare AA. SS. Maius, Propyl. p. 419.

Pl. XLVIII. From a MS. written by Matthew Paris (*circ.* 1250) in the Britiſh Muſeum. Cotton MSS., Nero D. I.

α. Pope Adrian I. receives a letter from Offa II., King of Mercia.

β. The Pope's ſanction having been obtained, the archiepiſcopal ſee is tranſ-ferred from Canterbury, in the " Kingdom of Kent," to Lichfield, in the " King-dom of Mercia." Eadulfus is conſecrated the firſt Archbiſhop of Lichfield.[508]

This tranſaction here recorded had an important influence on the ſubſe-quent hiſtory of the Engliſh Church in its relation to the Roman See. Cf. Hook, *Lives of the Archbiſhops,* vol. i. p. 243, *ſqq.*

---

[506] Compare AA. SS. Maius Propyl. p. 320, where this moſaic is figured and de-ſcribed ; and Muratori, R. I. S. tom. ii. p. 417.

[507] In this I follow Papebrochius (AA. SS. *ubi ſupra*), who further expreſſes his belief, that the principal figure in this group was intended by Calixtus for our Lord, but that this was conſiderably altered by Anaſtaſius, and *changed into the figure of the Virgin* here exhibited. A ſimilar change has been made in a moſaic of the fifth century. The original ſtate of this is delineated by

Ciampini, M. V. i. p. 200, the Saviour (with the *nimbus*) being ſeated on a throne, whilſt the Virgin mother ſtood near. " As this group is *now* before us, the erect figure is left out ; the ſeated one is converted into that of Mary, with a halo round the head, although in the original even ſuch attribute (alike given to the Saviour and to all the angels introduced) is *not* aſſigned to her." Hemans' Hiſtory, &c., p. 207. With what he ſays of the nimbus, compare what is ſaid above on Pl. XXVI.

[508] The crowns of the two principal per-ſonages in this picture have been deliberately

Pl. XLIX. [From the fame MS.]

α. King Offa gives inveftiture to Willegoda, firft Abbot of St. Albans.

β. The King and the Abbot kneel on either fide of the altar, on which is laid the charter beftowed by the king.

Pl. L. *The Council of Conflance.* "Erle Richard (of Warwick), and Robert Halain, Bifhop of Salifbury, with other worfhipful perfones, ambaffiatours of king Henry the Fifth to the general counfell of Conftance, are honourably and honeftly received by the pope and the clergy, by the Emperor Sygefmonde and the temporalte." [From a MS. of the fifteenth century. Cotton MSS. Julius, E iv.] The infcription is of later date than the MS.

Pl. LI. "Howe kyng Henry the VIth, beyng in his tender age, was crowned kyng of Englond at Weftminftre with great folempnytie." [From fame MS. as Pl. 6.]

The bifhops all wear copes.

Pl. LII. *The Coronation of the Emperor Sigifmund. α.* He is crowned by Pope Eugenius IV., *β.* The folemn cavalcade of the Pope and the Emperor, *γ.* The governor of the Caftle of St. Angelo awaits their approach.

Pl. LIII. to LV. Baffi Relievi commemorative of the Council of Florence, A.D. 1440.

Pl. LIII. The Emperor Palæologus, accompanied by the Patriarch of Conftantinople, and attended by the officers of his houfehold, *α.* Embarks at Conftantinople, *β.* Croffes the Adriatic in the Venetian Galleys, *γ.* Lands at Venice, *δ.* Is publicly received by Pope Eugenius IV., to whom he makes fubmiffion. [*This laft Scene is wholly imaginary, nothing of the kind having really occurred.*]

Pl. LIV. Pope Eugenius IV. and the Emperor Palæologus at the Council of Florence, July 6, A.D. 1440. The Cardinal Prefbyter, Julianus Cæfarinus, and other great Roman officials, are to the right of the Pope, Beffarion (Archbifhop of Nicæa) and others of the Greeks on the Emperor's right. The Emperor, *α.* Leaves Florence in State, attended by his Court; and *β.* Embarks at Venice for Conftantinople. [The figure ftanding on the left of the Emperor reprefents the Patriarch of Conftantinople, who died before the Council feparated.]

Pl. LV. Envoys from Æthiopia and from other Eaftern Churches, deputed (A.D. 1441) to attend the Council of Florence, and make fubmiffion to the Pope. They are received by Eugenius IV., who hands to Abbot Andreas, their fpokefman, the definitions agreed to by the Council.

The four Relievi above defcribed have been copied at Rome for the illuftration of this work. They were executed by Antonio Philarete, of

---

defaced, and redrawn in ink, within a comparatively recent period. They are reftored here to their original ftate by comparifon with the engravings of Strutt, M. and C. vol. ii. and with other drawings in the fame MS.

Of three crowns figured above (copied from later drawings in this MS), two (No. 2 and 3) are affigned to the Emperor, the third (No. 1) to the Emprefs.

Florence, at the command of Eugenius IV., and now form part of the great Gates of St. Peter's. In some important particulars they represent events not as they really did occur, but as according to Roman theory they ought to have occurred. For further particulars concerning them, see the Basilica Vaticana, of Valentini, Pl. XXII., &c. And for the true history of this Council, see Ffoulkes, *Divisions of Christendom*, part ii. p. 332, *sqq.*

Pl. LVI. 1. The Epitrachelion [348] of Bishop Nikita, † 1167 A.D. 2 and 3. The ἐπιμανίκια [350] of the same Bishop. 4. The ὠμοφόριον [355] of Archbishop Moses, † 1329 A.D.

Pl. LVII. A leathern breastplate [509] ("Rational") and girdle, found in a coffin in the Church of the Passion at Moscow. [This cannot be older than the tenth century, when Christianity was first introduced into Russia. From what later time it dates I have not the means of knowing. This is a wholly exceptional instance in the Greek Church of a direct imitation of the Jewish "Rational." But King (*Greek Church*, p. 39) states, that in Russia, two jewelled ornaments are worn upon the breast by Metropolitans, which "are imagined to be taken from the Urim and Thummim, on Aaron's breastplate." For a similar (local) usage in the West, in the twelfth century, see notes 256 and 263.]

Pl. LVIII. *Costume of the Greek Church.*

1. St. Sampson. He wears a φαινόλιον,[351] answering to the Latin chasuble, over the Sticharion (p. LXIII. v.), or white tunic. The ends of the Peritrachelion [144] (answering to the Latin Stole) are seen pendent under the Phænolion.

2. St. Methodius. In this Figure the Polystaurion [353] takes the place of the plain Phænolion: the Genual [510] is seen pendent (as in the next figure, that of S. Germanus) on the right side; and on the outside of the Polystaurion is seen the Omophorion,[355] which corresponds to the Pallium of the Roman Church, but is worn in the East by almost all bishops.

3. St. Germanus. The Sticharion, or Alb, is here distinguished by the λώρια,[146] or stripes proper to a bishop (Goar, *Euchol.* p. 110). He wears a Sakkos in place of the ordinary Phænolion, and thus marks [35c] his dignity as a Metropolitan. In other respects he wears the same vestments as those last described. [In Russia the Saccos is now worn by all bishops, See King's *Greek Church*, p. 40.]

Pl. LIX. 1. *The Patriarch Bekkos, in Walking Dress.* He wears on his head the outer and the inner καμηλαύχιον; and in his left hand carries the κατάσιον (also known as κάπιλλος), the strings of which (καμίλαβα) are seen pendent below it.

---

[509] This and the Plate last described are from the *Antiquités de l'Empire de Russie*, lately published by the Russian Government. The first volume of this work contains many ecclesiastical monuments of great interest.

[510] *Genuale* is the rendering given by Latin writers to ἐπιγονάτιον [349] as "hanging down to the knee," a distinctive ornament outside the Saccos,[367] worn by Patriarchs and metropolitan.

The long-fleeved coat, worn as a body-drefs, correfponds to the caffock of an Englifh clergyman. The outer garment is the Mandyas, with its three ftripes (ποταμοί, fee Note 343, p. 168). In his right hand he holds the δικανίκιον, or ράβδος. See Note 345, p. 168.

2. St. Macarius. This figure fhows the charaĉteriftic miniftering drefs of a Deacon, viz a clofe-fitting Sticharion (anfwering to the Alb of the Latin Church) and an Orarion (ὠράριον), or Deacon's Stole, having the word ΑΓΙΟC, thrice repeated, embroidered upon it. [This and Pl. LIX. are from Goar's *Euchologion.*]

Pl. LX. *Patriarch Nicon (circ.* 1650, A D.) *in his Cowl.* This Plate is from the fame fource as Pl. LVI. and LVII. The accompanying woodcut fhows the back of the fame Cowl.

Pl. LXI. This Plate is given with a view to the readier underftanding of the fhape, and relative pofition, of the various veftments and infignia now worn in the Roman Church, and defcribed in Appendix F. The central figure is from Bock *L. G.* Band ii. The figures of the Prieft and Deacon from Pugin's *Gloffary.*

Pl. LXIII. Four figures illuftrating the variations in the white drefs recognifed at various times, and in various branches of the Church, as fpecially appropriate to offices.of Holy Miniftry. That on the left is the figure of an Apoftle from the Roman Catacombs.[511] The next of St. James (wearing an Omophorion), from the Church of St. Sophia, at Trebizond, dating from the 14th century,[512] accidentally difcovered not long fince, by the fall of the plafter with which it had been overlaid by the Turks. The third is from a frefco

---

[511] After Aringhi *R. S.* tom. ii. p. 213.   certain *data*) to the Emperor Alexis III., *circ.*
[512] Texier and Pullan B.A. Pl. LXV. They   1350.
attribute the Church (though upon no very

at Florence, a group in which a prieſt (here repreſented) is ſaying the laſt office beſide a dying man. The fourth is a canon of an Engliſh Collegiate Chapter, and, as ſuch, has the Scarf (or broad Stole) worn, out of cuſtomary uſage, by Doctors of Divinity, cathedral dignitaries, and others. This prepared the way for the uſe of the Stole, which for the laſt twenty years, or there-abouts, has been very generally adopted in the Engliſh Church, preſenting nearly the appearance of the black *clavi* on the Tunic of the Apoſtle in this Plate, and in others figured in this Volume.

LIST OF WOODCUTS.

P. vi. The Adoration of the Magi. From the Cemetery of SS. Mar-cellinus and Peter. Aringhi, *R. S.* tom. ii. p. 117.

P. xv. A figure in the attitude of Prayer (comp. Mark, xi. 25 (ὅταν στήκητι προσευχόμενοι): Matt. vi. 5 ; Luke, xviii. 11, &c.), wearing a ſhort Tunic and a ſuperveſtment of peculiar ſhape. From the Cemetery of SS. Marcellinus and Peter. Aringhi, *R. S.* tom. ii. p. 111.

P. xxvi. Our Lord adminiſtering the Bread and the Cup to the Eleven Diſciples. From a Syriac MS. of the year 586, A.D. See deſcription of Pl. XXVI.

P. xliii. The Prophet Malachi. From the ſame MS. as Pl. XXVI. above deſcribed. For the " roll of a book " in the hand ſee p. xl., *ſqq.*

P. lii. [From a Drawing in Her Majeſty's Collection.] This repreſents the actual ſtate of the moſaic nearly two hundred years ago. A compariſon with Pl. XXXIII., already deſcribed, will be ſuggeſtive of the manner in which, as regards minor details, antiquaries vary in their repreſentation of the ſame objects. The *keys* in St. Peter's lap, for example, figured by Alemannus, are nowhere to be ſeen here. And the Pallium of Leo, arranged *more Romano* by Alemannus, has the older form (preſerved by the Greek ὠμοφόριον), as depicted in the preſent woodcut. And there are ſlight variations in the inſcription [513] (DN. CAROLVS REX in one ; DN. CAROLO REGI in the other).

P. lxxvi. An " Orante " (Female) in Dalmatic, and veil (*mafortis*). From the ſame ſource as the woodcut in p. xv, already deſcribed.

P. lxxxiv. Ancient Glaſs. From the Roman Catacombs.[514] This ſpeci-men is figured and deſcribed by Garrucci (*V. A.* tav. xxv. fig. 3), as follows :

A man, and a lady at his left hand, are here figured. They have their hands raiſed in prayer. Between them is the monogram ; and below this a " *volumen*," or ſcroll. On the ſpectator's left is a biſhop's throne, or chair of ſtate (*una cattedra) ;* above this, another monogram (which he deſcribes) ;

---

[513] BICTORIĀ is for VICTORIĀ, accord-ing to a variation of very frequent occurrence in Roman inſcriptions.

[514] From an engraving kindly lent to me by the preſent poſſeſſor of the ſpecimen, Mr. C. Wiltſhere.

behind it a mountain coloured green, from which flows a golden stream. On the top of this mountain is a tree, with fruit thereon. There is a superscription DIGNTIAS AMIC.[514a] Then after describing the dress, he goes on to say, that this had once been supposed to represent SS. Perpetua and Felicitas. But one of the figures, which, as he says, is clearly that of a man, he thinks is very like that of S. Laurentius, in tav. xx. 7 (it is difficult to trace the resemblance); and the female figure, he adds, may be St. Agnes. The dress does nearly resemble that attributed to St. Agnes in other specimens of glass, the fact being that it is the rich costume worn by Roman ladies of high rank at that time. A comparison of tav. xxvi. No. 11 and 12, in the same volume, suggests what I venture to think is the real explanation of the figures before us. They are man and wife, people of high rank: the "scroll" between them represents the *tabulæ matrimoniales;*[515] the coin just below the roll, the marriage dowry: the bishop's chair[516] is suggestive of the Church, and more particularly of the *Cathedral* Church, as we should call it; and the tree with its fruits, probably of the Tree of Life. I have a third explanation to mention, not my own, but that of a gentleman who, at a recent Church Congress, referred to this glass as an undoubted representation of *a priest vested in a Chasuble.* It is to be regretted that he did not give an explanation of the lady at "the priest's" side, or of the DIGNTIAS AMIC of the inscription. For myself I confess to some surprise, that anybody, having the slightest acquaintance with antiquity, should have ventured to assert, without any doubt or hesitation, that "*on this glass is depicted a priest, vested in just such a Chasuble as may now be seen in Ritualistic Churches.*"[517]

[514a] A mistake of the original workmen for DIGNITAS AMIC. The full inscription (for which these words stand representative) is DIGNITAS AMICORVM VIVAS CVM TVIS FELICITER. So in tav. ii. Or as on yet another specimen, DIGNITAS AMICORVM PIE ZESES CVM TVIS OMNIBVS BIBE ET PROPINA. By the phrase *Dignitas Amicorum,* we may understand either "*digni amici,*" or "honoured by all thy friends," ("Orgueil de tes amis." Gar).

[515] S. Augustine's Serm. xxxviii de Proverb. c. 31 (*apud Garrucci*) "Unaquæque conjux bona . . . . tabulas matrimoniales instrumenta

emptionis suæ deputat." Compare Martigny, D. A. C. *in voc.* "mariage."

[516] In the other specimens (figured by Garrucci, as above) in which man and wife are represented, the Church (and through this their Christian faith) is typically suggested by a pillar or column. [So Garrucci, a very learned author, whose work will repay a careful study.]

[517] Dr. Littledale. Report of Wolverhampton Church Congress (1867), p. 279. I have reproduced the engraving above described, that my readers may form their own opinion upon the matter.

N.B.—*The Plates, above described, as being from Her Majesty's Collection at Windsor, are from Coloured Drawings by Santo Bartoli and others, in which the Mosaic Pictures of the Roman Churches, and other objects of antiquarian interest, are depicted as they existed more than 150 years ago. The Collection was originally made for Cardinal Albano (afterwards Clement XI.), and is now the property of Her Majesty. These Drawings bear marks of having been very accurately copied, and contain a number of important details which are not to be found elsewhere.*

INDEX.

WORDS AND SUBJECTS.

N.B. Roman Numerals refer to the pages, and Greek Letters to the Notes, of the Introduction.

The larger Arabic Numerals refer to the pages of the later portions of this Treatise; and the smaller Arabic Numerals to the corresponding Notes.

K K

HAVE   HAVE
HEROTION
ET   VALE
AETERNOM
C CESTIVS   FILIAE
P   C

Boissard

Plate III

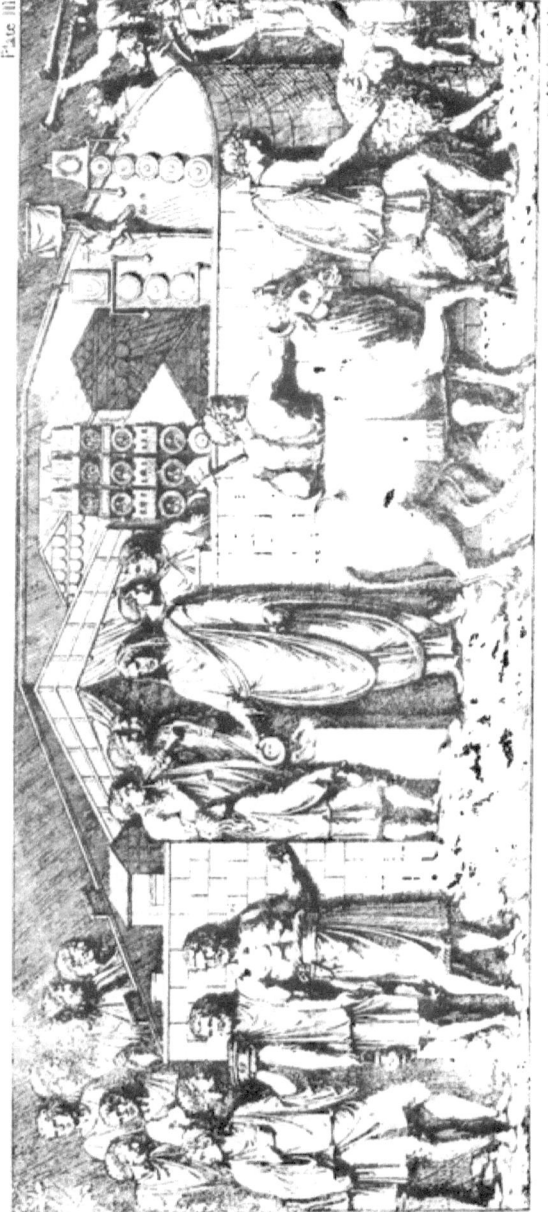

THE EMPEROR SACRIFICING

From the Column of Trajan

Plate IV

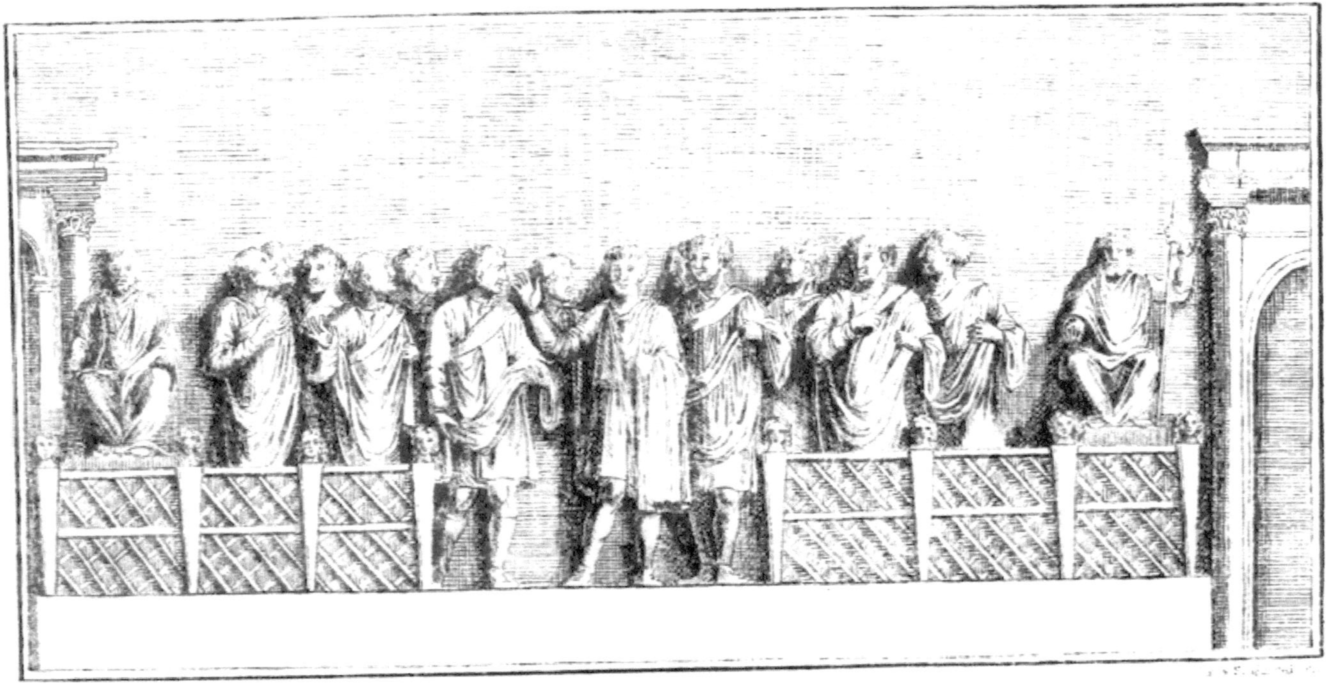

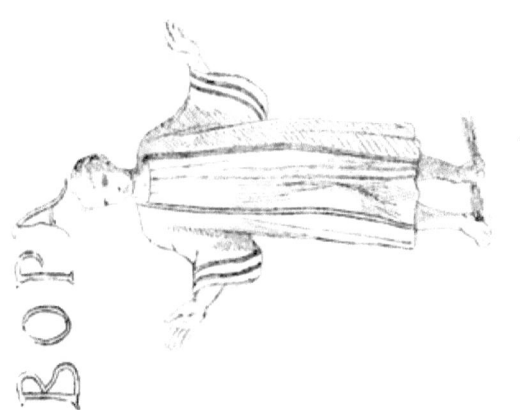

Du temps de Minerve d'Athènes.

Du temps de Minerve d'Athènes.

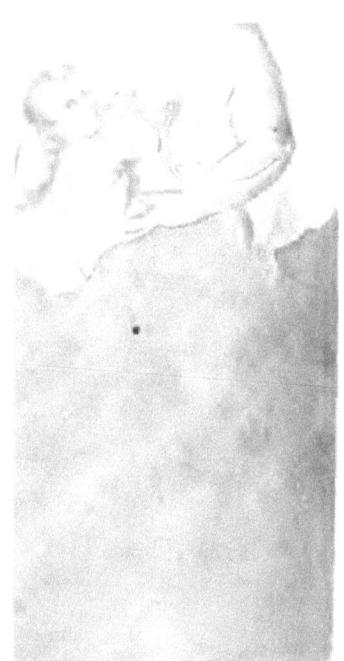

Days from Lunisolar Sun

Page A

THE CEMETERY OF MARCELLINUS AND PETER
At Rome

OUR LORD AS THE GIVER OF THE DIVINE WORD

FROM THE CEMETERY OF St AGNES AT ROME

Lang & Son, Lithomatic Ltd

Plate XV

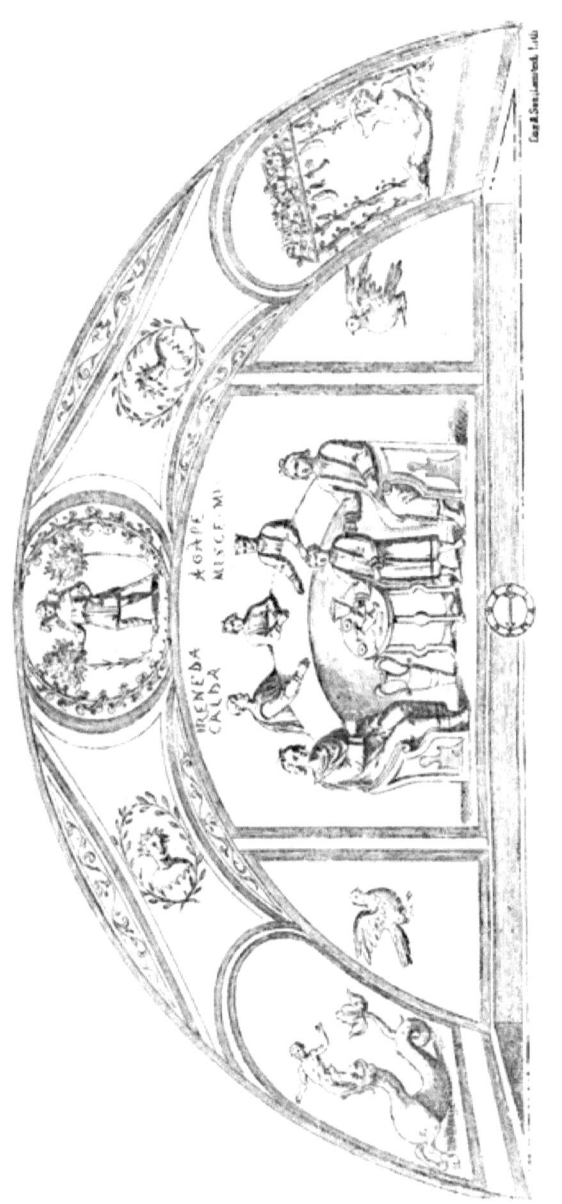

AGAPE
MISCE MI

IRENE DA
CALDA

FROM THE CEMETERY OF MARCELLINUS AND PETER

At Rome

ORDINATION OF A DEACON

From the Cemetery of S.t Hermes at Rome

Plate XVIII.

Plate XIX

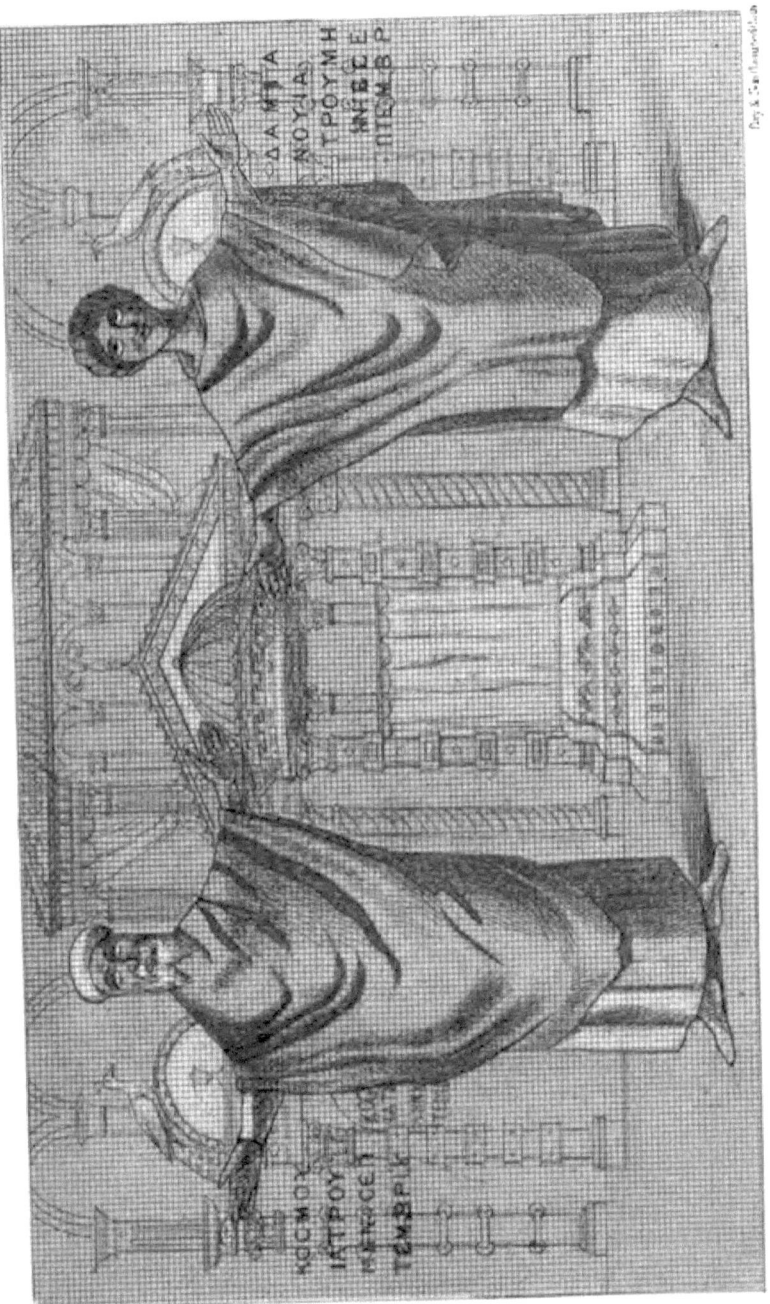

MOSAICS IN THE CHURCH OF S.ᵗ GEORGE, THESSALONICA.

Plate XX

ΒΑCIΛΙΟΥ
ΜΗΝΙ
ΑΤ
ΡΙΑΤ

ΦΙΛΙΠ
ΠΟΥCΠΙC
ΚΛΥ ΜΝ
ΙΟΚΤ
ΘΒΡΙΧ

MOSAICS IN THE CHURCH OF Sᵀ GEORGE, THESSALONICA.

Philip, Bishop and Martyr, and Basilius, Soldier and Martyr

Plate XXI

MOSAICS IN THE CHURCH OF S^T GEORGE. THESSALONICA.

Onesiphorus of Iconium and Porphyrius his Servant Martyrs

DIPTYCH OF BOETHIUS CONSUL OF THE WEST A.D. 510.
From Gori's Thesaurus Diptychorum

Plate XXII.

CLEMENTINUS CONSUL · FIVE BASE

Plate XXIV

IMAGINES AD VIVVM EXPRESSAE
EX AEDICVLA SANCTI ANDREAE
PROPE BEATI GREGORII MAGNI ECCLESIAM,
NECNON EX VITA EIVSDEM BEATI GREGORII
A IOANNE DIACONO LIB IV. CAP. LXXXIII. ET LXXXIV.
CONSCRIPTA.

ST GREGORY THE GREAT
His Father Gordianus and his Mother Sylvia

THE ASCENSION

From a Syriac M S written A D 586

EUSEBIUS
Bishop of Cæsarea

AMMONIUS
of Alexandria

from a Syriac M.S. of the Year 586 A.D.

Plate XXVIII

MAXIMIANVS

THE EMPEROR JUSTINIAN AND ARCHBISHOP MAXIMIANUS

From a Mosaic of the VIᵗʰ Century in the Church of Sᵗ Vitalis at Ravenna

S·LAVRENTIVS · S·PETRVS · S·PAVLVS · S·STEBIASVS ·

PELAGIVS · EPISC

IVR·ETVI·TEMPLIS·I

AMLEVIVS·XPISTI·

Amaniquo que mi in il corpo di ... e riservato di ... con la ... con il ... certi nomi la città di Gerusalem: ... sono rappresentati nelle ...de li Apostoli ... E'mira ... mini ... im Santo ... gli ... di Sacramenti ...

Mi ... intigro l'arco de la ... che ... il Presbiterio.

Plate *XXV*

SCS CORNELIUS PAPA AND SCS CIPRIANUS

A Fresco (8th Century) at Rome from De Rossi's Roma Sotterranea

Plate XXXI

S. XYSTUS PAPA ROMANUS AND STS. D. Perhaps
A fresco (8th Century) at Rome, from De Rossi's Imago Collection

A   Vultus imaginum suppleti ex alijs eorumdem temporum.

B   Historia renouata ad exemplum ab Antiquarijs olim exceptum cum desiuenet.

C   Tabula nullis notata litteris exceptorum inuria.

D   Nomen Pontificis desideratur.

E   Inscriptas tabella acclamationes seruauit Angelus Massarellus.

F   Ædificij descriptio verbis Anastasij Bibliothecarij.

G   Instaurati operis monumentum.

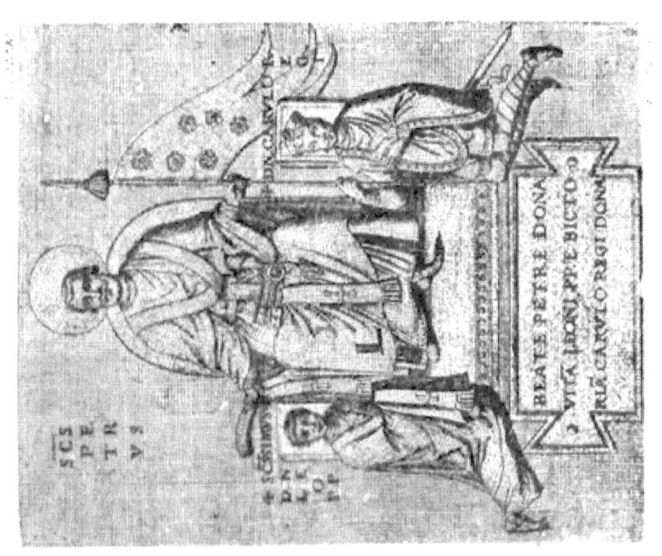

atcōdenbo eis clcues accelesiedi ē.

psctētu nuncaur ænct ponemßee.

atatōiōur ejs epr codiee[3]

Oeltoe psctct ens Incert pc[3]

Ecor calensatedia epis libellu.

jens catedia & pis cesosatteaui

Subdiaeconi patena[3] & caoliee[3]

ponat ostetdae super humesos

dum Inaeffæ psaceon fueh n?

otæhæ super collæ eo fum

super quof Inclynæœns cœpiœbuf

cumpollyce dexœeffe fœchueem

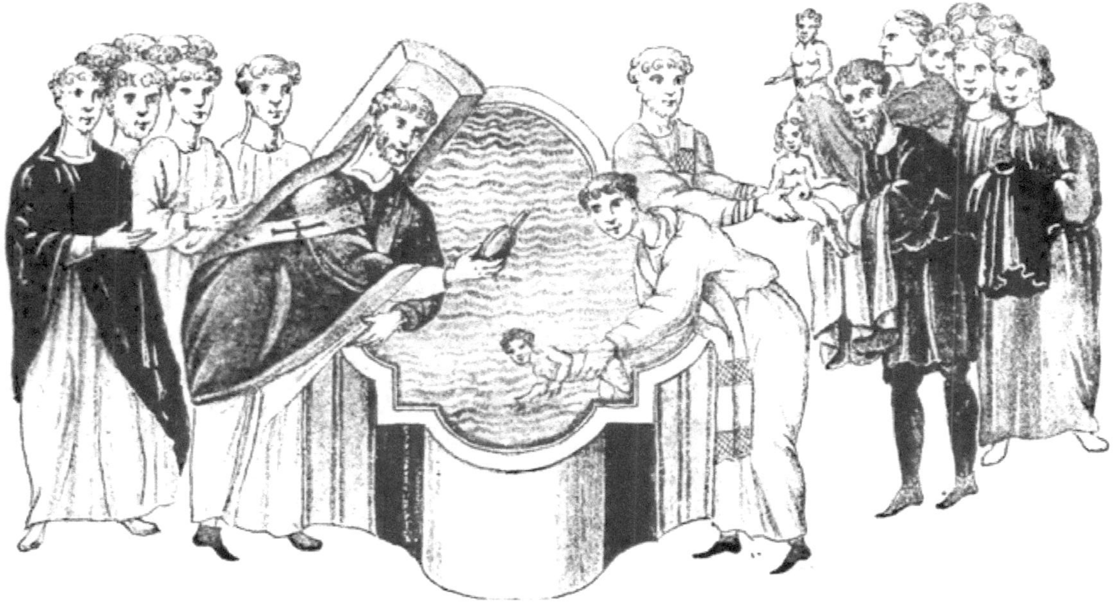

Day & Son, Limited, Lith

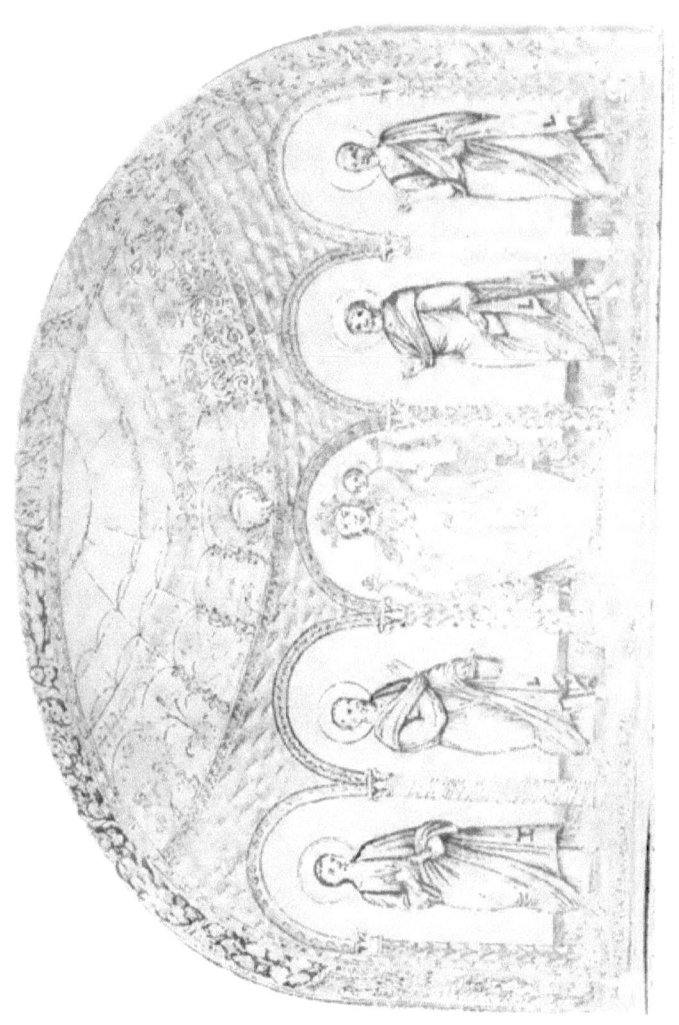

CHURCH OF S. MARIA NOVA AT ROME

Sedente Leone P.P. IV A.D. 847/ 855

POPE NICHOLAS THE FIRST & THE EMPEROR LEWIS II

a M.S partly of the IXe Century.

Plate XL

THE ASSUMPTION

A Fresco of the IXth Century from the hypogene Church of S Clemente at Rome

Plate XII

EGBERTUS, ARCHBISHOP OF TREVES

From a MS. of the X. Century

ST DUNSTAN.
From a M.S. of the XIth Century in the British Museum

POPE NICHOLAS II GIVING BENEDICTION TO ABBOT ADELEERO.

From a M.S. of the XIIth Century

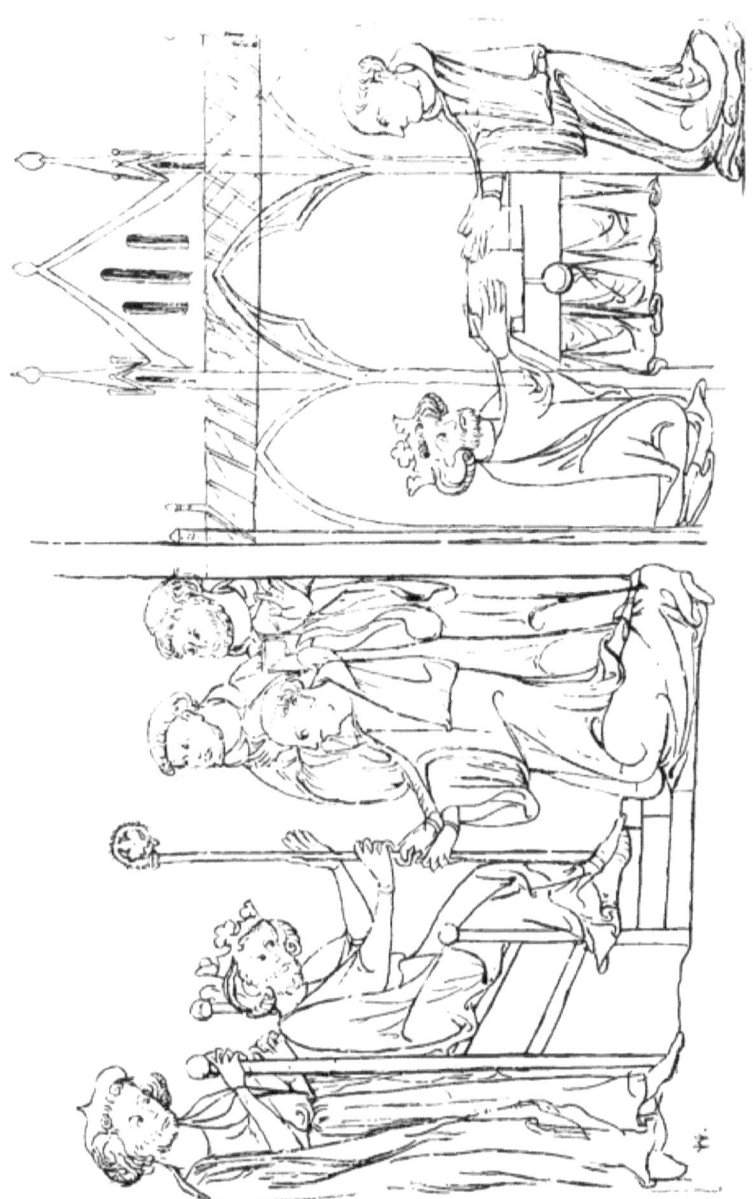

Plate 1.

RECEPTION OF THE ENGLISH AMBASSADORS,
AT THE COUNCIL OF CONSTANCE.
From a M.S. of the 15th Century.

Plate LI

HENRY THE SIXTH.

From a MS. copy

Plate LIII

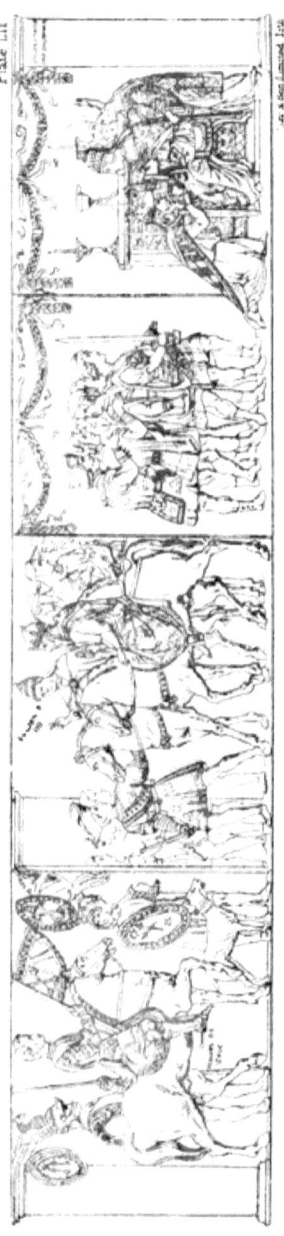

CORONATION OF THE EMPEROR SIGISMUND

And Procession to the Castle of Sᵗ Angelo

Plate LIV

THE COUNCIL OF FLORENCE

a Reception of Envoys from Eastern Churches. b Their solemn entrance into Rome

Plate XIV

Plate XIII

Plate 48.

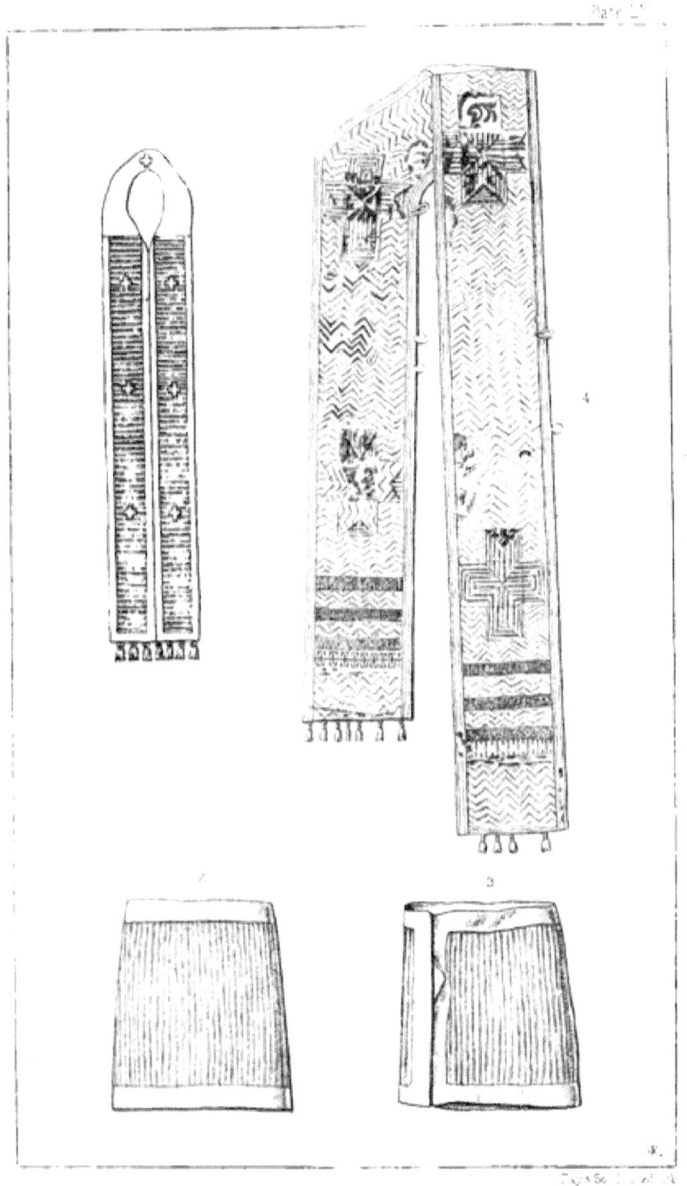

Epimachion. 2 and 3 Epimachia of Bp Nikita ＋1607 A.D.

4 Epimachion of Antony Moses ＋1520 A.D.

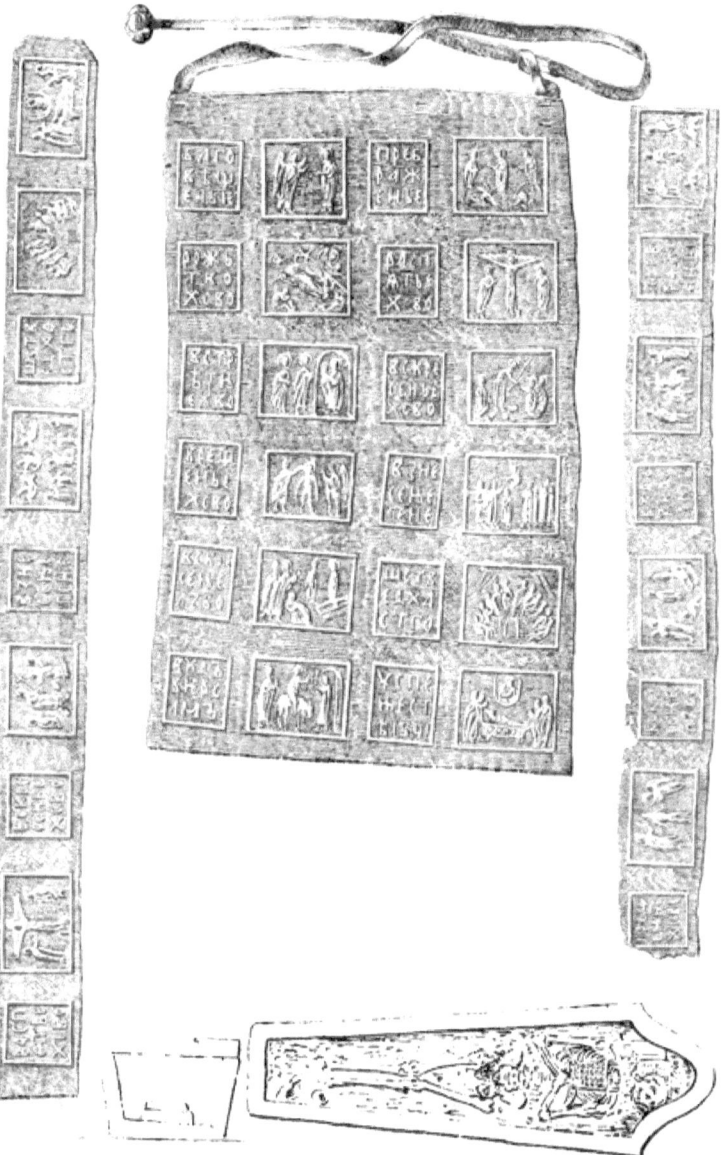

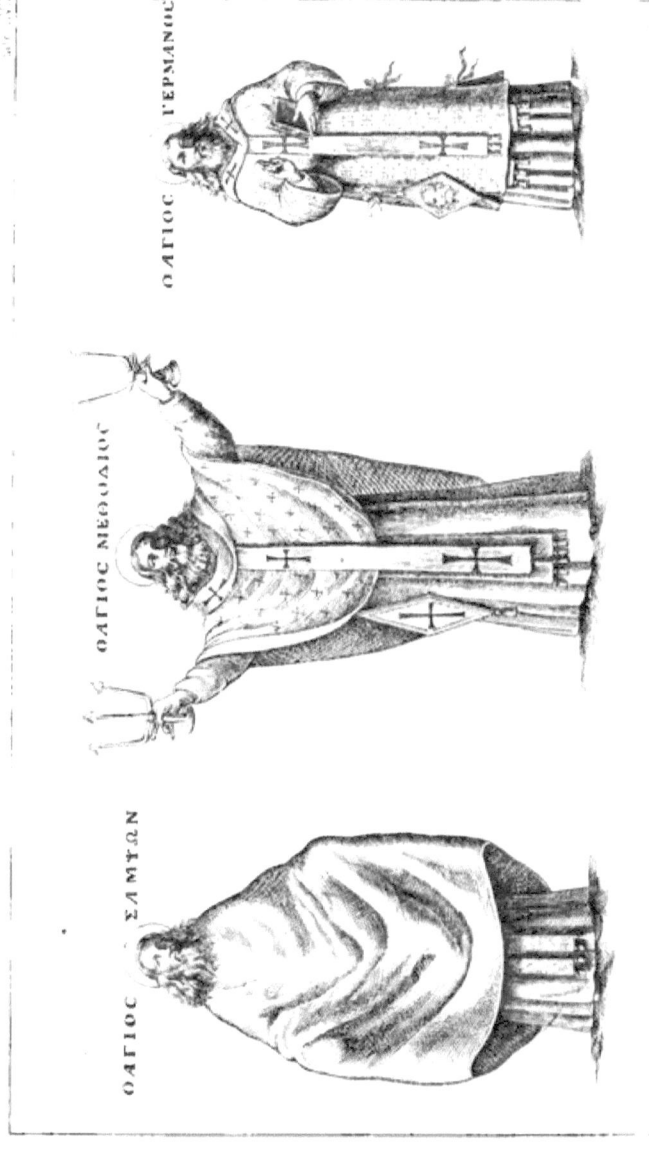

ΟΑΓΙΟC ΣΛΜΥΩΝ   ΟΑΓΙΟC ΝΕΘΘΔΙΟC   ΟΑΓΙΟC ΓΕΡΜΑΝΟC

SACERDOTAL VESTMENTS OF THE GREEK CHURCH

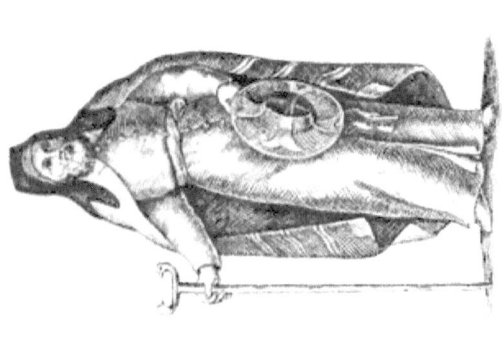

Ο ΒΕΚΚΟΣ ΠΡΙΑΡΧΗΣ

Ο ΑΓΙΟΣ ΜΑΚΑΡΙΟΣ

A GREEK PACRITHRCH
In Church Costume

A GREEK DEACON
with Sticharion and Orarion

Plate LX

THE PATRIARCH NICON. circ 1650 A D

The face is from an authentic Portrait . The Cowl here figured is still preserved

A Priest A Bishop A Deacon

ROMAN VESTMENTS

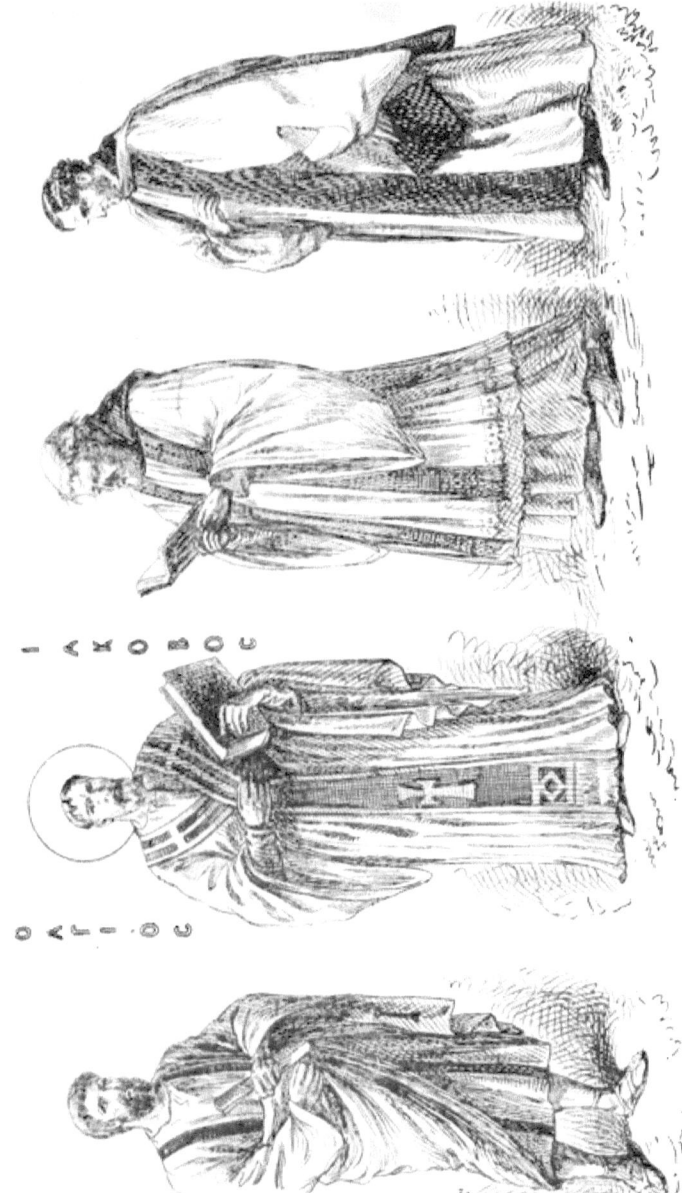